DAVID GARRICK AND THE MEDIATION OF CELEBRITY

What happens when an actor owns shares in the stage on which he performs and the newspapers that review his performances? Celebrity that lasts over 240 years. From 1741, David Garrick dominated the London theatre world as the progenitor of a new 'natural' style of acting. From 1747 to 1776, he was a part-owner and manager of Drury Lane, controlling most aspects of the theatre's life. In a spectacular foreshadowing of today's media convergences, he also owned shares in newspapers including the *St. James's Chronicle* and the *Public Advertiser*, which advertised and reviewed Drury Lane's theatrical productions. This book explores the nearly inconceivable level of cultural power generated by Garrick's entrepreneurial manufacture and mediation of his own celebrity. Using new technologies and extensive archival research, this book uncovers fresh material concerning Garrick's ownership and manipulation of the media, offering timely reflections for theatre history and media studies.

LESLIE RITCHIE is Associate Professor of English Literature at Queen's University, Ontario. She is the recipient of a Social Sciences and Humanities Research Council of Canada grant and has received fellowships at the Houghton Library, Harvard, and the Folger Shakespeare Library for her work on David Garrick. Ritchie's previous work includes *Women Writing Music in Late Eighteenth-Century England* (2008; 2016).

D1500073

DAVID GARRICK AND THE MEDIATION OF CELEBRITY

LESLIE RITCHIE

Queen's University, Ontario

CAMBRIDGE
UNIVERSITY PRESS

CAMBRIDGE
UNIVERSITY PRESS

University Printing House, Cambridge CB2 8BS, United Kingdom

One Liberty Plaza, 20th Floor, New York, NY 10006, USA

477 Williamstown Road, Port Melbourne, VIC 3207, Australia

314-321, 3rd Floor, Plot 3, Splendor Forum, Jasola District Centre, New Delhi - 110025, India

79 Anson Road, #06-04/06, Singapore 079906

Cambridge University Press is part of the University of Cambridge.

It furthers the University's mission by disseminating knowledge in the pursuit of education, learning and research at the highest international levels of excellence.

www.cambridge.org
Information on this title: www.cambridge.org/9781108469197
DOI: 10.1017/9781108661942

First published 2019
First paperback edition 2021

A catalogue record for this publication is available from the British Library

Library of Congress Cataloging in Publication data
NAMES: Ritchie, Leslie, 1970- author.
TITLE: David Garrick and the mediation of celebrity / Leslie Ritchie.
DESCRIPTION: Cambridge, United Kingdom; New York, NY : Cambridge University Press, 2019. | Includes bibliographical references and index.
IDENTIFIERS: LCCN 2018042528 | ISBN 9781108475877 (hardback : alk. paper) | ISBN 9781108469197 (paperback : alk. paper)
SUBJECTS: LCSH: Garrick, David, 1717-1779. | Mass media and theater–England–London–History–18th century.
CLASSIFICATION: LCC PN2593 .R58 2019 | DDC 792.02/8092–DC23
LC record available at https://lccn.loc.gov/2018042528

ISBN 978-1-108-47587-7 Hardback
ISBN 978-1-108-46919-7 Paperback

Contents

Figures

Tables

Acknowledgements

Warm thanks are due to the many people, institutions and organizations who supported the writing of this book. A Social Sciences and Humanities Research Council of Canada grant funded my archival research and the presentation of this work at conferences. The scholars of the Canadian and American Societies for Eighteenth-Century Studies, and the participants at the "Garrick and Shakespeare" conference arranged by Richard Wilson at Kingston University, have my earnest thanks for their discussions of and contributions to my research. I was fortunate to benefit from a sabbatical granted by Queen's University, Ontario, and from research fellowships at Harvard University's Houghton Library and the Folger Shakespeare Library, and enjoyed working in those lively research communities.

I am grateful for the kind assistance of librarians at the British Library, the National Art Library at the Victoria and Albert Museum, the Huntington Library, the Folger Shakespeare Library, the University of North Carolina Chapel Hill Research Collections, the Harry Ransom Center, the Garrick Club, and Harvard University's Hyde and Theatre Collections. Thanks to Queen's University's librarians, who support research in the eighteenth century by maintaining subscriptions to databases and journals in this field, by continuing to build our rare books collection, and by bringing the library into the classroom.

Thanks to my savvy research assistants Maya Bielinski, Elizabeth Brown, Katie Hunt and Emily Leach for their work on the databases and spreadsheets that made it possible to discern Garrick's degree of representation in the media. I am grateful to my Queen's colleagues, particularly Shelley King, John Pierce and F.P. Lock, with whom I've discussed various aspects of the book. Thanks also to April London, for timely advice; to Peter Walmsley, for continued support; and to Una D'Elia, for many conversations. Kate Brett at Cambridge University Press was a stalwart champion of this book, and she has my deep gratitude. Thanks to Eilidh Burrett for her help throughout the publishing process.

Lisa DeBoer prepared the index. Thanks to Damian Love, copy-editor, and to Lisa Sinclair, content manager, for their assistance. I appreciate the generous comments and criticisms offered by the anonymous peer reviewers.

The best saved for last: my love and thanks to my family, and especially to Brian, Owen and Alec.

Introduction

Mr. Garrick's Province was Praise; perhaps no Mortal ever enjoyed a
greater Share of it: We will leave it, not to Poetry but to History to
determine his Claims to it. The most singular Circumstance in Mr.
Garrick's Life, was that he obtained a greater Share of Applause than
any Man ever enjoyed, than any Man ever Merited . . . When Garrick
gave up his Breath, we supposed his Praises would cease. But there
were Reasons for their Continuation . . .

– *St. James's Chronicle*, 11–13 March 1779

From 1741, when he created a sensation with his novel interpretation of
Richard III, David Garrick dominated the London stage both as actor and
as progenitor of a new 'natural' style of acting. As part-owner and manager
of Drury Lane, one of London's two official theatres, from 1747 to 1776
he controlled hiring, actors' salaries and the plays and entertainments
offered there – many of which he also wrote or adapted himself from
various sources, including, most famously, Shakespeare. His image was
omnipresent: Garrick was artistically represented more times than the
King,[1] and amateur actors in London's "spouting clubs" energetically aped
his gestures and delivery. Garrick's fame, iconicity and his importance to
theatre history and Shakespeare studies are all well documented in period
sources and in recent biographies and works of theatre criticism.[2] What
remains unexplored is the question of whether Garrick's influential stature
is better understood as the fame garnered by an exceptional actor, or as
celebrity produced by media and market forces. I argue for the latter, and
view Garrick as an entrepreneurial manufacturer and mediator of his own
celebrity.

Garrick not only published advertisements, pamphlets, letters, poems
and essays which promoted his acting and his theatre, but, in a spectacular
foreshadowing of today's media convergences, he was also a proprietor of
papers, including the *St. James's Chronicle,* the *Public Advertiser,* the
Morning Post, and the *London Packet* – papers which, not coincidentally,

advertised and reviewed Drury Lane's theatrical productions. It was entirely possible for a theatre-goer in the 1760s to attend Drury Lane Theatre (partly owned and managed by Garrick) to see a play which Garrick had written or adapted, featuring a prologue or epilogue written by Garrick, in which Garrick himself was acting. That playgoer had likely been enticed to go to the play by an advertisement, puff or review written by Garrick, placed in a newspaper partly owned by Garrick. David Garrick possessed an almost inconceivable level of cultural power.

The influence Garrick wielded over the media was a recurring complaint amongst his contemporary adversaries: the *Theatrical Monitor* of 14 November 1767, for instance, complained bitterly of a "collusion of managers with news writers." Beyond mentioning his ownership of newspapers, however, modern critics have scarcely noticed this aspect of Garrick's celebrity. Mary Luckhurst and Jane Moody summarize recent work by theatre historians as mainly "concerned with fame (the nature of the exceptional life) rather than with celebrity (a concept which focuses attention on the interplay between individuals and institutions, markets and media)."[3] In Garrick's case, scholarship has followed the 'exceptional life' model, refreshing his fame rather than examining the social production of his celebrity. This focus on Garrick's exceptionality as a performer has led scholars to downplay the extent to which his carefully crafted puffs of various productions and actors (including himself) and his ability to quash opposition in print and on stage enabled public perception of his stature as a dramatic innovator.

This book will attempt to answer two multi-pronged, interconnected questions, the first of which is: how much of his own celebrity did David Garrick produce, directly and indirectly, by means of the media? The book examines Garrick's correspondence and contemporary media items written by or about Garrick to assign some quantitative basis to Garrick's mediation of his own celebrity. Which newspapers during the period 1741–76 were concerned with the reporting of dramatic or entertainment news? Of these, what share did newspapers owned by Garrick hold in the marketplace? Who comprised the target markets of these papers? How frequently do the papers and other print media refer to Garrick, and how often is Garrick the author of such references? How, in practical terms, did Garrick manage the production of his own celebrity?

The second research question asks: what strategies of self-representation did Garrick employ in the media, and what were their discernable effects? Further, to what extent can we define a secondary level of influence, exercised by Garrick over persons who owed him personal, political or economic debts? I ground my analysis of effect using not only the print texts identified above, but also readings of Garrick's prologues and epilogues, timely ephemeral pieces that address current theatric events; of cultural artifacts such as portraits, playbills, tickets and souvenirs that respond to developments in Garrick's public image; and of records of audience response, including the diaries kept by Drury Lane Theatre prompters Richard Cross and William Hopkins.

Previous Scholarship Concerning Garrick and the Media

The scholarly turn to consider the cultural import of celebrity has included numerous invocations of Garrick. Joseph Roach's book concerning celebrity, *It* (2007), touches on Garrick at numerous points[4]; Roach's earlier work, *The Player's Passion: Studies in the Science of Acting* (1985), offered a detailed study of eighteenth-century theories of acting and the expression of the passions, especially the work of Denis Diderot and its implications for Garrick's reputation as a 'natural' actor.[5] Fred Inglis's book, *A Short History of Celebrity* (2010), summarizes Garrick's role in professionalizing acting.[6] Leo Braudy, in *The Frenzy of Renown* (1986), sees Garrick as exemplary of the idea that "Greatness, no matter what its inner nature, appears to the world and to its greatest admirers as a performance that reaches beyond the grave."[7] Antoine Lilti's recently translated book, *The Invention of Celebrity 1750–1850* (2017), invites scholars to attend to the "mechanisms" of publicity that shape celebrity, and discusses Garrick's use of benefit performances to enhance his public image.[8] However, no extended study of Garrick's manipulation of the media yet exists. Closest to the mark is Cheryl Wanko's excellent book, *Roles of Authority: Thespian Biography and Celebrity in Eighteenth-Century Britain* (2003), which studies three contemporary biographies of Garrick. Wanko postulates that Garrick's authority was enabled by "an expanding London publishing trade and the increasing amount of attention the previous generation of performers had received in print," and defines his authority as "less actual power and more the perception of power and the acceptance of an actor as a person worthy of holding power."[9] Perception of power is itself powerful; but Garrick also did possess real media power, owning, contributing to and intervening in many media venues. It is only our view of that actual power that has been obscured, and biography is one of the culprits.

Biography is often a problematic evidentiary source, and it may be particularly so in Garrick's case: his first two significant biographers, Thomas Davies and Arthur Murphy, were men with whom Garrick

wrangled repeatedly in matters personal, professional and financial. Both
Davies and Murphy wrote their biographies to get out of debt, and their
biographies do not so much interrogate Garrick's celebrity as capitalize
upon his popularity. Davies, an actor-turned-bookseller who was co-
proprietor with Garrick and others in the St. James's Chronicle, had a
privileged view of many of Garrick's media interventions, but Davies only
teases his reader: "Those who can trace his [Garrick's] letters and essays in
the newspapers, will find many just observations and acute criticisms on
manners, customs, and characters."[10] Davies places Garrick's involvement
with the press early. "Sometimes he wrote criticisms upon the action and
elocution of the players, and published them in the prints. These sudden
effusions of his mind generally comprehended judicious observations and
shrewd remarks unmixed with that gross illiberality which often disgraces
the instructions of modern stage critics," writes Davies, of Garrick before
his London stage debut, circa 1740.[11] However, Davies declines to identify
Garrick's "acute criticisms."

As an insider who profited from the symbiotic relationship of print
media, theatre and bookselling, Davies was not motivated to expose the
workings of the industry. If some personal animus against Garrick persisted, it is likely that, having meted out this much praise, he was not
inclined to add to Garrick's fame as a writer by identifying his contributions with specificity. Or perhaps Davies regarded Garrick's media contributions as negligible alongside his other cultural work. Whatever his now
irretrievable reasons for withholding specifics, the biographer who could
have identified Garrick's additions to theatrical criticism did not do so. By
the time Davies's biography was published, just a year after Garrick's
death, many of Garrick's anonymous media interventions, restricted
during his lifetime to "those who [could] trace" them, as Davies put it,
were already fading fast from view. Murphy, a lawyer and playwright
whose biography was published in 1801, at a greater distance after Garrick's death than Davies's work, is less gracious and less accurate in several
factual points than is Davies, and even less inclined to consider Garrick as
anything but an actor and manager. Garrick's 'natural' talent in acting, and
to a lesser extent, in writing for the stage, is the focus of these early
biographies.[12]

Even leaving early biographers' self-interest out of the question, biography's customary progress and parade create a rhythm that is not appropriate to the study of Garrick's use of the media, which was extremely
consistent in approach throughout his career. Garrick's media use was
considered: responsive to negative media, conflicts of taste or theatre riots,

it was also proactive and managerial, often attempting to seed responses in the audience, and in the wider public that read about the theatre. Still, if their treatment of Garrick's involvement in the media is scanty, these and other contemporary biographies remain valuable sources of other information. In part, the biographies are confirmations and repositories of Garrick's concerted, life-long shaping of his media image – in some cases, echoing back to posterity words and images framed by Garrick himself. By examining the biographies alongside newspapers, pamphlets and correspondence, it is possible to trace some of Garrick's media interventions; these traces demonstrate that the convergence of media ownership and influence on stage and in print enabled Garrick to exercise real power over aesthetic and financial dimensions of the theatre market. For example, Garrick was and remains known for his infinite 'variety,' or his ability to play both comic and tragic parts, as well as the roles of manager, author and genteel, sociable man. As Wanko perceptively remarks, "Garrick's immense public presence seems more manageable [to biographers] when split into separate 'roles,'"[13] yet it was the overwhelming combinatory effect of these personae and their connections to media and markets that constituted his celebrity. *David Garrick and the Mediation of Celebrity* uncovers the means by which Garrick's interventions in contemporary media contributed to the ideal of variety as the apex of theatrical achievement, and the cornerstone of his celebrity.

Of modern scholarly works, George Winchester Stone, Jr. and George M. Kahrl's magisterial book, *David Garrick: A Critical Biography* (1979), has long had the last word on Garrick's relationship with the London press. While Stone and Kahrl cite Garrick's part-ownership of several papers[14] and acknowledge that public "suspicion of his power" over the press was "rampant,"[15] they categorically deny that Garrick exercised undue influence over public perception of his theatre. Garrick could and did place puffs in various papers, but, they say, paid for the privilege, which, they stress, was normal business practice for theatre managers and "open to *all* comers."[16] Subsequent works on Garrick have tended to follow this thinking. This study will correct assumptions that Garrick's involvement with the media was routine at several points.

Stone and Kahrl do not fully outline the times at which Garrick's shares in various papers were operative, or suggest how Garrick's periods of newspaper ownership might correlate with important, media-intensive incidents at Drury Lane Theatre. My work will mark a few notable incidents in Drury Lane Theatre during Garrick's reign, and plot media coverage against those occurrences. After identifying Garrick's periods of media ownership, I shall make an in-depth study of a theatrical incident with particular implications for Garrick's public image – the Battle of the Romeos (1750), in which Garrick's ardent Romeo was pitted against that of Covent Garden's handsome Spranger Barry – and contrast each theatre's management of the media in response to it.

Second, Stone and Kahrl presume that the press had the responsibility and the potential to make impartial observations. This misplaced, ahistorical faith in the freedom of the press leads them to misinterpret key documents pertaining to Garrick's influence over the media. For example, they interpret printer William Woodfall's letter to Garrick of 13 February 1776 as a sincere protest of Woodfall's journalistic impartiality. Woodfall writes: "It was not the object, what Mr. Woodfall would wish to print against his friend Mr. Garrick, but how far the editor of the *Morning Chronicle* found it absolutely necessary to go to save his character for theatrical impartiality–a character, by the by, which is the very basis of the paper."[17] An earlier letter from Woodfall of 18 November 1773 similarly insists, "my preserving inviolate my character for impartiality is of as much consequence to me as your preserving the character you have on the best grounds established, that of being the most capable actor, this or any other country ever produced."[18] Woodfall's letter and the "editor" persona he employs cannily signal that the *Morning Chronicle* needs to *display* the character of impartiality, which will be maintained by printing letters against Garrick from time to time.

The term "impartiality" appears to have borne quite a different meaning to eighteenth-century newspaper printers and publishers than it bears today. Impartiality was invoked to show that publishers had printed both sides of a question;[19] it in no way implied that both sides were given equal weight in the length, strength or frequency of their representation. To give but one example of this frequently voiced sentiment, see the *Gazetteer and London Daily Advertiser* for 27 January 1763. The printer, Charles Say, declares, "actuated by the steady principle of impartiality, we declare ourselves ready upon this, and all other proper occasions, to throw open our paper to whatsoever may be suggested on either side the dispute, provided a spirit of decency and good manners is adhered to, all *personal* and *illiberal* invective avoided, and our own safety in particular is not endangered," while remaining firmly on the "Town's" side of a theatrical riot, professing but not realizing impartiality. To return to Woodfall's letter, Woodfall as editor preserves not any real autonomy from Garrick, but rather, his public reputation for such autonomy. Even if one reads Woodfall's letter as a principled stand against Garrick's influence, the emotional and monetary ties of the Garrick–Woodfall association visible in Garrick's correspondence caution against belief that this feint had any lasting effect.[20] This project reads Garrick's correspondence closely, and demonstrates that there are further letters that might be reinterpreted in the light of Garrick's mediation of his own celebrity.

Stone and Kahrl further define media power as the ability to censor media content, and state that Garrick did not possess this power. This position is certainly at odds with contemporary perceptions of Garrick's influence on print media. Claiming that his criticisms of Garrick were unpublishable in all but two papers, in 1772 David Williams attacked Garrick in an anonymous pamphlet entitled *A letter to David Garrick, Esq. On His Conduct as Principal Manager and Actor at Drury-Lane.* Williams clearly believes that Garrick's extensive hold on the print media market amounts to censorship: "I happened to call on an acquaintance just as he had been disappointed of a share in one of the news-papers, by your having secured it to yourself."[21] Surprised that the wealthy Garrick should bother with this investment for "so trifling an object as the profits of such a share," it is only when he wishes to say some things to Garrick via the media, or what he calls "the present fashionable method," that the motive for Garrick's ownership becomes appallingly apparent: "I was not a little surprised to find myself so much restrained. Only two papers would receive any thing in which you were mentioned with blame," Williams remarks.[22] His summation, "You are a proprietor in several papers, and upon such terms with the proprietors of others, that they must not disoblige you . . . I no longer wonder that your name is ever inserted with honor,"[23] establishes eighteenth-century newspapers as a superlative tool for image management. Newspapers could saturate their audience with certain names and ideas on a regular basis, and silently exclude other voices.

As Williams's outcry hints, Garrick's power over the media did include the ability to preclude certain items from publication. This power was not restricted to those papers in which he had a share, but spread over a much wider constituency. Robert Bataille offers a corrective (1989) to Stone and Kahrl's assertion that contemporary journalists were impervious to Garrickian influence by suggesting that journalist and playwright Hugh Kelly did attempt to influence the public favourably on Garrick's behalf (though not demonstrably at Garrick's behest), out of a sense of gratitude for Garrick's influence in gaining Kelly's plays performances. While Bataille carefully concludes that it would be unfair to assume that the Garrick–Kelly relationship was "typical of Garrick's other professional alliances,"[24] it now appears that it is indeed suggestive of the ways in which Garrick exploited his personal networks to produce a trade in media favours. This book will map Garrick's media shadow, articulate the levels of influence which he appears to have held over various printers and producers of newspapers, and consider the validity of accusations such as Williams's that he blocked others' media access.

Stone and Kahrl's assumption that control of media would inevitably involve censorship of publicity Garrick considered to be negative in its representation of himself, his writing, or his theatre, is overstated. Garrick embraced negative publicity, generating it for himself, and responding to others' blasts with lively counter-attacks, misdirection or other forms of mediation. One of Garrick's first publications, *An Essay on Acting* (1744), was anonymously written in mock-criticism of himself. Self-manufactured anticipatory critique was a tactic that Garrick continued to employ throughout his career, as Ian McIntyre rightly observes in his entertaining biography, *Garrick* (1999): "Garrick's underlying instinct was to seek accommodation, to attempt to disarm opposition with facetious banter, to affect an ironic concession of the other side's case."[25] Garrick recognized that positive puffery was not the only or the most effective way of shaping public opinion, and his approach to negative publicity was not just about disarming the opposition. One of his most consistent strategies in self-critical works was to mention his diminutive height, a physical trait that ought to have excluded him from romantic leads according to contemporary typecasting. The title page of his *Essay on Acting* suggests Garrick is a "Pygmie"; elsewhere he calls himself "*a little fashionable Actor*" and punningly describes the *Essay* as a "short *Survey of Heroism in Miniature*."[26] The cumulative effect of these barbs reinforces the actor's skill in overcoming physical limitations. This book examines Garrick's production of negative publicity for himself and others, and demonstrates how his management of negative publicity produced beneficial effects for his reputation and that of Drury Lane Theatre.

If Stone and Kahrl's critical biography is the most resistant to considerations of Garrick's interventions in the media, McIntyre's biography is one of the most attentive to Garrick's ubiquitous media presence: "If newscutting agencies had existed in the eighteenth century, there would have been fierce competition to have Garrick as a client,"[27] he remarks. He also mentions Garrick's part-ownership of the *St. James's Chronicle*, writing "Garrick would find it a useful channel for the promotion of his interests over the years, and much of his occasional verse would appear there, as would many of his songs and prologues."[28] McIntyre's depiction of

Garrick's media war with the lawyer William Kenrick over Kenrick's libelous satire, *Love in the Suds* (1772), is another point at which Garrick's media influence materializes.[29] As these brief allusions suggest, this biography is much more alert to the extent of Garrick's interventions in the media than is the earlier work by Kahrl and Stone, or the biographies of Garrick by his contemporaries Davies and Murphy, but consideration of the mechanics or implications of those interventions is not its main concern.

A few scholarly articles that treat of Garrick's relationship with the media have appeared since the publication of McIntyre's biography. John Pruitt's article "David Garrick's Invisible Nemeses" (2008) summarizes and considers a sample of the anonymous satirical pamphlets written against Garrick. Focusing on the pamphlets' similarities and cumulative contributions to public discourse, Pruitt argues that "satirists began to evaluate Garrick by both social criteria and business endeavours: they investigated and questioned [Garrick's] identity as a virtuous gentleman and his business ethics as a perversion of true commerce."[30] These are indeed common themes amongst Garrick's detractors, but few of Garrick's media nemeses (with the possible exception of "Junius") were unknown to him, however anonymous their pamphlets appeared to readers outside the circle of theatrical cognoscenti. More importantly, pamphlets formed but one part of Garrick's variegated mediascape.

Stuart Sherman's article, "Garrick Among Media: The 'Now Performer' Navigates the News" (2011), considers suggestively "the reciprocal impacts – political, commercial, cultural – occurring day by day between press and playhouse"[31] brought into being by the temporal rhythms of the news. In contrast to the "profitably self-obsolescing" newspaper, Sherman writes, "Garrick worked differently, supplanting other actors' product with his own. But by severing the long thread of theatrical transmission and inherited roles – by breaking with the playhouse's tradition of tradition – Garrick forged a new and potentially reusable template of obsolescence, even of usurpation, that more than occasionally haunts his texts and gestures."[32] In two case studies (the 1763 Half-Price riots and the 1769 Stratford Jubilee), Sherman considers the press's potential to confer immortality upon performers.

These articles are the most media-centric of recent essays concerning Garrick, and they contribute to a trend in eighteenth-century studies to consider ephemeral texts, such as newspapers, more fully. Their materiality once enabled newspapers to circulate information about the theatre beyond its benches and boxes; now, paradoxically, it is their immateriality

that enables their scholarly circulation. The beauty of the virtual newspaper archive is that it permits one to look through either end of the
telescope: electronic databases illumine, at the micro level, content privateering, and enable searches for microbial ideas, or repeated phrases, or
pseudonyms; while at the macro level, they can show expansion of interest
in the development of genres such as the theatrical review, or in the
number of papers which devoted space to theatrical affairs.

Structure

At Garrick's first performance on the London stage, Thomas Davies
reports, the city's social geography reconfigured itself: "Goodman's-fields
was full of the splendor of St. James's and Grosvenor-square; the coaches
of the nobility filled up the space from Temple-bar to Whitechapel."[33]
Garrick's London debut was nothing less than a singular, cataclysmic
theatrical enlightenment. "Mr. Garrick shone forth like a theatrical
Newton," wrote Davies, "he threw new light on elocution and action; he
banished ranting, bombast, and grimace; and restored nature, ease, simplicity, and genuine humour."[34] Garrick's success in London was immediate,
according to his biographer.

   However, as I contend in this book, celebrity is an iterative form of
public recognition that is the product of repeated media exposures across
multiple media platforms. If we take this view, Davies's statement can be
read not just as contemporary witness to the birth of a new talent, but as
affirmation of the cumulative effects of the biographer's life-long exposure
to media representation of Garrick as a natural talent and immediate
success. Why should we take this perspective? Consider Figure 1. It is a
manuscript imitation of a rare newspaper advertisement announcing Garrick's first appearance on a London stage. The original document is rare
because Garrick was not yet famous; no one knew that an ordinary
newspaper playbill advertising yet another anonymous actor's debut ought
to be clipped out and preserved. This imitation newspaper article, produced by an unknown artist, was used to extra-illustrate a copy of another
biography of Garrick (that written by Percy Fitzgerald in 1868). Instead of
merely transcribing the words announcing the appearance of a "Gentleman" as Richard III, the illustrator's attention to italics and font size in the
faux type simulate the medium of transmission. This is a portrait of
Garrick *as* news. The faux document is an ingenious solution to the
extra-illustrator's problem of how to mark the moment when Garrick
burst from obscurity, when no extensive visual or verbal archive of the

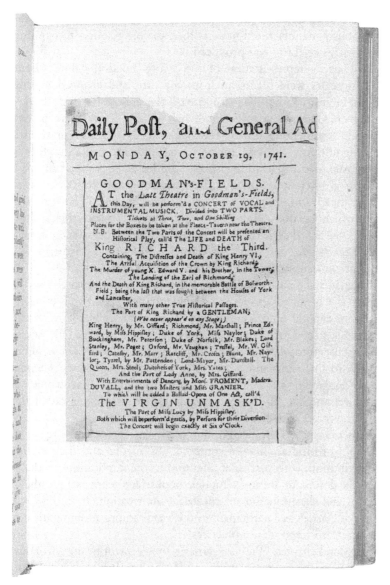

Figure 1 An extra-illustrator's representation of the news of David Garrick's debut, undated. PN2598.G3F5, copy 2 Ex. ill. vol. 1, pt. 1. By permission of the Folger Shakespeare Library.

actor yet existed. But it is more than that: by portraying Garrick as news, and obviously manufactured news at that, the image offers recognition of how Garrick's celebrity was produced.

Like Davies's representation of the actor's London debut, Garrick's media strategies were successful from the first, and changed mainly in scale and intensity rather than in approach throughout his thirty-five-year-long career. Garrick's acquisition of half of the Drury Lane patent in 1747 and his subsequent stature as manager do shift media representations of him significantly; likewise, his power to influence media increases with his new role of cultural impresario. Before his acquisition of the patent, Garrick is a different commodity: he is an actor, and he is able to move amongst theatres in order to increase his cultural capital and real earning power, which he does. Robert D. Hume's study of Garrick's time in Ireland, "Garrick in Dublin in 1745–46" (2014), elucidates in detail the strategic reasons for and results of Garrick's mobility in this period.[35]

The present study focuses primarily, though not exclusively, on Garrick's managerial years, from 1747 to 1776. Following two chapters that establish the historical context and evidentiary basis of this book, each subsequent chapter reflects upon one of the types of media intervention that Garrick staged in aid of establishing his own celebrity. This structure, which seems appropriate, given my findings about Garrick's consistency of approach to his media interventions, will, I hope, combat the tendency towards biography or a life-in-the-works approach that would drive towards yet another affirmation of Garrick's personal fame, rather than a look at the forces mobilized to construct his celebrity.

Chapter 1, "A View of London's Mediascape, circa 1741–1776," renders a historical account of contemporary media, and their audiences and distribution, with particular attention to the implications of the print industry's dominant business model, booksellers' congers, for the construction and dissemination of theatrical information. It finishes with a portrait of Garrick as a participant in this mediascape, outlining his media-reading and correspondence practices.

The second chapter, "Proofs: Garrick's Involvement in the Mediascape," identifies Garrick's media interests and ownership. It gives examples of the kinds of evidential proof that reveal the extent of his involvement, including ownership of newspapers; direct contributions to newspapers and other media; and social and economic transactional influences exerted upon other writers and media influencers.

Chapter 3, "Advertising and Brand Garrick: 'Infinite Variety,'" defines and discusses advertising costs and methods during the Garrick period. It considers direct, taxed advertising in periodicals, then limns untaxed methods of promotion, including reviews, occasional poetry, puffery and theatrical claques and cabals. Using contemporary promotional materials by Garrick and others, it shows the development of key aspects of the Garrick brand, including variety, or the ability to play comedy and tragedy, and ends with a survey of some commercial products that attempted to leverage the associational value of the Garrick brand.

Chapter 4, "A Short History of Negative Publicity," considers Garrick's deployment of negative publicity in aid of his own celebrity. It shows how he converted criticisms of his height into a new critical model that suggested to critics how they might judge and appreciate various aspects of his acting. It examines his mediation of negative publicity generated by others by means of published sick notes, and by the publication of his charity work. It then considers the best-known case of negative publicity in Garrick's career – William Kenrick's accusations of Garrick's homosexual desire for Isaac Bickerstaff – and shows in detail how Garrick exacted an apology in the papers for Kenrick's libel. The chapter concludes with a case study of Garrick's use of negative advertising techniques in the promotion of Joseph Reed's tragedy *Dido* as a means of protecting the integrity of his personal brand.

The fifth chapter, "Prompting, Inside and Outside the Theatre" considers the business practices at Drury Lane Theatre that had a discernable impact upon David Garrick's media representation and celebrity, moving from the division of managerial labour at Drury Lane to consider in-house communications, and Garrick's prompts to change, as discernable in the theatre diaries kept by the theatre's prompters Richard Cross and William Hopkins. It considers the Battle of the Romeos as a case study concerning the effects of dramatized theatrical competition on celebrity.

The book's conclusion takes a parting look at Garrick's media involvement post-retirement, and at Garrickian prints and their circulation, considering nineteenth- and twentieth-century extra-illustration of biographies of Garrick as processes of selection contained within a highly mediated visual archive designed to enhance Garrick's celebrity.

Garrick's deliberate, sustained management of multiple media platforms in constructing his own public image positions him as a plausible candidate for the position of the first modern celebrity. In the debate over whether or not Garrick felt the emotions he could display so easily, the anecdote cited most often is Denis Diderot's observation of Garrick's ability to separate acting from his own conscious emotional state:

Garrick will put his head between two folding doors, and in the course of
five or six seconds his expression will change successively from wild delight
to temperate pleasure, from this to tranquillity, from tranquillity to surprise,
from surprise to blank astonishment, from that to sorrow, from sorrow to
the air of one overwhelmed, from that to fright, from fright to horror, from
horror to despair, and thence he will go up again to the point from which he
started. Can his soul have experienced all these feelings, and played this kind
of scale in concert with his face? I don't believe it; nor do you.[36]

As Joseph Roach puts it, Diderot believes that he has found in Garrick a
perfectly conscious "acting machine"[37] capable of controlling and separat-
ing representation from affect. Consideration of David Garrick's consistent
attention to curating his public image in the media extends this idea and
elaborates the continuum between the late eighteenth-century stage and
page, showing that Garrick not only managed the consciousness of his
spectators on stage, but off it as well. Garrick's enduring reputation as the
'natural' actor, as the inventor of the modern Shakespeare industry, and as
the man whose upright domesticity and genteel friendships made acting a
respectable profession, are all propositions that benefit from a closer look at
his involvement with the media.

Corpus and Methodology

Lucyle Werkmeister's book *The London Daily Press 1772–1792* (1963)
concludes with an expression of "doubt that a really definitive history [of
the eighteenth-century press] will ever be written."[38] Among the difficulties facing the writer of such a history is Werkmeister's commendable
methodological recommendation that the researcher read the newspapers,
"all of them together, and that he should supplement this reading with a
reading of pamphlets, Parliamentary debates, Court records, and plays . . .
letters and diaries, litigations and semi-litigious actions, financial records,
and the memoirs, anecdotes, and early histories."[39] More recently, Richard
Schoch has reminded us, in *Writing the History of the British Stage,
1660–1900* (2016), that theatre history has "never been narrowly teleo-
logical but always dispersed and multi-directional," and that the divide
between theatre history and literary history is a product of twentieth-
century academic scholarship that has "no firm basis in prior scholarly
practice."[40] While it is neither a comprehensive history of the eighteenth-
century press nor of eighteenth-century theatre, this study heeds Werkmeister's and Schoch's calls for multidisciplinary reading. This book looks
at court records, financial records, plays, letters, prints and pamphlets, as

well as newspapers, to examine the available means of producing and circulating opinion within Garrick's mediascape, and to uncover some of the media interventions that Garrick's early biographers Davies and Murphy declined to identify, including Garrick's proprietary interests in newspapers.

To do so, I have read in several archives, as detailed in the acknowledgements, including the Victoria and Albert Museum's Forster Collection, which holds numerous letters written to Garrick that reveal his media reach, some of which were not published in James Boaden's edition of Garrick's correspondence. I am indebted to the work of David M. Little, George M. Kahrl and Phoebe deK. Wilson, whose edition of Garrick's letters was crucial to this study. The editors note that their collection comprises letters from "some three-hundred and forty correspondents . . . [from] familiar names in dramatic history [and] those high in state affairs and society" to "obscure but worthy citizens."[41] They contend that Garrick's correspondence "survives more by accident than by design. He kept about sixteeen hundred letters of his correspondents, largely for business purposes, or because he was proud of the friendships. Of his own letters he prepared and kept drafts and copies of barely one third of all extant letters, again mostly for business."[42] The editors estimate that this may represent "perhaps not more than one tenth of all he wrote,"[43] a fair estimate given Garrick's apparent ease in composition, love of people, and multiple commercial interests. Garrick's letters are by turns suave and brusque, erudite and playful, and they are a delight to read. However, beneath the disarming pleasantries, many of Garrick's letters function as strategic business intelligence, used to assess others' tastes and monitor his public representation.

Part of this book's argument is that media references to Garrick were copious, and that their number and frequency built the public idea of Garrick's celebrity: there are, therefore, copious assemblages[44] of opinion, references and epigraphs included, as material reminders of print's voluminous, unrelenting mediation of theatre. Developments in technology, including access to pamphlets via *Eighteenth-Century Collections Online*, and to databases of eighteenth-century newspapers, including the *17th–18th Century Burney Collection Newspapers*, aided my reading. So that this study could move beyond empirical presentation of archival material to identify and speak authoritatively about trends in Garrick's media representation, my research assistants and I created a dataset listing over 11,000 mentions of Garrick's name in the newspapers published between 1741 and 1779. Newspaper references are recorded locally in the text.

Examination of other theatrical ephemera (including the Folger Shake-speare Library, Harvard Theatre Library and Garrick Club collections, the Cross-Hopkins Theatre Diaries, and extra-illustrated biographies of Garrick), as well as scholarly works concerning the theatre, book and news-paper trades, round out the resources consulted.

Ease of access to newly available resources only renews my appreciation for previous media research, including work by Charles Harold Gray and Roy M. Wiles. It has also given me the dark suspicion that it would be entirely possible to frame a study about Garrick's representation in the press simply by drawing from Charles Burney's collection of news clippings about Garrick; or by mining references to papers and pamphlets cited in biographies of Garrick (which also often draw on Burney's clippings, which appear themselves to be preparation for a biography); or by drawing from news excerpted in standard reference works, such as the *London Stage* volumes. These frequently bur-nished items of news about Garrick are often presented neutrally, without reference to Garrick's agency in producing or promoting them. Where I have encountered an item of news within another collection or source, therefore, I have identified that source, in the belief that laying bare some of these ecologies of re-citation will further my argument about the reach and dur-ability of Garrick's media shadow. Wherever possible, I have supplemented or supplanted such sources with others less familiar, to demonstrate the remarkable breadth of Garrick's media exposure more fully. Likewise, when eighteenth-century newspapers repeat others' content, I have drawn attention to this act, in part because replication intensified Garrick's media exposure.

This book, in short, takes a historically informed approach to demon-strating the cultural construction of celebrity, and analyses fresh documen-tary evidence from contemporary newspapers and other media to show how David Garrick became an enduring cultural icon. Having outlined the book's aim, structure, corpus and methodology, before proceeding further, I will sketch the mediascape which Garrick so ably negotiated. Information about the London mediascape derives from several strands of scholarship: these include studies in the history of journalism, history of the book, theatre history, popular culture and studies of particular figures or publi-cations. What follows extracts elements from those fields, aiming for immediate utility to the reader rather than comprehensiveness. To com-prehend the degree of Garrick's influence over the media, it is necessary to assess the media available; their modes of distribution and ownership; their audiences (print and theatrical) and modes of social interaction; and then, to begin to consider some of the financial, aesthetic and organizational factors that drove Garrick's media strategies.

CHAPTER I

A View of London's Mediascape, circa 1741–1776

Upon the least favourable Calculation, the Number of those called Play-Followers, cannot be rated at less than twelve thousand in this Metropolis; and yet were I to allow the four and twentieth Part of these, a Capacity of determining on the Excellence, or Imperfections of a Performance, or a Performer, I am satisfied I should do the Public more than Justice.

> – [Samuel Foote], *A Treatise on the Passions,*
> *So Far as They Regard the Stage* (1747)

Jemmy [James Lacy] to David [Garrick]:

> ... you well know of our Slaves what a Gang,
> Who for Smiles and for *Stage* Orders will puff and harangue:
> Such resolute Champions, so ready at Call,
> To chatter at *Coffee-house, Ale-house,* or *Stall:*
> Who fear no exposing, no Duty refuse,
> But, as bid, will cajole, hector, scribble or bruise.
> – [William Shirley], *A Bone for the Chroniclers to Pick* (1758)

The word medium and its plural, media, used to identify "a channel of mass communication, [such] as newspapers" and "the reporters, journalists, etc., working for organizations engaged in such communication," emerged in the mid nineteenth century, according to the *Oxford English Dictionary*.[1] These words, however anachronistic, encapsulate eighteenth-century London's varied communications market. In this study, 'media' will refer to print media, including newspapers and other periodicals, playbills and single-sheet broadsides, print advertisements, pamphlets, books, music and prints. The term will also comprehend channels of mass communication, including theatrical performances, sermons and coffee-house reading practices. This chapter surveys the media available during the period of David Garrick's career, and considers their audiences and distribution, with particular attention to the implications of the print industry's dominant business model – booksellers' congers – for the construction and dissemination of theatrical information. An outline of Garrick's media-reading and correspondence practices concludes the chapter and situates Garrick within this mediascape.

Audiences and Readers

Two overlapping groups of cultural consumers inhabit Garrick's mediascape: the theatre audience; and the readers of periodicals and other print media pertaining to the theatre. To gain a sense of how much of London's population was influenced by the media, one must ask a basic question: approximately how large were these groups?

First, consider the theatre audience. Harry William Pedicord estimates that Drury Lane "held about 1,001 persons at capacity (and exclusive of any seating on the stage) in 1732, and that Garrick had enlarged it to hold at the outside 2,362 persons by 1762. Meanwhile, the rival house seems to have maintained its capacity at 1,335 persons (exclusive of stage seatings) until it was increased to 2,170 in 1782."[2] Assuming that both patent theatres were operating every evening at capacity, Pedicord estimates the maximum number of theatre patrons to be "2,336 persons nightly, 1732–47; 2,603 persons, 1747–62; and 3,697 persons from 1762 to the end of our period."[3] Assuming a regular theatre season of 180 nights produces a maximum of 665,460 viewings per season. I use the term viewings because one cannot map spaces in the theatre onto individuals, or assume that different individuals occupied those spaces each night. Many were dedicated theatre-goers, and attended nightly. London's population circa 1760 is estimated at around 750,000, so that one might say that there was almost enough room for everyone in London to attend the theatre each season in potential, but that was not the case, as many people were unable or unwilling to attend the theatre for economic, religious or other reasons.

Allardyce Nicoll chooses another way of measuring the theatre audience. Instead of Pedicord's nightly maximums based on the number of bodies accommodated in the physical theatre, Nicoll estimates audiences during the Garrick period using Samuel Foote's *Treatise on the Passions* (1747), which identifies a select group whom Foote calls "Play-Followers." Using Foote's claim that "the Number of those called Play-Followers, cannot be rated at less than twelve thousand in this Metropolis,"[4] Nicoll arrives at a theatrical audience of "about 9,000 at the start of the Garrick period, [which] rose to about 12,000 at the time when this actor took over the management of Drury Lane, and no doubt gradually expanded during the succeeding years. If the calculated population in 1750 is set against the figure of 12,000, this means that the theatres attracted at that time, some 1.7 per cent of the citizenry."[5] Foote's treatise sceptically judges that the number of cognoscenti is even smaller than the 12,000 "Play-Followers." Writes Foote: "were I to allow the four and twentieth Part of these, a Capacity of determining on the Excellence, or Imperfections of a Perform-ance, or a Performer, I am satisfied I should do the Public more than Justice."[6] According to Foote, fewer than 500 Londoners had the critical capacity to be true theatre critics. Whichever way one estimates the audience for London theatre at mid-century, it is a smaller group than that exposed to the city's burgeoning periodical press.

Just how extensive was London's periodical press during Garrick's career? Michael Harris estimates periodical output in the 1740s thus: "Allowing the five dailies an average circulation throughout the year of 1,500 copies per issue, the six thrice-weeklies an average of 2,500 copies, the five weeklies an average of 3,000 copies, and the two principal cut-price thrice-weeklies an average of 3,500 copies, the weekly sale would have amounted to 100,000 and the annual total to over five million copies."[7] Hannah Barker, working with Jeremy Black's estimate that 25,000 papers were produced each day in 1782 (including tri-weekly and weekly papers), and modifying that estimate using a contemporary source, arrives at an estimated readership of 250,000, or "a sizeable proportion of the London population, which was some 750,000 in 1780."[8]

These two overlapping groups, theatre audiences and periodical readers, were not just consumers of theatre-related media, but also producers of it. The same gentleman who sat in the pit and applauded Garrick's turn as Hamlet might well pen verses upon that performance that would be printed in a newspaper, and reprinted in a magazine or poetic miscellany. The gentleman in the pit might be a disinterested member of the public; but he might also be an aspiring playwright, hoping to smooth his way to the manager by paying out occasional poems in an economy of praise. He might be a fictional persona fabricated by a newspaper printer or a theatre manager. In part because that gentleman in the pit is not always who or what his periodical persona claims ("A By-Stander," say), I believe it is most instructive to begin not with the assumption of a public, but with an examination of the ownership structures underlying the media. Perhaps this study's most surprising conclusion is that the degree to which the eighteenth-century media can be said to represent public opinion has been exaggerated. Revealing Garrick's involvement with the tight circle of men who manufactured the news opens a hatch into a world rife with what today would be decried as conflicts of interest.

Congers; or Some Implications of the Business Organization of Eighteenth-Century Newspapers

Most newspapers were embroiled in the commercial interests of the congers of booksellers who owned and controlled them and used them to promote their other print products, including pamphlets, books, music, magazines and other newspapers of different bent or frequency. Competition in the eighteenth-century media was rarely as simple as newspaper versus newspaper, and the reason for that lies in the organizational structure of newspapers, which was based on that of the bookselling industry. Just as booksellers purchased shares in the copyrights[9] of various book or play titles for their lists, so too did they purchase shares in newspapers; it is often coalitions of booksellers and printers, rather than individuals, who are competing with one another in the news marketplace. Such coalitions were called 'congers,' as John Feather explains:

> The term 'conger' was first used in print by the maverick bookseller John Dunton in the late seventeenth century … as a term of mild abuse for a small group who called themselves the 'trading booksellers'. They were copy-owning and wholesaling booksellers … The group seems to have emerged in the period when the Printing Act was not in force (1679–1685) as a protective device for the copy-owners … By marketing their books through a few major booksellers, the copy-owners effectively ensured that those booksellers would not deal in piracies; if they did so there was the implicit threat of the loss of the far more profitable trade in legitimate editions.[10]

Importantly, Feather notes, members of congers were "competitors as well as collaborators; the conger never operated as a partnership, but rather as a group whose members worked independently of each other while also working collectively in defence of mutual interests."[11] Not only did booksellers form wholesaling congers, buying up books and reselling them to other retailers for a higher price, but they used the same model to form copyright-owning congers. At trade sales, usually held in taverns, members of a copyright conger could purchase fractional shares in the copyright of an individual book title, ranging from half-shares down to a sixty-fourth or smaller share in the case of extremely profitable titles.[12]

The Company of Stationers, the London guild of printers, stationers and booksellers, founded in 1403, and granted a royal charter in 1557, presents an even larger, older nexus of power and protectionism in the print industry.[13] Not all booksellers were members of the Company of Stationers; however, the point is that members of the print trade were accustomed to business practices that embraced collaborative business models intended to reduce their financial outlay, to reduce their risk, and to exclude other competitors from obtaining market share of a particular item. Their business structure was at once closed and protectionist, and yet flexible in the sense that collaboration on or co-ownership of a copyright or a share in a newspaper did not preclude the possibility of competition with one's collaborators on other fronts.

The conger model is visible in the operation of newspapers, where owners, who were predominantly booksellers, purchased fractional shares of a given newspaper. Michael Harris dates the beginning of booksellers' use of the conger model in newspaper ownership to the 1720s, and describes the motives behind this ownership model as "mixed," including "cash return" and "the newspapers' unique value as an outlet for trade advertisements."[14] Periodicals offered booksellers and printers a measure of economic diversification. If their books were flashy racehorses, on which they bet in the sense of investing substantial production costs, stockage costs and copyright shares on individual titles, periodicals were booksellers' reliable cash cows. Periodicals could be counted on for more regular infusions of money or interest, including profit dividends, and the promise of moving along print trade stock by advertising, excerpting or reviewing it.

Equally important to the ability to advertise in periodicals was the ability to block one's competition from so doing. Harris observes, "a share in one or more newspapers meant that the advertisements of competitors could be frozen out, and this negative influence caused a good deal of complaint."[15] Arthur Murphy, the playwright, lawyer and Garrick's early biographer, complained "when a set of booksellers are concerned in a newspaper, a *Monthly Review*, or a *Magazine*, they take every opportunity in the said productions of praising the works, in which they have a property themselves, and of decrying every thing that may prevent an increases of their own sale." Jeremy Black notes that Murphy "also complained about the difficulties that confronted him as the author of the *Gray's-Inn Journal* for which he lacked 'the advantages enjoyed by some of my brother writers. I have not had the happiness of being puffed in any of our common newspapers, nor have I stood well enough with the conductors of our magazines, to be admitted to the honour of furnishing them with an essay once a month.'"[16] As Murphy's protest hints, content, opinion, reputation and access to publication and advertising were all at the mercy of those who could purchase a place in the congers. Later chapters of this book further discuss advertising practices and their impact upon Garrick's reputation.

Robert L. Haig's detailed study of the *Gazetteer* has formed the basis of certain assumptions about the operation of newspaper congers; namely, the idea that no person was allowed to hold "controlling" interest in a newspaper by purchasing more than one share, and the idea that those who owned shares in one paper were precluded from owning shares in any other paper. Haig writes: "By the terms of the contract,[17] the property of the *London Gazetteer* was to be divided into twenty equal shares, of which each proprietor was entitled to hold only one. No individual, therefore, or small group, would be able to gain controlling stock in the paper ... no one who held interest in any other daily paper could become a partner in the new paper, and ... any partner who should later acquire such interest automatically forfeited his share in the *Gazetteer*."[18]

It is tempting, given the paucity of ledgers, minutes and accounts of eighteenth-century newspapers, to extrapolate from this account of the *Gazetteer* and assume that the operations of other papers were similar. However, even from examining the few other extant records, it appears that the ownership structure of the *Gazetteer* was not usual at all.[19] It was customary for the publisher or printer to hold more than one share in a paper, and common for shareholders to possess interest in other newspapers. As C.Y. Ferdinand notes, publisher John Newbery's will bequeathed to his wife "all my Right Shares Benefit and advantage that I am anyways Interested or Intitled unto of in or to all and every the Newspapers or papers hereafter to be printed called as follows that is to say the London Chronicle Loyds Evening Post the publick Ledger Owens Chronicle or the Westminster Journal the Sherborn or Yeovill Mercury," indicating a diverse portfolio of multiple newspapers.[20] Similarly, Salisbury bookseller and publisher Benjamin Collins owned shares in several London papers: the thrice-weekly *London Chronicle* (1757) and a daily, the *Public Ledger* (1760), both of which he initiated, as well as a one-sixteenth share in the *Rambler* (purchased 1757), a one-twelfth share in the *Gentleman's Magazine* (purchased 1755), and a one-quarter share in Ralph Griffiths's *Monthly Review* (purchased 1761).[21]

It does seem to have been usual for shareholders to be cautioned against holding interest in another publication that replicated the first's publication frequency: Richard Baldwin disposed of his share in the thrice-weekly *London Evening Post* before becoming a proprietor of the thrice-weekly *St. James's Chronicle*, for instance.[22] Part-owners in a weekly, however, could also possess shares in a daily paper, or in a monthly magazine, and frequently did, as the examples of Collins and Newbery above show. Indeed, even the *Gazetteer*'s 1748 agreement about exclusivity was soon broken, when in 1752 printer Charles Green Say began printing a weekly, which added an essay or two to content extracted from the daily *Gazetteer*: the 'new' paper was called the *Craftsman; or Gray's-Inn Journal*, which later changed its name to *Say's Weekly Journal*.

Say was not alone in this practice: recycling content across media platforms for maximum profitability was brought to a high art long before the internet era. Robert Dodsley was legendary for his efficient republication of poetry. "First," writes Harry M. Solomon, "a poem would be printed in his periodical; second, it would be reprinted when the separate issues of the periodical were bound and sold as volumes; and, third, the best poems would finally appear in Dodsley's future *Collection of Poems*. Finally, any poem sufficiently popular in the periodical or the *Collection of Poems* would receive a separate edition, just as other poems published by Dodsley in autonomous editions could feed the grander project without ever appearing in the periodical."[23] To keep this poetic circulation scheme afloat, Dodsley had his hand in a number of periodicals: the *Public Register*, the *Museum*, the *World* and the *Annual Register*, which he controlled, in addition to shares in the *London Evening Post*, the *London Magazine* and the *London Chronicle*.[24] Such concentrations of media ownership could work to the advantage of advertisers as well as to the benefit of writers' reputations. Collins's advertisers were offered a sweet deal: "all Advertisements inserted in the Salisbury Journal could, if desired, be inserted in the Ledger without additional expense"; and content such as Oliver Goldsmith's *Citizen of the World* essays appeared in both venues as well, Ferdinand notes.[25]

Periodicals were part of a porous print system. Publishers might maximize their profits on content not just by sharing news stories or items amongst their many print outlets, but also by borrowing from one another, with or without attribution. Small or low-end papers were "largely made up of miscellaneous items extracted from their full-priced competitors" which "emphasized the high level of uniformity in the content of the London papers and contributed to the ironing out of variations between individual publications," Michael Harris writes, noting that though "news borrowing could help to perpetuate mistakes, it also provided a rough-and-ready check on the accuracy of reports that were inevitably sifted by the process of selection. Repetition also guaranteed the widest coverage for items that passed through the circle of London papers into the provinces and beyond."[26] Such borrowing often crossed genre lines. Jeremy Black summarizes: "Newspapers took material from magazines and vice versa."[27]

Borrowing and reprinting was conscious, deliberate policy on the part of the papers' proprietors. The *General Evening Post*'s minutes for 27 September 1754, for example, show the committee advising their printer to print extracts from a publication in which they have an interest, and to purloin items from two other newspapers: "Mr. Say was desired to remember that he has had the first Volume of Postlethwayte's Dictionary some time, and as far as appears, without having made any Use of it, in the Manner that was intended. He is desired to give a Specimen of it very Soon, in the General Evening Post ... It is recommended to Mr. Say, occasionally to take from the World or Connoisseur, So much of those Papers as would conveniently come into the General Evening, Whenever he thought they would please his Readers."[28]

Given that the dynamics of news circulation were such that some more active, content-generating newspapers acted as nurseries for the news of the rest, it follows that a man need not own shares in all the papers to own a circulation of opinion greater than the sum of his shares. Owning a share in the *St. James's Chronicle* had just this effect for David Garrick, as that paper was frequently pillaged for content. For instance, an article lauding the appearance of historically informed theatrical costuming practices at Drury Lane was first printed in the *St. James's Chronicle* for 2–4 November 1762:

> *Drury-Lane.* Last Night the Reformation in Dress, of which we gave Notice in a former Paper, took Place as [sic] this Theatre in the Revival of the Second Part of King Henry the Fourth. The Beauty, as well as Propriety of the Dresses, gave great Satisfaction. The Old English Habits are, indeed, admirably suited to the Stile and Manners of the Plays of that Time, in which a Peculiarity prevails very remote from modern Dialogue and the present Fashions. The Effect of this Observation of the *Costume*, as the French call it, is very visible in the Representation of *Every Man in his Humour*; and will, we hope, for the future be strictly observed in dressing every Character of the Plays of that Age.

The article is reprinted in *Lloyd's Evening Post and British Chronicle* for 3–5 November 1762, with fewer capitals, and the French word "*Coutume*." The article appeared yet again in the *Gazetteer and London Daily Advertiser* for 5 November 1762, with minor variations.

Whether one views this business flow as opportunistic, plagiaristic or as printer-authorized content privateering, repetition engenders a number of ethical issues. An assertion repeated across multiple publications or genres breeds familiarity and comfort with that assertion, simply because it occupies more space in the public imaginary. Repetition across print platforms reads as verification of the item repeated, as well as amplification of its importance. The "Reformation in Dress" boasted of first in the *St. James's Chronicle*, in which Garrick was a proprietor, is reiterated so broadly that it seems to herald universal acclaim for a new epoch in theatrical authenticity. The French word *costume* is applied, seemingly everywhere at once, to describe theatrical dressing; interestingly, this usage predates the earliest instance of 'costume' to describe theatrical dress cited in the *OED*.[29] Garrick's "truly affecting" performance as the sick King, described later in the review, is likewise repeated, rolled in with this report of innovation at his theatre. Repetition of media content brought benefits to those who could control the manner in which their words and reputations were circulated.

The booksellers' interest in the newspapers drove newspapers' content, and not just in terms of advertising books and other print products. The prevalence of patent medicine advertisements in newspapers is traceable in part to the booksellers' interest in the papers. William Zachs's study of John Murray's career notes the necessity of product diversification in Murray's bookshop for the quick realization of capital: Murray sold "stationery, quills, ink, sealing wafers, calling cards, account books and diaries . . . beer and wine, fever powders, Irish linen, lecture tickets, lottery tickets, even woodcocks and partridges – anything to make a profit."[30] Such products were not unique to Murray's shop, and they were frequently advertised in the newspapers. John Newbery, for instance, bought the patent to Doctor [Robert] James's Powder and marketed it throughout the country, while Murray promoted Edward Galliard's pre-measured doses of a rival antimonial medicine.[31] Contrary to demonstrating a diversity of advertising revenue sources in the newspaper, patent medicine advertisements often represent more advertising space occupied by the same booksellers who hoped to drive the public to their shops. Zachs observes, "As both books and proprietary medicines were centrally manufactured and needed national advertising and distribution, the sale of one easily complemented the sale of the other."[32] Medicine, print books and news were entwined from early on in the eighteenth century, thanks to the ownership structures of the book trade. "Booksellers, who, it must be allowed, of all the modern Sages that this Kingdom has produced, best understand their own Interest," wrote "Democritus Minor" in the *St. James's Chronicle* for 2–5 May 1761, "seem so thoroughly to have considered the strict Union there is between the Soul and Body, that the same Shop which sells *Pills to purge the Melancholy*, now furnishes us also with a safe and speedy Remedy for almost every Kind of Distemper."

London theatre was a natural fit with booksellers' and publishers' asset mix. Theatre was centrally manufactured; it had natural print product extensions of its live performances in playbills and books of the play; it depended on printers to advertise its offerings; and, as Stuart Sherman observes, the temporal rhythms of press and stage were mutually reinforcing.[33] The power of convergence of these business interests could be felt at all levels, from large deals and close business and social associations down to passing stage jokes. David Garrick and George Colman's 1766 comedy, *The Clandestine Marriage*, has one such joke that may reveal larger business interests at play.

The Clandestine Marriage features a superannuated gallant, Lord Ogleby, who takes, amongst the many potions needed to oil his ancient carcass into motion, "cephalick snuff." "Cordial Cephalic Snuff" was a headache medication invented, sold and advertised in his newspapers by bookseller Benjamin Collins.[34] Its appearance on stage was not a positive product placement, however. Cephalic snuff's supposedly beneficial properties are mocked as Ogleby compares his ridiculous Swiss manservant, Canton, to the product. Ogleby says to Canton, "'Thou art like my rappee here, [*takes out his box.*] a most ridiculous superfluity, but a pinch of thee now and then is a most delicious treat … Thou art properly my cephalick snuff, and art no bad medicine against megrims, vertigoes, and profound thinking – ha, ha, ha."[35] Ogleby's last exclamations are sneezes of laughter, as he expels any serious thoughts from his brain. Cephalick snuff is at once identified as ridiculous, ineffective and unfashionable, thanks to its association with these characters. Why?

A quick look at the title page of the 1766 edition of *The Clandestine Marriage* reveals the names of its printers: T. Becket and P.A. De Hondt, R. Baldwin, R. Davis and T. Davies. Of these men, Becket, Baldwin, Davis and Davies were all co-proprietors with Colman and Garrick in the thrice-weekly newspaper, the *St. James's Chronicle*.[36] Benjamin Collins, printer and inventor of the Cordial Cephalic snuff, had no interest in that paper. Advertisements for Cordial Cephalic Snuff appear frequently in papers associated with Collins and his business associate John Newbery, including the *St. James's Chronicle*'s competitors in the thrice-weekly periodical market: the *Lloyd's Evening Post and British Chronicle* (see the

7–10 January 1763 issue for Newbery's advertisement for the product) and the *London Chronicle* (see the 21–24 July 1764 issue for a joint advertisement placed by Collins and Newbery); as well as the daily *Public Ledger*, which later published Collins's royal patent for the medicine (see 5 July 1773).[37] The joke on cephalic snuff is a small indication that the *St. James's Chronicle*'s owners, including Garrick and Colman, who wrote the joke, had no interest in promoting a medication that might enrich their media rivals, Collins and Newbery.

Scholarship Concerning Eighteenth-Century Newspapers

Scholarly work on eighteenth-century newspapers to date has focused on their material history, including their modes of manufacture, print runs and ownership; on their literary content; and on their involvement in politics and the creation of a public. As Michael Harris notes, this has led to "the construction of an eccentric chronological framework for the history of the press in which its development is defined largely if not entirely in terms of national politics."[38]

Without question, eighteenth-century newspapers often exhibit political biases, but consideration of these biases or of the politics of the day does not form a significant part of the present study. As the part-owner of a public playhouse, diplomatically courting clientele from various social strata, David Garrick could not afford to demonstrate an overt political bias in print, on stage or in his social relationships. An examination of his social circle turns up Tories like Samuel Johnson; radicals like John Wilkes; ties to the Whiggish Devonshires; and a close friendship with Edmund Burke. His policy of friendship to all parties was a celebrated part of Garrick's public image. The *General Evening Post* for 26–29 October 1771 enthused: "There is no man in England at this period who resembles the Roman Atticus so much as Mr. Garrick. He is on the most intimate footing of friendship with all parties; visits Lord Camden one day, and dines with Lord North on the next; never troubling himself about politics, he is beloved on every side, and renders incessant services to the friends of each, without once glancing to the nature of their connexions." Regarding Garrick's politics, Arthur Murphy wrote, "True to his King and the Constitution, he declined all disputes about Whig and Tory."[39] Whether motivated by practical business policy or by his own equable nature, no sustained political commitment on Garrick's part is visible in his correspondence, published works or representation in the media. Yet Murphy's conclusion was not so much that Garrick was apolitical as that he ruled a separate realm, comparable in importance to other openly politicized modes of national governance: "In his time, the theatre engrossed the minds of men to such a degree, that it may now be said, that there existed in England a *fourth estate*, King, Lords, and Commons, and *Drury-Lane play-house.* "[40]

Contemporary readers did not conceive of their newspapers in terms solely political, either: style and the character derived from style and the particular kinds of content emphasized in a paper mattered too, as shown in a scene from *The Drunken News-Writer* (1771).[41] The humour of this comic interlude depends upon the drunken news-writer Paragraph fracturing the news, reading a partial sentence from one article, and capping it with another, as in this example: "'A lady of rank and fortune has lately become enamour'd of' — 'a highly finish'd picture of a Roman gladiator.'"[42] Paragraph's monologue reveals the characters of several newspapers:

> *SCENE, a Room; a Table with a lighted Candle, Bottle and Glass, and several News-Papers. Enter PARAGRAPH (the News-Writer) drunk.*
>
> Let me see–(*sits down, and prepares to read the papers*) the *Public Advertiser*–right!–I like to take things according to order–*the Public Advertiser* is like—what?—Egad it is like a MADE DISH—full of *good things*, and of the most *opposite* qualities. –Yes!–The *Public Ledger* is *water-gruel* without *salt* or *butter*–and has neither *flavour* or *substance.*—The GAZETTEER,—or *the* NEW DAILY ADVERTISER–is like an UNFILLED HOGSHEAD— full of *sound*, and *empty*;—and the *Daily Advertiser*–pardon, O ye sons of trade, if I call the *Daily* a BASKET *of chips*—for it is dry, and fit only *for the fire* ... [Paragraph then remarks, of an article] 'Pshaw! that's a *lie*–for I wrote it myself—.[43]

Paragraph views news as a common stock of interchangeable parts, or, to use his metaphor, ingredients: the newspaper's style is the catalyst that transforms common ingredients into "good things." The interchangeability and constant recirculation of news, not the rigid stratification of political bias, is the dominant impression of the news visible in Garrick's day, and newspapers attain their characters not only from their political direction, but from their style and non-political content.

Garrick's career (1741–76) corresponds with an apparent lacuna in news history: after Robert Walpole's time, in which the government controlled newspapers, and before the 1780s, when Secret Service accounts strongly suggest a resurgence of government controls, through the quiet buying up of public opinion.[44] P.M. Handover writes, "Management of the Press had become systematic under Walpole after 1721. His ministry encouraged the foundation of pro-government newspapers, paid writers and distributed free copies, spending lavishly from secret service funds until the mid-1730s when the accusations mounted by opposition papers on the outlay of public money obliged a retrenchment."[45] Handover identifies the 1780s as the period at which government control of the press again began to exert itself. It was in this period that the *Morning Post* began, she suggests, to accept government monies to "pay for favourable publicity and to buy off unfavourable, and it became part of the duties of many senior public servants to do their share of 'managing' the Press by arranging for the supply of paragraphs."[46] Garrick's career, and his period of newspaper ownership, then, occupy a historical space when the booksellers' congers were the chief market force behind the newspapers, and – barring the discovery of new archival evidence to the contrary – when many papers were relatively free of government interference.

If historians have been interested principally in issues of political bias, there has been a further foreshortening on the newspaper in literary studies, focusing on those few papers featuring literary essays – *Tatlers*, *Spectators*, *Ramblers* and the like – rather than on the more prosaic advertising sheets;[47] and with more scholarly interest to date in London periodicals than in provincial papers, with some notable exceptions, such as the work of John Feather and Roy M. Wiles. In theatre history, newspapers have served as a source for cast lists such as those excerpted in the volumes of *The London Stage, 1660–1800*, and for ephemeral pieces such as prologues and epilogues. Finally, in journalism-centred histories of the press, the scholarly concern has been to build a narrative of increasing freedom of the press.

Hannah Barker gives an informative survey of works concerning the development of the British newspaper as depicting a progressive, Whiggish view of increasing press freedom: "The serious study of eighteenth-century newspaper history began in 1850 with F. Knight Hunt's *The Fourth Estate: Contributions towards a History of Newspapers, and the Liberty of the Press* [which . . .] depicted the emergence of press freedom in England and the eventual establishment of newspapers as the bulwark of British democracy: the 'fourth estate' of the constitution. Hunt's rather Whiggish interpretation of newspaper history – which presents the heroic struggle of the newspaper to wrest itself from the corruption of eighteenth-century politics – was soon followed by other studies in a similar vein."[48] Recent research, Barker writes, "continues to be dominated by the original Whig thesis mapping the rise of English newspapers from the mire of eighteenth-century corruption to the glorious independence of the Victorian age. This model of newspaper history has profound and misleading implications for the portrayal of the eighteenth-century press."[49]

Mid-eighteenth-century printers of newspapers, however, were less likely to state their "independence" or to insist upon the "freedom of the press" than they were, as William Woodfall did, to insist on their prerogative to "print both sides of the question," a phrase I read as betokening greater concern with commercial viability than with moral or intellectual liberty. Notably, the phrase "both sides of the question" in no way assumes a political question. Scholarly analysis of freedom of the press has been predominantly concerned with the press's ability to comment freely on political events; little corresponding analysis exists regarding the press's freedom to cover other kinds of news, including theatrical entertainment.

News Pamphlets

Studies of newspapers as a genre can neglect an important feature of the eighteenth-century news mediascape, for booksellers and printers not only had their hands in periodicals and books: they also printed and sold pamphlets, usually quarto booklets approximately thirty pages in length, pertaining to a single event or issue. Andrew Pettegree, considering the pamphlet's role in the news industry, remarks that the "apparent virtue of a newspaper, its regularity, became something of a burden," overwhelming the reader with volume and variety of incidents; pamphlets were superior because their single event descriptions could "offer proximate causes, explanations and draw lessons. The newspapers in contrast offered what must have seemed like random pieces from a jigsaw, and an incomplete jigsaw at that."[50] Their single-issue focus made pamphlets perfect for special interest groups, such as theatre critics, and small print markets, such as Foote's 500 theatre cognoscenti.

Pamphlets were usually one-off jobs for printers, who, as we have seen, formed congers that were notable for their flexibility and did not in any way preclude competition on other fronts with conger members. While publication in a newspaper might be difficult for those who could not afford a share or who possessed no other form of interest with shareholders, pamphlets offered an alternative mode of expression to those who could afford to print them, or who could write prose attractive or inflammatory enough to guarantee sales. A number of pamphlets pertaining to Garrick survive, and because they have been more accessible to date than newspapers in the archives, they are somewhat over-represented as expressive of public or contrarian opinion in biographies and in scholarly literature about Garrick.

As David Williams's pamphlet accusing Garrick of controlling access to news media, discussed earlier, shows, many of these pamphlets offer counter-discourses from the aggrieved or dispossessed: those who, like Williams, considered that their access to the press was denied by Garrick-influenced or -owned congers; or others like William Kenrick, who accused Garrick of cutting off playwrights' access to the stage. One might well assume Garrick's relationship with the media was completely adversarial and reactionary if one examined only pamphlets. That is not to say that all pamphlet writers were cranks, or that all were excluded from other forms of media; Garrick frequently used this mode of publication himself. Pamphlets need to be viewed in the total media environment, and especially alongside the periodicals they so frequently presume to correct, supplement or provoke.

Accessibility of Media: Costs and Spaces

Any study of the effects of media needs to consider its accessibility, as well as contemporary reading or viewing practices. The cost of purchasing a newspaper or a pamphlet during Garrick's career was relatively low, compared to the cost of other cultural experiences: just 3*d.* for a stamped newspaper, and double the price or higher, 6*d.* to 1*s.* 6*d.*, for a pamphlet, largely depending on its length. For a labourer in London making 12–18 shillings per day, a newspaper might be an occasional treat.[51] However, it was not necessary to purchase one's own newspaper or pamphlet to gain access to these media. One might club together with neighbours to purchase a paper. Alternatively, admission to a coffee-house, where one might have access to a newspaper, a pamphlet or a book of the play, as part of the coffee-house library, cost only pennies.[52]

Informed knowledge about theatrical events had a significant financial cost. If viewing the play, reading the papers and contributing to the public discussion about it form the basis of informed criticism, then, given that common theatre ticket prices circa 1746 were 5*s.* (boxes), 3*s.* (pit), 2*s.* (first gallery), 1*s.* (upper gallery),[53] one might say the minimum price of airing an informed opinion on the theatre in the late 1740s was roughly four shillings (pit admission, plus coffee-house admission and a drink). Robert D. Hume suggests that "a multiplier between two hundred and three hundred tends to give a rough but suggestive present-day equivalency in buying power."[54] In modern buying power, a would-be coffee-house and pit wit would have to spend about £40, or $80–100, to purchase his place in the detail-rich theatrical conversation of the day. Even before adding in the potential cost of purchasing a book of the play, this was a considerable splurge, and as such, supports Samuel Foote's view that London supported only a small group of regular theatre-going cognoscenti, though many persons of differing social ranks could and did attend the theatre. Reading about the theatre in the papers was considerably cheaper than attending the theatre on a regular basis. Some occasional theatre-goers undoubtedly bolstered their critical reputations by way of the coffee-house and reduced-fee late entry to the playhouse, rather than through full-price admission. It was less expensive to purchase a second-hand opinion via the media than to form one from first-hand experience in the playhouse. For those who could afford to attend the theatre only sporadically, the media did not just represent the theatre, it substituted as proxy for the experience.

Coffee-houses were important centres of dissemination for theatre-related discussions and print products. Markman Ellis's research concerning printed works inscribed with the names of coffee-houses "suggests that at least thirty different coffee-houses in London and the English university cities had book collections of some sort in the mid-eighteenth century" and that in London, these coffee-house libraries clustered around the Inns of Court, the Royal Exchange and the Strand and Charing Cross; alas, no copies of works inscribed with the names of the coffee-houses most closely associated with the theatres, including the Bedford and Slaughter's, remain, though there are plenty of inscriptions on the flyleaves of contemporary plays and works of criticism that show that dramatic works were on offer in coffee-houses.[55] Customers "expected a coffee-house to provide a range of newspapers" and the newspapers themselves were "often organized into files."[56] In some coffee-houses, newspapers were "regularly filed, kept from year to year, and are referred to in public and in private, like the records of law in Westminster-hall," Pierre Jean Grosley wrote in his 1772 book, *A Tour to London*.[57] The theatrical repertoire contained in a coffee-house library might reach back some way, supplementing current stage offerings. Coffee-house reading, as Ellis explains, was "a collective and sociable encounter" and included such practices as reading aloud, memorization and critical debates about quality and authorship attributions.[58] Brian Cowan observes that coffee-house sociability had advantages: it was less expensive and more spontaneous than a formal visit, and coffee-houses had early established a character as civil and genteel places for conversation amongst men, operating in public spaces outside the "traditional social economy of patronage and clientage."[59] Coffee-houses were also closely associated with the book trade: booksellers' auctions frequently took place there, and the extant minutes of newspapers indicate coffee-houses as locales for newspaper proprietors' meetings.[60]

Newspapers and pamphlets could function as extensions of the sociability of the playhouse and theatrical coffee-houses, generating conversation beyond their walls. Reciprocally, the coffee-house could generate discourse that found its way into print. The Bedford coffee-house, under the Piazza in Covent Garden, was renowned as a site of theatrical criticism. Garrick had a long history with the place, beginning with his early career as a wine merchant. He wrote to his brother Peter on 5 July 1740, "I have ye Custom of ye Bedford Coffee house, one of ye best in London by Giffard's means."[61] In a 14 November 1756 letter to the Reverend Thomas Franklin, Garrick demonstrates awareness of the value of coffee-house discourse as he voices concern at hearing that Franklin had circulated opinions critical of his character: "what you publickly said in ye Bedford Coffee house before Men of ye first Character for Letters & Integrity, convinc'd Me, that My Success was unpleasing to you."[62] One of Garrick's works is amongst the titles inscribed with the name of a coffee-house library, as Ellis notes, so Garrick may be said to have had both print and word-of-mouth presence in these sociable spaces.[63]

Garrick's surveillance of coffee-house discourse, in person and by means of report, was known to his contemporaries. The sixpenny pamphlet, *D-ry-L-ne P-yh-se Broke Open. In a Letter to Mr. G——* (1758), conjures up a crowd of critical opinions concerning Garrick, elbowing for space in London's coffee-houses:

> If you go into one Coffeehouse, you will hear a Knot of Criticks inveighing against you [Garrick] for not acting oftener; at the next, a Cluster of Youths, calling your Honesty in question, for playing so much more for yourself, than you did for other Managers—Away, to a third, and your Partiality to *B——*, and your Usage of *Q——*, are the Topicks of Conversation; when perhaps, at another End of the same Coffeehouse, *B——*'s Friends are condemning you for not doing him Justice; while Half a Dozen Friends, who are drinking Punch in the little Room behind the Bar, are d—g you for giving *B——* all the Parts, and swear you have clapp'd the Patent under your Pillow, given up yourself wholly to Ease and Pleasure; and, provided you reap the Fruits of a Manager, you are not solicitous for the Reputation of an Actor—Upon this, Proofs are brought in Defence of their Assertions—*viz.* Prologue at Opening of the House——Ditto to *Albumazar*—Chorus to *Henry* the Fifth—Your frequent Repetition of Characters of little Consequence, such as *Chamont, Hastings, Lothario,* Capt

Plume, Abel Drugger, Sir *John Brute*, &c. and your seldom appearing in those of greater, such as *Hamlet, Richard, Lear, Macbeth*, &c.—Thus they talk, thus they argue, and thus contradict each others [sic] Sentiments.[64]

Talking thus of Garrick is the fashion, the writer asserts, and the print news cycle and coffee-house discourse are mutually reinforcing. Addressing Garrick, writes that he'll consider Garrick impartially, and as "a Servant of the Publick":[65]

It is become a Sort of Fashion (and I don't doubt but you are vain of it) either greatly to abuse you, or extravagantly to applaud you. The Press swarms with Pamphlets address'd to you; and, how the Authors or Printers can find it worth their while to publish 'em, is a Matter of some Wonder. I cou'd wish my Countrymen had something of more Importance to shew their Concern about; but, as the Disorder is epidemical, no Wonder a Lover of the Theatre (as I am) has catch'd the Infection. I see others write as little qualified as myself, so I take up my Pen, and say with your Favourite, *Richard, With all my Heart, I'll not be out of Fashion.*[66]

Similarly, in the satiric green-room dialogue, *Hecate's Prophecy, being A Characteristic Dialogue Betwixt Future Managers, and Their Dependents* (1758), the Garrick figure, Fidget, is shown to have puffers positioned in all the coffee-houses to elevate his reputation. Fidget whispers, "Let's see your List o' *Puffers*. [Reads]——um-n-n-At the BEDFORD, *Pump-well*—GEORGE's, *Frothy*, –Tom's *Specious*-RAINBOW, *Mouthall*-M-m-Mouthall!" [Fidget strikes out the name of this last puffer for praising another actor, Mr. Sweet-tone, then continues naming his minions:] "COCOA-TREE, *Babble.* -CHILD's, *Bushy*—huh-SLAUGHTER's, *Listen*-Um-n-n *Lungs-Whisper-Browbeat,–Double tongue, &c.* "[67] Like a claque designed to boost applause in the theatre, these men insinuate Garrick's name into coffee-house discourse by brow-beating, babbling and whispering praise of the actor. The pamphlet also implies that Garrick and his partner Lacy ("Schemewell") have obtained nearly total control of London's newspapers by purchasing shares in them:

Enter PEERY running with a News-Paper.

PEERY.   Sir, Sir, Sir, Sir,–Pray, Sir, have you seen this, Sir?
FIDG.   [. . . . *catches it and reads*] "ELYSIAN FIELDS, *Feb. 31.* [sic]
"*We hear that Fidget ROSCIUS, Esq; Chancellor of the Theatrical Exchequer, was Yesterday elected Porter to King PLUTUS.*"
—Eph! Damn'em, I say. . . Why-I-aw-a-I thought you had *tyed up* this Paper.
SCHEM.   I!-not I-for it's the *only* one you know, that we are n't Sharers in!
FIDG.   Damnation![68]

Coffee-house wits had the satisfaction of knowing that they were talking to some purpose, for they were well aware that their opinions were monitored. Performative talk about theatrical performance in a coffee-house flush with spies from the theatres is a long way from Jürgen Habermas's cozy ideal of a democratized coffee-house as the site of "rational critical debate" of a "bourgeois public" carried on "without regard to all preexisting social and political rank and in accordance with universal rules."[69] Tying up the tongues of coffee-house wits and disrupting the circulation of theatrical news is part of Garrick's media influence, these pamphleteers assert.

Public houses or taverns, though less likely to maintain significant reading material on the premises than were coffee-houses, also served as sites for gathering and mediating news of London's theatres. Thomas Davies writes, of Hugh Kelly's arrival in London around 1763, that Kelly immediately grasped the growing market for theatre news and "conceived that the surest method to get employment as an author, would be to signalize himself by writing short essays and paragraphs in the news-papers. He constantly paid attendance at a public house within a few doors of Drury-lane theatre; in this place he learned from the lowest retainers of the stage the characters of the actors, or rather, he gleaned the idle and insignificant remarks which were made on their conduct in private life, as well as their professional merit. From what he gained in such company, and from such information, he treated the players with great and unexampled severity in the public prints."[70]

Access to media depends upon proximity to resources and the spaces in which news is disseminated as well as upon economic factors. Writers like Kelly would not have far to walk from the theatres to the presses: the theatres and much of London's print industry were located within easy reach of one another. Ian Maxted's book, *The London Book Trades 1775–1800*, considering the names of print trades associated with Fleet Street and the Strand, where the trade was concentrated, lists "55 engravers and 53 printsellers on Fleet Street and the Strand as well as some 30 music businesses located in the Strand alone," and, Michael Harris observes, "when the predominant booksellers and printers are added, the way in which the two thoroughfares became a primary artery in the general flow of all forms of print begins to take shape."[71] Both Bridges Street (the location of the Theatre Royal in Drury Lane) and Covent Garden are five minutes' walk from the Strand. This geographic overlap of two highly concentrated industries suggests that not only Kelly, but many other writers, booksellers and printers must have frequented the same coffee-houses and public houses as theatrical personnel, facilitating the transfer and manufacture of news about the theatres.

This was also David Garrick's neighbourhood, as Boaden observes: "Mr. Garrick through life resided constantly near the playhouse. The Great Piazza, James-street, Southampton-street, the Adelphi, were in succession rendered happy by possessing him. There was a fondness for him in this neighbourhood, that, as he passed through it, darted electrically from shop to shop; and his name was oftener resounded in Covent Garden than that of any other human being."[72] Garrick and his urban neighbourhood were mutually constitutive, as the print industry and its products supported the theatre, and theatre news supported the printers, publishers and booksellers on Paternoster Row and the Strand. Each was identified with the other from an early date: Samuel Foote wrote in 1747 of "an admired Dramatick Genius, who now resides in the Navel of the Metropolis"[73] and expected his readers to understand that this figure (described with Foote's customary irony) was Garrick. London's navel may have been an undignified description of Garrick's place of residence, but it unquestionably places the actor in the centre of theatrical discourse. In this part of London, in theatres, coffee-houses and booksellers' shops, theatrical and media geographies overlapped comfortably, and the most celebrated object in both theatre and media enjoyed the constant, visceral buzz of celebrity as he moved through these spaces.

Garrick's Media-Reading Practices

The sociable news-reading and news-gathering activities in public spaces such as coffee-houses and public houses remind us that unlike the often solitary activity of novel-reading, news-reading frequently brought people together. In material terms, this also tells us that the number of copies per issue of a given paper or pamphlet does not equate with its total number of readers. Michael Harris contends, "Contemporaries calculated that a single copy of a London paper could have as many as 20 readers and a popular weekly up to 40."[74] Though scholars' estimates of the number of second-hand readers vary, numerous accounts of contemporary news-reading practices certainly show that the number of readers exceeded the number of copies of newspapers and pamphlets printed. Garrick's correspondence shows him to have participated in the multiple-reader-per-copy mode of reading, sharing his papers with his brother Peter, among others.[75]

His correspondence also demonstrates his awareness of the reading habits of important taste-makers and patrons: Garrick knew, for instance, that the King "always sees ye *Publick Ad[vertise]r* "; and that Lord Spencer took all the papers of interest except the *Morning Chronicle*.[76] Knowing such preferences was actionable intelligence, useful for nurturing important social relationships. Garrick's knowledge of the King's daily reading habits enabled him to place a well-timed retraction in the *Public Advertiser*, before the King could be offended at a report of Garrick's visiting a friend in the country when he had been excused from court to recover from an illness. To William Woodfall, Garrick wrote hastily on 2 February [1777]:

> my old Friend Sampson has said in his *Public Adr* Yesterday that I was in London to visit Mrs B[arry] as I am here upon the [King]'s Business, & got leave to recover myself in ye Country–they may take it ill at St James's– could you desire him to say in an unparading paragraph from himself–*that he was Mistaken about Mr G–that he was in the Country & had been for some time in order to recover the great weakness which was caus'd by his late illness–* You or He will put it better & Modester for Me than that, which I have written upon ye gallop: pray let it be inserted in ye same paper tomorrow– HE [the King] always sees ye *Publick Adr*.[77]

Similarly, when Garrick passed on a scarce anonymous pamphlet, *The Case of the Unfortunate Martha Sophia Swordfeager*, to Philip Yorke, second Earl of Hardwicke, on 21 July 1771, he was not just lending out a salacious story of a woman tricked into a false private marriage. His selection pays a delicate compliment to Hardwicke's father, and acknowledges Hardwicke's taste for history and rarities. As Stephanie L. Barczewski writes, "Hardwicke was a prominent man in intellectual and antiquarian circles, as is evidenced by Horace Walpole's advice to Horace Mann in 1757: 'That family is very powerful; the eldest brother, Lord Royston [Hardwicke's title before he became the second Earl of Hardwicke in 1764], is historically curious and political; if, without its appearing too forced, you could at any time send him uncommon letters, papers, manifestoes, and things of that sort, it might do you good service.'"[78] Whether or not Garrick, who knew Walpole, received the same advice, he was clearly aware of Hardwicke's tastes. The pamphlet itself carries some of the burden of compliment.[79] Its preface notes that the woman's distress might have been prevented by the Marriage Act of 1753, of which the present earl's father was the chief architect. Hardwicke would have been pleased to read the rare piece, and doubly pleased to reflect on his family's role in preventing further such distresses. Garrick's sharp sense of others' periodical reading habits and tastes was used to good effect in promoting influential social relationships.

In addition to those who shared their newspapers, inside or outside the coffee-house, there were super-readers who regularly read several London papers. Barker remarks, "some people would almost certainly have read more than one paper. In addition, the circulation, and therefore the possible influence, of London newspapers was not restricted to the capital."[80] Garrick's own news-reading practices, as detailed in his correspondence, show him to have been a reader of several papers, whether in town or country or abroad. Whilst he was on the Continent in 1763–65, his letters mention Garrick reading the *London Chronicle*, glimpsing a *St. James's Chronicle* and "other papers" in Naples to read theatre news, and asking his brother George Garrick and George Colman to keep a stack of *St. James's Chronicles* for him to "rummage over when I come to England."[81] When he was out of London, visiting friends or staying in the country, Garrick directed his brother George or other friends to send him the latest news. In a 2 June 1750 letter, Garrick asks Somerset Draper to send him Fletcher's play *The Faithful Shepherdess*, "and the Monthly Review, if you please; and any thing else, will be diverting."[82] Similarly, on [28 April] 1767, he requests that George send him a parcel of news, in anxious terms that show his hunger for the papers:

> I have enclosed two franks, one for the letters, and one for 'The St. James's Chronicle' and 'The Public Advertiser,' which I beg you will send on Saturday next–both the papers of *that* day. Sir Edward Lyttleton's affair shocks me: I long to know the event … You will take care to put 'The Public Advertiser' and 'Chronicle' of Saturday into that frank which I have directed myself, and the letters into the other,—very cautious, you will say,—but, my dear George, a mistake might be made, so do not think me overwise in wishing to be sure of my newspapers, when I come into my Inn at Reading.[83]

Whether he was "long[ing] to know the event," keen to check the accuracy of a playbill, or curious to see his own words in print, there can be little question that Garrick was an insatiate reader of periodicals. References in his correspondence show Garrick to be a reader of, at various times, the *Dublin Mercury*, the *Dublin Journal*, the *Whitehall Evening Post*, the *London Chronicle*, the *Gentleman's Magazine*, the *Morning Chronicle*, the *London Packet*, *New Morning Post or General Advertiser*, the *Annales politiques, civiles, et litteraires*, the *Morning Post*, the *Public Ledger*, the *Critical Review*, as well as the previously mentioned *Monthly Review*, *Public Advertiser* and the *St. James's Chronicle*, among others.[84]

Garrick's pleasure in periodicals was only heightened by his understanding of the trade, which understanding increased in complexity throughout his career. On 15 December 1777, from Althorp, Garrick wrote to his brother George: "You need not send me any more papers unless it is the Morning Chronicle, which Becket will take care of, Lord Spencer has all ye Papers Except that, I shd be glad to know what he says of ye *Roman Sacrifice*, Mr Cumberland has written an excellent Epilogue for it & that B—— Master Y[ates] would not speak it—."[85] This letter shows Garrick's appetite for reading the representation of events in newspapers when he possessed inside knowledge of the back story (in this case, Yates's bastardly refusal to speak Richard Cumberland's epilogue). Garrick did not read the newspapers naively, as if they contained objective reportage, but with a well-informed ex-manager's interest in the representation of his theatre and its actors. Reading the papers was at this point, for Garrick, who had been actor, author, manager and newspaper proprietor, a delectable personal entertainment, affording him a trebled view, as if standing between the scenes, able to see at once the news now acting on stage, the responses of the newspaper's audience, and the machinations of those writing, producing and shifting the scenes of the whole production – in short, the kind of rarefied appreciation of one magician who fully understands exactly how it is done, for the tricks of another.

Correspondence and the Media

Garrick's correspondence was often considered fair game for publication in the media. Occasionally Garrick expresses astonishment at seeing some element of his correspondence in the papers, as he does when writing to his brother George from Paris on 12 November 1764: "I am told part of a Letter of mine about ye Duke of Parma &c was printed how came that about—I was supriz'd—."[86] More frequently, Garrick is the agent of such placements of his or others' correspondence in the newspapers, and suggests the inclusion or development of some part of a letter to his correspondent. Garrick writes to John Hawkesworth, one of the proprietors of the *Gentleman's Magazine*, circa December 1755: "You cannot imagine how Exactly We agree in our Sentiments of the *Duke de Foix*: Your Letter is a very agreeable Critique upon ye Performance, & might make a very good Letter in yr Magazine: I shall preserve it with ye hopes that You'll do Something with it."[87] Sometimes the suggestion is at the level of content, as it is in a letter to George Colman, dated Paris, 10 March 1765, regarding a tragedy called *The Siege of Calais*, which has "made ye

People Mad": "there is much merit in ye Play, & more luck in ye Choice of the Subject—I rejoice at the success, for Monsr de Belloy the Author of it is a most ingenious Modest & deserving man–his Genius is an honour to his own Country & would be to any other–You may mention something of this in ye St James's but not from Me—."[88] Other times, the letter or a part thereof is drafted ready for the periodical press. Garrick is particularly adept at doing this with his foreign correspondents – or at least, these are the instances that have been preserved, not surprisingly, as the option of private conversation was not available to these distant friends. There is evidence in the correspondence, too, of Garrick as a reader of his own publicity when authored by others. The correspondence shows him thanking Samuel Richardson on 18 July [1749] for the great "honour" done him in the last volume of *Clarissa*, which "flatter'd me extreamly."[89]

James Boaden, who first edited Garrick's correspondence, speculated that Garrick may have selected and preserved letters with an eye towards autobiography.[90] During his life, however, Garrick appears to have treated his correspondence as a stockpile of weaponry, to be unleashed in the media should an unhappy correspondent foolishly threaten to breach the cold war of unpublished letters. As Garrick wrote to the Rev. Mr. Hawkins on 20 September 1774:

> Notwithstanding your former flattering letters to me, which I have luckily preserved, you now accuse me of pride, rancour, evil designs, and the Lord knows what, because I have refused your plays, which I most sincerely think unfit for representation, and which (some of them, if not all) have had the same fortune with other managers ... Can you really believe that this unprovoked, intemperate behaviour can make me submit to your inquisitorial menaces? "Perform my plays or I'll appeal to the public!" If you will publish your plays with your appeal, I will forgive you the rest.[91]

Garrick retained an epistolary shield to guard against disgruntled playwrights, should they attempt an appeal to the public. Boaden's published collection and the Forster archive, both of which include letters written to Garrick, yield insights into Garrick's influence on booksellers, publishers and authors, as they show correspondence kept for the purposes of protecting his public reputation.

Garrick's letters also reveal an avid reader collecting an extremely valuable library over his career. The contents of this library, partly visible in letters, and partly glimpsed in auction catalogues, show the scope of

Garrick's reading and media involvement. The 1823 Saunders auction catalogue[92] is prefaced with a note on the state of the Garrick library after Eva Maria Garrick's death in 1823, by which time, Garrick's treasured collection of old plays had been donated to the British Museum, and other bequests made.[93] The Garricks read widely, and their library included books on gardening, architecture, cookery, classics, theatre, art, oration, music and poetry; there are memoirs, epigrams, plays, novels; there are works in numerous languages, and spectacular acquisitions such as D'Alembert and Diderot's *Encyclopédie* and a fine set of Hogarth's prints, down to a few sermons and prosaic works on trade, travel and medicine, as Nicholas D. Smith notes in his admirable recent study of the library, *An Actor's Library*.

Most important to understanding the degree to which Garrick read and participated in the periodical culture of his day, the auction catalogue shows that Garrick's library contained masses and masses of periodicals and pamphlets. Among the collections of periodicals are listed the *Bee*, the *Rambler*, the *Idler*, the *Spectator* (multiple editions), the *Tatler*, the *Guardian*, the *Adventurer*, the *Post Boy* (1709–19); the *Protester*, a Periodical Paper, "23 first Nos."; the *Mercure de France* (January 1768 – April 1778, 83 vols., wanting 9); the *Monthly Review*, odd numbers, 1771 to 1778, and vols. 48, 49, 56, 57; Arthur Murphy's *Gray's-Inn Journal* (2 vols., 1756); "London and other Journals, 2 vols 1727–35"; and "Magazines and Reviews, 52 odd numbers." Unfortunately for the purposes of documentation, the pamphlets were sold in lots, and titles and dates are not given, but there are hundreds:

> 1836 Pamphlets, 25 Poetical, by Goldsmith, H. More, Keate, Garrick, &c.
> 1837 Pamphlets 30 Poetical, chiefly anonymous
> 1838 Pamphlets 36 Poetical, chiefly anonymous
> 1839 Pamphlets, 20, chiefly anonymous
> 1840 Pamphlets, 20, Miscellaneous, Prose
> 1841 Pamphlets, 23, ditto
> 1842 Pamphlets, a bundle of French, Italian, &c.
> . . .
> 1867 Newspapers and Pamphlets, a bundle of odd, *various sizes*
> . . .
> 2678 A parcel of loose pamphlets, &c.[94]

Garrick read a wide range of periodicals and pamphlets old and new, many of which seem to have been retained by him for reflection, and curated or annotated.

Theatre in the News

Garrick's stage career occurred during a period of rising representation of the theatrical world in the newspapers. Describing the changes in newspapers' content from the 1720s to 1780s, Jeremy Black writes: "there was more non-political news, particularly items devoted to social habits and fashions. Literary, particularly theatrical, news had become a regular feature, and there was more economic news, though nothing approaching the percentage of non-advertising space devoted to it in modern 'quality' British newspapers."[95] Black's statement does not assign cause for this development: it could mean that consumers of papers demanded such changes, or caused them to come about by purchasing papers which delivered more non-political news. However, one must also consider the other end of the supply chain, and the idea that those persons who owned the newspapers had an interest in promoting and publishing non-political news. This is indeed the case. Garrick and his rival manager at Covent Garden, George Colman, were both proprietors of and contributors to newspapers, intensifying a trend that may have begun a decade earlier.

Garrick was not the first theatre man to purchase print influence: the actor Theophilus Cibber for a time owned a third of a tenth share in the *London Daily Post*, as is evident from British Library Add. MS 401.C.27, which includes a 1736 legal document signed by "The. Cibber," "Stampt in the presence of Robt. Turbutt [and] Edwd: Berry," recording the sale of this share to Henry Woodfall. The difference between Garrick's long-term purchases and Cibber's minuscule third of a tenth share lies not just in the scale of influence, but also in the uses to which that influence was put. This difference in ownership power was magnified by the actors' social networks: while Cibber had few resources but his father's surname, and had alienated much of the London theatre world through his atrocious personal behaviour, people were anxious to ingratiate themselves with the rising star, Garrick, particularly after his consolidation of power by patent purchase. Garrick was better positioned than was Theophilus Cibber to take advantage of the benefits of media exposure in the complex print world, and his media ownership and engagement were correspondingly greater in scale and impact.

In late eighteenth-century London, newspapers were not just about news: they were flexible yet protectionist business arrangements that enabled printers to cross-promote their other products, including those associated with theatre. Garrick was a constant, enthusiastic reader of newspapers and other periodicals. His correspondence furnished material to periodicals and was retained, in some cases, as protection against media misrepresentation. His letters show the depth to which he monitored not only his representation, but the media-reading habits of others, including the sociable reading practices of coffee-houses. The next chapter reveals the ease with which David Garrick was able to insert and influence media content.

CHAPTER 2

Proofs: Garrick's Involvement in the Mediascape

*Mr. Garrick hath always had considerable shares in the *property*, and very great influence in the *management*, of the PUBLIC ADVERTISER, the GAZETTEER, the MORNING POST, and the ST. JAMES's CHRONICLE; and hath always found *means* to keep in his interest the *illiterate* conductors of the CRITICAL and MONTHLY REVIEWS: but his hatred to genius hath kept him at perpetual variance with the GENTLEMAN's MAGAZINE, and the LONDON REVIEW, which are conducted by men of learning and abilities.

> – Editorial note in [David Williams], *A Letter to David Garrick, Esq. On His Conduct as Principal Manager and Actor at Drury-Lane. With a Preface and Notes, by the Editor*
> [2nd edn, 1778]

Drury-lane. On Thursday last, for the first Time, was performed at this Theatre, a new Comedy called *The Discovery* ... As to what relates to the Theatrical Representation, we must acknowledge that the Characters of the Play were all very properly and handsomely drest, and most excellently performed ... AS to Mr. Garrick, He was (to use the Stile and Language of Sir Anthony) most ex-tra-or-di-na-ri-ly ac-cu-ra-te in e-ve-ry Syl-la-ble which he ut-ter-ed.

[We can give no direct Answer to the Letter printed in Yesterday's Gazetteer, addressed to the Printer of this Paper, because the Charge is so dark we do not understand it. We shall therefore only repeat our former Assertion of being totally uninfluenced; and appeal to the Judgement of our Readers, whether the Letter and Paragraphs relative to the Theatres, inserted in this Paper, are not the best Evidence of our Impartiality.]

> – *St. James's Chronicle*, 5 February 1763

That David Garrick had breathtaking access to the newspaper press of the day, as well as to other media, is conclusive and inarguable, as it is apparent from a number of extant documents. I will identify each type of documentary evidence here, with reference to a few examples of the type, and pursue the effects of Garrick's interventions in detail as appropriate throughout the study. The kinds of evidence available to substantiate a claim of thoroughgoing media intervention on Garrick's part include evidence of Garrick's ownership of media; evidence of contemporaries' knowledge of Garrick's media ownership and influence; evidence of Garrick's direct contributions to the media; and evidence of transactional links, both social and economic, between Garrick and various media stakeholders.

Garrick's Ownership of Media

From approximately 1756 to the end of his stage career in 1776, David Garrick owned shares in several newspapers that covered theatrical news. The period 1762–1776 is the most media-intense of his career. Part-owners or sharers were termed "proprietors" in the extant records of newspapers. Accordingly, I use that term, not only for its historical accuracy, but also because it is redolent of proprietary interest in the newspaper's content. I will begin by discussing the strongest evidence of Garrick's media influence: his ownership of shares in newspapers. Certain documentary evidence exists of Garrick's proprietorship in the *London Packet*, the *Public Advertiser*, and the *St. James's Chronicle*; there is also evidence which strongly infers he held such interest in the *Morning Post*.

The minutes of the *London Packet* show David Garrick as part-owner of that newspaper.[1] In a meeting at Anderson's coffee-house on 8 January 1770, Garrick's friend, the bookseller Thomas Becket, agreed on his own and on Garrick's behalf that "each Partner shall Deposit the Sum of Twenty five Pounds in order to carry on the London Packet," signing for Garrick in absentia.[2] On a meeting of the partners at the Devil Tavern on 12 January 1770, Becket again signed "TBecket for D. Garrick Esq," thereby agreeing to a change in the paper's publisher and printer.[3] From the minutes of 6, 8 and 12 of January 1770, it is clear that Garrick was an existing, not a new, partner in the concern; therefore, we may extend his ownership in the paper conservatively back into 1769. As shown below, many of the *Packet*'s part-owners, like Becket, were also participants in the book trade. To judge by a reference in a satire called *The Theatres: A Poetical Dissection*, discussed later in this chapter, Garrick still seems to have had an interest in the paper in 1772.

The extant run of the *London Packet* (later the *London Packet; or, New Lloyd's Evening Post*) in the *17th and 18th Century Burney Newspapers Collection* archive during Garrick's career is thin – sometimes only a single

issue per month survives. It was issued thrice-weekly, first printed by
T. Evans; W. Woodfall's name appears on surviving issues from 1774,
and later T. Brewman appears as publisher. The paper dealt in a mix of
foreign affairs, reports from London and the House of Lords, letters to the
printer on topical subjects (including theatre), occasional columns containing theatrical intelligence, and the usual mix of advertisements for
pamphlets, books and patent medicines. No regular bills of the play appear
to have been placed in the *Packet*.

It is doubtful that Garrick still owned shares in the *London Packet* in
1778, when the *Packet* printed "*The importance of* PUFFS *and* PARA-
GRAPHS *continued; or,* ACT II,"[4] for while Garrick did not shy away from
negative publicity and even generated some of his own, there is a degree of
personal insult and invective in this piece which is inconsistent with the
control proprietors might exercise over content in their newspapers. In a
dramatized conversation between Garrick and the playwright and news-
writer Henry Bate, who was at this point working for the *Morning Post*,
Garrick's media and social influence is laid bare in scathing fashion:

GARRICK.   What! What! G—d dammé, are you not writing the paragraphs
    about my *illness* and *Cox-heath*? . . . you know, Bate, what I can do. *I'll tell
    the King of you*; and then, what will become of your pension?
BATE.   Sir, Sir, I was only musing how to put your hints into a proper dress. You
    used to have the goodness to bring the paragraphs yourself; and you always
    say that *no man can praise you exactly to your mind but yourself.*
GARRICK.   Ay, that's true enough . . .
BATE.   You had better dictate to me.

Bate's paper, the *Morning Post and Advertiser*, had on 7 August 1778 actually reported that Garrick was recovered from his "late alarming indisposition," an illness which, the Garrick character in the dialogue says with
regret, has made his right hand so gouty that he cannot write his own
publicity paragraphs. Bate takes dictation of a paragraph praising Garrick
as a "theatric Apollo (in capitals)," and then the two men discuss its
distribution, which includes a planned repetition of content:

GARRICK.   Let it be in thy paper directly, with some little error, that it may be
    inserted twice, in justice to *the importance of the subject*. At the same time be
    sure you get it into all the papers in which I have shares. I have them all,
    except two or three. G—d dammé, it is very hard to be obliged to go on
    buying to the end of my life.

The two conspirators then drum up another false paragraph to be inserted
in the *Morning Post*, this time concerning "Cox-heath," a British military

camp. The paragraph's intent is to show Garrick as a patriot, and a man of such fame that his name has become a watchword. The laudatory Coxheath story had run in the *Morning Post* on 15 August 1778: "The other Day Mr. Garrick visited several Military Gentlemen at the Camp at Coxheath, when, in compliment to that Gentleman, we hear the Pass-word was Shakespear, and the Counter-sign, Garrick!"

However, the *London Packet*'s satiric dialogue reveals that this is a staged event on two levels. The Garrick character cautions: "I have it ready – but observe, Bate don't put it in the day before I go there, and spoil it's [sic] effect." In case the reader misses the point, an editorial note advises: "*The reader is to observe, that this dialogue passed before Garrick went to Coxheath, where no notice was taken of him, though he had previously concerted a *trick* with some officers of the Surry militia." The casual complimentary linkage of Garrick, Shakespeare and patriotism intended by the exclamation in the *Morning Post* is exposed as calculated puffery. The Bate character warns his patron that the auctioneers Christie and Skinner "say that you should pay as they do, for advertising yourself," insinuating that Garrick's access to the *Morning Post* permitted self-promotion such as the Coxheath paragraph without the costs associated with formal advertisement.

This privilege has been gained, it appears, through a proprietary interest in the *Morning Post*. The Garrick character in the dialogue asks Bate, "Have I not bought a sufficient number of shares to secure thee in thy place at all events?" suggesting that Garrick currently, in 1778, owns shares in the *Morning Post*. Unfortunately, there is no further documentary evidence indicating the extent of Garrick's proprietary holdings in this paper. Yet in August 1778, though Garrick was no longer an actor or theatre patentee, he was still managing his celebrity in the media so actively that the *London Packet*'s satire had bite.

Garrick's longest stint as a newspaper proprietor was undoubtedly with the *Public Advertiser*. That Garrick owned shares in the *Public Advertiser* appears from a letter written to the publisher John Payne in 1756: "What can be ye Meaning, of a foolish Paragraph in our Paper about my being rob'd?–I could Wish that you would call at ye Printer of it, when you pass yt way, & let him know how ill I take it that they will mention my name without authority from Me–I look upon it as very unaccountable & disobliging."[5] The offending paragraph was this, from the *Public Advertiser* for 20 July 1756: "On Saturday last about Six in the Afternoon, David Garrick, Esq; was attacked by four or five Fellows on Foot, within twenty Yards of the Swan at Waltham-Green; but Mr. Garrick's Horse taking

Fright at their sudden and tremendous Burst of Oaths, ran away with him, by which Means he escaped being robb'd, and perhaps being very ill treated." Garrick's letter berates Payne for including this unflattering portrait of his retreat from robbers, and particularly for mentioning his name "without authority." Supposing, as the letter suggests, that this is an aberration, it follows that already in 1756 Garrick generally did exert some control over content, and over the ways in which this paper mentioned his name.

The *Public Advertiser*, as its name trumpets, was an advertising sheet featuring notices of lotteries, auctions and sales by the candle; advertisements for servants, books, medicines and stolen horses; properties for sale or lease; shipping, London and country news; letters to the printer, and other occasional pieces. The most prominently placed advertisements in this daily were for the entertainments offered by London's theatres. The *Public Advertiser* enjoyed the market advantage of being the official publisher of playhouse bills, and paid the playhouse for this valuable privilege, as is discussed further in the section on transactional evidence below. On any given day during the theatrical season, which ran from approximately September to May, a reader of the *Public Advertiser* would be likely to see David Garrick's name at least once – usually in capitals, on the top left of the newspaper's front page under the masthead, in the bills of the play. On 13 December 1756, for example:

> D R U R Y – L A N E.
> At the particular Desire of several Persons of Quality.
> At the Theatre Royal in Drury-Lane,
> This Day will be presented the Tragedy of
> H A M L E T,
> PRINCE of DENMARK.
> Hamlet, Mr. GARRICK;
> The King, Mr. Davies; Ghost, Mr. Berry; Horatio, Mr. Havard . . .

The example shows Garrick's customary typographical and positional prominence in the bill. Amusingly, the casting calls for Garrick, as Hamlet, to display murderous hatred for his future biographer, Davies (playing the King); Davies had not yet made the transition from actor to bookseller.

It would be difficult to overstate the degree of commercial exposure afforded Garrick by this newspaper. In the calendar year 1756 alone, Garrick's name appears over 300 times in the *Public Advertiser*, usually in advertisements for which the paper paid Drury Lane Theatre. This advertising sheet established Garrick as a theatrical commodity and a household name. Advertisements listing the bill of the play were not the only way in which Garrick was featured in the *Public Advertiser*; as we shall see, he was also the subject of letters, poems and other articles, and he contributed content.

This reciprocally beneficial long-term commercial relationship was not without its irritants. Garrick wrote to Henry Sampson Woodfall on 20 March 1773, pettishly complaining that he was prepared to give his shares in the *Public Advertiser* up:

> By what dropt Yesterday from our Friend Becket I imagine that I am but a poor caput Mortuum among my Brethren of ye Publick Advertiser–& what is worse I have a property the very reverse of that of a Boy's top, for the more I am whip'd, the less I spin. I must therefore desire you to dispose of *my* Share to any Gentleman [who has more time and talents to serve the] Paper & the Publisher, tho no one can wish better to both than Dr Sr Yr most humle [sic] Sert D: Garrick. I shall have no objection to give up the Dividend too which I have receiv'd.[6]

However he felt about his shares, Garrick was still contributing articles to the *Public Advertiser* in the two months before his death. Garrick's correspondence with Thomas Becket shows that he was writing an anonymous newspaper column for the *Public Advertiser* called 'The Whisperer.' This secret is referred to obliquely in the correspondence, and the column, which appeared on 26 December 1778 and 7, 8, 9 and 19 January 1779, does not seem to have been previously identified as Garrick's work. Given his usual pattern of convergence between ownership and direct contribution to a newspaper, it seems likely that Garrick retained his proprietary investment in the *Public Advertiser* until that time. Garrick's involvement with this paper, then, may be given the approximate time frame 1756–79. Henry Sampson Woodfall, who took over this paper from his father, Henry Woodfall, printed it for a long period (1758–1793), making this one of his many points of contact with Garrick.

If his relationship with the *Public Advertiser* is the longest running, then Garrick's closest newspaper association, or at least the one for which the most evidence remains, was with the *St. James's Chronicle*. By a stroke of good fortune, the *St. James's Chronicle* is one of the few eighteenth-century newspapers for which a substantial run of minutes survives (1761–1815). Its minutes illuminate Garrick's involvement in the newspaper. Garrick acquired a share sometime in 1762, when Thomas Davies held the share in trust for him, in secret. Garrick is obliquely noticed in the minutes as one

of "the two Secret Partners" on 29 September 1762 and as one of "the two
partners for whom Messrs. Thornton and Davies hold in Trust" on 24 June
1762. He is first mentioned by name in the 28 September 1763 minutes.
His earlier interactions with the paper had been managed quietly through
George Colman's interventions, as seen in the correspondence, and Garrick might well have been glad to remain a "Secret Partner" but for
difficulties with Davies. In a letter dated 6 August [c. 1763], Davies fumes
to George Garrick that his brother David has sent George Colman to
collect Garrick's dividends from the newspaper:

> What yr: Brother [David Garrick] said to Mr Colman yesterday, I confess
> has touched me very much, he had desired that Gentleman it seems to take
> up what was due to him from ye St. James's Chronicle; at the same time
> that he knew his share in that paper, was held by me, in Trust for him.
> What is this but to brand me as a fellow not fit to be trusted with ye receipt
> of his money? He did indeed some time since, insinuate there was some
> mistake in my account–Why then does he not point it out? I am ready to
> shew my books & to settle with him when ever he pleases.
>   So help me God I know of no mistake but what I long since
> mentioned to him of five pounds wch. my Srt. I imagined had over
> charged to him & wch. I told him then shod. be allowed—
>   If he is tired of his kindness in God's name, let him withdraw it but let
> him not endeavour to deprive me of that, by wch. alone I must get my
> bread, I mean <u>ye character of an honest Man</u>————This I write, that
> you may shew to Mr. Garrick. I am Sir, Yr. most obt
>   humble Servant
>   Thomas Davies[7]

In the manuscript letter, Davies's scrawl swells and becomes furiously
uncontrolled as it approaches the underlined accusation that Garrick has
cost him his honest reputation. Davies is right to be upset: his relationship
with booksellers in the newspaper's conger would undoubtedly have been
damaged by any imputation of distrust. Davies's difficulties in managing
money (he was later declared bankrupt, and the minutes for 29 April 1778
show the bookseller Vaillant making a "Claim upon Mr. Thos. Davies's
Share" that cost the proprietors three hundred guineas) necessitated Garrick's entrance into the paper in propria persona.

    Garrick's formal entry into the *St. James's Chronicle* as a shareholder is
late: he is not one of the founding members, who included Henry Baldwin
(printer), Robert Griffiths, Lockyer Davis, John Berkenhout, Christopher
Henderson, Robert Davis, Bonnell Thornton, Thomas Davies and
Thomas Becket. He joined when the newspaper was a functioning concern, avoiding start-up costs, such as the call for five more guineas per

partner made on 10 June 1761 as the paper struggled with a deficit in its first year of operation. 24 June 1762, the date at which Garrick's share is first referred to obliquely (still in trust to Davies), was also the first noted financial balance in favour of the partners, and though that positive balance was not distributed, by December 1762, the paper had begun distributing quarterly dividends to its proprietors. These dividends ranged from a low of £5 per twentieth share (25 March 1763) to the mid-teens in the late 1760s, and from 15 guineas to £20 per twentieth share through the 1770s, barring a few occasions when dividends were deferred to pay out legal costs or the executors of a former proprietor's estate.

For Garrick, this quarterly income (£80 at its height in the 1770s) was not a key component of his portfolio, when considered in purely financial terms. For a bookseller like Becket, who held 1½ shares, however, a regular influx of £120 was likely a godsend that helped to mitigate the irregular, unpredictable income of the book trade, in addition to the product placement opportunities a share in a newspaper might afford. As Richmond and Marjorie Bond note with reference to the *St. James's Chronicle*'s minutes, "Booksellers were able to advertise their merchandise in the paper on a very favorable arrangement … the Proprietors resolved that the Printer would be 'at Liberty to insert Partners Advertisements, not exceeding two per Week of each Partner's, charging such Partners Advertisements with the Duty only.'"[8] Paying only an advertisement's tax, and not its cost, was a substantial subsidy. Stone and Kahrl's argument that Garrick paid for the privilege of puffing himself in the papers is technically true in the case of the *St. James's Chronicle*, in the limited sense that Garrick would have paid the tax on official advertisements therein, but it ignores the proprietary advantage of subsidized advertisements and other opportunities for promotion besides taxed advertisements.[9]

The *St. James's Chronicle* minutes show that Garrick not only avoided start-up costs: he also avoided business meetings. His attendance record at the newspaper's quarterly General Meetings is dismal. Of the seventy-six General Meetings called during the period when he held a share in the *St. James's Chronicle* (1762–79), Garrick attended, at most, three partial meetings. In two of these cases, he is marked absent, though his signature appears at the conclusion of the minutes, probably indicating a late entrance. Both of these occasions were late December meetings held at the Bedford Head tavern in Southampton Street, less than a block away from his house at 27 Southampton Street; the timing and location may have made attendance easier or more attractive. A forfeiture charge was assessed for late and absent proprietors, and it appears that Garrick was content to pay to escape meetings. A receipt inscribed in Garrick's hand, "Baldwin's Account St. James's Chronicle ballanc'd Nov.r 25 1765," shows that he paid fourteen such fines for missing meetings in 1763–65, at 2s. 6d. each time.[10]

Garrick was twice voted (in absentia, on 21 December 1767 and 27 June 1777) onto the more active part of the newspaper's management, the smaller Committee of proprietors that met monthly with the printer, Henry Baldwin, to assess monthly accounts and discuss important matters such as legal charges pending against the paper, or financial disbursements to a former proprietor's executors. However, Garrick is marked absent for all Committee meetings as well. If this was a strategy on his fellow proprietors' part to goad him into more frequent attendance or active management, as in the earlier resolution of 24 June 1765 on Garrick's return from the Continent, "that Mr. Garrick be summoned to all General Meetings in future," it failed.

Even if he had the time or inclination to attend, the busy theatre manager had no real need to be present. His friend, the bookseller Thomas Becket, was a steady attendee of General Meetings, and a near-constant member of the Committee. Any news Garrick required of the paper's operations would have been available from Becket, the printer Baldwin or fellow proprietors George Colman and Bonnell Thornton, with whom Garrick was in frequent contact. Just as in his co-management of Drury Lane Theatre, where he was content to leave daily business management to his partner James Lacy and the theatre's treasurer, Garrick was content to leave the management of the newspaper to the printers and other proprietors more closely associated with the book trade.

Thomas Becket did look out for Garrick's interests: on 1 November 1770, Becket summoned a special General Meeting, at which those present resolved "that the Theatrical Journal Inserted in the St. James's Chronicle last Thursday, be for the future omitted." The original resolution still visible in the minutes gives a livelier sense of the proceedings: "Resolved, that the Printer has been very culpable in admitting the Theatrical Journal, No. 1 though at the repeated Instance of the whole Body of Partners, and that all future Numbers shall be omitted – ." This accusatory phrase is lightly struck out and followed with the explanation, "(this Cancelled by desire of the printer)." It seems that on this occasion, the printer and the proprietors were at variance about what constituted saleable, printable news. That proprietors with financial interests in the theatres opposed its inclusion suggests the *Theatrical Journal* was unflattering or otherwise unwelcome. Neither Garrick nor Colman was noted present, but Becket's action was clearly a defensive intervention under-taken to benefit one or both theatrical managers. Unfortunately, the *Burney Newspapers Collection* does not have any numbers of the *St. James's Chronicle* for October 1770, so unless there is a clipping of this incendiary *Theatrical Journal* in a scrapbook or extra-illustrated volume somewhere, the exact nature of the censored theatrical content will remain a mystery. Still, Garrick's man Becket looked after this problem, and the proprietors trumped the printer, who won only the minor victory of having the accusation of his culpability lightly struck out in the minutes.

The minutes of the *St. James's Chronicle* show the paper as a profitable enterprise, if somewhat precariously so, as the loss of a shareholding proprietor could affect profitability adversely whilst the share's consider-able value was paid out to the deceased's beneficiaries. There was a financial advantage to maintaining stability in the membership of a newspaper conger for all proprietors. It is interesting to speculate on the opportunities that this may have afforded Garrick, who did not depend on dividend income, and who thus may have been able to leverage other conger members' dependence upon stability. By 25 [July] 1775, however, Garrick was growing tired of this investment, or at least of its publisher, Henry Baldwin, as he wrote to his fellow proprietor George Colman:

> I have been insulted greatly–first to have a Paper, in which I have a property [the *St. James's Chronicle*], abuse me for puffing myself, & then I am suppos'd the Author of a paragraph, or letter in ye Morng Chronicle [see 23 June and 12 July], which the Printer himself almost avows, & which by my honor, I never heard of till you mention'd it to me:
> I have done my Share to ye paper, nay I have told that worthy Gentle-man Mr Baldwin, that I would look out things whenever he was in want of Nonsense–but I give ye matter up now, & as he may be assur'd I will trouble myself no more about it, he may abuse me as fast as he pleases–I don't expect mercy from such Gentry for past Services. This you may say or read as you please.[11]

Garrick is not protesting that it is untrue that he has puffed himself – his protest is that a paper in which he has a property has abused him for puffing. A proprietor ought to be free from such nuisances, especially one who writes for the paper, as does Garrick, who states that he has contrib-uted his "Share" of "Nonsense." Further evidence of his direct contribu-tions to this and other newspapers appears below.

Comparing the extant lists of proprietors in the three newspapers for which we have convincing evidence of Garrick's proprietorship reveals a

Table 1 *Garrick's Network of Co-Proprietors in Newspapers*

Public Advertiser (as of Dec. 1766)	London Packet (as of 12 Jan. 1770)	St. James's Chronicle (as of 14 March 1761)
Robert Baldwin (1/20)	Robert Baldwin	Henry Baldwin (3)
Thomas Becket (1/20)	Thomas Becket	Thomas Becket (1.5)
Edward Dilly (1/20)	George Colman	Dr. John Berkenhout (1)
[David Garrick]	Thomas Davies	George Colman (1; +
James Hodges (1/20)	Lockyer Davis	1 in trust for Baldwin)
H. Thomas (1/20)	David Garrick, Esq.	Thomas Davies (2; + 1 in
Edward Rivington (1/20)	Christopher Henderson	trust for David
Henry Woodfall (2/20)	Thomas Lowndes	Garrick)
Henry Sampson Wood-	James Macpherson, Esq.	Robert Davis (1)
fall (1/20)	P. Thompson	Lockyer Davis (2)
	Caleb Whiteford	Christopher
	Henry Sampson	Henderson (1)
	Woodfall	William Jackson (1)
	William Woodfall	Thomas Lowndes (1.5)
		Bonnell Thornton (4; +2
		in trust for anonym-
		ous proprietor)

core group of Garrick's most frequent media collaborators. As evidence of ownership (ledgers and minutes) is so thin, it is not possible to compare ownership across precisely the same time period. However, the large degree of overlap in proprietary personnel shown in Table 1 strongly suggests that ownership in one newspaper in no way precluded ownership of another.

These lists of newspaper proprietors show that Garrick had long-standing business associations with several prominent London printers and publishers, including the Baldwin, Dilly, Davis, Davies, Becket, Rivington and Woodfall families – in some cases, as with the Woodfalls, through multiple generations. Proprietorship in these newspapers and participation in the larger print networks of his fellow proprietors facilitated the placement of news items concerning Garrick and other persons associated with Drury Lane Theatre.

Garrick's ties with these men streamlined publication for Drury Lane playwrights when it came time to print a book of the play. To Elizabeth Griffith, Garrick wrote of her play's fate: "You may depend upon It's being acted in this sea[son] or ye next & you may also depend upon selling the Copy of it directly upon my assuring the Bookseller that I had received it– nay I will find the bookseller if necessary–."[12] Who published Elizabeth

Griffith's play, *The School for Rakes*? Garrick did not have to look far: Griffith's play was published by Garrick's co-proprietor in the *Public Advertiser*, the *London Packet* and the *St. James's Chronicle*, Thomas Becket. The play's title page advertised the theatre ("As it is Performed at the Theatre-Royal in Drury Lane"), and newspapers in which Becket and Garrick were proprietors advertised the book of the play. The *Public Advertiser* for 14 February 1769 advertises the play's sixth night, a benefit "For the AUTHOR," as well as Becket's publication of the book of the play that day at noon.[13] In modern business parlance, a situation in which a business owns its suppliers or different stages of the production path is known as vertical integration. Garrick's seamless vertical integration of theatre and print media yielded indisputable advantages for those whom he had an interest in promoting.

Covent Garden authors were not necessarily shut out of this network: note that Garrick's friend and rival manager (1767–74) of Covent Garden Theatre, George Colman, appears on two of the lists of newspaper proprietors. Contemporaries, when they commented on Colman's co-ownership of papers with Garrick, interpreted this not as a balance of power, but as evidence of collusion in the entertainment industry, or a cabal between the principal London theatre managers, as Francis Gentleman's identification of Garrick and Colman as "united BUBBLE MASTERS," discussed below, shows.

Contemporaries' Knowledge of Garrick's Media Ownership; or, "Cobweb Politics"

Garrick's media ownership and networks amongst publishers, taste-makers and other persons of influence were well known to his contemporaries. That this influence was known seems not to have decreased its efficacy or power; if anything, because its full extent was never articulated by anyone, though verifiable instances of influence emerged constantly, contemporaries' understandings of Garrick's influence may have been magnified by a feeling that his influence reached, iceberg-like, into unseen depths. Dispersed, incomplete information about Garrick's media holdings in reliable contemporary sources presents the first problem in ascertaining the extent of Garrick's media influence.

A second problem is that contemporary critiques of Garrick's media influence have not received their scholarly due. Many writers concerned to expose Garrick's media involvement chose satire as their mode, and the tone of these exposés has led scholars to discount such critiques as the grumblings of the aggrieved. *The Theatres: A Poetical Dissection*, by Sir Nicholas Nipclose, Baronet [Francis Gentleman] (1772), is one such text. In his *Dissection*, Gentleman, once favoured by Garrick, now complains bitterly of a media cabal involving George Colman and Garrick. Gentleman's satiric poem discloses a media structure that chokes off access to print and effectively replicates the theatrical patent structure at the level of the press.

Though Gentleman's satire has never received critical consideration as a measure of Garrick's press influence, the historical context suggests that it should be taken seriously. Francis Gentleman was perfectly placed to assess Garrick's involvement in the newspapers, as he had "superintended" (edited) the *London Packet* – in which Garrick was a proprietor – for a period beginning in 1770. Gentleman knew how the press ran, because he had helped to run it. Ventriloquizing Colman, Gentleman writes:

> "The LONDON PACKET (49), the St. JAMES'S join
> To vend the puffs which I and DAVY coin:
> We, pleaders like, though at the public bar
> We wrangle fiercely, wage no hostile war;
> Behind the curtain we shake hands and smile,
> United BUBBLE MASTERS of this isle."[14]

Gentleman's footnote (signalled by the number 49) explains that the *London Packet* and the *St. James's Chronicle* are "Two evening papers, of which the managers are proprietors; therefore every defence of their impositions and absurdities, however vague, is greedily admitted: indeed we believe every thing favourable is written by *themselves*, for certainly no other person, save a fool or a flatterer, would undertake so impracticable a justification."[15] As superintendent of the *London Packet*, Gentleman must have known the origin of much of the content given him to insert in the paper. Content in the two papers derives directly from their owners, and content-sharing across these two papers is principally motivated by their common ownership, Gentleman contends. The apparent competition between Colman and Garrick as rival theatre managers is nothing but a theatrical pretense, framed to disguise their common interests in manipulating and fooling or 'bubbling' the public.

Other critics besides Gentleman laboured to make Garrick's media networks more widely visible. The *Theatrical Monitor*, a specialty newspaper in existence for only seven months, written in the acidic style of William Kenrick, printed the following verses on 16 December 1767.[16]

Like Gentleman, the poet argues that there is substantial commercial collusion in the theatre world:

> Sir, Please to admit in your paper part of a discourse supposed to pass not long since between Mssrs. Garrick and Colman.

> GARRICK. Friend Colman, we've hum'd all the wits of Town,
> Since we brib'd every paper to puff our renown,
> And all cutting reflections from critics to hush,
> ('Twas an excellent way) their productions to crush ...
> But we (who are callous) self-int'rest still aiming,
> May safely go on, now we've stop'd all their blamings,
> You, writing of plays without fear of rebuking,
> While, my prologues and epilogues give them a puking.[17]

This state of affairs prompted the Monitor to choose a newspaper format to combat Garrick's and Colman's grasp on the periodical press, combining pamphlet-like focus on a single issue (theatre) with the repeated exposure afforded by a newspaper. However, the Monitor complains three days later, "Complaints in fugitive unconnected news papers, though repeated, have answered no purpose, but that of emboldning [sic] the managers to contrive to put a stop even to those channels, which ought to be considered as Public ones." The Monitor's description of his newspaper's "fugitive unconnected" character contrasts with the combinatory power of Garrick's media networks. Indeed, the Monitor rages, even the fugitive numbers of the *Theatrical Monitor* have been menaced by Garrick's interest amongst publishers: "Mr. G—— has by his emissaries *meanly attempted* to influence the publisher [William Bingley], to drop the publication of the d——d Monitor, as he pleased to call it."[18] Whether for this or some other reason, Samuel Bladon did replace Bingley as printer of the *Theatrical Monitor* for its final three issues in March and April 1768. The *Theatrical Monitor*'s last issue of 16 April 1768 offers an exposé of Drury Lane's profits, including one last kick at Garrick's media holdings: its speculative balance sheet identifies puffing newspapers allied with the theatre as "Other advantages," in addition to the estimated annual house receipts of £41,148:

> Other advantages there are to be added, such as paid by the Gazetteer and
> Public Advertiser, for the honour of publishing an account of the

plays and puffs ——	———	———	100	0	0
A share in the St. James's Chronicle			60	0	0

The Monitor, with his isolate, fugitive oppositional paper, could hardly hope to compete against such market forces. While it is difficult to trust in the maturity of someone who rhymes "rebuking" with "puking," the Monitor does have an informed, accurate grasp of the value of Garrick's media holdings.

Similarly, an article in the *Westminster Magazine* of March 1773 attempted to flush out Garrick's media connections. "A.B.," the writer of "The Character of David Garrick, Esq.," memorably describes Garrick's network of booksellers, writers and publishers as lice: "The Naturalists tell us, that no animal is so lousy as a louse . . . It is no wonder, therefore, if the greatest of parasites should be pestered with a swarm of petty parasites . . . a Brother George, a Becket, a Griffin, a Hiffernan, a Packer, a Fawcett, a Lieutenant Bickerstaff, and a Parson Lloyd."[19] "A.B." names names, hoping to discount this swarm of authors as the potential source of diverse critical opinions, by revealing Garrick as the common host of all these media-borne parasites.

The "lousy" article offended at least one person, who immediately seized upon the impolitic idea of redress through the press. A subsequent letter from Garrick to this person, Captain Edward Thompson, written [?4 March 1773], shows Garrick attempting to manage Thompson's interventions in the media on his behalf: "Upon Second thoughts I would not insist, if I were You, upon ye Editor's making an apology for inserting ye Character of Me in ye Westminster Magazine—it will be going too far, & occasion some Scribbling about it, should You quarrel. a Word to ye Wise."[20] Garrick's letter to Thompson, of course, bears out "A.B."'s contention that Garrick did not just own newspaper shares and influence: he also 'owned' several writers whom he could muzzle or unleash at will.

As "A.B."'s letter and other sources demonstrate, Garrick's contemporaries knew that he possessed significant influence over many writers. George Colman, in his anonymous pamphlet, *A Letter of Abuse, to D—d G———k, Esq.* (1757), christened this tactic of employing a clutch of "Hackney-Scribblers" to write both for and against Garrick with the delightfully appropriate name "Cobweb Politics."[21] Colman's image of writers wound up together in a partially visible tissue of fictions fabricated for Garrick is an apt metaphor for Garrick's media and social networks and the public's knowledge of their existence. Another near-contemporary, James Boaden, justifies Garrick's interest in the media in terms of his profession. Garrick, Boaden writes,

> paid great regard to the press, he even meddled with newspaper property, he anticipated attack sometimes, was irritated by it at others, and never practised the policy of being silent. But his self-love as an actor was not alone to account for this. He was the proprietor of a concern, that flourishes

but by the 'popular breath;' to engage the public mind, therefore, about *himself* and his *theatre*, was essential to the triumph of both. He had writers who were engaged in his *interest* in such vehicles, and he wrote in them himself.[22]

Garrick's media ownership and his influence over particular writers were apparent to his contemporaries. Further examples of such associations are explored in the later chapters of this book, which describe Garrick's characteristic techniques for creating and mediating publicity.

Garrick's Direct Contributions to the Media

Garrick's involvement as a contributor to publications associated with his cobweb of writer-allies was public knowledge, too. Robert Lloyd began the *St. James's Magazine* in September 1762, and in an introductory poem, "The Puff: A Dialogue Between the Bookseller and Author," Lloyd establishes the magazine's draw by dropping contributors' names:

> "And then your interest might procure
> Something from either CONNOISSEUR.
> COLMAN and THORNTON, both will join
> Their social hand, to strengthen thine:
> And when your name appears in print,
> Will GARRICK *never* drop a hint?"[23]

Lloyd was hoping to capitalize on Garrick's knack for witty occasional verse. Garrick's poems were widely published, with and without attribution, in magazines and newspapers, as well as being circulated privately in his social circle, often with images of himself or other gifts.

These verses include prologues and epilogues, many of which enjoyed a significant second life outside the theatre, as well as verses written for particular occasions, epitaphs, songs and retaliatory satiric epigrams.[24] Mary Etta Knapp's *Checklist of Verse by David Garrick* catalogues many of these pieces. Her checklist identifies 269 pieces of occasional verse, 164 prologues and epilogues, 5 theatrical skits, and 39 songs, most with multiple publication venues. Knapp's list shows that Garrick's media reach in light verse alone extended over thirty-three publications, including, during his life: the *Universal Visiter*; the *Universal Magazine*; the *Scots Magazine*; the *St. James's Magazine*; the *St. James's Chronicle*; the *Gentleman's Magazine*; the *Whitehall Evening Post*; the *Annual Register*; *Lloyd's Evening Post*; the *Bath Chronicle*; the *Weekly Magazine; or Edinburgh Amusement*; the *Morning Chronicle*; the *Fugitive Miscellany* (1774); the

Muses' Mirrour; *The Repository: A Select Collection of Fugitive Pieces of Wit and Humour*; the *Whitehall Evening Post*; the *London Magazine*; Dodsley's *Collection of Poems by Several Hands* (1748); the *Westminster Magazine*; the *European Magazine*; the *Warwickshire Journal*; the *Town and Country Magazine*; *Poetical Amusements at a Villa near Bath*; the *Public Advertiser*; the *Royal Magazine*; the *Bath Journal*; the *London Chronicle*; the *Theatrical Monitor*; the *Morning Post*; the *Lady's Magazine*; the *Public Ledger*; and *The Court of Thespis*. It is worth listing this media spread in detail, as Knapp's list (1955) has not received the attention such careful bibliography deserves, and as its typescript edition of corrections and addenda (1974) exists only in a few archives.[25] The impressively lengthy list of venues in which Garrick's verse appeared establishes Garrick as an author, ubiquitously so. Consider that these thirty-three publications appeal to different classes, as they range from cheap advertising sheets to literary collections and records of high society functions. Then, note that these are publications targeted at different genders. Finally, bear in mind that many poems and occasional pieces were printed in more than one of these venues. A sense emerges that Garrick's name, writing and reputation were inescapable elements of eighteenth-century culture, even if one never attended the theatre. Considering Garrick as an actor alone is insufficient to account for the large space his name occupied in Britons' cultural imagination and in contemporary media.

Garrick's correspondence shows that he was as attentive to managing the appearance of his writing in these publications as he was to managing his stage appearances. Writing to Horace Walpole on 6 October 1757 concerning some admiring lines he had written about the poet Thomas Gray, Garrick shows how sensitive he is to the printing and positioning of individual articles within a newspaper:

> –they were printed in ye Chronicle of last Saturday, but very inaccurately & they were thrust into ye most Obscure Corner of ye Paper—As I am at such a distance from Mr Gray, I cannot know his Sentiments upon ye Occasion, but You have my free Leave to dispose of 'Em, as You shall please, for they and their Author are always at Yr Service.[26]

Attention to these poems elucidates Garrick's networks of personal influence, as many of the pieces are written "to" or "on" or "for" particular friends.

Garrick needed to see the reception his writing received, whether this meant reading reviews, or even creating scenarios by which he could gauge reception and know his audience's "Sentiments upon ye Occasion."

Richard Cumberland vividly describes the delight Garrick took in managing the media reception of performances at Drury Lane. With spritely wit that veers nearly into cruelty, Garrick reads aloud a review of Cumberland's new play, *The West Indian* (1771), to the playwright:

> Garrick was extremely kind, and threw his shield before me more than once, as the St. James's evening paper could have witnessed ... One morning when I called upon Mr. Garrick, I found him with the St. James's evening paper in his hand, which he began to read with a voice and action of surprise, most admirably counterfeited, as if he had discovered a mine under my feet, and a train to blow me up to destruction. 'Here, here,' he cried, 'if your skin is less thick than a rhinoceros's hide, egad, here is that will cut you to the bone. This is a terrible fellow; I wonder who it can be.' He began to sing out his libel in a high declamatory tone, with a most comic countenance, and pausing at the end of the first sentence, which seemed to favor his contrivance for a little ingenious tormenting, when he found he had hooked me, he laid down the paper, and began to comment upon the cruelty of newspapers, and moan over me with a great deal of malicious fun and good humor–'Confound these fellows, they spare nobody. I dare say this is Bickerstaff again; but you don't mind him; no, no, I see you don't mind him; a little galled, but not much hurt: you may stop his mouth with a golden gag, but we'll see how he goes on.' He then resumed his reading, cheering me all the way as it began to soften, till winding up in the most professed panegyric, of which he was himself the writer, I found my friend had had his joke, and I had enjoyed his praise, seasoned and set off in his inimitable manner, which to be comprehended must have been seen.[27]

The manager did not stop his promotional efforts with just one planted review. Cumberland wrote to Garrick from Dublin on 2 October 1771: "I watch your operations with a friendly eye, and see my poor "West Indian" receive early honours ... I never thanked you for the paragraph you sent me from the Public Advertiser, relative to the degree, and I believe I am to thank you, not for the sending it only."[28] From his sending of the paragraph to Cumberland, it appears that Garrick not only was interested in the transactional business benefits of media promotion; he also wanted playwrights to know of and appreciate his efforts. That Cumberland acknowledged Garrick's promotion of his work so gratefully and graciously may be one reason for the length of their productive relationship.

Although many of Garrick's contributions to the media were anonymous, they were not impermeably so. There were those like Cumberland who had their 'anonymous' reviews read aloud or sent to them; and then there were those who, like the actress Catherine Clive, immediately knew Garrick's style when they read it. Clive writes playfully to the small, dark-eyed actor of his 'anonymous' newspaper column, "The Mouse in the Green Room," which appeared in the *London Packet* and the *Morning Chronicle, and London Advertiser*.[29] "I *had* read the mouse in the green room, and I knew its face the moment I saw it, *a pretty little black eyl']d fellow*; it is admirably done."[30] The column dished up "all the politicks, conspiracies, gossipings, and vanities of *this little wicked world*" (Drury Lane Theatre's green-room) from the perspective of a resident Mouse, who asked to be paid only in cheese parings by the printer. The Mouse promised that not even "the high and mighty little great Mock Monarch himself" (Garrick) would escape notice.[31] Garrick's authorship of this column is confirmed in a letter to the *Morning Chronicle*'s printer, William Woodfall: "I shall Send You Mouse ye first soon –."[32]

There were plenty of clues for Clive, or indeed any alert reader, to find, any one of which would have sprung the mouse-trap. On 30 November 1775, the Mouse wrote a short green-room dialogue for Mrs. A—n (Abington), Mr. K—g (King) and the Manager (Garrick). King warns the Manager that Abington, an actress who had come in for criticism on her frequent feigned illnesses and self-importance in previous "Mouse" columns, now smells a rat, and suspects the Manager of being the Mouse. The same article works in a compliment to Garrick, suggesting that his presence on stage as Richard III and Macbeth is the only remedy for a house thinned by the popularity of *The Duenna* at Covent Garden: "if Roscius is not an actor in Drury-lane, three times a week, it is not your painted glass, and fine fangled cieling [sic] and boxes will do your business," says the King character, reminding readers of recent renovations to the theatre. Even the printer, Woodfall, gets in on the joke, promising his readers that he will not compromise his "*impartiality*" by "feeding or hiring any underlings of any theatre, to give hints to the prejudice of their employers" and "shall continue to entertain his readers, tho' his Majesty of Drury-lane, or their dignities of Covent-Garden, should put him under the bar of their empire."[33] In his last will and testament, delivered in the 27 April 1776 *Morning Chronicle, and London Advertiser*, the Mouse asks that his remains be interred "near the temple of Shakespeare, belonging to D. Garrick, Esq, at H—n [Hampton]." The Mouse even penned an elegiac poem, "*On seeing Mr.* GARRICK *every night at the* Theatre," in the 1 October 1776 *Morning Chronicle*, following Garrick's retirement:

> WHEN fav'rite bodies sleep within their graves,
> They say, their souls are still attendant slaves;

They hang and dwell with pleasure round the tomb,
Nor care to leave the old corporeal room.
So Garrick's soul frequents his house of fame,
And haunts the place where he obtain'd his name.

THE MOUSE.

It was not a difficult disguise to penetrate.

Clive's letter shows that Garrick's writing was identifiable to those who knew him or his work, and indicates that his anonymity in the media may not always have been secured through the use of pseudonyms, even if he could keep himself from the pleasures of reading aloud or revealing his identity through pointed insider allusions (such as those concerning Abington in "The Mouse in the Green-Room") or clues given to a few friends. The 'sport' of secrecy was appealing to Garrick, but sport required a spectator. A letter to George Colman of [15 February 1767] reveals Colman colluding with Garrick to conceal their authorship of faux criticisms from their common friend, Thomas Becket: "Poor Becket is very angry with Baldwin for abusing What we act, & he prints–pray keep up ye Ball, we shall have some sport with him."[34] Becket, normally an insider privy to Garrick's media secrets (such as Garrick's initially secret interest in the *St. James's Chronicle*), is here the object of fun, as he believes that the anti-Garrick writing in Baldwin's paper is genuine. It is lucky that Garrick did indulge in these asides; had he truly been capable of keeping a secret, instead of requiring a select audience to appreciate the sport involved in his media maneuvers, they would be more challenging to trace.

Garrick's correspondence shows that he was able to contribute articles directly to numerous newspapers, including papers in which he was not a proprietor. Many such contributions were made anonymously or pseudonymously, and are identifiable through examination of letters written to Garrick, including many not published in Boaden's collected correspondence. Rather than listing the papers by title, and perhaps thereby promoting the erroneous idea that he had the ability to insert content in all of these papers at all times, examples of Garrick's content-mongering are dated and discussed below; other instances will be examined in later chapters.

Garrick's direct contributions to newspapers predate his most intensive period of media proprietorship, and evidence of them is available just five years into his acting career. To Somerset Draper on [2] January 1746, Garrick writes that he has published some verses in George Faulkner's newspaper, the *Dublin Journal*, and is now ensuring their wider media distribution: "I see the *Farmer's Letters* are publishing in London; I told you, I believe, Mr. Brookes was the Author; I writt some verses on him, which were printed in Faulconer's Paper, and were liked: I have promised them to Harnage, and let him have them when you see him."[35] Draper, Garrick's friend, twenty years older than he, was a brewer, whom Garrick may have met, Ian McIntyre speculates, during his days as a vintner. Draper was also a partner of the publishers Jacob and Richard Tonson, and for Garrick, he performed "negotiations with managers and actors, looking after his investments, keeping an eye on his house when he was away."[36] The letter to Draper demonstrates how entwined were Garrick's social, business and publishing networks, even at this early date. Likewise, a letter to his brother on 1 September 1752 closes by directing George to send on some verses to Charles Corbett's paper, the *Whitehall Evening Post*: "I have Enclos'd You half a dozen Lines upon ye affair between *Withers* & my friend *Dr Garnier*, if you like 'Em put 'Em into ye Penny post seal'd up, the Publisher of ye Whitehall I dare say will put 'Em in, if not there will be no great loss—say Nothing of 'Em to anybody, be sure—."[37] The dates of these contributions suggest that Garrick early saw the value of content placement in the media, and later intensified a proven practice through proprietorship and his social and economic networks.

Amongst the newspapers to which Garrick contributed directly are the *St. James's Chronicle*, and Edward Say's paper, the *Gazetteer*. A letter of January 1765, written to George Colman while Garrick was away on the Continent, shows the ready access both men had to media networks, as Garrick casually asks a favour: "I could be glad that something was put into the St James's Chronicle, or into Say's paper for my friend *Mon[n]et*." [38] Similarly, Garrick's flattering letter of 14 June 176[5] to Jean Baptiste Antoine Suard models his ability to leverage media influence and his social networks so that they become mutually reinforcing:

> I have sent you the sketch of Preville [French actor Pierre Louis Dubus], which I wish more worthy of your acceptance. Our little friend Colman (who hopes you have receiv'd his Terence, and which is much approv'd of here), begs that I will print it in the St. James's Chronicle, which perhaps I may next week. My servant has copy'd it, and has made some mistakes. I beg that you will correct any that I may have made in my description of the characters Preville performs, and omit any part of it which may not please you. I am very sincere in this request, for, without a compliment, you are *mihi magnus Apollo*.[39]

In just five sentences, Garrick suavely praises Préville's acting, Suard's critical judgement, Colman's abilities as a translator, and his own abilities as a writer, while highlighting his media access and influence, which last were substantiated when the article appeared in the *St. James's Chronicle* for 22–24 June 1765.

Garrick's direct contributions to the media of articles, letters, poems, reviews and other pieces were frequent and well known. His identification as author increased his media exposure across numerous print platforms, and extended the theatre's cultural reach. His occasional adoption of pseudonyms was not always undertaken for the purpose of anonymity, as Garrick enjoyed the game of being found out in his thin narrative disguises. The practice of generating his own publicity, for himself and for the theatre and its actors and associated playwrights, began early in his career, and intensified as his media networks grew.

Transactional Links between Garrick and Media Stakeholders

For David Garrick, whose business was the promotion of the theatre's social pleasures, social transactions were just as likely to yield financial benefits and media access as were his commercial dealings. A sampling of Garrick's transactional links with media stakeholders appears below, ranging from formal business arrangements such as long-term advertising contracts, to social events and friendships that provided inside business intelligence.

Garrick's extensive dealings with the Woodfall family via his role as newspaper proprietor have already been observed. Another aspect of this notable financial relationship with personal and professional benefit for Garrick was Drury Lane Theatre's receipt of payments from the newspaper printed by Henry Sampson Woodfall, the *Public Advertiser*. This paper enjoyed the status of official printer of Drury Lane's advertisements, and boasted of its exclusivity and accuracy: "*To prevent any Mistakes in future in advertising the Plays and Entertainments of Drury Lane Theatre, the Managers think it proper to declare, that the Play-bills are inserted, by their Direction, in this Paper* ONLY," emphasizes a note beneath the playbills in the *Public Advertiser* for 1 January 1765.

What was the cost of obtaining up-to-the-minute, accurate bills of the play? The manuscript "Accounts in [the] Public Advertiser 1765–1771"[40] shows, in the debts column for December 1765, an amount owing to the playhouses of £200, as well as "Drury Lane Advertisements – 54.16.6"; in December 1767, expenses listed include "Playhouses 150" and "Drury Lane Advertisements 60.6"; December 1768 records expenses including "Playhouses 150" and "Drury Lane Advertisements 68.8"; December

1769 records an expenditure of £100 to the playhouses, and "Drury Lane Advertisements 64.9." Expenditures are also recorded for 1770 and 1771. The amounts paid to the playhouses were variable.[41] The usual cash flow wherein advertising generates direct income for a newspaper is inverted: the paper pays the playhouse for the privilege of advertising dramatic productions.

An agreement between newspaper and playhouse dated from the first issue of the *London Daily Post and General Advertiser*, the paper later renamed the *Public Advertiser*,[42] so Garrick did not negotiate this arrangement, though he certainly exploited it to the full. The editor of the *London Daily Post* informed his readers on 4 November 1734 that, at the managers' request, and for the convenience of the populace, all playbills for the Hay-Market, Drury-Lane, Covent-Garden, Lincoln's-Inn-Fields and Goodman's-Fields theatres would now be available in the *Post*:

> As there is no Reason to doubt, that all Coffee-Houses, and other Places of Publick Resort, as well as many Private Families, will take in this Paper, such Persons as shall please to favour it with their Advertisements, need not question their being more generally read, than if inserted in any other; it being observable, that those Papers which contain the greatest Number of PLAY-BILLS, and other Accounts of Publick Diversions, are always most called for.
>
> NOTWITHSTANDING the Advantages this Paper will have above any other, Advertisements of a moderate Length, which require no Preference, will be inserted at Two Shillings each.

Whether it was true that newspapers with playbills sold better than ones without, or merely a persuasive attempt to structure the public's reading and advertising habits, the *London Daily Post*'s notice suggests that the newspaper–playhouse benefit was mutual. The list of places at which advertisements were taken in for the *London Daily Post* in 1734 neatly maps connections between the print and theatre industries: would-be advertisers could send copy to the office in Covent Garden Theatre, a bookseller's, a pamphlet printer's, or go directly to the newspaper's printer.

F. Knight Hunt alleges that "dramatic intelligence cost the Journals much more than foreign News,"[43] and supports this bold statement by reproducing the 1773 statement of expenses for the *Public Advertiser*.[44] If dramatic news consistently cost more than foreign news, this might justify the period's frequent metaphors describing theatre managers as heads of state or monarchs. Indeed, theatrical managers including Garrick (a self-described "Mock Monarch") would seem to have exceeded heads of state and foreign affairs in the economic hierarchy of news, for they held sway over the news most costly to acquire, and most sought-after by readers.

That entertainment news was a hot commodity appears by other newspapers' challenge to the *Public Advertiser* in posting their own play-bills: by the 1770s, bills of the play were published in the *Morning Post, and Daily Advertiser,* the *Gazetteer and New Daily Advertiser,* and the *London Courant, and Westminster Chronicle.* Even after his retirement, Garrick's influence was still sought by those in the print trade seeking the advantage conferred by advertising the stage's offerings. Henry Bate of the *Morning Post* wrote to Garrick on 13 September 1776, to obtain his influence on a decision by the new owners of Drury Lane to renegotiate the placement of playbills in certain newspapers: "I have taken the liberty of applying to you for your interest with your successors relative to the playbills: the object would be considerable to me, and I think their end would be fully answered in advertising with us. You hinted some time ago, that Linley spoke something of the playbills being given in common to the four papers; if you cannot serve the Morning Post in particular, favour that plan as much as possible, and you will much oblige me."[45] Bate seeks Garrick's interest, either in an exclusive contract for the *Morning Post,* or in one that will level the competition by distributing the playbill information amongst four papers.

Bate's request for the newspaper playbill contract was merely the latest in a flurry of favours. Bate had already paid for his influence by flattering Garrick in the *Morning Post.* As Wilfred Hindle notes, Bate's friendship with Garrick was "responsible for the *Morning Post* 's flattering description of the farewell season in which Garrick 'retired, crown'd with unfading laurels, amidst blinding tears and acclamations of the most brilliant theatre that ever assembled; –all ranks uniting in their invocations for the future happiness of a man who has so repeatedly and essentially contributed to theirs.'"[46] Bate's fulsome tributes had been sown when Garrick produced Bate's comic opera, *The Blackamoor Wash'd White,* in February 1776, despite fierce opposition. John Genest describes the riot that ensued. Bate, he writes, was

> the conductor of a most scurrilous newspaper, called the Morning Post; in which abuse was daily vented on private and public characters – the Farce itself was probably as trifling as Bate's other productions; but people were determined to damn it out of dislike to the author ... Garrick acted to sweeten the dose, but it would not go down.[47]

Though it would prove difficult to assign a monetary value to these transactions, Bate and Garrick obviously understood the meaning of quid pro quo, and sought to assist one another.

A similar trade in favours enabling media access appears in Garrick's relationship with Hugh Kelly. Kelly assumed editorship of the *Public Ledger* sometime in late spring or early summer 1765, which "helped him establish himself with Garrick more thoroughly than any flattering poem could have done, for Kelly's control of the *Ledger* allowed him to support Garrick and Drury Lane on a regular basis with favorable reviews of Garrick's productions," Robert Bataille argues.[48] There is evidence in the correspondence that Kelly did attempt to insert a favourable review of Garrick's adaptation of *The Chances* into the *St. James's Chronicle* (see the letter of 22 April 1773); when Baldwin, then the editor, cautioned him to "avoid prejudice or gross partiality," Kelly instead promised Garrick that he would send his account to the *Morning Chronicle* or *Morning Post*.[49]

Garrick also used his social networks to censor and discipline writers who might adversely affect his portrayal in the media. The sight of a letter passed on by a friend was enough to goad one W. Jackson into pleading to Garrick that he was not the author of criticisms made in the *Public Ledger*:

> Doctor Schomberg yesterday favoured me with the sight of a card which he had received from you. It contained a complaint that I had made use of your name in a very unfriendly manner in The Ledger. Whoever, Sir gave you that information, made a very improper use of my name ... That two or three unfavourable pieces have gained admission into the paper, I admit. That my pen gave them existence your candour I trust, will permit me to deny ... I have exerted my influence with the printer to obviate any complaint of the kind in future.[50]

Jackson's letter is dated 28 August 1778, and the date is significant: even after Garrick's retirement from the stage, even outside the theatrical season, a word from a friend intimating that Garrick was not pleased was enough to set in motion a quiet chain of social influence intended to produce improved representation of the Garrick name in this newspaper in future.

Ethical Considerations

Our present-day expectation of a free press, guided by ethical consider-ations governing the publication of information, is far removed from eighteenth-century media practices. Journalist Ian Hargreaves states, "jour-nalism is defined, to some extent, by the institutions within which it is created," and contends that "we need many and competing cultures of ownership if our news media are to be truly diverse and, consequently, as a whole, trusted."[51] Eighteenth-century newspapers do not lay claim to any independent status, nor could they, since their ownership structures were hopelessly, openly entwined with the printing, patent medicine and entertainment industries. Far from representing competing cultures of ownership, the overlap in proprietors and other personnel suggests collusion. Neutrality and objectivity were never the objectives of those writing and printing newspapers at this period; these newspapers tend to represent the interests of their proprietors, not the populace.

The modern British "Editors' Code of Practice," enforced by the Press Complaints Commission from 1 January 2012, likewise has no eighteenth-century counterpart. While the press did strive for and enact some modes of correction, such as amending erroneous playbills, accuracy and verifiability of facts were not operationally necessary. Eighteenth-century notions of gentility and personal honour were not bound by anything like current privacy laws, especially concerning the reprinting of correspondence. Printers would have found laughable the idea that they should maintain independence from those persons covered in their pages. Far from pursuing ideals of transparency regarding their sources or methods of newsgathering, their sources were often concealed. We have already seen that content-sharing practices were condoned, even encouraged, by newspaper proprietors.

Ethical considerations in modern press organizations and publishing houses include decisions about what topics receive coverage, and how much and what kind of coverage they receive. Here lies some common ground with the mid-eighteenth-century media, in which questions such as 'Is entertainment news really news?' and 'How much notice should actors receive in the newspapers, and why?' were warmly contested. The writer of a note "To the PUBLISHER" (dated 16? November 1756) criticizes newspapers' excessive coverage of theatrical matters:

> It is impossible, Sir, that every performer in a theatrical exhibition can deserve elaborate commendation, nor can such commendation be of any credit to your paper, because the enlightened part of mankind must withhold their assent; and certainly it can be of no service to the lowest class of your readers, because they are not thereby informed of the principles of a just and well regulated taste.
>
> To give assistances to the faculty of the mind, just mentioned, and to make the gross of mankind not altogether irrational in their enjoyments, but on the contrary to awaken in them some idea of truth and propriety, in the art of dramatic poetry and the business of an actor, was, I imagine, the primary intention of the plan of your paper. And this, and this only, can justify the allotment of so much room in the Chronicle to imaginary heroes, who, most assuredly, are not so much the objects of public attention, as the importance of a man to himself may make the players dream they are.[52]

The interests of proprietors, printers, "imaginary heroes" and theatrical managers were known to be interconnected, but any sustained action by critics upon this knowledge appears to have been contained by the very structures that evinced it. The *London Magazine* for October 1776 contains an essay on theatrical criticism that demonstrates knowledge of the dilemma. To obtain access to the theatre was necessarily to be influenced to write praise; yet to write theatrical criticism without such access was impossible:

> The news-paper *critics* are another great cause of the degeneracy of the stage; for as the established morning papers are connected with the man- agers, this insect tribe are connected with the players, and now and then they have the honour of being noticed by the managers themselves. –These hyper-critics are composed of three descriptions of men . . . –the managers, their flatterers, friendly acquaintance and a few independent persons. – Editors of papers, persons connected with the second rate performers; and scribblers looking for favours, or for a dinner, from every person concerned or connected with the theatres, from the managers down to the lowest frequenters of Jupp's, these are the authors of the theatrical critiques, or criticisms. The first in general will surely *praise* the managers and *abuse* the deserving performers; and if the independents were capable of giving an able judgment, the news-paper printers would refuse their productions. The second class never tell truth; because they are *bribed* by orders, dinners, &c. to stifle it, to abuse all young performers, and daub their benefactors. And the last class, the most despicable of all, setting up without *capital* depend for all their information on the understrappers of both houses; and of course, misrepresent, abuse, extol, and blunder without end, and without mercy.[53]

In his involvement with the media, David Garrick played a long game. While it is not possible to give conclusive start and end dates for all of Garrick's media interactions, this chapter confirms there is abundant evidence demonstrating that Garrick managed the media every bit as much as he managed the theatre. His direct media influence is most intensive in the period 1762–76, when he possessed proprietary interest in several newspapers. Garrick's media influence, however, is not confined to this period or to newspaper ownership exclusively. As his correspondence and contemporary comment indicate, Garrick's personal influence over authors, printers and publishers, and other taste-makers was substantial. John Brewer convincingly argues that as culture was increasingly com- modified during the eighteenth century, "the marketing of culture became a trade separate from its production."[54] Surprisingly, David Garrick ran counter to this trend. Whereas the commodified cultural market was expanding and diversifying to produce diverging strands of producers and marketers, Garrick's media involvement shows that he sought the benefits of convergence and vertical integration, and maintained an active presence in every level of the stratifying cultural market.

David Garrick used his unparalleled imbrication within the mediascape to promote certain consistent messages concerning his appearance, his acting abilities and his personal character. To borrow from modern advertising parlance, the words "David Garrick" connoted not just an actor, manager, writer or person, but a "brand." The next chapter articulates the kinds of advertising available to Garrick, and demonstrates his use of each in building his personal brand.

CHAPTER 3

Advertising and Brand Garrick: "Infinite Variety"

O BRAGG   Advertishe it, and what is advertishe it, my Dear?
AP MEAGRE   It is as much as to say put it in the Papers.
                    – *The Theatrical Manager: A Dramatic Satire* (1751)[1]

Before this court I *Peter Puff* appear,
A *Briton* born, and bred an *Auctioneer*,
Who for myself, and eke a hundred others,
My useful, honest, learned, bawling Brothers,
With much Humility and Fear implore ye,
To lay our present, desp'rate Case before ye.
                    – Prologue to Samuel Foote's play, *Taste* (1752), lines 1–6,
                    "Written by Mr. Garrick, and spoken by him in the Character
                        of an *Auctioneer*"; printed in the *London Magazine, Scots
                            Magazine* and *Universal Magazine* (1752)

I Will not say, I on one stage have seen
A second *Roscius*; that too poor had been;
But I have seen a *Proteus*, that can take
What shape he pleases, and in an instant make
Himself to any thing, be't that, or this,
By voluntary metamorphosis!
                    . . .
Thou rul'st our smiles and tears! nature made thee
To shew her cunning in epitome;
T'express thy all would ask a better pen,
Thou art, tho' little, the whole map of men.
    – "To Mr. GARRICK," *Ladies Magazine* (1752), *Gentleman's Magazine* (1752)[2]

What counted as advertising during the period of Garrick's career? Jeremy Black astutely observes that "Advertisements were part of a system of intelligence, not isolated curiosities."[3] To read eighteenth-century advertisements for the hilarious twang of anachronism alone is to underestimate their power. Determining what was understood to be direct advertising by Garrick's contemporaries establishes the extent to which Garrick finessed the conventions governing this "system of intelligence" in mediating his celebrity. This chapter defines advertising in an eighteenth-century context and discusses advertising costs and methods during the Garrick period. It considers direct, taxed advertising in periodicals, then limns untaxed methods of promotion, including reviews, occasional poetry, puffery and theatrical claques. Citing contemporary promotional materials by Garrick and others, it shows the development of key aspects of the Garrick brand, including variety, or the ability to play comedy and tragedy, and major and minor parts; liveliness of eye; vigorous action and elegance of gesture; pleasing vocal modulation; and skillful interpretation of Shakespearean drama. The chapter concludes with a survey of commercial products that attempted to leverage the associational value of the Garrick brand.

What is Advertisement?

From a commercial standpoint, advertisements were treated differently than other newspaper content, beginning with their status as taxable items. "Advertisements were made subject to taxation in 1712, at the rate of one shilling each, a duty renewed in 1743, and doubled in 1757 ... These increases helped to push up the price charged for advertisements ... advertising rates rose in general after the Stamp Act of 1725, though duty on advertisements was not increased," Black summarizes.[4]

The cost of inserting a formal advertisement in a newspaper remained relatively stable during Garrick's career, rising by only a shilling. In the *London Daily Post, and General Advertiser* for 5 December 1743, H. Woodfall, Jr. advises, *"Advertisements of a moderate Length are taken in for this Paper at Two Shillings each."* J. Meres, printer of the *Daily Post*, advertised the same rate on the same date. Towards the end of Garrick's acting career, in January of 1776, H.S. Woodfall, long having dropped the 'Junior' from his name, announces that advertisements "of a moderate Length" may be placed in the *Public Advertiser* for three shillings each. His brother William Woodfall's *Morning Chronicle and London Advertiser* of 29 March 1776 offers the same rate, and promises a rapid turnaround, an acknowledgement that advertisement could be just as time-sensitive as news: "Advertisements of a moderate length will be generally inserted in this Paper the Day after they are sent, if delivered to the Printer before TEN o'clock at Night." The modest increase in price was driven in part, James Raven explains, not just by advertising duties, but by other business costs controlled by the Stamp Act, which "determined that the only legal source of supply for newspaper-stamped paper was the warehouse of the

Commissioners of Stamps in Serle Court, Lincoln's Inn, to where unsold papers also had to be returned to claim a rebate."[5]

As a working definition, I propose that in the newspaper trade during the Garrick period, 'advertisement' refers to paid paragraphs printed in a periodical for a specified time, with the aim of selling a good or service by describing the properties of that good or service, naming its provider, and often the location(s) for its purchase. In addition to the overt appeal to a consumer to purchase a good or service, advertisements are generally identifiable, by the 1740s, by their visual format: by their moderate length (usually ten to twelve lines),[6] and by their visual separation by horizontal rules from other newspaper content and from each other. They may include illustrations, such as the lovely miniature ships that sail over announcements of sales by the candle, and distinctive typography ranging from manicules and asterisks to capitals and heavy type, but neither illustration nor distinctive typography is usual or necessary in the majority of newspaper advertisements during the period of Garrick's career, with the exception of the playbills printed in periodicals. Bills of the play had their own semiotics, in which meaning was accorded to the order of actors' names, and the font size and type in which they were presented.

It is this identifiability of the newspaper advertisement as a distinct form that first inspires, then stymies one would-be contributor of a "Burlesque Advertisement" to the *Bath Advertiser* in March 1760. The printer objects that the form of the writer's satire will incur taxation: "The Author of the Burlesque Advertisement will be pleased to remark that the inserting a Piece of Poetry has no Duty to be paid to the Government for it; but an Advertisement, serious or not, has a Duty of Two Shillings charged on it. If the Author will give it another Form, instead of an Advertisement, (which must be paid for) we shall with Pleasure comply with his request."[7] The inference is that promotional material may be inserted in a newspaper without tax consequences, as long as it does not *look* like an advertisement. This may be one of the only points in history in which occasional poetry could enable tax evasion.

Though distinctive typography was not a necessary or definitive feature of all advertisements during the Garrick period, certain typographical conventions were common across several print formats associated with the theatre, including but not exclusive to direct advertisements. In theatre playbills, both those printed in the newspapers, and those posted separately, the size of type used for each player's name and the order of the names in the bill were jealously watched by players. A stalwart, longtime member of Drury Lane's company, and an infrequent complainer,

Thomas King wrote to Garrick on 13 November 1772 of his improper representation in the playbill:

> I asked for a bill of "The Merchant of Venice;" for I *thought* I recollected, that *character*, song, and *name of the performer*, were contained in *one* line. I found it to be true. I should not have made the remark, but as I came to the house, the first name that struck me was that of Reddish, which took up to itself the whole line. I could hardly believe that it was intended to be first in the bill. On examination, I found it was *not* the first; but really, to make room for the lines devoted to him, my character and name were thrust so close under the title of the play, that it required some attention to find them. I made the remark to the *prompter* (thinking him only to blame) and added – "These things have ever been, in my opinion, below notice; but as I find other performers think them of consequence, I shall henceforth endeavour to have my right!["] As I am a man I meant not to glance at you.[8]

If the normally stoic King was prepared to protest at his misrepresentation in the bills, then it is clear that conventions of font size and precedence were widely understood as meaningful by both players and periodical readers.

Capital letters were likewise legible to readers as both promotional and merit-based accolades for performers. The writer of *A Letter to David Garrick, Esq; on Opening the Theatre* (1769) avows: "The bill may be looked upon as a sort of scale of theatrical merit, and the public has thus a criterion to judge of the abilities of performers. The importance of the part, and the size of the letters in which the names are printed, are sufficient to put the talents of a performer out of all dispute."[9] However, audiences' reliance on capitals as synonymous with capital talent and parts might also be exploited. In 1744, "Mr. Neither-Side" writes that a theatre manager is like a "Jockey," handicapping his authors in type just as one might load a racehorse with weights: "if one favorite Actor's or Actress's NAME is in CAPITAL LETTERS in the Play-bills for the Day, 'tis sufficient to bring a House: And I am very sorry to say, by the Madness or Folly of the Town, he has too often succeeded."[10] In the pamphlet *A Defence of Mr. Garrick, In Answer to the Letter-Writer. With Remarks upon Plays and Players, and the Present State of the Stage* (1759?), "A Dramatic Author" objects to the idea that players may be brought into Reputation by printing "their Names in large Letters in the Play-Bills," a technique he likens to putting children on stilts to represent adults.[11]

With these exceptions – the assumption of merit and rank from precedence, font size and type – direct advertising about the theatre may be distinguished from other formal advertisements of the mid eighteenth century. One might speculate that periodical readers learned how to interpret and advertisers how to exploit the commercial implications of order and typographical variation in part from reading playbills. Name order and typographical variation continue to distinguish top actors from bit players in modern cinema posters; the movie trailer, too, has its prefiguration in announcements of new plays in rehearsal. The *Public Advertiser* for 24 January 1757 whets the audience's appetite: "There is now in Rehearsal at Drury Lane and will be performed some day next week a new Dramatic piece of 2 Acts call'd The Author written by Mr. Foote."

Other advertising, in the broader contemporary sense of making something known to the public, or what we would now call promotion, could elude taxation and perhaps even a few readers' detection as promotional material by employing different rhetoric and formatting than did standard advertisements. One such format was "fake news," or promotional material that appeared to form part of the paragraphs grouped under headings such as "London News" or "Extraordinary Intelligence." Arthur Aspinall notes that "occasionally the [tax] assessments were challenged by the publishers: an unintelligent clerk might fail to distinguish between a newspaper paragraph and an advertisement, or might be guilty of other error."[12] A clerk might be forgiven, however, for failing to draw a distinction that was so cunningly elided by the interested parties who placed the paragraph. London printers were co-proprietors with the theatre managers in various newspapers, and proprietors could include or block content. Further, theatrical intelligence was a valuable commodity, and any revenue lost by disguised advertisements (assuming that there was no off-the-books fee handed to the printer for inserting such paragraphs) might be recovered by other advertisers eager to include their notices in a paper made popular by its reliable access to theatrical news. Examples of deceptive, non-taxed promotion are discussed further below.

Given that direct advertising was taxed and legislated, one might think it would prove easy to determine how much money each newspaper made from advertising, and from whom, and when, but unfortunately, the "statistical records of the Stamp Office have not been preserved," Aspinall writes; if they had, they would have shown eighteenth-century newspapers' rise and fall "as revealed by the amounts paid by each newspaper for advertisement duty. The Audit Office papers in the Public Record Office [A.O. 3/950 seq], however," do show "the gross annual produce of the advertisement duty and the pamphlet duty, collected by (*a*) the head office in London and (*b*) the country distributors of stamps; ... annual lists of newspaper publishers in London, the names of the London newspapers which they printed, and the outstanding balances of advertisement duty owed by these publishers at the end of each financial year."[13]

From Aspinall's Audit Office-derived information, we can see that Garrick's career took place against a backdrop of rapidly expanding advertisement revenues. In 1741, when Garrick first took the stage, the gross advertisement duty in Great Britain was £4,058 12s. 0d. By 1779, the year of Garrick's death, it had grown to £36,956 10s. 2d.[14] These numbers suggest that the volume of advertisement was growing, or that collectors were getting better at enforcing and collecting duties, or both. Within this environment of increasing frequency and expense in advertising, Garrick enjoyed distinct financial advantages: as a newspaper proprietor, he had subsidized advertisement costs, paying only the tax on any ads he placed, in the case of the *St. James's Chronicle*, while the *Public Advertiser* actually paid the playhouse for the privilege of publishing its playbills.

Formal advertisements were the most direct means of making known a good or service, though they were costly; fortunately, aside from printing bills of the play, David Garrick had little need for such bald consumer appeals. There were subtler and more genteel avenues to promote himself and his theatre using his publishing community network: occasional poetry; reprinting or summarizing prologues, epilogues and other material from plays; or inserting paragraphs of theatrical news, letters or reviews. If these alternative forms of advertising fooled the skimming gaze of tax collectors, most readers still knew promotion when they saw it. They called it "puffery."

Puffery

A puff is not just good publicity, but "inflated or unmerited praise or commendation," whether performed or printed, as in "an extravagantly laudatory advertisement or review."[15] Examples of this use of the noun and verb 'puff' in the *Oxford English Dictionary* derive from plays which mock the practice of puffery: Henry Fielding's *The Author's Farce* (1730) and Samuel Foote's *The Patron* (1764).[16] In both plays, puffers are paid for promoting the playhouse. The alliance of the theatre and puffery is telling. One writer in the *General Evening Post* for 7–9 February 1771 opines that while booksellers and publishers indulged in puffery, the playhouse perfected it: "If players, however, and patentees did not invent puffing, they have of late certainly much improved it, and by their own constant use of the art may be supposed to have contributed greatly to the extension of its application, which, till lately, was very much confined to quackery in physic and literature, but now is made assistant to every species of imposture, and become of itself a real branch of business."

Though their presence was probably paid for or otherwise negotiated, puffs were not taxed as advertisements, nor did they look like advertisements.[17] They were more likely to appear in the guise of news or reviews, such as this 14 December 1762 review article in the *St. James's Chronicle*. The article, which appears in the first year in which there is evidence for Garrick owning a proprietary share in the paper, ecstatically praises Garrick's revival of John Fletcher's 1624 play, *Rule a Wife and Have a Wife*:

> Our Little-great-manager, though too often guilty of exhibiting Nonsense and Pantomime, seems however to entertain much Affection for the nobler Parts of the Drama, and has (it is said) in his Possession, the finest Collection of old Plays in the Kingdom. Let him therefore polish some of these inestimable Jewels, and expose them to publick Admiration! Let him open to himself new Veins of Applause, and surprise us more and more with the Exertion of his Talents, in other Characters, equal to Leon, Benedick, and Kitely!

A puff, excessive in its diction, punctuation and claims, also exceeds the promotion of a particular good or service proffered in a standard advertisement. Puffs promote the diffusion of positive affect. This paragraph shines a happy glow not exclusively on the adaptation of Fletcher's play, but on adaptation generally, on old British plays, and on Garrick's management and taste, even as it slips in mention of his acting talent in three of his best-known roles. This praise endeavours to leaven criticism of Garrick's neglect of the work of new playwrights by noting his "very judicious Alterations," and by trading on nationalist pride in noble old English dramas. The puffer, if not the "Little-great-Manager" himself, was someone with knowledge of Garrick's extensive private library of old plays. And, given Garrick's relationship with the newspaper in which it appeared, this puff was subsidized promotion.

Just as repeated exposure of Garrick's name in the front-page playbills of the *Public Advertiser* made him a household word, so did repeated puffs of Garrick, by himself and others, build a particular representation of the actor's attributes. A newspaper clipping from the Forster Collection, titled "October 19, 1751. *A Dramatic Piece of Theatrical Affairs*," presents a typically honeyed piece of Garrickian puffery. In a scene set at the popular site of dramatic critical discourse, the Bedford coffee-house, Mr. Drury and Mr. Newcome (newly arrived from the country) discuss Garrick's reputation:

D.   *Garrick's* a Genius.
N.   A Son of Nature.

N. . . .
We have found out in the Country; that it is not the largest Calf, that makes the best Veal.

D. For my Part, I think an Actor tall enough, if he can reach your Heart.

N. . . .
. . . he is equally our Admiration in Tragedy or Comedy; born to display the Sublime as well as the Ridiculous in human Nature!

D. . . .
The Thing is this, the Greatness of his Soul in Tragedy, or the Liveliness of his Fancy in Comedy, may ingage all your Attention, and not leave you Time to spend a single Thought on his Deficiency in Person but meer Gracefulness of Action, and tender Delivery, however engaging, can never take such an entire Possession of an Audience; for which Reason, I believe, we must not wish to see our little Hero in *Beville*, or Lord *Townly*.

N. . . .
. . . don't you think our Theatrical Stage is in a fair Way of arriving to great Perfection, since Mr. *Garrick* as Manager as well as Actor, labours to make the Dramatical World flourish? I could wish to see the *British* Stage vie with the *Athenian*!

This anonymous drama puffs Garrick's natural genius as an actor, reiterates his exquisite skill in tragedy and comedy, praises his liveliness and gracefulness of action as well as his labour as a manager, while it builds recognition of his person, emphasizing Garrick's short stature: all key components of the Garrick brand.

Puffery did not go undetected or unchallenged. Contemporary essays endeavour to alert the public to the techniques of theatrical puffery, expressing the hope that the public might then judge plays and players on their own merits, independent, or at least aware, of commercial influence. A column in the *Morning Chronicle*, "The Scenic Spectator," by one "Lemuel Launce," condemns puffery as "INFAMOUS Chicane!" and "the paltry subterfuges of theatrical pride," and mentions recent short news articles or "cards" testifying to the powers of various actors as "too vainly *constructed* to proceed from any but interested people."[18] In identifying the elements of puffery, by enumerating or parodying them, such criticism presumes that the puff, like a formal advertisement, might prove a genre discernable by means of its rhetoric, style and content. Exposing a puff's author was important to deflating it, for revealing the "interested people" behind a puff was crucial to investing the public with a cautionary sense of the words' commercial intent.

Critics were thus keen to link Garrick's name with puffery. Samuel Foote's anonymously published *Treatise on the Passions* (1747) attacks

Garrick's reputation as an actor as the product of puffery, using caustic hyperbole to enhance his point: "this Nonpareil, this Phoenix of the Imagination has been puffed as high as the Breath of Popularity can blow him."[19] Foote's *Treatise* is one of the first to premise that Garrick's reputation as a writer supplements his celebrity as an actor, and that Garrick's authorial reputation is also the result of puffing interest: "his Friends, apprehensive that their little Hero's airy Castle will have a Tumble, from a Consciousness of the Weakness of its Foundation, endeavour to prop it by a collateral Pillar; and now, forsooth, he is to commence Poet."[20] Foote acknowledges the power of puffery and social networks in creating market anticipation for Garrick's acting and writing. He implies that Garrick's glowing reputation in one field of cultural production warms his reception in another:

> No matter for that tho', he is a great Actor, and must be of consequence a great Writer; private Assurance has been before given that such a Thing is on the Anvil, that my Lord ——, and Dr. ——, and Mr. — have seen it, and pronounce it great; thus the Town is prepared, and up flies the Curtain, there may be seen the poor deluded Audience with lack-lustre Eyes gazing at their *Roscius*, applauding as heartily, as if *Nero* was the Performer, and Death was to be the consequence of Dislike.[21]

Puffery prepares perception, Foote argues; it establishes a positive mood around an actor, a writer or a performance, and genially goads critical reception.

Frustration with the inability to name and pin down specific puffers permeates critiques of Garrickian puffery. The "Cobweb Politics," as George Colman phrased it, of theatrical interest created a large field of probable suspects: indeed, a whole galaxy of them, as this accusation of "gainful idolatory" in the *Public Ledger* for 7 October 1765 grimly states:

> The Planet of a Theatre, when surrounded by his lick-spittle satellites of sycophants, in all the flutter of self-puffing or servile incensing, to raise importance by exciting public observation, in order the better to secure the gratifications of vanity and avarice, is another glaring instance of the gross application of this fashionable art [puffing], to the acquisition, by artifice, of gainful idolatry from the infatuated and ignorant; who, like true bubbles, so become puffed out of their pence and their praises.

Unmasking a puffer's identity could restore a directional vector to the puff's diffuse aura of glamour, revealing the puffer's interest in constructing hyperbole with commercial implications. Yet such unmasking was frequently impossible, given the profusion of theatrical "satellites" devoted to promoting their interest with Garrick. The restricted market for drama – two patent theatres in London – only intensified playwrights' need to puff Drury Lane's manager, in order to smooth their plays' path to his stage. The bitter author of the pamphlet, *Brief Remarks on the Original and Present State of the Drama* (1758), fulminates that Garrick has orchestrated this praise-fuelled monopoly on reputation and production with Machiavellian cleverness:

> Well ROSCIUS knows, that a Competitor in Merit would create a Competition in *Profit*; and that there is no Screen for Monopoly so subtle as a popular and *allow'd Pre-eminence*; therefore keeps himself trumpeted to the very highest Note of Fame . . . either in Sock or Buskin . . . lest his Divinity should be farther question'd, how assiduous he becomes to catch the public Ear? What incessant Pamphleteering is employed to deify him? . . . the Conduct of ROSCIUS has hitherto been ever treated in Extremes; either sanguinely attack'd by some disgusted Playwright, (whose Virulence defeated his Charge) or else rapturously blazoned by his own *Hirelings*, to keep an eternal Mist of Panegyric before the Eyes of Candour and Examination–But where's our Spirit of Resistance? Independency? *Native* Judgment? if this, our *Stage-Machiavel*, our AMURATH! can so post his *Janizary*-Scribblers as to occupy all Quarters of the Town, and discipline each modest Mind into Subjection.[22]

The writer concludes by urging "un-brib'd" pens to examine the stage with "Moderation and Justice."[23]

Garrick, meanwhile, deflected some of the negative associations of puffery by jovially confessing to his participation in the airy economy of encomiums, appearing as "Peter Puff" in his self-authored prologue to Samuel Foote's play, *Taste* (1752). With masterly irony, Garrick, as puffery personified, cautions the audience, "*Before you buy, be sure to understand.*"[24]

The puff's soft appeals, eschewing a direct commercial ask while building public recognition of Garrick's attributes as actor, writer and manager, combined powerfully with the efforts of the many "*Janizary*-Scribblers" concerned to further their interest with Garrick. Diffuse, yet consistent praise, apparently from multiple, unidentifiable sources, was positive media exposure that played to Garrick's benefit. Even if the puffery was recognizable as puffery, surely so many writers, who agreed on so many points, could not be all wrong?

Claques and Cabals

Puffery's live-action corollary in the theatre is the claque: a group of interested persons, paid or not, who attend the theatre to drive up applause and approbation for a piece, an author or an actor. Whereas puffery can mask itself in anonymity or pseudonymity, a claque is bodily present and visible – and sometimes, violent and armed.[25] Long before advertising research confirmed that positive peer reaction drives consumers' adoption of new products, those in the theatre industry knew that to propel a play to the author's night and beyond, encouragement of the audience might prove necessary. Conversely, a cabal might form to damn a disliked author, play, actor or theatre.

James Boswell's *London Journal* shows the formation of a damning cabal underway. On 19 January 1763, Boswell and two friends, Erskine and Dempster, went to David Mallet's new tragedy of *Elvira*, determined to damn it. They disapproved of Mallet's changing his last name from Malloch, in denial of his Scots background. The men wandered London, ate beefsteaks,

> and drank damnation to the play and eternal remorse to the author. We then went to the Bedford Coffee-house and had coffee and tea; and just as the doors opened at four o'clock, we sallied into the house, planted ourselves in the middle of the pit, and with oaken cudgels in our hands and shrill-sounding catcalls in our pockets, sat ready prepared, with a generous resentment in our breasts against dullness and impudence, to be the swift ministers of vengeance ... We hissed [the prologue] and had several to join us. That we might not be known, we went by borrowed names. Dempster was Clarke; Erskine, Smith; and I, Johnston. We did what we could during the first act, but found that the audience had lost their original fire and spirit and were disposed to let it pass. Our project was therefore disconcerted, our impetuosity damped. As we knew it would be heedless to oppose that furious many-headed monster, the multitude, as it has been very well painted, we were obliged to lay aside our laudable undertaking in the cause of genius and the cause of modesty.[26]

Boswell's damning cabal was damped because it was opposed by a larger claque that protectively encircled *Elvira*'s author, David Mallet. Edward Gibbon's *Journal* reports that Gibbon took his place with the author and thirty friends in the pit, "ready to silence all opposition"; however, Gibbon contends, "Notwithstanding the malice of a party, Mallet's nation, connections and indeed imprudence, we heard nothing but applause."[27]

The clash of claques carried on outside the theatre. The next day, still enamoured of the witty sallies they had drunkenly concocted the night before, Erskine and Boswell "threw" their observations on *Elvira* into "pamphlet size," and took the corrected copy to Flexney, who as "Mr. Churchill's bookseller," they presumed was interested in incisive criticism.²⁸ Earlier that day, Boswell had met with Garrick, and the two had indulged in mutual admiration ("the man whom from a boy I used to adore and look upon as a heathen god–to find him paying me so much respect!" Boswell gushes) and settled on a date to drink tea together.²⁹ Boswell then brought his pamphlet to tea: "I called at Mr. Garrick's, who said there were half a dozen as clever things in the *Strictures on Elvira* as he ever had read," Boswell concludes with satisfaction.³⁰

A reading of Boswell's *Critical Strictures on the New Tragedy of Elvira, Written by Mr. David Malloch* (1763) explains why the manager might have received comments damning a play produced at his theatre with comparative calmness. Boswell mocks the play's dullness, anachronisms and borrowings, but flatters the performance: the "incomparable Action of that universal Genius Mr. *Garrick* alone, saved this Act from the Damnation it deserved."³¹ Boswell also praises the epilogue, written by Garrick, as "fraught with Humour, and spoken with Spirit ... some of the Lines contained an exquisite and severe Criticism on the Play itself."³² Despite Boswell's critique and an intervening riot, *Elvira*'s author received the profits of three author's nights and the play appeared twelve times that season. Garrick profited directly from the presence of both claque and cabal in the theatre, as well as indirectly, from Boswell's published praise of his acting and writing, obtained at the small cost of a compliment and a cup of tea.

While there is no indication in Boswell's and Gibbon's accounts of the *Elvira* affair of his exerting influence on either party's formation, Garrick was suspected of encouraging other claques, and not without reason. Any author who had even a single play produced at Drury Lane Theatre was entitled thereafter to free run of the house. To put this boldly, Drury Lane's audience was padded with authors who owed something to Garrick for staging their plays, creating what was in effect a powerful in-house claque for the actor-manager. Boaden suggests that Garrick's acceptance of Tobias Smollett's farce *The Reprisal* "brought his enemy to his feet ... Smollet, in fact, absolutely found a niche for the manager in his *History of England*; thus making a public atonement, in a work of truth, for the wrongs he had done him in a work of fiction."³³ Authors were not the only ones to receive such favour: publishers, too, seem to have been at least occasional beneficiaries of Garrick's largesse. Boswell wrote to Garrick on 18 September 1771, "Mr. Donaldson, who published the last edition of Shakespeare, is a prodigiously happy man, on your having inscribed him among the freemen of Drury-lane Theatre."³⁴ Garrick's free hand with the freedom of the house created an audience of practitioners with professional motivation to discuss his theatre's performances in person and in print. Garrick created his own body of obliged critics, and did so in a manner that conferred professional prestige and recognition upon the group. He endeavoured to keep them under his watchful eye, writing about his theatrical productions, even when his relations with individuals became strained. Garrick's correspondence with Arthur Murphy and Robert Dodsley after disagreements reassures each man of continued access to the theatre, and reveals the values each party assumed were embedded in the designation "freedom of the house."

In a pet about Garrick holding on too long to a farce he had given him to consider, Arthur Murphy wrote the manager from the Bedford Coffee-house on 27 February 1754 to return his pass to the theatre. Murphy's letter shows that playwrights given the freedom of the house held a material ticket to assure their entrance. His letter also indicates that Murphy had put his ticket to use in publishing reviews of Drury Lane's productions under the pseudonym 'Ranger' in the *Gray's-Inn Journal*:[35]

> I must acknowledge myself indebted to you, and I therefore take this opportunity to return my best thanks for the inclosed ticket, which Ranger has found very useful in his Saturday compositions. As I do not foresee any farther occasion for this obliging passport, I am not willing to trespass too long upon your civility.[36]

Garrick's high-minded return denies Murphy has done him any favours as a reviewer: "as I thought you were above an undue Influence, I never meant ye Tick[e]t as ye least Tye upon The Liberty of Your Pen or Conversation."[37] Their breach was patched when Garrick produced the neglected farce, *The Apprentice*, in January 1756, and it proved a success. Murphy's mutually beneficial ties with Garrick and his theatre continued, though as Little and Kahrl wryly observe, the Murphy–Garrick relationship is best described as "a lifelong dispute, punctuated by brief, but never lasting, intervals of friendliness."[38]

The playwright and publisher Robert Dodsley had earned his theatrical passport twice over: upon Drury Lane Theatre's production of his satiric farce *The Toy-Shop* (1735) in the benefit season of 1757; and with *The King and the Miller of Mansfield* (1737), staged in 1755–56.[39] Following a long public fight over Garrick's refusal to stage Dodsley's tragedy *Cleone*,[40] Garrick wrote on [?18 October 1759] that Dodsley might be angry with him, but was nonetheless welcome to retain the "Liberty of the house":

> I am told, that You have complain'd of my giving orders to the Doorkeepers to refuse You admittance into our Theatre:–

> Since I have been Manager, Every Author, from ye highest to ye lowest, who has wrote for our Stage has had, & Shall have, the Liberty of the house–It is their Right & not to be taken away at ye Caprice of a Manager: therefore You may Enjoy it freely without being Oblig'd to Me; a Circumstance wch will give You no little pleasure, as You have lately boasted wth some Warmth that you never *was* oblig'd to me—[41]

In fact, the obligations flowed both ways: Dodsley had previously published Garrick's occasional poetry in several publications in which he held a proprietary interest, including the *Museum; or, Literary and Historical Register*, the *World*, the thrice-weekly *London Chronicle*, the *London Magazine* and his *Collection of Poems by Several Hands*.[42] Dodsley was, to paraphrase Foote, one of the "collateral Pillars" that propped up Garrick's reputation as a poet. In offering Garrick his tragedy, the publisher probably had sanguine and not unreasonable expectations of a trade in favours.

Those expectations were never met. Though Dodsley revised the tragedy repeatedly, Garrick refused to take it. Worse, as James Tierney relates, Garrick not only attempted to drive down Dodsley's profits by appearing in *The Busy Body* against *Cleone* once Dodsley's tragedy was finally staged at Covent Garden, but spread bad reports of *Cleone* in the place most likely to house theatre critics.[43] George Anne Bellamy, who played Cleone, told Dodsley that Garrick "had anticipated the damnation of it, publicly, the preceding evening, at the Bedford Coffee-house, where he had declared, that it could not pass muster, as it was the very *worst* piece ever exhibited."[44]

Dodsley was defended in print. In addition to a one-fifteenth share in the *London Evening Post*, Dodsley was proprietor with William Strahan in the *London Chronicle* from 1757. Criticisms against Garrick and early advertisements for the print edition of *Cleone* flew into the newspapers. The most serious accusations suggested that Garrick had rewarded John Hill for publishing a pamphlet-length diatribe against *Cleone* by producing Hill's farce, *The Rout*. "The Theatre" column from the 7–9 December 1758 *London Chronicle*, reprinted in *Lloyd's Evening Post and British Chronicle* for 8–11 December, assures Dodsley that Hill's malevolent pamphlet "may indeed, gratify the person [Garrick] for whose use it was principally written. But it will never justify his refusal of a piece, which, had it been acted at Drury-Lane, would, in some degree, have compensated for all the bawdy that has been there exhibited." The writer promises that Dodsley will have opportunity for revenge-reviewing once Hill's farce, "dullness wrapped in the Veil of Charity, at Drury-Lane," appears.

Whether or not he was behind the appearance of that news item, Dodsley clearly believed that there had been a pamphlet-for-production exchange of favours between Hill and Garrick, and that Hill had worked swiftly and assiduously to damn his play. To William Shenstone, Dodsley wrote on 20 January 1759:

> You ask me who is the Author of the Remarks on it [*Cleone*]? Dr. Hill, the precipitate Dr Hill; who came to see it acted on Saturday night, wrote his Criticism on Sunday, printed it on Monday, and with great Good-nature publish'd it on Tuesday morning, the third day of its being acted, & two days before the Play its self was printed: such was the industry exerted in predjudicing [sic] the Town against it. But he did not miss his reward; Mr. Garrick brought on for him, some days afterward, the Farce call'd the Rout, which was damn'd the second Night.[45]

A reading of Hill's anonymously published pamphlet *An Account of the Tragedy of Cleone* (1758) supports Dodsley's insinuation that the pamphlet served the manager. The pamphlet reinforces Drury Lane's reputation as the popularly recognized centre of "all good playing" and faintly praises the "other" house's production of *Cleone* as well rehearsed, while declining to advertise either Covent Garden or George Anne Bellamy, the principal actress, by name: "The most accustom'd play could not be perform'd with more decency and punctuality in its parts, at the best regulated theatre that was ever open, that of Drury-lane, than this new piece was at the other; and the actress just named [Bellamy is *not* named] was not only right but excellent; not only proper, but original."[46] After summarizing the plot, Hill rejects it, saying "'tis impossible to overlook its weakness and improbability"; the characters are "all idiots"; the language "wants the true Promethean fire, which is the character of proper Tragedy"; the tragedy wants dignity, and "the author has raised horror and detestation, where he meant only to have excited pity."[47] One could hardly have blamed Dodsley for retaliating against Hill and Garrick in the newspapers.

Remarkably, it was Dodsley, writing to his co-proprietor Strahan on 12 December [1758], who put an end to this paper war by blocking anti-Garrick content in the *London Chronicle*, citing ethical and market-based considerations. Garrick, he says, has many friends:

> As Mr. Garrick has not treated me with all the civility I could have wish'd, in the affair of my Play, I am apprehensive the Letters in our Paper, censuring his conduct, may be thought by several to come from me, which is an imputation I would chuse to avoid. I should be sorry to be the occasion of any injury to his Character as a Man, tho' he refus'd to favour mine as a Writer. Besides, Mr. Garrick has doubtless many friends, who

I think will all be disgusted with a Paper that should persist in endeavouring to cast an Odium upon him. Perhaps, therefore, in prudence it might be better to forbear all personal reflections: for my own part, I do not feel at present the least disposition to Revenge, but on the contrary could wish his behaviour might be forgotten.[48]

Though Dodsley's politic note to Strahan put a period to wrangling in the newspapers, his disappointment over Garrick's behaviour did not abate. Garrick failed to keep Dodsley "in the house," and as a result, lost his own entrée into Dodsley's publication networks. The *Cleone* affair revealed a tenuous balance of power between print and social networks. Dodsley's use of his media base to defend his tragedy and reputation against Garrick's denigration of both may well have been the inspiration for Garrick's own intensification of proprietary interest in periodicals in the 1760s.

Garrick's return letter to each spurned playwright denies, in print, that freedom of the theatre implied favours due its manager. However, both Murphy's and Dodsley's attempts to return their tickets suggest that they received them with expectations of attendant transactional obligations. The writer of the pamphlet *Stage Policy Detected* (1744) described such dependencies like this: "The Author, from seeing his Play prefer'd to others, becomes the Manager's assur'd Associate; and as People of his Turn are often necessary at a Theatre, he becomes his Bosom Friend and Table Companion ... provided he will do as well as he can, all the dirty Work allotted him, instead of a Prison, his Patron's safe Asylum for his Refuge."[49] Conferred upon grounds of professional merit, freedom of the house produced a tangible body of critical playwright-practitioners whose opinions were policed by their fellows and by personal interest and obligation: in short, a managerial claque.

A claque lacks the direct commercial appeal of a conventional advertisement, and manifests instead as a sociable alliance that noisily promotes or, in the case of a cabal, derides performances. Yet thanks to its visibility and embodied presence, a claque's promotional influence could be considerable, and could extend its influence into print. Having identified some modes of advertising and promotion available in the mid eighteenth century, let us turn to the product being promoted.

Brand Garrick

Ahistorical though it is to use the early twentieth-century term "brand" to describe the defining marks of an eighteenth-century product, it is the most appropriate, practical term to describe the constellation of

market-oriented attributes associated with the name David Garrick in
contemporary media. Brand identity "consists of the combination of the
name, logo, symbols, design, packaging and image or associations held by
consumers."[50] Brand Garrick stood, with remarkable consistency,
throughout the actor-manager's career, for:

- variety, or the ability to play comedy and tragedy, and major and
  minor parts
- nature, or the ability to produce a sense of affecting truth in performance with apparent ease
- brilliancy and liveliness of eye
- perfection of (small) proportion
- vigorous action and elegance of gesture
- pleasing vocal modulation and transitions on stage; and off stage, bluff,
  friendly, broken speech[51]
- prologue-smithery, epilogue-mastery, and play-writing and adaptation
- harmonious domestic life and genteel reception of aristocratic favour
- nationalism, British drama and Shakespearean drama

Like sedimentary rock, these positive brand attributes accrued in layers,
over time, across various media, their repetition and recombination
deepening the impression of Garrick's natural genius, geniality and desert
of good fortune, and obscuring their own origins, which often owed much
to Garrick's mediation. As David Williams sneered in *A Letter to David
Garrick, Esq. On His conduct as Principal Manager and Actor at Drury-Lane*
(1772): "That posterity to which men of merit look forward for a just and
honourable name, will be looking back on that which you had formed to
yourself . . . your invention is for ever employed to make yourself the sole
object of public notice."[52] The actor-manager's brand attributes are neatly
collated in this letter from "A Collection of Original Letters from a Young
American Gentleman in London, to His Friend," printed in the *Town and
Country Magazine* (1774). The writer, ostensibly a young American,
describes Garrick as one of the sights one must see whilst in London.
Garrick is, he writes,

> an universal actor. It is difficult to say whether he acquits himself with
> greater propriety in tragedy or comedy, or whether he more forcibly excites
> the tears of sympathetic affliction, or the risible muscles of mirth and
> pleasantry. His person, though rather under the middle stature, is finely
> proportioned; his countenance is expressive; his eye vivacious and marking;
> his voice clear and articulate; its tones as various as his situations; and his
> action invariably apposite to character and incidents.[53]

The writer calls attention to Garrick's "regulation" of Drury Lane Theatre "since the year 1747" and asserts "his knowledge and experience in all the arcana of the drama are so deep, that no manager has ever been at the head of a theatre for so many years with such extraordinary success and applause as he has met with and obtained."[54] It is unsurprising to see lavish accolades at the apex of Garrick's extraordinary career; what is remarkable is how early each of these attributes began to be stressed, singly and in combination, and how their consistent application in the media continues to influence scholarship.

"The king's name is a tower of strength"

The actor's name began to factor into advertisements and playbills just over a month into his first London season. In this brief span, Garrick leaps from being announced as an unknown "Gentleman" in his 19 October 1741 debut as Richard III, to being styled as a celebrated performer of a particular role, to becoming a recognized name. Garrick's transition from unknown to name-brand draw is so rapid that it can actually be seen in a single newspaper: the 24 November 1741 *London Daily Post, and General Advertiser*. In one advertisement, for the Goodman's Fields production of *Pamela*, he is the unnamed "Gentleman who performed King Richard." The farce that follows *Pamela* is Garrick's *Lethe*, though he is not named as author. In the advertisement below, for his benefit on 26 November, Garrick is mentioned by name three times: first, as the actor "Mr. Garrick (Who perform'd King RICHARD)"; second, as a novelty, appearing in a part for the first time: "The Part of Lothario by Mr. GARRICK, (*Being the first Time of his appearing in that Character*)"; and third, as the commodified object of a theatrical benefit, who distributes benefit tickets from the Bedford coffee-house and "Mr. Garrick's Lodgings in Mansfield-street, Goodman's Fields." After 26 November 1741, barring the time he spent travelling abroad, Garrick's name remains in the periodicals' playbills until his retirement in 1776. His near-daily name exposure in the *Public Advertiser*, discussed in the last chapter, garnered the benefits of name recognition, with ever-increasing exposure as the newspaper's circulation widened: by the 1770s, James Raven suggests, the *Daily Advertiser* "sold well over three thousand copies per day."[55]

Conceding that the rest of the acting company was necessary to fill out the dramatis personae, contemporary observers clearly felt that the Garrick name was *the* draw to Drury Lane: "Drury-Lane play-house is generally looked upon as unrivalled by Covent-Garden," wrote Edward

Purdon, the vexed author of *A Letter to David Garrick, Esq; on Opening the Theatre* (1769),

> your single name has given it a degree of lustre, which no efforts of the manager of the other house could ever attain to. You may say in the words of Shakespear,
>
> > The king's name is a tower of strength
> > Which they upon the adverse faction want.[56]

Garrick's star, Purdon opines, shines so brightly that it is reflected by lesser satellites: "such is the veneration of the town for the modern Roscius, that the most pitiful players who act on his theatre, derive a lustre from his name."[57] Recognition and approbation of the Garrick name served his theatre and its company; the actor was not the sole beneficiary of his celebrity's fiduciary value.

What did that name connote? Let us examine some of the attributes of Brand Garrick.

"Those Eyes!"

Garrick's large, dark eyes were, critics judged, crucial to the actor's expression of emotional range. Richard Cumberland wrote that "his eye was so penetrating, so speaking, his brow so moveable and all his features so plastic and accommodating, that wherever his mind impelled them, they would go, and before his tongue could give the text, his countenance would express the spirit and passion of the part he was encharged with."[58] Fanny Burney, the novelist whose family was upon intimate terms with the Garricks, wrote in her journal of 8 May 1771 that Garrick's eyes bedazzled her:

> I never saw in my life such brilliant, piercing Eyes as his are–in looking at him, when I have chanced to meet them, I have really not been able to bear their lustre. I remember three lines which I once heard Mrs. Pleydell repeat, (they were her own) upon Mr. Garrick speaking of his Face:
>
> > That mouth, that might Envy with Passion inspire,
> > Those Eyes! —fraught with Genius, with sweetness, with Fire,
> > And every thing else that the Heart can desire—[59]

Garrick's penetrating, brilliant, fiery, lustrous, ingenious, speaking eyes were exercised mightily by a scene in a tragedy written by another Burney family friend, Samuel Crisp. Crisp's play *Virginia* (1754) is given its stroke by two words and a look: when Claudius claims Virginia as a slave born in his house, pleading his case before Appius,

Garrick, representing *Virginius*, stood on the opposite side of the scene, next to the stage-door, with his arms folded across his breast, his eyes riveted to the ground, like a mute and lifeless statue. Being told at length that the tyrant is willing to hear him, he continued for some time in the same attitude, his countenance expressing a variety of passions, and the spectators fixed in ardent gaze. By slow degrees he raised his head; he paused; he turned round in the slowest manner, till his eyes fixed on *Claudius*; he still remained silent, and after looking eagerly at the impostor, he uttered in a low tone of voice, that spoke the fullness of a broken heart, "*Thou traitor!*" The whole audience was electrified; they felt the impression, and a thunder of applause testified their delight.[60]

People did not follow Garrick's gaze only because his eyes were large and lustrous; they did so because consistent media representation of Garrick's eyes, like the description of his movements as Virginius, taught them to look to his eyes as a locus of emotion. Tobias Smollett's "Dramaticus" letter in no. 455 of the *Champion* (reprinted in the *Gentleman's Magazine*, 1742) is at the forefront of this trend, praising Garrick's ocular control as part of his ability to remain in character: "When three or four are on the Stage with him, he is attentive to whatever is spoke, and never drops his Character when he has finish'd a Speech, by either looking contemptibly on an inferior Performer ... or suffering his Eyes to wander thro' the whole Circle of Spectators."[61] Whereas lesser performers might exchange glances with individuals in the audience, by riveting his own gaze on the dramatic scene, Garrick directs the gaze of the whole theatre. Yet even when his attention is directed to other actors, the audience's attention is filtered through their awareness of his presence, for to discern the object of Garrick's attention, one first had to look at him and assume some measure of his physical attitude to look where he was looking.

Minute attention to Garrick's least glance on stage was encouraged, notably, by Garrick himself. Just three years into his career, Garrick anonymously issued a pamphlet entitled *An Essay on Acting: In which will be consider'd the Mimical Behaviour of a Certain fashionable faulty Actor, and the Laudableness of such unmannerly, as well as inhumane Proceedings. To which will be added, A short Criticism On His acting Macbeth* (1744). This pamphlet, which is discussed further in the next chapter, defines acting as the imitation or assumption of mental and bodily emotions by means of "*Articulation, Corporeal Motion,* and *Occular Expression.*"[62] The eyes, Garrick writes, "must *Speak*"; his analyses of his own portrayals of Abel Drugger and Macbeth in this tract highlight moments dependent upon meaningful ocular expression, such as the "*unsettled Motion* in his Eye" Garrick judged requisite to Macbeth's disordered perception of the air-drawn dagger.[63] In this early pamphlet, Garrick defines the art of acting as dependent upon ocular expression, and models criticism that depends on critics' observation of how actors use their eyes to depict character.

In a second anonymous one-shilling pamphlet, entitled *Reasons why David Garrick, Esq; Should Not appear on the Stage, in a Letter to John Rich, Esq;* (1759), the writer – Garrick again – claims to be so blinded by Garrick's skill in the role of Ranger that he cannot even see the other players on stage, a conceit carried to ludicrous heights: "I would willingly see Mr. *Strictland*; the character, who gives title to the Comedy, yet am I herein debarred, by Mr. *Garrick's* instrusion [sic], for when he appears on the stage, I am so blinded, either by prejudice or admiration, that I can see no body else; I can hear no body else; I can bear no body else." The pamphlet suggests that Garrick engrosses the audience's gaze whenever he appears, whether as Abel Drugger, Hamlet or Macbeth, and the only solution to break his monopoly on their gaze is to "exclude him from the stage, that other people may have their turn to shine; for if we did with him, as *Juliet* says of *Romeo*, Take him, and cut him out in little stars . . . Mr. *Garrick* would possibly glitter every atom and particle of him; and like a looking-glass, broke into ten thousand shatters, every brittle shatter would glitter, and sparkle still."[64] The author playfully invites Garrick to respond to his criticisms, and promises that if he answers, "we shall subscribe a submissive acknowledgment of our fault in the daily adver-tiser."[65] Garrick's anonymous writings assured his audience that his eyes drew all eyes, and engrossed all attention.

Detractors knew that in Garrick's vanity over his best feature, they had found a blind spot, and they probed it mercilessly. *Hecate's Prophecy* (1758), for instance, reveals Garrick actively promoting the distribution of images that prominently feature his chief asset. A minion enters, carrying a bust representing the actor, and the Garrick figure, Fidget, complains in Garrick's characteristic off-stage stutter that the sculpture's "*Eyes* look *blind*-I that that-that's the Reason I-I always prefer a *Print.*"[66] This critic concludes that Garrick's patronage of artists and interventions in the print market (discussed later in this book) were carefully cultivated to complement his image as the actor with speaking eyes.

In the final five years of Garrick's career, David Williams observed that Garrick's declining powers could be indexed by the lack of lustre in the actor's eye:

> Your eyes have lost the power of imitating softness, if they ever had it. That fine, bewitching liquid, which passion sends out to the eye of youth, cannot

be imitated by any old man. The eyes of age express only experience, cunning, and watchfulness. When you have a raree-shew to exhibit; and you peep, from your hole under the stage, as a spider from his recess; when you dart your glances to every part of that web, by which you would deceive and amuse the public; when you catch half-views of an audience you insult; shew a mingled anxiety and consciousness of guilt; and pop in at your hole, from fear of being hissed;—.[67]

The collapse of the actor's wide range of eye-borne emotions to a narrow streak of avaricious, anxious cunning is the ocular proof that Garrick's day is over, Williams asserts.

Garrick's supporters, however, saw no diminishment in the power of his gaze, even after his retirement, when it continued to instruct and inspire other actors. In a presentation copy of a prologue from the amateur theatricals at Wynnstay, inscribed by Garrick "1777 The Wynstay Prologue when I was there–written by W Griffith," the aristocratic amateur performers express a

> keen wish that natural desire
> To taste what Garrick's presence must inspire
> From each just motion some instruction draw
> Feel Shakespears Fire; & copy natures Law
> To watch the meaning Glances as they fly
> And catch correction from that speaking Eye
> That Eye which erst in wondrous Magick drest
> Call'd forth each Passion of the human brest,
> Enraptured nations gazed, & blest the Art
> That pleas'd the fancy and improv'd the Heart[68]

The "speaking Eye" that Garrick himself lauded as necessary to good acting is gracefully praised in this complimentary prologue, which returns the phrase to its author. Griffith's tribute to Garrick was in turn reported in the *Public Advertiser*, the *London Chronicle* and at length in the *Morning Post and Daily Advertiser* for 11 October 1777 as an "Extract of a Letter from Chester, Oct. 7":

> For this fortnight past there have been a great resort of ladies and gentlemen at Wynnstay, the seat of Sir Watkin William Wynne, Bart. among whom were Mr. and Mrs. Garrick, whose affable and polite behaviour to every one challenges their highest esteem. Mr. Garrick is in perfect health, in great spirits, and is the life of the company. – On Thursday evening there was performed a play, or rather two farces, in order to shew Mr. Garrick the theatre ... The theatre and design of the performance was kept an entire secret from Mr. Garrick till the moment of the company's being conducted there; the house was most elegantly illuminated, and filled with a very

brilliant audience. The instant Mr. Garrick entered the theatre, he was received with peals of applause; a medley overture struck up; at the end of which, Mr. Griffith, of Rhual, came forward, and spoke a most elegant and masterly prologue, written by himself, complimenting Mr. Garrick on his great attention to Shakespear's plays in particular, and echoing the regret of the whole world for the great loss they have sustained in his retiring from the stage.

The anonymous letter printed in these Garrick-owned and -influenced papers insists that even in his genteel retirement, Garrick remains the centre of regard. His professional expertise reverses the usual flow of artistic patronage, and the aristocratic amateur performers of Wynnstay now strive to please his eye – "To watch the meaning Glances as they fly / And catch correction from that speaking Eye." Garrick might have left the London stage, but thanks to his media presence, he was still very much in the public eye.

Garrick's penetrating eyes are an instantaneous identifier of the actor in contemporary prints – the visual corollary of Charles James Fox's bushy eyebrows, or William Pitt's bony nose – but never more eerily do they speak than in the Robert Edge Pine print depicting Garrick's death mask (Figure 2). The death mask is presented in a vertical plane, as if the actor were standing facing the viewer, but the gravity-struck flesh of the dead actor's face melts outwards horizontally, distorting the familiar visage's contours into something uncanny.[69] Most distressing, what should be blank, empty eye sockets in the mask are freshly planted with eyes, in a wild, white-walled stare, as if the actor's gaze has outlived his body. Pine's image of live eyes in a dead face is unforgettably grotesque. Yet it is also a fitting memorial, for Garrick himself puffed the speaking eye as essential to expressing the passions. If Garrick's gaze outlived his body, it is in part because his interventions in the media taught audiences to value it.

"Shakespeare's best commentator"

The intricately woven relationship between Garrick and Shakespeare, which began with Garrick's turn as Richard III and arguably reached its apex with the Stratford Jubilee in September 1769 and the ensuing successful run of the Jubilee pageant on stage at Drury Lane, is a key feature of Garrick's brand identity. Vanessa Cunningham has explained this aspect of Garrick's reputation ably, at book length.[70] In addition to Cunningham's book, and Michael Dobson's landmark study *The Making of the National Poet* (1995), a wealth of scholarly essays has taken into

Figure 2   Robert Edge Pine, Garrick death mask with eyes inserted, 1779. Pine's image of
live eyes in a dead face is a grotesque yet fitting memorial to Garrick, who puffed the
"speaking eye" as essential to expressing the passions. By permission of the Folger
Shakespeare Library.

account Garrick's interpretation of Shakespearean roles, his influence upon the editing of Shakespeare's plays, and his place in the inception of the Shakespeare industry.[71] I do not aim to rehearse this complex body of work, but rather to ask how eighteenth-century media contributed to one aspect of the Garrick–Shakespeare nexus, which reinforced the public conception of both men as national icons renowned for their natural genius: the recurrent insistence that Garrick is Shakespeare's "best commentator."

Variations on the sentiment that Garrick's actions provided a meaning-ful gloss on Shakespeare's characters abound, and some predate the "best commentator" formulation. To choose just one example from those who consider Garrick's action as edition, one might cite Richard Rolt's doggerel *Poetical Epistle from Shakespear in Elysium, to Mr. Garrick, at Drury-Lane Theatre* (1752), which has Shakespeare cry out to Garrick:

> "THOU art my living monument; in THEE
> I see the best inscription that my soul
> Could wish: perish, vain pageantry, despis'd!
> SHAKESPEAR revives! in GARRICK breathes again!"[72]

However, after the phrase terming Garrick "Shakespeare's best commen-tator" appears, and it appears long before the Stratford Jubilee, there is a virtual explosion of remarks citing or expanding on the idea. Tracing the "best commentator" stream of critique illustrates how much this phrase and our understanding of Garrick's legacy in Shakespeare studies owe to the media.

The phrasing that identifies Garrick as Shakespeare's "best commen-tator" appears to have been brought into vogue by Arthur Murphy.[73] Murphy, a.k.a. Charles Ranger of the *Gray's-Inn Journal*, please recall, is the man who tried to return his freedom-of-the-house ticket to Garrick on 27 February 1754; the same man mollified and brought back into the theatre by Garrick's acceptance of his farce, *The Apprentice*. By 20 April 1754, their dispute resolved, Murphy was back to publishing puffery like this letter ostensibly written to Ranger by one "G" in no. 79 of the *Gray's-Inn Journal*:

> I cannot forbear mentioning the obligation which the public has to the genius of Mr. Garrick, who has exhibited with great lustre many of the most shining strokes of Shakespear's amazing art; and may be justly styled (as he was once called by you) his best commentator: for it is certain, he has done our poet more justice by his manner of playing his principal charac-ters, than any editor has yet done by a publication.[74]

Despite Garrick's protestations to the contrary, Murphy's puffery does suggest a "Tye" upon his pen, and one that had lasting effect. Murphy had a fondness for this well-turned phrase, and re-used the "best commentator" remark across multiple media formats. The phrase reappears in a pamphlet, *A Defence of Mr. Garrick, In Answer to the Letter-Writer. With Remarks upon Plays and Players, and the Present State of the Stage* (1759). The anonymous writer ("A Dramatic Author") lauds Garrick for bringing forth more productions of Shakespeare's plays. There are plenty of clues that Murphy is this Dramatic Author, including references to the *Gray's-Inn Journal* and to his play *The Orphan of China*, as well as the occurrence of his trademark phrase: "Before Mr. *Garrick* took upon him the Management, we knew little more of our favourite Dramatic Author than his *Hamlet, &c.* but such is the Esteem paid him by this his best Commentator, that there is scarce a Play of his, which has not been got up to the best Advantage."[75] In *News from Parnassus*, an introductory piece for the opening of Covent Garden Theatre on 23 September 1776, Murphy dramatized the phrase. The venal publisher and newspaperman Vellum is told of Garrick's recent retirement:

RANTWELL   Roscius, you know, has left the stage; is not Shakespeare
        hugely angry?

. . .

VELLUM   This is bad news . . . No abuse in it: truth is a dull drug; I'll say in the
        paper that Shakespeare never thought him a good actor: he preferred
        Betterton, and Booth, and –
BOCCALINI   He says the reverse, and calls him his best commentator.[76]

Murphy reuses the phrase again in his biography of Garrick. Meanwhile, the *Gray's-Inn Journal* numbers circulated and were reprinted, and a host of other writers picked up Murphy's memorable phrase – some filching the phrase entire, others expanding on its implications.

Editors of Shakespeare and his contemporaries frequently invoke Garrick's performances as interpretations parallel to their own efforts. Following on Murphy's first identification of Garrick with Shakespeare using this phrase in 1754, Peter Whalley, in his edition of *The Works of Ben. Jonson* (1756), gratefully acknowledges Garrick's assistance in lending him rare copies of Jonson's plays to prepare his edition. However, Whalley notes that Jonson's characters – with the exception of Abel Drugger – lack the advantage given Shakespeare's characters "from the best action and expression that ever added grace and energy to the stage. And in thus wanting Mr. Garrick's performance, he [Jonson] wants that living explanation, which no comment of the most learned critic can possibly give."[77] The editor Elizabeth Robinson Montagu, though she gives credit to learned print commentators for preserving Shakespeare's genius, also praises performance, saying Shakespeare's "very spirit seems to come forth and to animate his characters, as often as Mr. Garrick, who acts with the same inspiration with which he [Shakespeare] wrote, assumes them on the stage."[78] George Steevens, in an "Advertisement" for general assistance in the preparation of his new edition of Shakespeare's work, writes in the *London Chronicle* for 1–4 February 1766: "He is happy to have permission to enumerate Mr. GARRICK among those who will take such a trouble on themselves; and is no less desirous to see him attempt to transmit some part of that knowledge of Shakespeare to posterity, without which, he can be his best commentator no longer than he lives." Finally, John Monck Mason's edition of *The Dramatick Works of Philip Massinger* (1779) teases Garrick in the prefatory address: "you must not expect to hear of the Quickness of your Conception, the Justice of your Execution, the Expression of your Eye, the Harmony of your Voice, or the Variety and Excellency of your Deportment."[79] Mason's jocular tone emphasizes how these components of the Garrick brand, including Murphy's assertion that Garrick has "been stiled the best Commentator on [Shakespeare's] Works," had been burnished to a hackneyed sheen, yet remained so closely bound to the actor's image that Mason felt he had to cite them.[80]

Not only did scholarly editors of Shakespeare and his contemporaries cite and dignify the phrase, but the "Shakespeare's best commentator" formula quickly became part of the very definition of 'Garrick' in contemporary reference works concerning the stage. David Erskine Baker's first edition (1764) of *The Companion to the Play-house*, which proceeds in an alphabetized dictionary-style format to define the careers and contributions of stage authors and actors, adds a professional veneer to Murphy's phrase, which it cites: "*Shakespeare* has been transmitted down to us with successive Glories; and you, Sir, have continued, or rather increased, his Reputation. You have, in no fulsome Strain of Compliment, been stiled the best Commentator on his Works."[81] Francis Gentleman's reference work *The Dramatic Censor; or, Critical Companion* (1770) likewise reinforces the sensible effects of Garrick's exemplary representation of Shakespeare: "Mr. GARRICK shews uniform, unabating excellence; scarce a look, motion or tone, but takes possession of our faculties, and leads them to a just sensibility. As SHAKESPEARE rises above himself in many places, so does this his greatest and best commentator, who not only presents his beauties to the imagination, but brings them home feelingly to the heart."[82] Any reader looking up 'Garrick' in contemporary dramatic dictionaries would be told, definitively, that the actor was Shakespeare's best commentator.

It was a phrase that felt increasingly apt and true because of its scholarly associations with editions and works of reference, and also thanks to its popular ubiquity.[83] Readers of *The Companion to the Play-house* or *The Dramatic Censor* had probably already encountered the phrase in the newspapers; if not in the *Gray's-Inn Journal*, then in the *St. James's Chronicle*, that Garrick-owned paper which printed poems containing the phrase with suspicious regularity. Consider this entry, printed on 21 December 1765:

> On Shakespeare's Commentators.
>
> . . .
>
> Shakespeare's best Comment would you know,
> In Spite of Envy, will I shew;
> Justice shall own it good:
> See Garrick! And in him you'll own
> Shakespeare's strong Sense is clearly shewn,
> Each Tittle understood. C.M.

Or this rollicking puff of a recent portrait of Garrick by Thomas Gainsborough, from the "Poet's Corner" of the 1 January 1767 *St. James's Chronicle*:

> Occasioned by seeing the Picture of
> Mr. Garrick painted by Gainsborough.
>
> Ye Warburtons flashing, ye dogmatic Johnsons,
> Forbear upon Shakespeare to publish your Nonsense:
> Wou'd you read with Precision his masterly Page,
> Burn your Notes, grub your Pens, and repair to the Stage:
> There Garrick reveals all his Spirit and Nature,
> And plainly points out who's the best Commentator.

The message of Brand Garrick could not be more consistent or better exposed: the idea Garrick was Shakespeare's best commentator was frequently iterated and remained steady no matter what the media context.

Praise poems of Garrick appear so frequently in contemporary media that the "panegarrick" is practically a genre unto itself. The occasional poem concerning Garrick's powers of expression that had the widest geographic distribution, travelling transatlantically via the newspapers, also quotes Murphy's "best commentator" phrase. Murphy describes the poem's inception: Mr. Shireff, a deaf and dumb painter of miniatures, moved to London with letters of introduction to members of the arts community, including Caleb Whiteford. Murphy writes, "When any of Shakespeare's plays was performed, and, particularly, when Garrick acted, young Shireff was sure to be present, professing that he was the actor whom he best understood. When the play was over, he used to act in dumb show the whole of Garrick's performance, and expressed an earnest wish to be introduced to so fine an imitator of nature."[84] Accordingly, Murphy explains, Whiteford wrote "in Shireff's name a short copy of verses in commendation of the actor's extraordinary powers, and conveyed them to Mr. Garrick."[85] Murphy reprints the verses in his biography.[86]

The verses are shown as they appeared in the *Public Advertiser* for 2 January 1772, with an introduction that cites Shireff, not Whiteford, as author. "A Young Gentleman (deaf and dumb from his Birth) having been at Drury-lane Theatre on Monday last, to see Mr. *Garrick* perform the Part of *Hamlet*, was questioned as to his Opinion of the Performance, upon which he wrote the following Lines":

> When Britain's ROSCIUS on the Stage appears,
> Who charms all Eyes, and (I am told) all Ears;
> With Ease the various Passions I can trace,
> Clearly reflected from *his* wond'rous Face;
> Whilst true Conception with just Action join'd
> Strongly impress each Image on my Mind:
> What need of *Sounds?* when plainly I descry
> Th' *expressive* FEATURES, and the *speaking* EYE;
> *That* Eye whose bright and penetrating Ray
> Does *Shakespear's* Meaning to my Soul convey.—
> Best Commentator on GREAT SHAKESPEAR's Text!
> When GARRICK acts, *no* Passage seems perplext. C.S.

Note the poet's casual reference to Garrick's "*speaking* EYE" as well as his absorption of Murphy's "Best Commentator" phrase. Whether Shireff or Whiteford is the author, the occasional poem demonstrates how fragments of puffery might recirculate in popular media until their origins were at last decently obscured. From its appearance in the Garrick-friendly *Public Advertiser*, the poem was reprinted in London magazines and provincial papers, even appearing in the 11 June 1783 *Freeman's Journal* of Philadelphia.[87] Following this, not only did Murphy cite the poem citing his phrase in his biography of Garrick, but the reviews of Murphy's biography then used the Shireff anecdote and poem as publicity for Murphy's book.[88] His compliment to Garrick continued to do good work for Murphy long after the actor's death.

Garrick was Shakespeare's best commentator. This idea, once spread across dramatic, scholarly and popular media – to say nothing of visual depictions of Garrick in Shakespearean roles – attained the gravitas of a received truth. Curiously, despite Arthur Murphy's obsessive and easily traced self-quotation, it seems also to have veiled its own roots as venal praise resulting from Murphy's obligations to the manager.

"Infinite variety"

Another aspect of the Garrick brand, variety, neatly complements the concept of Garrick as Shakespeare's best commentator. Shakespeare was celebrated as a writer whose mastery exceeded generic categories such as tragedy or comedy, just as Garrick's range of interpretive abilities was not confined to one walk of characters, or one genre of drama. In a letter to the Reverend Joseph Warton, 15 June 1756, Garrick appreciatively repeats the elegant compliment paid him in Warton's *Essay upon the Genius and Writings of Pope* (1756): "We therefore of Great-Britain have perhaps more reason to congratulate ourselves, on two very singular phenomena; I mean, Shakespear's being able to pourtray characters so very different as Falstaff, and Mackbeth; and Garrick's being able to personate so inimitably a Lear or an Abel Drugger. Nothing can more fully demonstrate the extent and versatility of these two original geniuses."[89] By playing Shakespeare's varied characters, Garrick efficiently annexed Shakespeare's reputation for variety and amplified his own reputation as an actor of breadth. He was regarded, as an occasional poem printed in the *Ladies Magazine* indicates, as a "*Proteus*"

> . . . that can take
> What shape he pleases, and in an instant make
> Himself to any thing, be't that, or this,
> By voluntary metamorphosis!

Garrick's varied acting range was lauded as "universal." As the *Ladies Magazine* poet put it, Garrick epitomized mankind's variety: "Thou art, tho' little, the whole map of men." Garrick's understanding of the importance of variety informed myriad aspects of his career and self-presentation. As a manager, David Garrick understood the need to tempt an audience's appetite with "infinite variety," just as Cleopatra did with the fickle

Antony.[90] Variety stimulates hunger for further novelty and change, not only in lovers, but also in consumers. Garrick vigorously asserted his theatre's variety in repertoire, actors, entertainments, scenes, costumes, music and other changeable elements in the media, often in direct advertisements or playbills. This typical advertisement in the *Public Advertiser* for 27 November 1770 stresses variations in the play text, in costumes and scenes, amongst other allurements:

> In consequence of some Alterations made in the new Comedy, called 'Tis well it's no Worse, acted last Night at the Theatre Royal in Drury-lane, it was performed to a crouded Audience, and was received with very great Applause. – The Tragedy of Zara (by particular Desire) will be performed To-morrow: Zara, Mrs. Barry, Osman, Mr. Reddish, and Lusignan, Mr. Garrick – The Masque of King Arthur, by Dryden, and the Music by Purcell and Dr. Arne, with new Scenes, Dresses, &c. will be revived the latter End of next Week at the same Theatre.

Equally typically, the advertisement claims these innovations have been instigated by the audience ("by particular Desire"), and they are described as well received, the better to stoke a warm reception.

Even off stage, as Oliver Goldsmith remarked in the poem *Retaliation* (1774), Garrick was renowned for his changeable nature. Goldsmith describes members of the Club to which he, Samuel Johnson, Garrick and other luminaries belonged, as different foods or dishes. He writes: "Our Garrick's a sallad, for in him we see / Oil, vinegar, sugar, and saltness agree."[91] Elsewhere in the verses Goldsmith is critical of Garrick's changeability when it manifests as superficiality or narcissistic pleasure in his own performances, but this image presents variety as an harmonious, balanced aspect of his character. Variety was deeply engrained in the Garrick brand, from his acting to his writing, and from his theatre's repertoire to his private persona.

Garrick perceived of variety as valuable, and encouraged its representation as a desirable stage commodity. Variety emerges as a desirable component of Garrick's self-presentation as an actor in one of his earliest extant letters, written to his brother Peter *ante* 29 December 1741:

> You perhaps would be glad to know what parts I have play'd, King Richd–Jack Smatter in Pamela–Clody fop's fortune—Lothario fair Penitent–Chamont Orphan–Ghost Hamlet–& Shall soon be ready in Bays in ye Rehearsal & in ye Part of Othello—Both which I believe will do Me & Giffard great Service–I have had great Success in all, & 'tis not yet determin'd whether I play Trajedy or Comedy best ... As to playing a Harlequin 'tis quite false—Yates last Season was taken very ill & was not

able to begin ye Entertainment so I put on ye Dress & did 2 or three Scenes for him, but Nobody knew it but him & Giffard; I know it has been Said I playd Harlequin at Covent Garden but it is quite false.[92]

Garrick's concern was to negotiate a swift exit from his failing career as a wine merchant by offering his brother evidence of his acting ability. Initially presented as a test of his powers to see which dramatic genre his acting best suits ("'tis not yet determin'd whether I play Trajedy or Comedy best"), his range becomes an argument for the viability of acting as a career. The more roles he can play, the greater "Service" it will do both Garrick and his manager, and the more financially viable this questionable employment might seem to Garrick's business-minded brother. The final sentences show Garrick's attentiveness to the cachet of various dramatic genres. Even as he argues range to be an advantageous commodity, he is quick to limit his participation in pantomime to a larky secret, reassuring his brother that it was only the once.

Not playing Harlequin differentiated Garrick from John Rich, the famous actor-manager known as Lun, who had played Harlequin since 1717, and who built a reputation and a fortune upon pantomime. Once manager, Garrick sought to distance the image of Drury Lane Theatre from the idea of pantomime. He attempted to position Rich's Covent Garden Theatre as the site of down-market spectacles and pantomimes, and Drury Lane as the house of Shakespeare. Note the words "sought" and "attempted." Garrick's marketing of Drury Lane as pantomime-averse in no way reflected the theatre's actual repertoire. Robert D. Hume asserts that "the array of mainpieces offered by the two patent companies between 1714 and 1761 was close to identical," and shows that Rich staged abundant Shakespearean productions, while Garrick, during the fourteen years he was in direct competition with Rich, staged many pantomimes.[93] Hume argues that Rich, the supporter of spectacle and pantomime, was the true theatrical innovator of the two, and concludes: "John Rich did not compete with David Garrick. Rather, David Garrick competed with John Rich–often not very successfully."[94]

However closely the two theatres matched repertoire in actuality, Garrick was nonetheless successful at fostering the abiding idea that Rich's theatre offered cheap thrills and Drury Lane offered high culture. Garrick's marketing of this concept begins with the paratexts heralding his first season as manager, "The Prologue and Epilogue, Spoken at the Opening of the Theatre in Drury-Lane 1747." The prologue, written by Samuel Johnson and spoken in the theatre by Garrick, enjoyed repeated print exposure: first printed as a sixpenny pamphlet (Robert Dodsley was one of its retailers), it was then reprinted in the *Gentleman's Magazine* for October 1747, in Dodsley's *Collection of Poems* (1748) and, as Pierre Danchin observes, in various spouting companions and poetic collections in the 1770s, including Davies's *Miscellaneous and Fugitive Pieces* (1773).[95]

The prologue's poetic history of the stage begins by celebrating the immortal Shakespeare. Johnson next traces drama's devolution through what he views as the rule-bound work of Ben Jonson and Restoration drama's obscenity, until Virtue quits her reign over the modern stage, usurped by Folly, Pantomime and Song. The prologue positions Garrick's Drury Lane Theatre as friendly to Shakespeare, and hostile to mere entertainments such as pantomime, albeit with Johnson's caveat acceding to the power of popular taste: "The Drama's Laws the Drama's Patrons give / For we that live to please, must please to live" (lines 53–54). With power comes responsibility, and it is the audience's responsibility not to cry out for "Follies," but to support "rescu'd Nature, and reviving Sense; / To chase the Charms of Sound, the Pomp of Show, / For useful Mirth, and salutary Woe" (lines 57–60). Certain kinds of morally "useful" variety in the repertoire receive cultural approbation, while others are painted as immorally sensational: comedy and tragedy are welcome at Drury Lane; song and dance, less so.

Johnson's prologue next establishes Garrick as a figure who will serve the public taste, even if he believes it to be folly. Garrick, in the sixth stanza, is given lines that reflect with sympathetic humour upon the curse of his new managerial role: "Hard is his Lot, that here by Fortune plac'd, / Must watch the wild Vicissitudes of Taste" (lines 47–48). The prologue cleverly premises a no-fault situation in which the manager himself would never choose entertainment over drama of substance, or at least should never be faulted for so doing, for he is "Fated" to serve the public: "let not Censure term our Fate our Choice, / The Stage but echoes back the publick Voice" (lines 51–52).

The prologue was Johnson's work, but it was printed largely without Johnson's name affixed to it, and sold by reference to Garrick's performance of it; sold, even, as a proxy for Garrick's voice. An advertisement for the sixpenny printing of the prologue in the 8 October 1747 *General Advertiser* reads: "Mr. GARRICK being disabled by Illness from Speaking the PROLOGUE when it was demanded, hopes this Publication will be considered as a Proof of his Desire to compensate the Disappointment." An advertisement in the *General Evening Post* for 31 October – 3 November 1747 listed the prologue as a selling point for an issue of the

Gentleman's Magazine. Garrick, as its speaker, remained closely associated with the prologue and its position on variety in the theatre's repertoire – a position he solidified three years later with a self-authored and delivered prologue to open the theatre in 1750. In it, Garrick amplifies Johnson's earlier claims, declaring, "Sacred to SHAKESPEARE was this spot design'd" (line 25), and protests that only unwillingly will he and his company "change the nobler Scene / And in our Turn, present you *Harlequin*" (lines 29–30) to avoid an empty house.[96] Prologues and epilogues provided Garrick with performative and print opportunities to differentiate his theatrical product – however illusory that differentiation – from others on offer, and to define what kinds of variety in the repertoire ought to receive cultural approbation.

Variety, embodied in the actor, continued to concern Garrick through-out his career. One of the ways Garrick assessed the appetite of his audiences, particularly early on, was through correspondence. An audience member confirmed Garrick's sense of himself as equally adept in either comedy or tragedy, and showed the pleasure audiences took in observing Garrick's bravura leaps from one genre to another, and in his subtle transitions from one passion to another. Joseph Smith, a clergyman, wrote to Garrick on 25 January 1741: "I was charmed in particular with your sudden starts into passion & quite in raptures at your fine recovery out of it. But you are not made for tragedy only: the Sock becomes you as much as the buskin."[97] From the outset of his career, Garrick felt that variety was a signal part of his identity as an actor, and had this confirmed by audience response. Later, in the 1760s, Garrick observed several actors at the Comédie-Française, and said disparagingly of Préville, "I did not see ye variety I expected—He has ye same looks in Ev'ry part I saw him Act & throws a kind of drunken folly into his Eyes wch in some parts would have a fine Effect, but to be us'd continually is a proof of confin'd talents."[98] His critique shows the degree to which Garrick supported the concept of variety of expression as essential to the finely differentiated display of characters.

Garrick's ideal of embodied variety began with the eyes, and included vocal inflection, attitudes and action. Baker and Reed's *Biographia Dramatica* lyrically commended to posterity the pleasing variation in his vocal tones: "His voice was clear, melodious, and commanding ... it appeared to have a much greater compass of variety than either [Mossop or Barry]; and, from Mr. Garrick's judicious manner of conducting it, enjoyed that articulation and piercing distinctness, which rendered it equally intelligible, even to the most distant parts of an audience, in the

gentle whispers of murmuring love, the half-smothered accents of infelt
passion, or the professed and sometimes awkward concealments of an aside
speech in comedy, as in the rants of rage, the darings of despair, or all the
open violence of tragical enthusiasm."[99] His variety of action was likewise
legendary. There are so many iconic portraits of Garrick holding dramatic
attitudes, and stilled into a contemplative genteel figure, that it is urgent to
recall that Garrick was famous for his action and busyness on stage.
A petulant rant from the *Memoirs of Charles Macklin* protests against this
busyness as upstaging:

> if, while one person speaks, in an interview of business, which every well
> wrought scene is, another pays not attention, but chases, struts, stalks, and
> pulls out his handkerchief, wipes his face, puts up his handkerchief and pulls
> it out again; varies his gait–walks up the stage, and down the stage, and across
> the stage, it is a breach of good manners; it is an interruption, a contempt,
> and an injury to the other actor; a little pitiful, avaricious ambition in the
> fellow that does it, and a total contradiction to the ways of nature.[100]

The actor's constant, various motion on stage drew attention as surely as
the constantly reiterated aspects of the Garrick brand retained it in
print media.

Garrick's alternation between comedy and tragedy had a practical
component: like many actors, he found tragedy exhausting to play, and
his characteristic busyness on stage could have only exacerbated tragedy's
emotional and physical demands. To offer himself respite from tragic
leads, Garrick conceived of a season's repertoire as a series of paired,
genre-contrasting pieces, as seen in this letter of 17 August 175[1] to
Somerset Draper: "I intend playing Coriolanus and the Rehearsal, alter-
nately—All's Well, &c. and Merope, in the same manner: and then I shall
present you with Don John and Sosia, into the bargain; besides new plays
without number."[101] It was restorative for the actor – but how did he
condition audiences to appreciate variety in role and repertoire, without
appearing lazy or manipulative?

Garrick built audiences' understanding of tragic roles as laborious. He
told the readers of periodicals the deleterious effects that acting several
tragic roles in succession had upon his health, while displaying a sporting
attitude to pleasing audiences and serving fellow actors by offering to
appear in less arduous roles. Garrick's letter to James Quin, printed in
the *General Advertiser* for 30 March 1747, apologized:

> I am sorry, that my present bad state of Health makes me uncapable
> of performing so long and laborious a character as <u>Jaffeir</u>, this Season. If you

think my playing in the <u>Farce</u> will be of the least service to you, or any
Entertainment to the Audience, you may command,
    Your humble Servant,
    D. Garrick.

It was the more necessary to emphasize in the media that acting tragedy
was hard work because of the perception of Garrick's acting as easy and
natural, which might have led audiences to assume that there was little
exertion needed. Not so! Tragic roles, as the *General Advertiser* for
24 March 1744 advises, take energy. Mr. Ryan, an actor whose benefit's
profitability was threatened by Garrick's illness, thought it worthwhile to
change his benefit's repertoire to retain the star: "Mr. *Garrick's* Indisposition having rendered him Incapable of Acting any Part that requires
Energy, obliges me to Change the play, & add the Farce of *Miss in her
Teens*, in which he may be able to perform." Such notes heighten tragedy's
cultural value by consistently representing it as the most artistically
demanding dramatic genre, from a practitioner's perspective.

Similar strategies were deployed to accustom audiences to seeing Garrick in minor roles. Garrick's anonymous *Essay on Acting* (1744) describes
the challenge of playing Abel Drugger, a minor role for which he became
well known. Garrick devotes two pages of minute detail to describing
Drugger's reaction to dropping the urinal, anatomizing the complex
movements that best show the character's mute terror, from holding one's
breath to inverting the toes and convulsing the fingers, showing readers the
labour that goes into creating "the compleatest low Picture of *Grotesque
Terror* that can be imagin'd by a *Dutch* Painter."[102] Drugger is a low
masterpiece in miniature, and ought to be appreciated as such, the comparison with detailed Dutch interiors suggests. Garrick emphasizes his
interpretation of Drugger in *Reasons why David Garrick, Esq; Should Not
appear on the Stage* (1759) yet again. His pattern of repeatedly stressing the
critical pleasures inherent in attending to his meticulous performance of
this minor part suggests that one of Garrick's aims in these anonymous
pamphlets was to heighten audience appreciation of his work in
minor roles.

Some writers agreed that Garrick could add interpretive lustre to small
parts as well as leads. One anonymous pamphleteer wrote in 1758 that it
was better to see the actor-manager more frequently in smaller and comic
roles than in infrequent tragic turns:

> Yourself I could wish to see oftener, but in lighter parts: and I think I could
> point out a way wherein we might have that pleasure every night; and yet

not add to the fatigue of your profession. 'Tis rash to say you excel in one species of acting, for you have shewn the world a genius, which is equally capable of all. You are at least as eminent in the easier parts of comedy, as in the fury of sublimer passions; and there are characters, the spirit of which is lost to us, because they are acted by those who do not understand them … You must not conceive to see you every day would make you cheap: this is the fate of inferior performers.[103]

Garrick's portrayal of minor roles drew criticism, nonetheless. Edward Purdon complained (anonymously) in 1769 that hearing Garrick in minor parts was a major infraction of audience expectations: "notwithstanding the great reputation of Drury-Lane play-house, I have generally observed that plays are better acted at the other house. You are satisfied to reap the profits of a reputation already established, and now leave all the capital parts which you alone are capable of performing to the satisfaction of the town to wretched substitutes, who could hardly deliver a message with tolerable grace."[104] As this criticism suggests, promoting the concept of variety had benefits, but required constant management of the repertoire and the media: too many important roles and Garrick would be viewed as selfish and avaricious; too few, and he was cheating the public.

Prints of Garrick embrace variety in their impressive number, and in the variety of poses and roles portrayed therein, while some thematize variety in and of themselves. Comedy and Tragedy consistently feature in Garrick's iconography: to name but a few instances, they are visible in a portrait of a wigless Garrick by Johann Zoffany (c. 1763); in the frame of J. Collyer's popular engraving of Thomas Gainsborough's portrait (Figure 3); and the portrait painted in Italy in 1764 by Pompeo Batoni, commissioned by the actor, shows Garrick gesturing to a page of masks with varied expressions in the 1736 edition of Terence's *Comedies*.[105]

No image speaks more eloquently to the actor's self-representation as variety embodied than Sir Joshua Reynolds's 1761 canvas, "David Garrick between Tragedy and Comedy" (Figure 4). The composition, as has been widely noted, plays on the classical choice of Hercules,[106] recast so that Garrick must choose not between Virtue and Pleasure, but between a hectoring, stern Tragedy, and a smiling, buxom Comedy. Comedy is clearly winning, as she pulls a grinning Garrick into her scenic space. David Mannings notes that the painting was exhibited publicly at the Society of Artists exhibition in London in May 1762 before its purchase by the second Earl of Halifax, and provocatively suggests that Garrick may have inspired the composition and subject.[107] What can be said with certainty is that Garrick personally requested and distributed Edward Fisher's prints of this

DAVID GARRICK Efq.^r

Published by G. Kearsly, N.º 46 Fleet Street. 1.Nov.º 1776.

Figure 3   Joseph Collyer, after Thomas Gainsborough, "David Garrick Esqr.," 1776.
A subtle visual reference to Garrick's consistent association with tragedy and comedy
appears in the frame. By permission of the Folger Shakespeare Library.

image to friends in Paris in 1764, as this book's final chapter relates, thereby
promoting this image of himself.[108] Visual identification of Garrick with the
figures of Tragedy and Comedy endured even after his death: Thalia and
Melpomene are seated on the actor's monument (1797) in Westminster

Figure 4   Edward Fisher, after Sir Joshua Reynolds, "David Garrick between Tragedy and Comedy," 1761. Fisher's prints of Reynolds's representation of Garrick as variety embodied were distributed by the actor himself. © Victoria and Albert Museum, London.

Abbey, just below the actor, who is caught in dramatic action thrusting aside stage curtains, with a medallion of Shakespeare visible behind his head. Garrick's gravestone lies symbolically at the foot of Shakespeare's monument.

Garrick's long campaign to represent variety as acting's difficult yet desirable apex bore fruit, as most writers embraced the idea in their analyses of his achievement. An article in the *London Museum* for January 1770, "An original Critique on the Merits of Mr. Garrick as an Actor," shrewdly equates Garrick's universality with his efforts to build his reputation around the assumption that variety in a player is the ultimate theatrical attainment: "As no actor, perhaps, ever arrived to such a height of reputation, so none has ever taken greater pains to extend and preserve it. The contrasted characters he has often played, in the course of one night—such as *Lear* and *Fribble*, *Lusignan* and *Chalkstone*, with his present attachment to the stage, though fluctuating between fifty and sixty, are incontestable evidences of this assertion."[109] Garrick's capacity to sustain a variety of roles is meant to evince youthful vigour, and this critic views this as a strategic defence of his reputation.

Murphy's biography takes a clear retrospective view of the manager's interest in varying not only his own roles, but Drury Lane's repertoire. Murphy asserts Garrick "knew that variety is the ruling passion, the *primum mobile* of the public mind."[110] Murphy depicts Garrick attempting to balance comedy and tragedy; the demands of living writers with the promotion of old English authors; and the constant public demand for novelty:

> Whenever Garrick appeared in any of his capital parts, either in tragedy or comedy, he was sure of attracting crowded audiences. Aware that variety was necessary, he devoted his time every summer to our best English authors. This was his constant plan, and it must be allowed to be the true ambition of a manager, as from that source the public derived a two-fold pleasure; their love of novelty was gratified, and they saw with pride the literary merit of ancient times.[111]

The most fitting tribute to Garrick's reputation for variety is a description of his retirement from the stage penned by the "Old Comedian" who wrote *The Life and Death of David Garrick, Esq. The Celebrated English Roscius* (1779). In this account, Garrick has not one final performance, but two – one comic, and one tragic. Of his final appearance in Don Felix in *The Wonder,* the "Old Comedian" writes, "never were the passions of love, jealousy, rage, &c. so highly coloured, or admirably set off. In short, he finished his comic course with as high a theatrical climax, as he did his tragic one in *King Lear*, a few evenings before."[112] The paired final performances provide an apt double ending for the actor who embodied variety.

Things Go B-tter With Garrick

The strength and positive nature of the multivalent Garrick brand meant that David Garrick's name and endorsement were valuable commodities. Eighteenth-century media are replete with products advertised to leverage this associational value.

Not surprisingly, publications related to the theatre, acting, Shakespeare and other aspects of the Garrick brand frequently invoke the Garrick name in dedications to imply the actor-manager's endorsement, acknowledge his patronage or annex positive association. Luigi Riccoboni's *General History of the Stage* (1754, second edition) carries a dedication from Riccoboni complimenting Garrick on his performances, followed by a note from the translator praising Garrick's "Dignity and Power, Variety, and Elegance, of Harmony and Feeling [. . . and the] Fire, that native Spirit that glows in all his Parts, that double Portion of the Promethean Heat, that animates the little Lump of Clay."[113] Nor does the translator leave Garrick's skill as a manager or talents as a writer unmentioned. He ties these characteristics to the improvement of the nation's taste in drama: "It has been less the Custom of the *English* to invent, than to improve . . . there is no doubt but that, under a Manager so judicious and so indefatigable as he . . . it will continue to rise in Excellence."[114] Such reverent invocations of key components of Garrick's personal brand accrue credibility thanks to their reliance upon an already familiar image of the actor, even as they consolidate his media image.

Robert Sayer and John Smith's *Dramatic Characters, or Different Portraits of the English Stage* (1770) similarly touches on the exemplary nature of Garrick's career as actor and author with this dedication:

> In search of a Patron for this Little Work, I find no one to whom I can so properly Inscribe it, as to a Gentleman, who has rendered the English Stage, not only famous, by those universal Talents which no other Actor either Ancient, or Modern is recorded to have possess'd; at least in an Equal degree; but who, as an Author, has Enrich'd the Roll of the English Drama, with several Characters Equally excellent, and Admir'd.[115]

Smith's dedication to his series of engravings of actors and actresses cites Garrick's universality or variety, his contribution to the formation of a national identity, and his work as author.

Numerous authors reworked the dedication, that conventional form for seeking artistic patronage, as a supplication made to the monarch of Drury Lane, rather than to an English noble. What is novel about dedications to Garrick is not simply their authors' application to an accomplished meritocrat rather than a born aristocrat, but how often the dedications themselves are advertised in newspapers, to the extent that advertised dedications to Garrick sometimes supersede the products they promote. Such advertisements suppose that a dedicatory gesture to Garrick was a saleable feature, worthy of promotion. The *London Packet* for 17 April 1772 advertised two very different works from the same author, each with a dedication to Garrick as its prime feature: "Dedicated to GARRICK, COLMAN, and FOOTE, With an humorous Address to the Readers, EPIGRAMS of MARTIAL, &c. . . . As also, A SERMON ON THE KING'S ACCESSION, preached Sunday October 25, 1772, dedicated to Mr. Garrick." The *Epigrams* dedication trades on Garrick's reputation for repartee, and the work includes several epigrams and riddles which take Garrick as their subject.[116] The Rev. William Scott's sermon dedication awkwardly acknowledges the popular acceptance he hopes will be the effect of using Garrick's name:

> But if They [the public] are pleased to think well of The SERMON upon the strength only of YOUR *Name*, I am proud in congratulating Myself on the honour done to Me for *their* Good Opinion of it, and of the Opportunity given Me to testify at once my gratefull Acknowledgements both to THEM and YOU . . .[117]

Several editors of Shakespeare employed dedications that acknowledge Garrick's authoritative stage interpretations of Shakespeare as part of their advertising. The *London Chronicle* for 8 January 1774 carried an advertisement with a double dedication: "Dedicated to DAVID GARRICK, Esq; BELL'S Edition of Shakespeare's ACTING PLAYS . . . together with two speaking portraits of SHAKESPEARE and GARRICK." Garrick's name and portrait both speak for the value of Bell's edition of Shakespeare in this widely dispersed advertisement, which appeared in papers from the *Gazetteer and New Daily Advertiser* to the *Morning Post and Daily Advertiser*. The dedication inside Bell's second edition praises Garrick's interpretation of Shakespeare, and accredits Murphy's conception of Garrick as Shakespeare's best commentator to "the public voice": "if we pronounce you the best illustrator of, and the best *living comment* on, SHAKESPEARE, that ever has appeared, or possibly ever will grace the British stage, it is merely echoing the public voice, and concurring with that unparalleled unanimity of praise, which, during so long a course of years, hath attended your incomparable merit."[118]

Illustrations of the actor seem the principal inducement to buy certain books and magazines, judging by the prominent mention plates of Garrick receive in advertisements. The title page for a volume of plates intended to accompany Bell's 1774 edition advertises the availability of extra prints of Shakespeare and Garrick: "*A few prime Impressions of the complete Set of Prints, consisting of 41 striking Dramatic Subjects, including the much-admired Likeness of the Author, and of David Garrick, Esq; are preserved on Proof Paper, and will be sold for Cabinet Furniture, or to bind up with any other Editions*, At One Guinea and a Half per Set."[119] *The Universal Museum and Complete Magazine of Knowledge and Pleasure* for December 1768 advertised in the 3 January 1769 *St. James's Chronicle* that its latest issue was "Ornamented with a fine Print of David Garrick, Esq; an exact

Representation of the Rhinoceras and Porcupine; and a new Song set to Music," placing Garrick's image amidst a confluence of curiosities that were expected to sell the magazine. Even after his retirement, prints of the actor received top billing in printers' efforts to move stock. The *London Packet; or, New Lloyd's Evening Post*, another newspaper in which Garrick was a proprietor, advertises on 17–20 October 1777: "The NEW ENG-LISH THEATRE, Was this day published, price only 6d. Ornamented with the portrait of Mr. GARRICK, in the character of Demetrius." Prints of Garrick in private dress and *en role* were also advertised widely; these items and their re-circulation in extra-illustrated books are discussed at length in the final chapter of this book.

Garrick's head even became a recognized sign to advertise the sale of print products associated with the theatre. "Garrick's Head" swung over the shop of printer, bookseller and publisher William Griffin in Catharine Street, in the Strand. The sign's name appeared in Griffin's publications, beginning around 1766, as part of the direction to his shop. Garrick's correspondence shows that the two men knew one another well. Griffin published and sold works by members of Garrick's circle, including Bickerstaff, Cumberland, Murphy and Goldsmith.[120] His shop occasionally sold theatre tickets, as it did for Bickerstaff's author's night of *The Padlock* (printed by Griffin) at Drury Lane, advertised just below the playbills in the 9 November 1768 *Public Advertiser*.[121]

The sign of Garrick's Head illuminates another corner of the cobweb connecting printers and the famous actor-manager. Griffin, from 1775, was proprietor and publisher of the *Morning Post* – a paper in which it is likely that Garrick possessed an interest, as previously discussed. Griffin had earlier attempted a periodical called the *Gentleman's Journal, Or Weekly Register of Politics, Literature, and Amusements,* a sixpenny pamphlet, printed on Saturdays, that was to contain "remarks upon the Theatres," according to an advertisement for its third and fourth numbers in the *Gazetteer and New Daily Advertiser* for 10 December 1769.[122] This journal appears to have lasted only a month, and unfortunately no copies remain to enable an assessment of how closely it followed the theatre or promoted the work of Drury Lane playwrights on Griffin's list. Griffin did have ready access to theatrical information. A notice in the *New Morning Post, or General Advertiser* for 13 November 1776 indicates that Griffin for a time printed Drury Lane's playbills, for the paper notes an "emolument settled on the printer of the play-bills of Drury-lane Theatre, bestowed by the friendship of Mr. Garrick on Mrs. Griffin's late husband." Griffin might be said to have operated under the sign of Garrick in more ways than one.

Garrick was present, tickled and embarrassed, at the raising of his street sign, as he writes in a 9 September 1749 letter to the Countess of Burlington:

> as I was walking along, I saw a number of People togeather [sic] about a Bookseller's Shop; My Curiosity lead me to make one & I just came as a Man was getting up a Ladder to hang on a Sign for the Shop, which was New & fitted up very handsomely; I jostled in amongst the Crowd to See whose head had the honour of being Exalted; when behold, I saw my own, & My Name written about it, in Letters as tall as Myself; You may imagine I was much disconcerted to be thus caught; however I slunk away as fast as I could, & I believe was lucky enough not to be known by any present, or seen by any, who might have given out that I was superintending the work ... some minor wit, has written a Satirical Poem upon it, in which he very gravely says, (& I am told dully too) that he does not think my writings are Sufficiently sublime to entitle Me to be a Sign; I am very much of his opinion, & hope he will print his Sentiments, that I may (good or bad,) send 'em for your Entertaint [sic] at Londesburgh.[123]

Though disarmingly cloaked in modesty, as he professes to be of the same opinion as the poet who deems his writing insufficiently sublime for his head to figure as a sign, Garrick's appetite for further print publicity on the occasion of the raising of the "Sign of Garrick" materializes at the letter's close.[124]

In addition to a host of Garrickian souvenirs, from medals to watch-papers, consumers could also enjoy porcelain Garrickian collectibles, including tiles and three-dimensional figures. Heather McPherson has shown how mass-produced "porcelain collectibles, in conjunction with paintings, engravings, and print media, enhanced and reified the public image of the actor" and served as "surrogates and as commemorative objects and repositories of memory and feelings."[125] Many porcelain figures were based on extant prints or drawings, though the complex transfer of a print into a three-dimensional figure suggests, McPherson says, that supplementary drawings may have been made of live figures, or based on observation of live performances.[126] McPherson hypothesizes that Garrick may have had a hand in commissioning porcelain figures, given that he possessed prints by a prominent porcelain producer, Thomas Frye, but concludes that there is no evidence corroborating Garrick's direction in the production of his image in porcelain.[127] However, porcelain items were advertised in papers in which Garrick was proprietor: the Derby Porcelain Manufactory advertised "upwards of 1000 curious Figures of different Attitudes and Sizes" for sale in the *Public Advertiser* for

6 January 1757; the Bow Porcelain Company's bankruptcy sale was announced in the 12 March 1764 *Public Advertiser*, and so forth. Mention of Garrick's name does not appear to form part of the advertising tactics of porcelain manufacturers, who instead appeal to the variety of objects available for viewing to entice consumers into their shops to experience the objects' intimate tactile appeal – and, one imagines, the pleasurable thrill of recognition at finding the diminuitive actor represented in this glossy miniature world.

Garrick's name was even invoked to sell patent medicines. As the most famous alumnus of a profession that prized vocal clarity, Garrick was an inspired choice as a spokesperson for throat lozenges. "[BY] HIS MAJESTY's ROYAL LETTERS PATENT. IRWIN's Fruit Lozenges, and Black Currant Drops . . . well known for their great efficacy in curing of colds, coughs, and hoarseness" were endorsed in the 10 November 1778 *Morning Post and Daily Advertiser* by "David Garrick, Esq. who returned thanks for saving his life." Whatever health benefits he enjoyed from the lozenges in the months before his death (and it must be admitted that he did not die from a throat ailment!), their advertisement also benefited a newspaper in which it is likely that he held proprietary interest.

This survey of some of the forms of advertising David Garrick employed to promote himself and those associated with Drury Lane Theatre demonstrates the actor-manager's savvy exploitation of media. From cultivating an in-house claque of playwrights interested in promoting the manager, to writing puffs and prologues for (and occasionally, against) individual actors and playwrights, Garrick worked around the constraints of a system that attempted to identify and tax print advertisements. With such strategies at his fingers' ends, with his unparalleled access to print media, with a gleaming brand image and a guaranteed market, thanks to the protection of a theatrical patent, how could David Garrick lose? Mostly, he didn't. The next chapter examines some rare instances of negative publicity – some levelled at Garrick, some cannily authored by him – to explore how even negative publicity strengthened Garrick's hold on celebrity.

CHAPTER 4

A Short History of Negative Publicity

On a late Dinner at Serle's Coffee-House.

M-p – y, F – te, G—k, man, monkey, and beast,
To turtle and venison sat down at a feast:

. . .

While bumpers went round in a brisk circulation,
F – te leering about made this shrewd observation:
"We each of us drink – but with different views;
I wish to promote – render Bacchus his dues;
Lawyer M-p-y the worm of conscience to still,
And G—k to conquer the dread of the bill."
– MYSO-SCURREAE, in the *Theatrical Monitor* October 1768;
reprinted in the *Whitehall Evening-Post*, 4–7 February 1769

The Theatrical Monitor and his Correspondents, are perpetually harping on the avarice of Mr. Garrick. How far the charge may be just in private life, I know not; but as a Manager ... the town have been entertained with greater variety, and with more expence, than they have been by the Managers of Covent-garden. If Mr. Garrick is that niggardly soul he is represented by his enemies to be, it excites my wonder, that he is able to form a company of any kind of players for the season ...
– "CANDIDUS," *Whitehall Evening-Post,*
Or London Intelligencer, 17–19 January 1769

I would not wish that You should spare me;–the Chiefs of Every profession must be Yr game, & when I am less taken Notice of, it will be ye best hint for Me to retire.
– David Garrick to publisher William Woodfall, 6 November [1773][1]

This chapter attends to Garrick's use of negative publicity to define the means by which Garrick transcended, and even exploited, a defect of person – his unheroic short stature – in an era of highly typed stage personae. After considering Garrick's deployment of negative publicity in aid of his own celebrity, the chapter examines his timely mediations of negative publicity generated by others. First, it looks at Garrick's responses to the negative personal critiques most commonly levelled at the actor-manager: accusations of his unwillingness to perform; and insinuations of avarice, and the neglect of artistic principles for monetary gain. Next, it considers the best-known case of negative publicity in Garrick's career – William Kenrick's public slur insinuating that the actor engaged in sodomy – and details how Garrick exacted an apology for Kenrick's libel in the media. It concludes with an analysis of the promotion of a tragedy written by the ropemaker and playwright Joseph Reed, arguing that Garrick carefully controlled the negative promotion surrounding Reed and his tragedy to protect his own and his theatre's brand equity.

Shortness Considered

David Garrick was short.[2] He was also "little," "a *Puppet Heroe*," "a Pygmie," "a Tom Thumb," etc., according to the pamphlet entitled *An Essay on Acting: In which will be consider'd The Mimical Behaviour of a Certain fashionable faulty Actor*, published anonymously by Garrick in 1744.[3] Garrick's height ought to have prevented his acceptance as an actor of serious heroic roles. Fellow actor James Quin disparaged Garrick's performance as Othello on precisely these grounds: "There was a little black boy, like Pompey, attending with a tea-kettle, fretting and fuming about the stage, but I saw no Othello,"[4] he wrote. Similarly, Samuel Foote sniped, "I am afraid frail Nature has been a little unkind . . . such is the Folly of the Million, that they expect a more than ordinary Appearance from a Man, who is to perform extraordinary Actions . . . they are dissatisfied, when they see a Bulls-Pizzle, a dried Elves-Skin, in *Falstaff*'s language, bullying a Congregation of Heroes."[5]

Garrick's shortness rendered his body neither serious nor heroic of itself. It had to be defended, as it was in Garrick's *Essay on Acting* and in Tobias Smollett's article, "The Character of Mr. Garrick," where Smollett contends: "Mr *Garrick* is but of middling Stature, yet, being well proportion'd, and having a peculiar Happiness in his Address and Action, is a living Instance that it is not essential to a Theatrical Hero to be six Foot high."[6] Media interventions turned potentially career-limiting negative messages about Garrick's shortness into discussions of Garrick's acting technique and his rivals' limitations. Shortness became part of the Garrick brand, but reframed: not as limitation, but as perfection of proportion and concentration of emotionally affecting action.

From his *Essay* to his later anonymous works such as *Reasons why David Garrick, Esq; Should Not appear on the Stage* (1759), *The Fribbleriad* (1761), and *The Sick Monkey* (1765), Garrick's repeated use of self-generated negative publicity suggests that he esteemed it an effective marketing tool. Before turning to examine its deployment in the *Essay*, one should perhaps ask of the modern marketing scholarship that studies quantifiable effects of negative publicity: is it? Is any publicity good publicity?

Negative publicity can benefit an individual or organization under certain conditions. In a study that measured the sales spike in the week following a book's review in the *New York Times*, Jonah Berger, Alan Sorensen and Scott Rasmussen determined that "negative publicity can sometimes increase purchase likelihood and sales" by "increasing product awareness or accessibility."[7] "Whereas positive reviews always increased sales," they write, "a negative review hurt sales of books by well-established authors but helped sales of books by relatively unknown authors."[8] The study's authors found that as consumers' memory of the initial publicity faded, what remained was not the negative valence of that publicity, but product recognition.[9] While this modern study was carried out in a vastly more media-rich environment and considered literary rather than dramatic reviews, its findings about the lingering consumer awareness of a product after it is exposed via negative publicity are suggestive. As we saw in the survey of eighteenth-century advertising practices, positive theatrical reviews and puffery worked to increase product awareness and positive brand associations with Garrick and those associated with Drury Lane Theatre; negative theatrical publicity resulting from cabals, riots or bad reviews could enhance audiences' awareness likewise. Modern marketing research suggests that perhaps, as an instance of negative publicity faded, its initial negative valence need not have maintained a negative impact on the theatre or Garrick's reputation.

The *Essay on Acting* promotes awareness of the actor as a specific kind of entertainment product, and it does so in part by using a negative marketing technique: not trumpeting Garrick's name, but erasing it. Garrick's name is erased (G——k) no less than eight times over the twenty-seven-page pamphlet. Such erasures are common to eighteenth-century writing, and are usually used, as Janine Barchas notes, to mark "pauses, rhetorical transitions, approximate syntax, and moments of aposiopesis."[10] Aposiopesis is surprisingly effective in advertising: as Charles R. Duke and Les Carlson put it, "word fragment completion, show[s] significant product information retention from print advertising."[11] The work of filling in the blanks blazes Garrick's name on the reader's brain. Each iteration associates the Garrick name ever more cozily with fashion, modern taste, novelty and popularity, referring to him as the "*little fashionable Actor*" and the "*favourite* Actor" who is the "*little sweet Nut*" of "the Town."[12] These associations of Garrick with refined taste are frequently nested with diminutives.

These desirable attributes are presented, not in a promotional puff, but in a complexly ironic negative review purportedly written by a self-styled critic of taste who for "twenty Years, or more" has "made the STAGE, and ACTING, [his] Study and Entertainment."[13] This narrative persona's views are ostensibly contra-Garrick, as in his opening salvo, "I shall present my Readers with a short *Treatise* upon ACTING, which will shew 'em what ACTING *ought to be*, and what the present *Favourite* in Question *is not*."[14] However, the document's heavy irony and the narrator's Bayesian insistence upon the importance of minutiae satirize the narrator's pretensions to taste and work to praise Garrick. Consider the narrator's critique of the costuming in *Macbeth*: "Mr. *G———k* 's Dress is very faulty too; *his* Coat should be *Banquo's*, and *Banquo's* his; and for this Reason; *Red* and *Gold* suits the Dignity of *Macbeth*, and at the same Time implies, a more *principal* and *exalted* Character, without derogating, or taking from the Rank of *Banquo* in *Red* and *Silver*."[15] After lengthily wrangling this idea to the point of absurdity, the narrator concludes, "SO much for *Dress* and *Figure*; now I shall proceed to the more difficult and physical Parts of the Character, and shall consider the *Action*, *Speaking* and *Conception* of our *modern Heroe*."[16] The disquisition upon dress establishes its own superficiality, and this conclusion effectively dismisses "dress" and "figure" as equally inconsequential. Though the verbal irony that should resonate in the phrase "*modern Heroe*" intimates "that Garrick's "*Action*, *Speaking* and *Conception* " will be condemned next, in shifting the argument from "figure" or physical appearance to consider intellectual and kinetic inter-pretation of character, the narrator lays the ground for confirming Gar-rick's virtuosity in those areas.

The negative positioning of the *Essay*'s narrative persona is important, for in addition to promoting product awareness, negative publicity is also perceived by consumers to be more believable than is positive publicity: "A robust finding in the impression formation literature is the negativity effect; that is, people place more weight on negative than positive infor-mation in forming overall evaluations."[17] One reason for this so-called negativity effect, suggest Ahluwalia *et al.*, is that "negative information is considered more diagnostic or informative than positive information."[18]

Readers approach the *Essay*'s content less sceptically because it is presented negatively, and are taken unawares by praise. In considering Garrick's portrayal of the desire for revenge as depicted in the contrasting roles of Macbeth and Abel Drugger, the narrator fumes, "If an Actor, and a *favourite* Actor, in assuming these different Characters with the *same Passions*, shall unskillfully differ only in *Dress*, and not in *Execution*; and supposing him right in *One*, and of Consequence absolutely ridiculous in the *Other*. Shall this Actor, I say, in Spite of *Reason, Physicks*, and *common Observation*, be caress'd, applauded, admir'd?"[19] Common observation was that Garrick's performance in these two roles was not restricted to a costume change, but varied as much as could be desired. Thomas Davies described Garrick's Macbeth as possessing an "ardent look, expressive tones, and impassioned action,"[20] as opposed to the "awkward simplicity [. . . that] bespoke the ignorant, selfish, and absurd tobacco-merchant."[21] Davies's criticisms, which appear in his biography of Garrick (1780), adopt the terms of criticism Garrick proposed earlier in the *Essay*, focusing upon the actor's action, interpretation and gaze. As mentioned in the previous chapter, the *Essay* raises the question of variety only to position it as a desirable attribute, visible to all in Garrick's impressive range.

The efficacy of the *Essay*'s satire is not dependent upon readers' knowledge of its authorship. It was published anonymously, but even if readers became aware of Garrick's authorship, the *Essay*'s negative presentation of his talent offers a charming pose of humility. More importantly, satire, considered from an advertising perspective, is remarkably effective. Research on humour in advertising indicates that "satire is the most effective type of humor for gaining recall and comprehension of an advertising message."[22] Satire was a popular eighteenth-century mode, and by using it in his sixpenny pamphlet, Garrick ensured that readers would remember what they read. Indeed, most literary critics have interpreted the *Essay* as canny anticipatory critique, following Thomas Davies's lead:

> the guarding against distant ridicule, and warding off apprehended censure, was a favourite peculiarity with Mr. Garrick through life . . . I remember when he first acted Macbeth, he was so alarmed with the fears of critical examination, that during his preparation for the character, he devoted some part of his time to the writing a humourous pamphlet upon the subject . . . He knew his manner of representing Macbeth would be essentially different from that of all the actors who had played it for twenty or thirty years before; and he was therefore determined to attack himself ironically, to blunt, if not to prevent, the remarks of others.[23]

Davies is not wrong, but the *Essay*'s aims are decidedly more ambitious than preparing audiences for a new interpretation of Macbeth. The *Essay* constructs several essential attributes of the Garrick brand. First, it builds recognition of Garrick's name and person: Garrick – he's the short one. This concept is reinforced by twelve repetitions of the word "short" and related synonyms, as well as by humorous references to scale, such as the narrator's objection that Macbeth's daggers "are near an Inch and half too long, in Proportion to the Heighth [sic] of the Murderer."[24] Invoking Garrick's shortness increases recognition of the actor's figure; it anticipates figure-based criticisms such as those made by Foote and Quin; and it recentres critique upon the interpretation of character by means of action, speaking and conception. Second, the *Essay* begins the focus on the power of Garrick's gaze that animates much later criticism of his acting powers. Most vitally, the *Essay* insists on the novelty and uniqueness of a Garrick performance. "How are we degenerated in Taste!" the narrator exclaims, "That our Theatre shall be crowded with Nobility, Ladies and Gentry, to see Macbeth Burlesqu'd, or Be–g–k'd, which are synonimous [sic]."[25] The coinage "Be-Garricked" implies there is something distinctive about Garrick's treatment of a role; that the actor is not subsumed by the role, but produces a performance that revels in what Lisa Freeman characterizes as "staged contests between interpretable surfaces,"[26] the surfaces here being "Garrick"; the performance text of *Macbeth*; and particularly, the performance of the role to which the audience is accustomed, "James Quin as Macbeth." Garrick's pamphlet stages the contest between these surfaces, prompting the reader to first imagine, then dismiss, any preconception of Macbeth-as-Quin:

> *Valour* and *Ambition*, the two Grand *Characteristicks* of *Macbeth*, form in the *Mind's Eye* a Person of *near six Feet High, corpulently Graceful, a round Visage, a large hazel Eye, aquiline Nose, prominent Chest*, and a *well-calv'd Leg*, rather inclin'd to that which is call'd an *Irish Leg* ... I mention this only to prove that Mr. G———k is not form'd in the least, *externally*, no more than *internally*, for that Character, and tho' there are many Figures in the World would become it very well ... the nearer they approach to it, they will the better *look Ambition, Heroism*, and *Murder*.[27]

The narrator's implication that Quin "looks Murder" and personifies Macbeth internally and externally, blasts Quin's reputation and bolsters Garrick's simultaneously. Quin, who had been convicted of manslaughter following a fatal duel with William Bowen in 1718, is, the narrator hints, typecast as a murderer, whereas Garrick must interpret the role skillfully, by overcoming the barrier of his short body. "Burlesquing" the six-foot-high phantom that lurks in the audience's imagination positions Garrick as an edgy iconoclast, and allies him with modernity and novelty. First you see the short actor; then his remarkable interpretive skill renders his height immaterial.

That the *Essay*'s primary purpose is to shape the Garrick brand also appears from its furtive attempt to manage previous negative publicity concerning an ongoing dispute between Garrick and fellow actor Charles Macklin. Garrick, Macklin and a group of other actors had left Drury Lane in the spring of 1743 because their salaries were in arrears, and agreed not to return to Charles Fleetwood's management individually until he struck a deal with them all. In December 1743, Garrick returned with the other actors – all but Macklin, whom Fleetwood believed to be the rebellion's instigator, and refused to accept. A furious Macklin lashed out at the "deserter" Garrick in the papers and in pamphlets.[28]

Garrick' *Essay* cautiously attempts to mollify Macklin. The narrator praises Macklin's extensive study for the part of Shylock, and reminds the reader (and theatrical managers) of Macklin's "*Genius*" and commodity value, stressing the ample returns gained from "crowded Theatres, and *unequall'd Applauses*." He writes cagily, "I shall not enter into the Reasons why he is at present excluded the Theatre, but shall only, as an Advocate for the Publick, say that I wish for *their* Sake, that there were many such Actors as him upon *both* Theatres."[29] The *Essay* is not a stand-alone manifesto on the art of acting; it is part of Garrick's ongoing effort to influence public perceptions of his character.

Garrick's control of various media did not inevitably involve suppressing negative publicity. As he wrote to the newspaper publisher William Woodfall, "I would not wish that You should spare me;–the Chiefs of Every profession must be Yr game, & when I am less taken Notice of, it will be ye best hint for Me to retire." Garrick's self-inflicted barbs concerning his diminutive stature, in the *Essay on Acting* and after, heighten the public's sense of his skill as an actor. Even Foote was obliged to admit "this Defect adds greatly to the Merit of *G*. for if by the Force of Action, he can conquer a first Prejudice, which is generally obstinate, it proves him possessed of a Genius, that few, very few Actors have been blessed with."[30] The motifs of Garrick's shortness and perfect proportion as recognizable yet immaterial to consideration of his talent, stuck fast to his public image, and are visible in all Garrickian biographies, beginning with the first extended treatment of the actor's life, by an "Old Comedian":

> Mr. Garrick was less than the middle size, but so well proportioned, that tho' his person was not calculated to express a superior degree of dignity, yet it was formed to exhibit the highest grace. In the most exalted characters, it carried an air of great elegance, in the most humble, a degree of much ease. It was happily suited to the gaiety of youth, and the infirmities of age; the frolics of a [R]anger, or the distress of a Lear. 'Tis not a little surprising that the generality of people, when they talk of a hero, always annex the idea of six feet high, as if greatness of soul was confined to eminence of person![31]

Murphy's *Life* sings the same refrain: "Like Betterton he did not rise above the middle size, but he was of a delicate frame, his limbs in just proportion; his voice clear and melodious, and his eyes looked the very soul."[32] While William Hogarth's famous sketch comparing the body proportions of Garrick and Quin is often used to illustrate Garrick's perfection of proportion, this image did not circulate in public prints until the nineteenth century. By that time, Garrick and the early biographers who drew on his *Essay on Acting* had already prepared the public for the reception of the caricaturist's sketch as an objective measure of Garrick's perfect, small body by reframing negative attitudes towards his shortness as a positive brand attribute.

"Sick – Sick – Sick –"[33]

The Rev. Charles Burney's collection contains a plethora of notes published in the newspapers excusing Garrick from performance on grounds of illness – a seemingly eccentric thing to collect, but one that proves revelatory of Garrick's strategic self-representation in the media. Typical examples in Burney's collection include a line ripped from a newspaper, manuscript-dated 12 February 1771: "Mr. Garrick is better, but still confin'd to his House," and a second short paragraph, hand-dated 18 February 1771: "It is said Mr. Garrick intended to have appeared in the Character of Bayes this Week, but going out too soon, has relapsed again; and tho' he is at present much better, it is feared he will not be able to perform any Character for some Time."[34] Though these are both late-career examples, the Burney and the Forster Collections' scrapbooks and the *17th and 18th Century Burney Newspapers Collection* demonstrate that publishing notes like these was a consistent part of Garrick's mediation of his public image throughout his career. Previously, we saw how Garrick used such notes to fashion public understanding of tragic roles as laborious. It is worth considering Garrick's published sick notes in greater depth, because even as they excused the actor from performing, his notes were working hard for the actor's public image.

Whatever puffs the papers might contain, the playbills printed therein were supposed to be denotatively correct, naming the correct performers in the correct parts. At bottom, published sick notes are simply supplements to the playbills, inserted to prevent the anger of audience members who might otherwise attend the playhouse specifically to see Garrick play. Fanny Burney, who noted in her journal for 1 October 1771 that she had gone to the playhouse to see Garrick play Kitely, was one such disappointed audience member. Already at the theatre, once she received "a Bill, importing that dear Creature's being taken suddenly ill, & being unable to Act," she wrote, "Sorry, disappointed & provoked we tore out of the House faster than we had into it. We have, however, heard that he is much recovered."[35] Published sick notes reinforced Garrick's celebrity, for they assume the sort of response displayed by Fanny Burney to be general amongst audiences, and promote this expectation.

Updates on the precarious state of Garrick's health were given out regularly, not just to excuse cancellations, but preventively, to explain why he would not be featured on the playbill. In the 1758–59 season, notes of Garrick's illness perform their own long-running drama. A newspaper clipping hand-labelled 1 October 1758 gossips, "We hear that Mr. Garrick was taken so ill on Wednesday night, while he was playing King Lear, that it was with great difficulty he finished the part." Fortunately, by month's end, the *Public Advertiser* for 28 October was more sanguine about Garrick's health, if still vague as to the date of his reappearance: "Mr Garrick, who has been indisposed, will appear again on the stage, the beginning of next week." But Garrick's illnesses persisted, and the *Public Advertiser* was forced to announce on 6 January 1759, "The Tragedy of Antony & Cleopatra is deferred till Tuesday next, in order to give the principal Performers a necessary respite" in order that those to whom it had advertised Garrick's Anthony might not claim falsity in the playbill. On 14 February 1759, the *Public Advertiser* puts it about that a performance was "deferred on account of the indisposition of a principal Performer," to which Burney adds, "At the bottom of the D Lane Bill. Mr Garrick being still indisposed with a Cold & hoarseness, the Guardian is deferred till tomorrow."[36] From Charles Burney's annotations, it appears that an apology for non-appearance was expected, and noticed if omitted: "April 18. 1745 For Mr. Yates The Provok'd Husband. Lord Townly by Mr Garrick. On the Night, Mr Giffard played Lord Townly, on account [of] Mr Garrick's illness. No apology in the Bills."[37] As this clipping and the account in Fanny Burney's journal show, Garrick's notes enjoyed a double circulation: in the bills within the playhouse, and in the newspapers.

Burney's personal collection of Garrick's sick notes, while impressive, actually downplays the volume of media representations of Garrick's illnesses. There is scarcely a year in which the public is not notified of its disappointment at not being able to view the actor. It is for their own good, the public is assured, that they are deprived now, to secure Garrick's future performances, as in this report from *The Theatre* (no. 6, manuscript-dated 1759): "we believe the public may spare him till he recovers his voice; for if he attempts Richard, or any of the ranting heroes till he is better, we shall be the more disappointed, as he will injure himself and us."[38] Published sick notes establish Garrick as a rare resource, and point up the effort requisite to major, particularly, tragic roles, as previously noted. Burney selects this news for preservation: "At the bottom of the Bill. Monday. March 1. 1756. The fourth Night of Athelstan is deferred till Thursday, as the principal Character is too fatiguing to be acted two Nights together."[39] This reference to fatigue is notably destitute of any apology whatever. Instead, the note seeks to educate the audience in the value of seeing a tragedy performed, and to promote acting as valuable, difficult work. Cumulatively, the notes are both exculpatory and aggrandizing, implying that despite his constant battles with ill health, Garrick was able to overcome affliction and valiantly serve the public.

Critics were wont to attribute miserliness with his public appearances to Garrick's love of ease or to deep strategy to increase his worth. One pamphleteer, "E.F" (thought to be Samuel Foote), asserts that "as an artful Manager, whose Business it is to keep our Appetites sharp sett," Garrick appears rarely, "For the greater the Resentment shown at your not acting, the greater your Honour as an Actor, and the greater your Finêsse as a Manager; since it is a Proof that you are the only necessary Ingredient in all our Theatrical Entertainments; and that without You all the rest is languid and insipid, scarce worthy the Name of Diversion."[40] This point's acuity is reinforced by the frequent appearance of Garrick's excuses of illness in commodity-based advertising sheets like the *Public Advertiser*. The pamphlet writer pertly asks the manager to look into his own interest, and command himself to perform more often: "Though, Sir, Mr. *Garrick*, the Manager, and Mr. *Garrick* the Player, are really one and the same Person, yet they must always be considered separately, and in different Lights: for we have, and always shall have, an incontestible Right, while there is such a Player as Mr. *Garrick*, to ask Mr. *Garrick* the Manager, why Mr. *Garrick* the Player is not ordered to entertain us."[41] Later, in a mock-advertisement c. 1773, Foote openly parodied the convention, announcing that his "Primitive Puppet-Shew" had to be deferred "on account of the illness of a principal performer."[42]

Constant circulation of news of the state of Garrick's health in the press created a sense of his cultural value, and kept the actor's image before what was portrayed as a sympathetic and caring public. The anonymous writer of the pamphlet *A Letter of Compliment To the ingenious Author of a Treatise on the Passions, So Far as They Regard the Stage* (1747), writes (in response to Foote's *Treatise*) that the actor's illness is "a public Calamity" for which a devoted public ardently desires a cure:

> The Indisposition of Mr. *G.* which alas is *real!* is a public Calamity; and there are Numbers who wou'd divide a plentiful Fortune, if that Sacrifice cou'd purchase him the Constitution and Strength of an *Hercules*. But when a Malady critically interferes to encrease the Value of a Jewel, by its not being made too common, what Remedy can be apply'd to this extreme Disaster?[43]

The public was reminded that while other actors might malinger, Garrick's illnesses were genuine. Mrs. Barry, a notorious malingerer, is indirectly admonished in the 25 March 1774 *Morning Post and Daily Advertiser*: "Mr. Garrick's appearance last night in Abel Drugger, which was to have been Mrs. Barry's evening, arose from the lady's being taken most danger-ously ill on Wednesday night last, and therefore prevented from performing ... We could not but lament to see Mr. Garrick scarce recovered from a violent fit of illness, himself so circumstanced, as to be under the disagreeable necessity of thus stepping forth at a moments notice, to fill up the gap at the hazard of a life so valuable to the admirers of our refined drama." Readers could participate in such calamities know-ledgeably, as they were kept minutely informed of Garrick's medical treatments, recoveries and relapses: "Mr. Garrick is so well recovered as to be able to ride abroad; and, by the last letters from Bath, we are told, that his health will be speedily re-established," readers of the 17 March 1769 *Lloyd's Evening Post* were reassured.

Garrick's health even formed the subject of lengthy published panegyr-ics, such as William Combe's poem, *Sanitas, Daughter of Aesculapius. To David Garrick, Esq.* (1772). In the poem, various characters request health from Hygeia and Apollo, and unworthy supplicants are turned away. One hack who "From many a different author stole" prays:

> "O let me frequently appear,
> In Public, or in Gazetteer;
> Either in epigrammic fun,
> In essay, ancedote [sic], or pun,
> As thou shalt deem, O pow'r divine,
> My genius fitted most to shine."[44]

Apollo, who hates such "blockheads," turns him down. Melpomene next successfully intercedes for Garrick, and Apollo wipes away a tear and decrees that all will be well.[45] The author notes that the poem was read privately by Garrick before publication:

> The following poem was sent to Mr. Garrick in his late illness, with the impression of Sanitas, or Hygeia, goddess of health, prefixed to it. The polite reception he was pleased to give it, has so far excited the author's vanity, that he now submits it to the inspection of the public; and he flatters himself he shall, in some degree, conciliate their esteem, in sending health to a gentleman, who, by his personal exhibitions, his literary productions and his close attention to the morality of the stage, has so long and so judiciously blended the most liberal instruction with the most exquisite entertainment.

The poem's public sale and distribution assume broad public interest in "sending health" to the actor. Over a period of thirty years in the limited London theatre market, audiences might have grown understandably weary of seeing the same actor again and again. Garrick's published notes of illness accomplished immediate advertising ends, but also were the means by which a culture of care was cultivated around the actor, by depicting acting as laborious, and a ubiquitous resource as rare.

Advertising Acts of Charity

As this chapter's epigraphs indicate, accusations of avarice dogged the actor-manager almost from his career's inception, creating one of the most tenacious challenges to the Garrick brand. The writer of *A Letter to Mr. Garrick, on His Having Purchased a Patent for Drury-Lane Play-House* (c. 1747), cites Garrick's love of power and money as the chief motivations for his taking up management:

> whatever Proofs you may have given of your Love of Power, and a Restlessness in remaining in a Station which could not be looked upon as in the least beneath that of any Man who ever trod the Stage, I am tempted to believe you have been chiefly instigated by another Passion, which (or the World is much mistaken) has no less a share in your Composition than

Ambition: It is said of you, that as few Men at your Years ever attained to so much Perfection in the Capacity of an Actor, so scarce ever any Man at your Years, was so well acquainted with the Value of Money.[46]

Garrick is such a miser, he writes, that "on the least Diminution, tho' for the necessary Expences of Life, [he] feel[s] Agonies like those of parting with ... Vital Blood."[47] Garrick sought to mediate such accusations by publicizing his acts of charity.

My aim is not to question Garrick's moral intent in various acts of charity, but rather to observe the probable effects that publicizing certain acts of charity had in mediating his image. In the mid eighteenth century, there was nothing socially or morally untoward about public displays of charity. Such display, thought to encourage emulation and devotion, was encouraged. As Sir William Ashburnham said in a sermon in support of the London-Hospital, true charity "opens it's hand without reluctance, and distributes with ease and pleasure ... letting it's *light shine* in public monuments of beneficence, that by *seeing such good works men may glorify our Father which is Heaven.*"[48] Advertising charitable benefit performances at Drury Lane Theatre and reprinting news of Garrick's personal acts of charity built a print monument of the actor-manager's beneficence, and helped to moderate perceptions of the self-made man as selfish by demonstrating that he was willing to share the fruits of his success with the less fortunate.

Theatrical benefits at Drury Lane supported many causes, including the Middlesex Hospital, the British Lying-In Hospital, the City of London Lying-In Hospital, and various penurious individuals, families and victims of misfortune. On each occasion, Garrick was published as the author of charitable acts across several media platforms, including posted playbills, newspaper playbills, occasional verse and accounts in the periodicals, his good works advertised in venues from the stage to the church (see Figure 5). Though other actors of Drury Lane Theatre and the theatre itself undoubtedly accrued goodwill from these performances, they were less often acknowledged in print than was Garrick. This trend began early. After a disastrous fire in Cornhill on 25 March 1748, several public measures were taken to relieve the affected families and businesses, including a donation of £1,000 in relief funds by the King, and a public listing of bankers who would receive charitable donations on behalf of the sufferers, creating an organizational flow similar to modern disaster-relief operations.[49] As Drury Lane's prompter Richard Cross noted, one measure designed to raise funds for the fire's victims was a benefit performance of

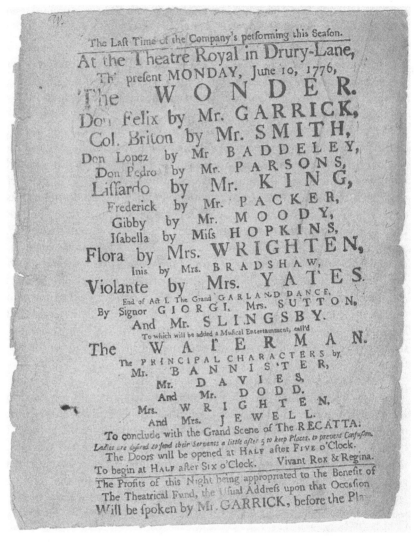

Figure 5   Playbill for Garrick's last performance in *The Wonder*, 10 June 1776, advertised as a charitable benefit for the Theatrical Fund. Harry Ransom Center, The University of Texas at Austin.

Lear and *The Double Disappointment* on 23 April, "for ye. Sufferers by ye. fire in Cornhill," which earned an estimated house take of £210. The *General Advertiser* for 2 May 1748 then duly reported: "Last Week Mr. Garrick paid to Mr. Belchier, Banker in Lombard-street, £208 1s.

being the whole Money received at the Benefit Play of King Lear, which he most generously gave for the Relief of the unhappy Sufferers by the late most dreadful Fire in Cornhill, etc. without deducting any Charges whatsoever."

Charities also appealed to Garrick to hold performances to benefit their regular operations. The order appointing Garrick a Perpetual Governor of the British Lying-In Hospital for Married Women in 1758 is still extant,[50] and his performance to benefit this charity that year was advertised assiduously. Garrick is the sole named performer in the *Public Advertiser* playbills for 1, 3 and 4 April 1758: "For the Benefit of the British Lying-In Hospital, In Brownlow-Street ... MUCH ADO ABOUT NOTHING. Benedict by Mr. Garrick. With Entertainments as will be express'd in the Bills of the Day. Tickets to be had at the Hospital in Brownlow-street, near Long Acre and of Mr. Varney at the Stage-door." Appropriately, Garrick appeared as Benedick the married man to benefit a maternity hospital for married women.

The reception of such charity was bruited in the media: the *Public Advertiser*, in which Garrick had a proprietary interest, was frequently the vehicle of expression of public thanks for his charitable actions, as it was on 21 December 1761:

> Mr. Lacey and Mr. Garrick having, in the most generous and polite manner, given the Profits of that very brilliant House which honoured the Performance of *Every Man in his Humour* with their Presence on Friday last at the Theatre Royal in Drury-Lane, as a Benefit to the British Lying In Hospital for Married Women in Brownlow-Street; Long-acre; the Treasurer of that Charity, in the Name of the Governors and Subscribers, takes the first and this public Occasion to return his sincerest Thanks to the Managers of that Theatre for this Instance of their Benevolence to an Institution, whose particular Utility, at this Time, from the seasonable Assistance it affords to the Wives of Soldiers and Seamen, and to the Wives of others of the industrious Poor; must, at the same Time that it gives Satisfaction to Mr. Lacey and Mr. Garrick, recommend the farther Encouragement of so extensive and useful a Design to the Attention of the Humane and Beneficent.

Charity offered exceptional opportunity for positive publicity, for, thanks to its religious significance, it could escape periodicals' six-day news cycle. News of charitable acts might circulate on Sundays in sermons, whether delivered piping from the pulpit or read in family devotions. Occasional sermons given in aid of a particular charity were often printed to further benefit the charity, as were histories of charitable organizations; the names of the charity's patrons appear conspicuously in such publications' front matter. David Garrick's name circulated widely in published charity sermons, frequently marked for special notice with asterisks denoting his generous contributions or an honorary position, such as a governorship. Readers of the history, *An Account of the British Lying-In Hospital, for Married Women, in Brownlow-Street, Long-Acre,* would be reminded, with a storm of asterisks, that David and his brother George were "Governors for Life" (***) of this respectable organization, which provided married women with accommodation, food and medical help during childbirth.[51] Similarly, an amount listed in ledger style is credited to Garrick (accorded *** again) and his co-patentee James Lacy in Thomas Francklin's *Sermon Preached at the Parish-Church of St. Anne, Westminster, on Thursday, May the 10th, 1758, Before the Governors of the Middlesex-Hospital, For Sick and Lame; and for Lying-in Married Women.* The "Produce of the Benefit Play Given by Mess. *Garrick* and *Lacy*, Dec. 21 1757" is listed at £158 17s.[52] Published sermons listing Garrick as a charity's benefactor or governor gave readers an opportunity equivalent to peering into the collection plate.

Garrick's characteristic trades in publicity-related favours with the publishing community can be glimpsed in these published sermons, too. Thomas Francklin, whose sermons record Garrick's generosity, had married Eva Maria and David Garrick in 1749, and since that time, had had plays produced at Drury Lane. Charles Green Say, who inherited his father Edward's printing business, including printing the weekly *Gazetteer*, to which Garrick contributed, not only printed the history of the British Lying-In Hospital mentioned above, but further sermons that hymned the Garrick name.[53] John and Francis Rivington, relations of Edward Rivington, a proprietor in the *Public Advertiser* alongside Garrick, printed the sermon by Thomas Morell discussed below. The same printers who circulated Garrick's name and dramatic works in their workday periodicals circulated news of his good works in reading fit for Sundays.

His theatre's repeated benefits for lying-in hospitals may have helped Garrick to mediate criticism linking his childlessness with accusations of avarice. A scrapbook clipping hand-dated 1766 gives a sample of this virulent strain of negative publicity:

> WHY, G——k, should you get each year a play?
> You get no children – have no nurse to pay.
> Is thy soul fir'd with glory?—mount the Stage
> Again, like *Baron*, charm a grateful age.
> But quit the pen,—lest injur'd Authors blame,
> And swear you write from Av'rice, not for Fame.[54]

The epigram's writer accuses Garrick as manager and author of engrossing the repertoire to himself, an act considered the more reprehensible since he has no children for whom he must provide. However, though associating with these charities may have benefited the childless actor's image, Garrick himself made no statements that might substantiate a reading of his support of child-centred charities as compensatory. Perhaps Garrick simply supported lying-in hospitals because they were numerous, necessitous and a popular cause. One of the few indicators of his intent regarding charity benefits appears in a letter to Robert Smith of 12 December [1775?]. Garrick writes, "The Theatre Royal in Drury Lane gives two Charity Benefits a year to the Hospitals, & they take their Turn in Succession – there are two fix'd for this, & two for the next, & how they go on afterwards I cannot say, not having the Book with Me –."[55] The letter is notably devoid of warmth, and makes it plain that the theatre's charitable work was strictly controlled. Spreading charity around to various hospitals in turn to achieve maximum exposure for the theatre while keeping the costs of appearing charitable practicable seems to be the manager's main concern.

One of the charities to which Garrick lent his name as an individual, rather than as a theatrical manager or performer, was the Sons of the Clergy, an organization that assisted with the costs of apprenticing and supporting the sons and daughters of necessitous Anglican clergy. The Sons of the Clergy held an annual sermon and concert at St. Paul's Cathedral, and processed from there to a feast at Merchant Taylors' Hall. The organization, now called the Sons and Friends of the Clergy, still hosts a similar annual fundraising event. As a steward, Garrick was responsible for underwriting the expense of the event's rehearsals and feast. There, he mingled with his fellow stewards – a powerful set including the Archbishop of Canterbury, the Duke of Devonshire, and notable divines – and heard a concert featuring music by Handel and Boyce.

The event, and Garrick's charitable participation in it, were advertised at least seventeen times between 16 April and the concert on 16 May 1772, in five newspapers: the *London Evening Post*, the *Gazetteer and New Daily Advertiser*, the *Daily Advertiser*, the *General Evening Post* and the *Morning Chronicle and London Advertiser*. Good publicity for the charity was also good publicity for its steward. Garrick was again named as steward upon publication of Thomas Morell's occasional sermon: *A Sermon Preached at the Anniversary Meeting of the Sons of the Clergy, in the Cathedral Church of St. Paul, on Thursday, May 14, 1772.*[56]

However, one protester had sharp words for Garrick's stewardship of the Sons of the Clergy charity. "Tanaquil" began by asking Garrick to give the charity a benefit performance, writing in the 11 May 1772 *Morning Chronicle*, "your complying with this hint will ennoble your character in the eyes of the public." When no benefit performance was forthcoming, civility evaporated. Negative charges appeared in the 16 May *Morning Chronicle*, followed by this "Card" in the next issue:

> Another CARD. To David Garrick, *Esq*; The great falling-off in the collection for the Sons of the Clergy, elucidates the propriety of a former address to you in their behalf, and at the same time shews the necessity of a second. The receipts on the
>
> | | |
> |---|---|
> | 1st Day (at the Church) | 150 l. |
> | 2d Day | 130 l. |
> | And at the Hall | 576 l. |
> | | |
> | Amount to | 896 l. |
>
> Which shews that this collection is less than the last year's, as that was less than the preceding. The prospect is alarming to the present Clergy and their offspring; will not your regard for religion and its Ministers, blow the embers of that compassion, which always exists in your bosom? Shall it be said, that when you was Steward, their collection did not equal that for *supposed penitent Prostitutes*? Or is it the intention of the Great to recommend *prostitution* to the *Daughters of the Clergy*, to put them in a way of obtaining more liberal succours, than they can expect in cultivating their chastity and virtue? Once more in their behalf, I call upon you to give them a benefit; you need not publish it to be for them; but your *acting* for them, will soon shew your kindness to the defenders of religion, and that a man of your virtues will always be ready to encourage and support the virtues of others. TANAQUIL.

The correspondent's pseudonym, Tanaquil (a Roman prophetess), implies a female authorial persona. She refers to the rich charitable support for the Magdalen Hospital for repenting prostitutes, and shows how openly competitive social patronage networks for charities could be by wisecracking that a lack of like support for the Sons of the Clergy means that "the Great" are recommending prostitution to clergymen's daughters.

Tanaquil's emphasis on chastity and virtue also offers a sideswipe at Garrick's lifetime governorship in the Lock Hospital, which treated men, women and children suffering from venereal disease. In supporting the Lock Hospital and its treatment of a disease bearing significant social stigma, Garrick was ahead of many of his contemporaries. As Linda E. Merians observes, venereal disease was not a fashionable cause: "British society did not embrace this charity hospital as warmly as it did some of the others. The Lock Hospital had significantly fewer annual and lifetime governors than other charity hospitals."[57] Garrick supported the Lock Hospital through benefit performances: five are recorded in the Cross-Hopkins Theatre Diaries, beginning with the 9 April 1750 performance, which Richard Cross notes as "Benefit for ye increase of a fund for ye support of a publick Charity [Lock Hospital]." The three performances for which the diaries record estimated returns include amounts of £160, £160 and £210 for the charity. There is truth to Tanaquil's complaint that Garrick's exertions for the Sons of the Clergy in 1772 did not match his earlier results.

Moreover, Tanaquil is correct to observe Garrick's activity as an actor in benefit performances on behalf of other charities. Garrick appeared in all five Lock Hospital benefits personally – as Fribble in *Miss in Her Teens*, 9 April 1750; as Osmyn in *The Mourning Bride* on 22 May 1753; as the prologuist to *The Schemers; or Ye City Match* on 15 April 1755; as Lord Chalkstone in *Lethe* on 13 December 1758; and as Abel Drugger in *The Alchymist* on 15 December 1762. Not appearing as a performer to benefit the Sons of the Clergy charity was a departure for Garrick, and according to Tanaquil, Garrick the genteel private individual was less effective an agent of charity than was Garrick the actor, as her italics indicate: "your *acting* for them, will soon shew your kindness."

Tanaquil's suggestion that, should Garrick give the Sons of the Clergy a benefit, he "need not publish it to be for them" must have fallen upon incredulous ears. Failure to advertise a benefit's charitable recipient was likely to provoke complaints of managerial greed, by giving room for speculation that Garrick was extending the benefit season for personal gain. Actors' benefit performances usually rewarded an individual; but by appearing in an advertised charity benefit, Garrick might deflect critiques of acting out of avarice by aligning the display of his person with charity. As the manager's letter above indicates, charitable benefits at Drury Lane were negotiated to achieve maximal visible distribution amongst various charities, leaving little room for unpublished acts of charity. Whether due to Tanaquil's ungrateful implication that Garrick was less capable an agent of charity as a gentleman than as an actor, or to other factors, Garrick did not act as steward for the Sons of the Clergy again.

Garrick may not have engaged with Tanaquil in the papers, but George Steevens, writing under the pseudonym 'Animadvertor'[58] in the 18–20 May *General Evening Post*, leaped in to defend the manager against accusations of avarice:

> It has been Mr. Garrick's good fortune to have every dunce in the whole republic of letters his constant enemy, and therefore it is no wonder that

incessant attacks are made upon his reputation. Exposed as a manager of a theatre to continual importunities from the numberless blockheads who fancy themselves possessed of extraordinary abilities, the news-papers become filled with the grossest scurrilities against him, when he is compelled to reject their trash; and as no one scribbler will be persuaded into a belief of his own stupidity, he naturally enough endeavours to conceal his disgrace by fastening a charge of avarice on Mr. Garrick ...

Steevens's defence starts with spirit, implying that Tanaquil is nothing but a rejected would-be playwright; however, it then executes a twist, as if to demonstrate that Steevens has Garrick's back by stabbing him in it:

That Mr. Garrick sets a just value upon money, like every sensible man, and omits no warrantable opportunity of increasing his fortune, I shall readily admit; but is that prudence which is highly laudable in all the rest of mankind culpable alone in him? and must he, to avoid the imputation of avarice, launch out into a boundless ocean of prodigality?–No private gentleman in the kingdom lives with more elegance than this *miserly* manager: his town-house, his country-house, his equipage, his mode of entertaining company, all bespeak a disposition the most liberal. Besides, in what point of proper expence do any of his rival patentees exceed him? In what acts of generosity is one of them his equal? To what deserving object is his purse ever shut, or his interest ever refused?

Steevens's reinforcement of the conceit of Garrick as an *arriviste* was a defence that Garrick probably would have preferred to do without. However, Garrick had at that moment a much more difficult case of negative publicity to negotiate: William Kenrick's insinuations that Garrick possessed same-sex desire for the playwright Isaac Bickerstaff, who had been publicly accused of sodomy.

Mediating William Kenrick's *Love in the Suds*

Garrick deployed carefully delimited negative publicity to benefit himself and those associated with his theatre; he also used print and performance to mediate negative publicity from critics whose slings and arrows he could not entirely suppress. Those persons who took the trouble and expense to attack Garrick in print included actors, rival managers and taste-makers of the *ton*. Garrick's most vituperative, vociferous detractors, as Steevens's letter hints, were playwrights; in particular, playwrights who had had at least one play accepted by the actor manager,[59] and had hopes of a dramatic career raised, then dashed, or, more frequently, indefinitely suspended. As Davies put it: "in his treatment of writers, [Garrick] carried his politeness to excess, and in the first ardor of his friendship he was apt to promise more than he found it possible afterwards to perform."[60] Yet, Davies remarks, "[t]he man to whom nature has denied the genius to compose a play or a farce, may have abilities to strike out a very poignant satire. He who is an utter stranger to dramatic poetry, may sting with an essay, wound with a paragraph or bite with an epigram."[61] One such disgruntled playwright was William Kenrick. While Kenrick was a paranoid, libelous rascal, he was also, about Garrick's control of the media at least, not wrong.

Literary enmity can derive from any number of slights, real or imagined, and a manager's refusal to produce one's play might ignite a bitter burning in many a playwright's breast. However, over his long term as theatrical manager, Garrick adopted a rational, humane and consistent approach to the problem of refusing a play. Lasting estrangements upon his refusal of a script seem the exception rather than the rule. Garrick's letters to play-wrights are patient and polite; they cite practical reasons for refusal; and they are highly individualized: no playwright suffered the indignity of a form rejection letter. This letter of 24 July 1765 to George Graham about his tragedy *The Duke of Milan* (1765) is characteristically attentive to the script's stage-worthiness:

> I was greatly oblig'd to you for giving me so much time to consider the Tragedy, You put into my hands – I read it carefully before I went my Journey into Essex & since my return I have considerd it a second time – the result of Which, tho it may not raise me in your Opinion as a good Critick, will not I hope, lower me as a man of Sincerity—My judgement of the Duke of Milan, is, that not with standing there are many striking Passages in it, there will be certain dangers in representing it – the Charac-ters and construction of the Fable are greatly deficient, the language tho' often Poetical is seldom dramatic, & the Catastrophe will want the effect which it ought to have upon an Audience . . . [62]

Garrick rejects Graham's tragedy because it will not play well: it lacks dramatic structure, language and effect. Garrick softens the blow, as he often did, with a kindly offer to meet in person to discuss the play. Spurned playwrights infrequently contest Garrick's evaluations; when they do, they enlist outside interlocutors, if possible of rank and station, as Joseph Reed attempted to do. But even in these protests, there is little sense of clashing aesthetic values: instead, the source of aggravation is Garrick's control of access, not just to performance on Drury Lane stage, but to all avenues of publication and public approbation. When spurned authors air their griefs publicly, it is not Garrick's taste, but Garrick's media reach that they protest.

William Kenrick's name is familiar to many scholars, though lately not so much because of his translations of Rousseau, his legal work on adultery and divorce, or his best-selling conduct book, *The Whole Duty of Woman* (1753),[63] but because of a pamphlet entitled *Love in the Suds* (1772), which figures in discussions of homosexuality and masculinity in the period by Robert Fahrner, Charles Conaway and Michal Kobialka.[64] The circumstances that led to the pamphlet's release extend back over several years. Kenrick had some limited dramatic success at Drury Lane, staging a comedy called *Falstaff's Wedding* (1766) which played for just one night, and *The Widow'd Wife*, another comedy, which ran for nine nights in 1767. There was a wrangle over the profits arising from *The Widow'd Wife*, another about the non-performance of *Falstaff's Wedding*[65] and another about the timing of the staging of Kenrick's next play, *The Duellist*, culminating in an angry exchange of letters on 15 June 1772 in which Garrick invited Kenrick to meet him at the Green-Park coffee-house, with a friend, to discuss these matters. Kenrick interpreted this as an invitation to a duel or a beating, not a meeting, and declined to show up.[66] By late June 1772, Kenrick's ire broke forth in pamphlet form.

Love in the Suds is an extended dramatic monologue in verse, in which Roscius, the Garrick figure, pleads for the return of his beloved Nyky – the playwright Isaac Bickerstaff. Bickerstaff frequently altered plays for Garrick, and enjoyed considerable success in the comic opera genre. Bickerstaff had recently fled London for France, following his unfortunate propositioning of a soldier, who then blackmailed Bickerstaff by posting this advertisement in the 30 April 1772 *Daily Advertiser*:

> Whereas on Tuesday Night last, between the Hours of Eight and Ten, a Gentleman left with a Centinel belonging to Whitehall Guard, a Guinea and a Half, and a Metal Watch with two Seals, the one a Cypher, the other a Coat of Arms, a Locket, and a Pistol Hook. The Owner may have it again by applying to the Adjutant of the first Battalion of the first Regiment of Foot-Guards at the Savoy Barracks, and paying for this Advertisement.

This seemingly innocent lost-and-found note was given a scandalous gloss in the *Gazetteer and New Daily Advertiser* for 2 May 1772:

> An advertisement has appeared, giving notice, that the gentleman who left his watch, seal, and rings, &c. with a soldier, may have them again, by applying to the Savoy. The history of this watch, &c. is this: a *gentleman* grew enamoured, the other night at Whitehall, with one of the centinels, and made love to him; the soldier being of that rough cast, who would rather act in the character of *Mars*, than a *Venus*, not only rejected the

lover's suit, but seizing him, threatened to take him immediately to the Guard-room. The affrighted enamorato, to avoid the consequences of exposure, with the greatest precipitation gave the soldier his watch, rings, and other valuables, for his liberty. The centinel, rejoicing at his good fortune, soon after tells the corporal, the corporal the serjeant, the serjeant the adjutant, and he to the whole corps of officers. The articles of ransom were examined; one was a mourning ring of a lady who died at Gibraltar; and the watch had its maker's name; he was applied to, and he instantly declared to whom he had sold it, about two months since, a man of some fame in the literary world. Here at present the incident rests; and there is no doubt but the honest soldier will become intitled to the whole, as it is presumed the owner will scarcely apply for a return of them.

Garrick, meanwhile, had received an abject letter (in French) from Bickerstaff. His endorsement, "From that poor wretch Bickerstaff. I could not answer it"[67] shows, perhaps, understanding of the social necessity of distancing himself from Bickerstaff.

In *Love in the Suds*, Kenrick insinuates that Garrick displays same-sex desire for Bickerstaff.[68] It is a curious libel in the sense that David and Eva Maria Garrick had one of the century's most famously happy marriages, and were never parted for a day of their twenty-eight-year union. Without seeking to diminish the pamphlet's importance to histories of sexuality or masculinity, I must observe that Kenrick's allegations about Garrick's sexuality seem almost incidental in comparison to the weight the pamphlet's verses and Scriblerian footnotes give to Garrick's control of the stage and the press. The charge of sodomy against Bickerstaff is the occasion for Kenrick's pamphlet, but it is not its main subject.

Kenrick's strategy is to identify Garrick's networks of privilege in the publishing industry, usurping Garrick's voice to enhance his claims' credibility. He begins the attack by asserting that the writer Christopher Anstey and Garrick have exchanged puffs. Roscius is made to say: "the author of the New Bath Guide / Up to the skies my talents late hath cried" and Kenrick adds in a footnote, "The compliments passed between these celebrated geniuses indeed were mutual; Mr. A commending ROSCIUS for his fine acting, and ROSCIUS in return Mr. A. for his fine writing."[69] This is true. The newspaper flattery to which Kenrick refers appears in the *General Evening Post* for 9–11 May 1771. "*Mr. ANSTEY to DAVID GARRICK, Esq., on meeting him at a Friend's House*" takes up the familiar theme of variety, and refers to Reynolds's picture of Garrick between Tragedy and Comedy: "I ne'er yet as with truth could tell / Where most your various pow'rs excel," Anstey writes; while "*Mr. GARRICK's*

Answer," printed directly below it, commends Anstey's "choice verse."[70]
This is just the beginning of Kenrick's sketch of Garrick's trade in media
favours.

Next, Kenrick portrays Thomas Becket, Garrick's printer of record and
fellow newspaper proprietor, as a submissive spaniel, ready to bark out
flattery:

> Tho' shambling BECKET,* proud to soothe my pride,
> Keeps ever shuffling on my right-hand side;
> What tho', with well-tim'd flatt'ry, loud he cries,
> At each theatric stare, "See, see his eyes!"
> What tho' he'll fetch and carry at command,
> And kiss, true spaniel-like, his master's hand . . .[71]

With deadly aim, Kenrick identifies praise of Garrick's eyes as rote puffery
produced by this member of Garrick's media claque. Paul Hiffernan, too,
is charged with writing on Garrick's behalf; and the editors of the *Critical
Review* and *Monthly Review*, Archibald Hamilton and Ralph Griffiths, are
identified as Garrick's friends. Hiffernan did write innumerable verses in
Garrick's defence, as we will see shortly, and Garrick was on such terms
with Ralph Griffiths of the *Monthly Review* that in one letter he submits an
article to Griffiths, secure of its acceptance, asking Griffiths to add notes as
he pleases, and waiving the desire to see any proofs, so confident is he of
the consonance of their views.[72]

Garrick's relationship with Thomas Becket was so intricate that it
requires a lengthy aside. As we saw in the second chapter, Becket held
shares in newspapers for Garrick, and attended meetings of the proprietors
at which he signed for Garrick and acted in his interest. Becket sold to
Garrick, often collecting packets of books, magazines and newspapers from
his shop and Garrick's town house to post to Garrick in the country.[73]
Becket also served as a one-man news service, directing Garrick to articles
of interest in the newspapers.[74] Garrick's patronage of Becket included
insertion of advertisements and reviews of Becket's list in the papers, casual
recommendations in familiar letters, and traditional patronage endorse-
ments.[75] Becket's booklist was built of Garrick's social circle, including
Charles Burney, Marie Riccoboni, Jean Monnet, George Colman and
others. Becket's business was so entwined with Garrick's name by the
mid-1760s that Garrick sometimes had to conceal the connection, as he
did with *The Sick Monkey*, a fable written anonymously by Garrick to
herald his return to England from the Continent. Garrick writes to George
Colman on 8 March 1765: "I would have Becket be in ye Secret & print

it but not publish it under his name for it may be suspected ... I have given some of my friends, whom I love, a little fillip–for Heaven's sake take care to be Secret–when Becket gives it to be publish'd, he must swear the Printer to Secresy for fear of offending Me."[76] (Becket complied: it appeared under the imprint "J. Fletcher.") Becket assisted Garrick in publishing his work in the newspapers or under Becket's imprint, anonymously or not, as occasion demanded; and Garrick could fob off theatrical complainants using Becket as his middleman. Kenrick's assessment of this mutually beneficial partnership is correct, and calling Becket a spaniel, as Kenrick does, is actually a step up from Garrick's private name for Becket, which was the "Worm."[77]

Most damningly, Kenrick directly names the newspaper editors whom he believes curtail authors' access to the press, and insinuates that they are willing to go to great lengths to protect Garrick. To lure Nyky back to Drury Lane to patch plays for him, Roscius promises his friends' united press influence will defend Nyky from criminal charges of sodomy and from public infamy in the newspapers:

> HARRY WOODFALL, BALDWIN, EVANS, SAY*
> My puffs in fairest order full display;
> Impartially insert each friendly PRO,
> Suppressing ever[y] CON of every foe;*
> For well I ween, they wot that *cons* and *pros*
> Will tend my faults and follies to expose.[78]

With heavy irony, Kenrick's footnote identifies these four men as "*Editors and printers of news-papers, well known to the public for their impartiality in regard to ROSCIUS."[79] These men were anything but impartial: all had significant ties to Garrick and to the theatre business. Henry Sampson Woodfall printed the *Public Advertiser*, which printed daily playbills, and he owned shares in the *London Packet*, the paper begun by George Colman, to which Garrick contributed. Henry Baldwin was printer of the *St. James's Chronicle*, in which Garrick owned a share. Thomas Evans printed the *London Packet*; and Charles Greene Say printed the *Gazetteer* and the *Craftsman, or Say's Weekly Journal* – the *Gazetteer* was a daily which at this point also printed the playhouse bills. The special relationship between the playhouse managers and the *Gazetteer* and the *Public Advertiser* was public knowledge: these papers were mentioned in the 5 November 1772 *Morning Chronicle* as Garrick's "tributary papers" and the public was told in the 15 October 1772 *Morning Chronicle* that the managers "receive a considerable annual stipend for the play-house advertisements, and who are by article bound down not to insert any letter, essay, or paragraph relative to the theatres, unless it is signed by the Managers in person, or their Prompter."[80] The *Morning Chronicle* accuses the managers of creating a media shadow in which the newspapers duplicate the playhouse patent structure, creating, in effect, patent newspapers which do the managers' bidding. Advertising revenues and the market advantage resulting from advertising grant them the same kind of powerful control in the press as is afforded by licensing in the theatre. To return to Kenrick's pamphlet: so far, Kenrick has identified, quite correctly, two monthly reviews, five papers and several booksellers and printers as hostile to anti-Garrickian discourse.

Kenrick then uses the space of the pamphlet to do what he complains he could not in these partial papers: bring one of his "suppressed" verses face to face with panegyric about Garrick from Harry Woodfall's "tributary" paper, the *Public Advertiser*, so that verses pro and con Garrick appear together for readers to evaluate. The panegyric, Kenrick asserts, was "suggested probably to ROSCIUS himself by his brother GEORGE the attorney."[81] Legal discourse frames both poems, and both take up the common trope of Garrick's acting as consummate Nature. In the poem allegedly by Garrick, Nature brings a legal action against the actor, saying that she is ruined by his ability to imitate any man whom she creates, and powerless to create another like him:

> Nature against G——— Notice of Process.
>
> *Dame Nature against G———now by me*
> *Her action brings, and thus she grounds her plea.*
> *"I never made a man but still*
> *You acted like that man at will;*
> *Yet ever must I hope in vain*
> *To make a man like you again"*
> *Hence ruin'd totally by you,*
> *She brings her suit, &c. &c.*   B. Solicitor for the Plaintiff.

On the page in *Love in the Suds*, Kenrick's "CON" effects a visual balance, and in Kenrick's view, restores balance of opinion. A less charitable reading might observe that it is a parasitic parody that relies upon proximity for effect. Kenrick's poem makes the Garrick persona say to Nature that though he's often played the fool on stage, in life, he's never acted as a man:

> Nature against G——— Defendant's Plea.
>
> *For G——— I without a fee*
> *'Gainst Nature thus put in his plea.*

"To make a man, like me, of art,
Is not, 'tis true, dame Nature's part;
I own that Scrub, fool, knave I've play'd
With more success than all my trade;
But prove it, plaintiff, if you can,
That e'er I acted like a man."
Of this we boldly make denial.——
Join issues, and proceed to trial.   A. Attorney for the Defendant.[82]

The "*defendant's plea* would have appeared in the same paper," Kenrick writes, "but the cause was obliged to be removed by *certiorari* to another court."[83] As the term *certiorari* refers to a judicial review by a higher court, Kenrick here promotes the idea that papers like the *Public Ledger* and the *Whitehall Evening Post* are higher courts, open to dissenting views, for these are newspapers, "in which ROSCIUS is not a sharer, and hath not yet come up to the price of their silence."[84] Publishers did take sums for silence.[85] Kenrick identifies the *Morning Chronicle* as one of a select group of noisy papers, and has Roscius blurt: "Curse on that Morning-Chronicle; whose tale / Is never known with spightful wit to fail."[86] Just three London papers are open to publishing dissenting dramatic opinion, according to Kenrick's pamphlet. The pamphlet itself is likewise positioned as a high court, in which Kenrick gives his wit a fair hearing, in a more spacious argument than a guerilla war fought with anonymous newspaper epigrams would allow.

Kenrick, who styled himself "Dr. Kenrick, L.L.D." and had continental legal training, must have known the contentious nature of his pamphlet: in publishing it, he was not only taking a financial, but a legal risk, as the pamphlet dances on the edge of libel. In addition to his desire to limn Garrick's pernicious hold on the media, financial reward may have motiv-ated Kenrick. The pamphlet appears to have been a hot seller, running through five editions from June to August, at 1*s*. 6*d*. per quarto copy, also available in folio. However, Kenrick was accused of churning editions, and without records of the print run, the sales output remains indeterminable. The pretended legal action of the pamphlet's opposed epigrams was soon followed by a real one: Garrick began proceedings at the Court of King's Bench on 7 July, just a week after the first edition was advertised.[87] King's Bench is both the local court for Westminster, and the highest court of common law, meaning that it was a court from which Kenrick could make no *certiorari* referral to delay or extend proceedings.[88]

Kenrick's identification of Garrick's media contacts was perceptive in that he fingered the right suspects, but that is no guarantee against Kenrick propounding an exaggerated sense of Garrick's media influence. Let's turn to one of the three papers Kenrick favours as the "higher court" in *Love in the Suds*, the "spightful" and "wit"-ty *Morning Chronicle*, printed by William Woodfall. This was the newspaper that carried the majority of the Kenrick–Garrick dispute. I will evaluate Kenrick's claim that this paper was impartial[89] by considering factors indicative of influence within an eighteenth-century newspaper:

- article placement or position
- typography
- column inches and space
- coverage, as indicated by number of articles
- type of article, and its style and tone
- advertising of related products
- circulation of ideas, indicated by citations and reprinting
- responses in consumer behaviour

Finally, we'll turn to Kenrick's claim that Garrick's influence in news media precluded his ability to express dissenting dramatic opinion.

First, to set the scene: it is summer. The patent theatres, Drury Lane and Covent Garden, are closed, though Foote's summer season at the Haymarket is underway, and the parks are advertising fireworks and concerts. As Robert Haig contends, newspapers were more willing to entertain "nonpolitical subjects ... during the summer season, when Parliament was not in session and when news and advertisements were less plentiful."[90] There was space for an entertaining satirical debate to unfurl in the slow summer news cycle.

The *Morning Chronicle* is a four-page daily: the size does not vary, for as Jeremy Black observes, newspapers "could not be readily contracted or expanded as late twentieth-century papers can be, both because of the nature of the Stamp Duty, which was linked, however imperfectly, to size, and because [of] the limited capacity of each printing unit."[91] The first page of the *Morning Chronicle* typically carries entertainment advertisements, shipping news, patent medicine and book advertisements, and the beginning of a major letter or editorial essay that concludes on page 2. Pages 2 and 3 contain international, London and country news, as well as correspondence and epigrams, which spill, with more advertisements and shipping news, onto the fourth page. Habitual readers would know roughly where to look for the information they wanted, but would have the pleasure of disentangling what George Crabbe called the newspaper's "motley page"[92] for themselves.

In a modern newspaper, placement of an article on a section's front page above the fold is a certain signal of its importance; informational hierarchies are not signified as rigidly by article positioning in an eighteenth-century newspaper. As much of the content in this paper in particular was generated by advertisement and correspondence, there was considerable flexibility of content. On the front page of the *Morning Chronicle* for 1 July 1772, Kenrick's advertisement for his newly printed pamphlet immediately follows on the entertainment news and is highly visible on the first page, but this is not interpretable as a certain sign of favour.

As advertising was payable to newspapers by the number of lines of type one took up, there is a sense in which readers might equate columnar space with influence. The epigrams and letters in which the Kenrick–Garrick news war over *Love in the Suds* was conducted were probably not purchased as taxable advertisements. Even if some of these articles were paid puffs, it is extremely unlikely that one would ever find proof of that, for two reasons: "Few ledgers of eighteenth-century newspapers survive," as Hannah Barker reminds us, and Lucyle Werkmeister "discounts the importance of such documents since they were subject to periodic inspections by the Stamp Office, and therefore likely to have been falsified and not to have included 'illegitimate' transactions, such as the insertion of puffs."[93] Still, there is a visible skirmish for spatial supremacy in this paper war. Around 18 July, at which point Kenrick had been legally charged in King's Bench (on 7 July), the debate occupies almost half of page 3, and appears fairly evenly balanced. By 21 July, the public imagination had been seized, almost all of page 3 was occupied, and the editor had begun to ask correspondents, politely and humorously, to put an end to it. The next day, 22 July, it looks as if Garrick's forces have won the day; but later in August, Woodfall began printing sections of Kenrick's letter to Garrick as a four-day serial. Examining the battle's occupation of the space of the newspaper shows the degree to which the public was exposed to the dispute: whether they enjoyed or tolerated it, nearly a quarter of a significant daily is taken up with related content.

The number of articles on a given topic yields a rough measure of exposure and influence. From 29 June through 31 August, the "impartial" *Morning Chronicle* published 53 pro-Garrick and 53 pro-Kenrick articles. What could look more impartial than a pie graph divided down the middle? However, if one considers advertisements for Kenrick's pamphlet, and Kenrick's sideswipes at Garrick's defender, Paul Hiffernan (insults which evolved into a separate dispute), as contributing to his total, then the balance of articles shifts noticeably in Kenrick's favour. This, of course,

Table 2 *Pro-Garrick vs. Pro-Kenrick Representation in the* Morning
Chronicle, *29 June – 30 August 1772*

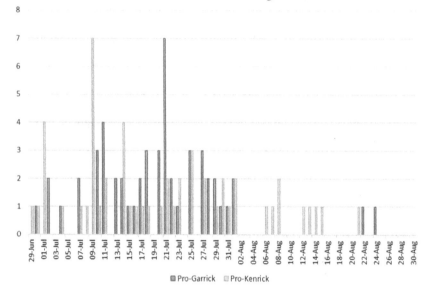

is a blunt measure of influence, unable to account for the type of article, or its tone, influence, length, credibility or timing.

By presenting the number of articles on a dateline (Table 2), one can see the relative degrees of coverage held by Kenrickians and Garrickians in the *Morning Chronicle.* The timeline of the dispute itself was this: on 15 June, there was the angry exchange of letters and the failed duel or meeting; on 17 June, Kenrick floated what he called an "embrio" advertisement for his work, not yet published; it was advertised as available from the printer, John Wheble, on 1 July; and on 7 July, Garrick took legal action, reported in the "partial" *Craftsman, or Say's Weekly Journal* for Saturday 11 July 1772 in this manner: "Yesterday Mr. Dunning made a motion in the Court of King's-Bench, for a rule to show cause why an information should not be granted against the Author of Love in the Suds, when the Court was pleased to grant a rule for the first day of next term."[94] Subsequent editions of Kenrick's pamphlet included a new letter to Garrick that spoke to this legal action, and again complained of his hold on the press. Kenrick blusters,

> it was with more indignation than surprize I was informed of your having used your extensive influence over the press to prevent its being advertised in the News-papers ... by what right or privilege do you, Sir, set up for a

licenser of the press? That you have long successfully usurped that privilege, to swell both your fame and fortune, is well known … by what authority do you take upon you to shut up the general channel, in which writers usher their performances to the public?[95]

In innuendo-laden language, Kenrick suggests Garrick can defend himself with "a ready pen and a long purse. The press is open to the one, and the bar is ever ready to open with the other. For a poor author, not a printer will publish a paragraph, not a pleader will utter a quibble. You have then every advantage in the contest."[96] Yet, as you can see in Table 2, in the *Morning Chronicle*, judging by the number of articles (mainly smutty epigrams and short letters under classical aliases), Kenrick's side of the debate was clearly ahead. Kenrick's allegation that Garrick prevented his advertising in any papers is an overstatement, for the pamphlet was advertised in four different papers, with advertisements appearing twenty times between 29 June and the end of August. If one adds the direct paid advertisements that appeared in the *Morning Chronicle* to the chart plotting news items in the pamphlet war, one can see in Table 3 that each advertisement for Kenrick's pamphlet is accompanied by a spike in Kenrickian contributions to the newspaper.

Table 3 *Pro-Garrick vs. Pro-Kenrick Representation in the* Morning Chronicle, *29 June – 30 August 1772, with Advertisements for* Love in the Suds

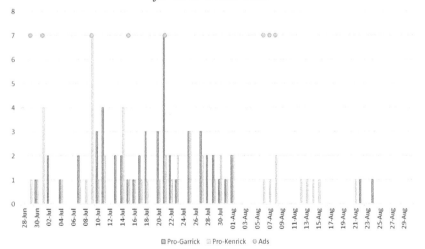

Kenrick's strategy of preparatory puffs did not go unnoticed by the Garrick camp. A letter *"To the Poetaster, Gog-Magog"* in the *Morning Chronicle* of 18 July refers to Kenrick's

> *two principal puff-schemes* to enforce the sale of a *neglected pamphlet;* which are to give out, that either power has ordered a low prosecution to be commenced against its author; or that influential interest has been made with the printers of news-papers to prevent its being advertised . . .
>
> Most truly lamentable K—k's grown –
> Has then our *critique* wrote his *libel* down?*
> Print off the *new title* pages, and *large-bill* the town!
>   *It is recommended to him, to serve as a proof of his
>   candour, to annex a copy of it to some of the many
>   editions he means to strike out of really but one!*

The mid-August table entries refer to the *Chronicle*'s reprinting of sections of Kenrick's letter to Garrick. This met with a resounding, significant silence. Citations, reprinting and circulation are amongst the best indicators for assessing the spread and potential influence of a given article or topic. One indicator that Kenrick may be correct about Garrick's media reach is the unusual restraint shown in not reprinting the *Morning Chronicle*'s wittiest sallies in other papers. In the 21–23 July issue, the *Middlesex Journal or Universal Evening Post* digests the news: "That Garrick has been infamously traduced by Kenrick, every impartial man must allow; and that Kenrick's insinuations, like his affections, are even below contempt, every man of spirit knows. Perhaps there is not, in the whole literary circle, so contemptible a character as that of (Lord help us!) DOCTOR Kenrick!!!" By digesting this news under the heading *Morning Chronicle*, this account suggests its restriction to that paper. The *Middlesex Journal* was one of only three other papers (besides the *Morning Chronicle*) to carry advertisements for Kenrick's pamphlet (11–14 and 16–18 July; and 6–8 August). This outburst has the air of an editor covering his bases – the more so when one considers that the printer is none other than John Wheble, who printed Kenrick's pamphlet. Normally, a printer would promote a pamphlet he had printed in the paper in which he held an interest. Wheble's surprising action may have been grounded in fear of being named in a libel action.

Was Kenrick correct in arguing that Garrick's influence over other newspapers, and over his confederacy of writers, affected the insertion of Kenrick's advertisement and news of his publication, in other papers? In a word, yes. Garrick wrote to Richard Berenger on 10 [July 1772] in terms which demonstrate his knowledge and approval of a concerted group effort:

What shall it be said my dear Friend that I turn my back upon my Antagonist now, I who have fought face to face

Et militavi non sine Gloria

no no - we shall clip the wings of Calumny & make defamation peep through timber, as ye Blackguards call it –

   I am very proud to see all ye world friends & foes join against this most consummate S—l [Scoundrel?] to do me Justice.[97]

One of those writers, besides Hiffernan already mentioned, who wrote under the name "Mother Shipton," was the ropemaker-playwright Joseph Reed, who in a rare moment in which he was not feuding with Garrick, tried to curry favour by inserting pro-Garrick poems under the name "Benedick."[98]

Kenrick's idea that other newspapers were shut against him also seems correct, judging from the available evidence. Though it is an overstatement to say that he was not allowed to advertise, there does seem to have been a closing of the ranks in papers that had previously printed work by Kenrick. The *Public Advertiser*, which had carried advertisements for Kenrick's 1768 *Poems Ludicrous, Satirical, and Moral* in its 19 March 1768 issue and for his translation of Abbé Millot's *Elements of the History of England* (7 February 1772), did not advertise *Love in the Suds*. There is a large gap between this last advertisement, and any mention of Kenrick or his works until 8 April 1773, when his *Dictionary* is advertised. The *St. James's Chronicle*, which had previously printed Kenrick's occasional poetry, as on 1–3 December 1768, did not mention his name. The *Gazetteer* likewise makes no mention of Kenrick whatever from 1 July to 23 November 1772. All of these papers that excluded Kenrick in the summer of 1772 were produced by the men named in *Love in the Suds*: "HARRY WOODFALL, BALDWIN, EVANS, SAY."

But on 23 November 1772, Kenrick's name appeared in all these partial papers, as the author of a public apology. The apology by the Author of *Love in the Suds* was carried in the *Public Advertiser* and the *Gazetteer* for 23 November; and in the *St. James's Chronicle* for 24–26 November. It also appeared in Kenrick's favoured paper, the *Morning Chronicle*. Garrick may have withdrawn his legal action against Kenrick at King's Bench,[99] but in the newspapers, Kenrick was made to abase himself before all the partial editors whom he had abused in his pamphlet.[100] Like Samuel Foote, whose theatrical seasons at the Haymarket were permitted to run in the summers while the patent theatres were closed, Kenrick was permitted his brief summer season in the papers to profit from his pamphlet, until

Garrick exacted an apology before the public who had returned to the town for the new theatrical season. The multiple spaces occupied by Kenrick's November apology corroborate his views on Garrick's firm hold of contemporary media.

Despite his self-representation as a critic, Kenrick was no disinterested observer of Garrick's manipulation of the media. Oliver Goldsmith's *Retaliation* (1774) echoes Kenrick's critique of Garrick's media reach, even while it implicates Kenrick in the "Cobweb Politics" of those theatrical writers who trade in Garrick's economy of praise:

> Of praise, a mere glutton, he [Garrick] swallowed what came,
> And the puff of a dunce, he mistook it for fame;
> 'Till his relish grown callous, almost to disease,
> Who pepper'd the highest, was surest to please.
> But let us be candid, and speak out our mind,
> If dunces applauded, he paid them in kind.
> Ye Kenricks, ye Kellys, and Woodfalls so grave,
> What a commerce was yours, while you got and you gave!
> How did Grub-street re-echo the shouts that you raised,
> While he was berossia'd, and you were beprais'd?[101]

Whether in puffery or in satire, Goldsmith writes, those who traded in words about Garrick invariably raised themselves. The verbal currency used to manufacture Garrick's celebrity transmutes itself, in a single line ("What a commerce was yours, while you got and you gave!"), into real currency and shared financial and reputational gain.

While critical discourse of freedom of the press has been predominantly concerned with the press's ability to comment freely on political events, the case of William Kenrick's pamphlet *Love in the Suds* suggests that a similar discourse regarding the ability to comment freely on the entertainment industry was already extant in the 1770s.

Puffing Reed the Ropemaker's Play

As manager of Drury Lane Theatre, David Garrick had an interest in promoting *Dido* (1767), a tragedy by the ropemaker-playwright Joseph Reed, yet this interest was tested by Reed's troublesome personality, and his insistence on a particular kind of self-representation in the media. Analysis of Reed's case offers a fitting cap to this examination of negative advertising, for it shows how Garrick used paid advertisements in concert with other strategies, including occasional poetry, fake news and puffs, to promote a certain image of the play and its playwright. Garrick's positioning of Reed as a surprising prodigy of the lower classes met with opposition from Reed, who had previously employed a similar marketing strategy himself, but who viewed this positioning as inconsistent with the dignity of tragedy. The conflict between the two men and their ideal public images exposes the normally hidden machinations of theatrical promotion, and provides insight into Garrick's ability to protect the integrity of his personal brand under the assault of negative publicity.

Joseph Reed was a country[102] ropemaker who settled in Sun Tavern Fields.[103] According to a mock-autobiography published in the *Universal Museum* (1764), Reed attended a country grammar school for a short time before the deaths of his father and elder brother forced him to take up the family business. He borrowed from the local circulating library Shakespeare's plays, which he read in secret, for fear of his Dissenting mother's displeasure.[104] His background echoes Garrick's own short stint of schooling in Lichfield, and reluctant apprenticeship as a wine merchant. By the time the two men met, around 1758, Garrick had largely effaced his trade origins. Reed, still a ropemaker, now also possessed significant literary aspirations and connections – he knew Johnson, Whitehead, Capel and others from Garrick's circle, and he drew on this community, particularly upon Fielding, for ideas and support. Reed wrote a burlesque mock-tragedy, *Madrigal and Trulletta*, which Theophilus Cibber staged for one night, 6 July 1758; a farce, *The Register Office*, produced successfully at Drury Lane in 1761, based on Fielding's employment office; and later, infamously, the opera of *Tom Jones*, staged at Covent Garden in 1769.[105]

Reed's tragedy *Dido* has a tenuous textual history. Arthur Murphy claimed erroneously "it was never published."[106] Lynette Eckersley's *Oxford Dictionary of National Biography* entry attempts a correction: "Joseph Ritson prepared it for press in 1792, but it was not printed and distributed until 1808. Unfortunately, no copies of this printing exist as they all perished in a fire at Nichols's printing office before distribution and the work was never reprinted."[107] This is also incorrect. One copy survives: the copy now at the Huntington Library, once belonging to J.P. Kemble, which bears a manuscript note from John Nichols on the title page: "For Mr Jones (The only Copy saved from the Fire)."

Unlike *Beowulf*, *Dido* is not a mighty work saved from the pyre for the ages. In the manner of a bad French tragedy, everything exciting occurs off stage, action is summarized, and the audience knows the ending. Reed's prose is turgid with archaisms. Garrick wrote to Reed, "I fear the language would rather appear, from the affectation of obsolete words, to ridicule Shakespeare than seriously to imitate him ... I hope that you will excuse my plain dealing upon the subject, as mistakes in our affairs are so frequent, & equivocal expressions are too apt to create misunderstandings."[108] This insistence on virtuous plain speech and open, honourable action – to which both men lay claim – dogs Reed and Garrick's disputes over the play, which were long: this letter, already Garrick's second refusal, is dated 18 July 1761, and *Dido* was not produced until 1767. Having demonstrated that the play is extant, I will trace *Dido*'s tortuous route to the stage to contextualize its later marketing.

After Garrick's second refusal of the play,[109] Reed enlisted five friends to "get the piece cramm'd down the managers throat": Johnson, Capel, Churchill, Mason and Whitehead.[110] Neither Johnson nor Churchill co-operated. Johnson reportedly later complained, "I never did the man an injury; yet *he would read his Tragedy to me*."[111] Garrick objected that this court-of-appeal approach would set a difficult precedent. Reed countered that there was a precedent already: Murphy's *Orphan of China*, which Garrick had accepted after a referral to Whitehead. Garrick refused *Dido* a third time, though Reed offered to underwrite its financial success. Reed then decided to see if John Rich would take *Dido* for Covent Garden. Rich read the play and, according to Reed, offered to exhibit it, but then died. Rich's successor, John Beard, would not take the play. Reed suspected Garrick had influenced Beard, and "openly made use of very warm, even virulent expressions, arraign'd him of duplicity & injustices in regard to my play ... and even threaten'd to publish his Letters in an appeal to the Town."[112] Garrick regarded this threat as ungenteel, and after it, the two were no longer on speaking terms. When Garrick left to recover his health on the Continent in 1763, Reed offered the tragedy to Garrick's co-manager, James Lacy. Lacy refused it. Reed's autobiography in the *Universal Museum*, published at this time, shows a man desperate for an advocate:

> What then, in the name of compassion, would you advise me to do? I am thinking, for novelty's sake, to publish an advertisement in the following words, which, if you approve of, I must beg your insertion of it.
> W A N T E D,
> A Patron, of sound judgment and poetical discernment. He must be a lover of the Muses, and not so wrapped up in the national infatuation of cards, horse-racing, and luxury, as to be entirely insensible of the concerns of genius and science. He must have sufficient influence to procure (no matter at which house) the representation of a tolerable play. Such a person, who has humanity enough for the generous undertaking, by applying to the publisher of this Magazine, may have the glorious opportunity of raising

from obscurity a dramatic genius, which may probably be a credit to his
patronage, a delight to the stage, and an honour to his country.
    I am, your humble servant,
    DRAMATIS PERSONA.[113]

This hopeful advertisement remained unanswered. When Garrick
returned to England in 1765, Reed approached him again. How to explain
such persistence?

Even after his initial success with *The Register Office*, Reed continued his
career as a ropemaker. He did not pursue dramatic aspirations as a means
of escaping trade. Indeed, it seems to have been part of Reed's personal
brand to publish widely that he could make both plays and nooses. Just as
a publisher might advertise other publications and his place of business on
a novel's endpapers, Reed made his address, name and self-description in
various publications do double duty to advertise his rope business. Reed
published a pamphlet addressed to Tobias Smollett, written by "A Halter-
Maker." In the preface to his mock-tragedy *Madrigal and Trulletta*, his
trade, place of work and name are all mentioned. And, in what may be the
world's most tasteless instance of product placement, the "hempen bard"
wrote an epilogue for his mock-tragedy in which one of the characters
produces a noose on stage. Reed refused the Garrickian narrative of
upwardly mobile tradesman-turned-dramatist, preferring instead a refreshing alternation of two trades: "I hate a lazy Life," he wrote, "and must have
my Hands or Head employed. When my *hempen* Calls are brisk, I *am not
at Home to the Muses*; but when my Trade grows dull, I am glad to receive
their Ladyships."[114]

Reed's motivation for pursuing a production at Drury Lane is captured
in his repeated use of the word "popularity." As Reed employs it, popularity seems derived from Johnson's first dictionary definition, "a state of
being favoured by the people," and connotes not only possessing a happy
personal reputation, but beneficial financial prospects.[115] This double
hope appears in his letters to Garrick. In 1765, he writes, "If the piece
succeed, my popularity must necessarily increase my business; wherefore to
keep me under the hatches another year will be a double disadvantage";
and in 1766, he returns to the theme:

> To be kept another year in obscurity must totally annihilate my character as
> a dramatic writer, and greatly hurt me as a Tradesman; as the increase of
> business is dependant on popularity ... Publication in your theatrical
> Gazette, 'that the quarrel which had long subsisted between our celebrated
> Roscius and the Halter maker was some months ago amicably comprised, in
> consequence of which Queen Dido will this season make her appearance on

the Stage of Drury Lane theatre,' would put me upon so respectable a
footing, that I shall not doubt of doubling my calls in the Hempen way this
winter.[116]

Reed surprisingly insists on the relation of his two characters of dramatis
persona and ropemaker, and positions Garrick's acceptance of *Dido* as a
weighty transaction that can confer the monetized popularity necessary to
drive his two careers. His use of the term "popularity" offers a period-
specific partial synonym for celebrity, though it overlooks celebrity's
iterative construction (means) in favour of its assumed financial gains
(the end).

Hoping to interest an actor in a new role[117] and by that means get his
play staged, in 1765 Reed read *Dido* to William Powell, who convinced
Garrick to look at it again. Reed sent Garrick a revised version of *Dido* to
read during Passion week, but that September Garrick denied ever receiving it. Fortunately, Reed had another copy. Garrick offered to let *Dido* play
in the summer, if it had been suitably altered; Reed objected "the
Town ... will have a mean opinion of it merely from its coming out at
such a time."[118] Garrick's brother George then intervened: *Dido* would
not do for the regular season, but, if Reed "would consent to try it at a
benefit either for Holland or Powell, in case it should be well received he
would bring it in a favorable part of the ensuing season"; to this, Read also
objected: "I could not agree to such proposals, as the first appearance of the
play at a benefit must be its utter destruction."[119]

Reed's refusals, which sound exasperatingly stubborn and impolite even
when heard in the self-righteous tone of his own vindication – a manuscript thrillingly entitled "Theatrical Duplicity" – nonetheless demonstrate
a thorough understanding of the limitations of marketing a new play in the
off-season. The *Public Advertiser*'s usual theatrical advertising duopoly
showing playbills for Covent Garden and Drury Lane becomes in the
spring benefit season a proliferation of individual advertisements for actors'
benefits. Compare, for instance, the front pages of the *Public Advertiser* for
24 January 1767 (three advertisements: one each for the Haymarket,
Drury Lane and Covent Garden) with the *Public Advertiser* for 24 May
of the same year during benefit season (nineteen advertisements: two for
operas, three for concerts, five for actors' benefits at Drury Lane, and nine
for benefits at Covent Garden). In the benefit season, the individual actor/
beneficiary, not the house, is the unit of competition and the focus of
advertisement. As actors chose the repertoire for their benefits, and generally paid house expenses, by placing *Dido* as a benefit, Garrick might

minimize his financial risk, and avoid the imputation that this addition to the repertoire was to his taste – crucial, since the town knew that he had been refusing the play for years.[120] Garrick seems to have toyed with the idea of releasing an "Epigram" on the subject, and drafted these lines:

> When Garrick play'd your former Play,
> How did you puff and praise away!
> But now you've chang'd your Plan.
> His Worth was then without compare,
> You bellow'd forth the Matchless Player,
> The Manager and Man!
>
> Now you abuse, and bounce, and huff,
> To make him take more wretched stuff,
> But <u>Crab</u> you'll never force him;
> He knows should he receive your Play,
> Again you'd puff and praise away,
> But all the Town would curse him.[121]

Reed refused a benefit season performance because he wanted the cultural consecration of a regular-season acceptance, and the chance at an extended, lucrative run for his play: popularity, in a word.

Reporting that Paul Hiffernan had sent him another play called *Dido*, Garrick pressured Reed to take the benefit season offer. They then quarrelled over whose benefit it should be: as Powell was the means of effecting reconciliation with Garrick, Reed favoured Powell, but Garrick gave it to Holland, the senior actor, and insulted Reed by asking him to shorten the play.[122] Reed convinced Holland to risk taking *Dido* for his benefit, and on 2 January 1767, Holland and Reed read the play to Mary Ann Yates in the green room, when Powell entered, offended at not having been invited. At this point, Reed had alienated nearly everyone in the London literary and theatrical world: Johnson, Churchill, Garrick, Rich, Beard, Hiffernan, Foote, and now, even the actors on whom he was depending. He had not just insulted Powell, who was shut out of the green room; but Holland, who knew he was Reed's second choice; and Mary Ann Yates, who knew that Dido had been written not for her, but for Susannah Cibber, who had died before the play could be produced.

At last, by mid-February 1767, it was time to advertise the performance, which was less than a month away. On 26 February, Reed writes, "Mr. Garrick, Mr Holland and I had a meeting at the Theatre to draw up a public paragraph for the Public Advertiser . . . I produc'd one which I had previously written: 'A new Tragedy call'd Dido will be acted at the Theatre

Royal in Drury Lane on Saturday the 28th of March. The Managers, with the consent of the Author, have given the first night to Mr Holland. This Tragedy would have made an earlier appearance, if the success of the new pieces already exhibited had not render'd its representation before the benefits impracticable: but notwithstanding the lateness of the season there will be a sufficient number of nights left open for the run of this play.'"

Reed's effort to secure "a sufficient number of nights left open" for his play to make an extended run by forcing through his own advertisement was doomed.[123] First, as a benefit piece for and featuring Holland, there was little likelihood that the play could get an extended run during the benefit season, when each beneficiary played in his or her own favourite piece.[124] Second, Garrick owned a share in the newspaper in which the advertisement would appear, and he rejected Reed's paragraph, saying, "it would be a gross imposition on the public, as it was not literally true for the agreement was to try the piece at a Benefit."[125] Holland, too, may not have been pleased by the tangential position his name occupied in an advertisement ostensibly promoting his benefit.

Garrick countered with his own advertisement, giving Holland's name the prominence customary for a benefit: "A new Tragedy call'd Dido (written in imitation of Shakespeare's style) will be acted for the first time on the 23d day of March for the benefit of Mr Holland to whom the Manager, with the consent of the Author, have generously given up the profits of the first nights representation."[126] Having reasserted Holland's dignity on the front page of the *Public Advertiser* for 24 March 1767, Garrick then skewered Reed's dignity on page four:

> To the Printer
>   Sir,
>   As I imagine there is not a better Trumpeter of Intelligence political or theatrical in this puffing Metropolis than yourself I am surprised that you have not given us one Blast yet for the Dramatic Phenomenon which will shortly appear at the Theatre Royal in Drury Lane. Don't imagine, Sir, that Genius & Wit are Plants only growing in and about Covent Garden; the New Tragedy of *Dido* sprang complete in five Acts, in Imitation of the Style of Shakespeare, (as Pallas from the head of Jupiter) from the Pericranium of a *Rope Maker*, living in Ratcliff Highway. We have had Poetry and successful Plays from Threshers, Bricklayers, Stone Cutters, & Tallow Chandlers, but never from a Rope Maker.–Limehouse, Wapping and Ratcliff Highway are up in Arms for the Honor of their Neighbor and Friend–The Author, we hear, is much respected for his Probity & Modesty, and we hope we shall have equal proofs of his Ingenuity next Saturday, or

his Probity and Modesty will stand him in very little Stead at the Cockpit Royal in Drury Lane.

> There is no Shuffling: there the Action lies
> In its true Nature, and we ourselves compell'd,
> Even to the Teeth and Forehead of his Faults,
> To give in Evidence.   SHAKES.

A Friend to Merit in every Station
P.S. We hear that a particular prologue from a very rich ground is prepar'd from the old Prologue Manufactory to be exhibited by *Tom King*, Salesman.

This curious piece is overtly identified as a puff, which deflates its efficacy, especially as *Dido* is not the principal object of its puffery. It identifies Reed as a freakish "Phenomenon," a lower-class talent comparable to a figure like Stephen Duck, the thresher-poet. Instead of expanding upon the author's merits, or entreating the fashionable town to honor the house with their attendance, the puff suggests that Drury Lane will erupt in Cockpit-like riotousness, once crowded with the boisterous inhabitants of "Limehouse, Wapping and Ratcliff-highway," who are "up in arms." This is not the language to fill the boxes. Finally, there's the sly quotation of *Hamlet*, in which the King reflects that in heaven, his actions will be shown in their true nature, as giving evidence of his faults. The "there" that is the afterlife in the King's soliloquy is repositioned in the advertisement as Drury Lane, so that the quotation intimates that the "action" of performance will give evidence of Reed's faults.[127] The puff invites play-goers to compare Reed's "Imitation" of Shakespeare's language with the original, and the remark about the tragedy springing readymade from his pericranium hints that the language will not prove the only thing that is derivative. Last, the quotation insinuates to readers the advertisement's origin: the most famous Hamlet of the day. Garrick is the best Hamlet, the best manager ("A Friend to Merit in every Station"), and the best prologue-smith ("the old Prologue Manufactory"). This is not a puff for Reed.

Reed knew it, and was incensed, noting, "Burlesque is not the species of writing to recommend Tragedy to public favor."[128] Reed knew burlesque: he had penned *Madrigal and Trulletta* as burlesque, designing "to expose the *Buckram* of the *modern* dramatic Diction."[129] The puff's diabolical cleverness is that Garrick trades in the same images and tone with which Reed had marketed his mock-tragedy. Reed is cast, by the puff, as one of his own dramatis personae: the Grub-street hack of *Madrigal and Trulletta*,

"A wilful murderer of sense in rhyme," who is said to have had a tragedy turned down by Garrick. In his burlesque, Reed had defended the manager against such foolish authors, and flattered Garrick in an obsequious footnote:

> *DAVID GARRICK, Esq; an actor, and manager of the theatre in Drury Lane, in the 18th century. This great man, though not above five feet six inches in stature, was the most celebrated, and universal performer, that ever trod the *British*, or any other stage in the known world. In all his theatrical personations he was so exact a copyer of nature, that it was a proverb in his day, with the best judges of the stage, *nature and* GARRICK *are the same.*
>
> This note, my readers are desired to remember, is made for the benefit of the lovers of drama, in the year two thousand and upwards. It would be an affront to the above gentleman's merit and universality, to add a note, to inform the world who, and what he is; or even to suppose that his memory would not outlive his theatrical performances, at least, a brace of centuries.[130]

Given that Reed's puffery of Garrick in *Madrigal and Trulletta* had been so lavish (and prescient), Garrick's public dismissal of Reed, thinly disguised as a puff, must have stung.

Reed correctly observes that Garrick's prologue for *Dido* is the object for which the puff raises anticipation, noting that though it is "a manifest puff on the Prologue, it could be of no service to the play." Publicity for the prologue need not have been problematic, as Garrick's prologues were sought after by playwrights, who conceived of them as effective marketing, since prologues frequently appeared in the newspapers during or near a play's run. However, Garrick's prologue for *Dido*, though much applauded in the papers,[131] appears not to have been published until his collected poems appeared in 1785.[132] This surprising omission from his usual practice may indicate Garrick's lasting irritation with Reed. Garrick's prologue continues the burlesque on Reed begun by the newspaper puff:

> Now to the Rope-maker I come again,–
> Who having spun much hemp, now spins his brain:
> This *hempen* produce any test will stand;
> This, of his brain, may prove a rope of sand;
> But should this spinning of his head deceive him,
> This hempen manufacture may relieve him!
> . . .
> And should he fail to please, poor scribbling elf–
> O—then he makes a rope to hang himself.[133]

A rope is implied as a prop in Garrick's prologue, suggesting a parody of Reed's noose-bearing epilogue in *Madrigal and Trulletta*. Garrick's insinuation that Reed may go hang himself metaphorically or in actuality is barely masked aggression.

Performance of both prologue and play was pre-empted in the *Public Advertise*r by an anonymous[134] anti-Reed poem signed "Cotton Whipcord." When Reed attended rehearsal the day before his tragedy was to open, the performers had heard the poem and were "in a bustle … Mrs Yates declar'd if any part of them [the verses] should be hollow'd out while she was upon the Stage, that she should not be able to get the better of her confusion"; Reed immediately suspected Garrick: "So critical a publication in the Managers' paper gave me a strong suspicion that a certain manager was concern'd in it."[135] The verses appeared in two of the manager's papers: in the *Public Advertiser* on 27 March, the day before the play opened, and in the *St. James's Chronicle* for 24–26 March, two days previous to opening. They continue the puff's motifs with even more brutality:

> The Critics all, who look'd upon her,
> Declaring candidly, 'pon Honour,
> In Terms indeed not over civil,
> Dy was a Morsel for the Devil.
> (lines 89–92)

Reed sent a noose to the critic, care of the newspaper.[136]

Whether out of curiosity to see the worst tragedy ever staged, or to hear Garrick's unpublished prologue, audiences came out for *Dido* that spring, three times. According to Reed, *Dido* was applauded as performed on Saturday 28 March 1767, and according to the treasurer's books, Holland profited: £201 8*s*. 6*d*. after house charges of £67 1*s*. 6*d*.[137] Garrick's letter to his brother George of 5 April drips with disgust at the town's bad taste in supporting Reed's tragedy: "And does 'Dido' please? Good God!–and will they come twice to see it? Good God!"[138]

After these performances, Reed's tragedy sank from public view. Reed may have been paid to never exhibit the play again. On 11 February 1768, Drury Lane's prompter William Hopkins wrote a memorandum: "By the Manager's order I ask'd Mr [Joseph] Reed what he had a benefit for the next night. His answer was The Managers give it him for his withdrawing *Dido* and on account of *The Register Office* and to clear them from all demands he had upon them whatever."[139] Though Reed claims in "Theatrical Duplicity" that he never received the author's benefit money from

Dido, it seems from Hopkins's memo that he was literally paid to stop pressing *Dido* forward. The ropemaker was restored to his proper walk, farce, his aspirations to heroic tragedy checked.

A volume of letters published in 1820 reveals a twisted coda to the ropemaker's tale. Having discerned the power of managers, Reed seems to have made an untimely grasp at buying into the theatre business. On 6 July 1769, Reed wrote to George Colman:

> I have this afternoon been warmly advis'd by a Friend to endeavour to purchase the Share of yr deceas'd Colleague in the Property of Coventry [sic] Garden Theatre; but as it is so hazardous an Undertaking, I am resolv'd not to proceed in the affair without your Advice, nay let me add without your Concurrence. A theatrical Connexion with you were
>
> a Consummation
Devoutly to be wish'd,
>
> as from a Consciousness of your Integrity, & the Rectitude of your Management, I am convinc'd it would be my Inclination as well as Interest to continue your fast Friend & Ally; but I would not ever think of such a Purchase, unless my being a Partner in the Property would be agreeable to Mr. Colman.
>
> As therefore Mr. Powell's theatrical Property will, in all Likelyhood, be dispos'd off [sic], I could wish you would favour me with your Sentiments on the occasion. If I can have the Preference, I should endeavour to make the Bargain advantagious to Mrs Powell, by an Annuity besides the stipulated Price.
>
> As I have thus freely unbosom'd my Intention, I have only to desire of you to keep the Subject of this Letter a Secret. I should not have made so recent an application, if I had not been assur'd by my friend there was no time to be lost.[140]

At the bottom of this letter, in Colman's hand, is the dismissal: "no Sale."

David Garrick did not shy away from negative publicity. He created it, managed it, overwrote it, performed it and dished it out to others, who, lacking his media access and his theatrical patent, could not control their message and its distribution as fully as he could. The next chapter considers, in addition to negative publicity, what other prompts to change the actor-manager considered in adapting the media's representation of himself and his theatre as occasion demanded.

CHAPTER 5

Prompting, Inside and Outside the Theatre

Real talents stand not in want of daily, hurtful, nauseous panegyrics
in prose and verse; which, not content with giving common praise,
must even – to deserve their hire – change the *full of the leaf*, into the
very *budding of the spring*!
> – "The PROMPTER before the Curtain!" [David Garrick],
> *Morning Post, and Daily Advertiser*, 21 December 1776

DICK: ... But come the news; the news of the town, for I am but just
arrived. Has any thing been damned? Any new performers this
winter? How often has Romeo and Juliet been acted? What new
plays on the stocks? Come, my bucks, inform me, for I want news.
> – Arthur Murphy, *The Apprentice* (1756)[1]

David Garrick's business practices as manager and co-owner of Drury Lane
Theatre were intricately bound up with his constant negotiation of media
representations of himself and his playhouse. Garrick's hand is visible in
the marketing of Drury Lane's productions, as well as in preparing and
managing audience response to plays and actors. One *Public Advertiser*
article for 15 December 1772, for instance, prompts the public to receive
Garrick's new adaptation of *Hamlet* by telling them that it was exactly
what all the "best Critics" longed for:

> As the best Critics and warmest Admirers of Shakespeare have long wished
> that the great Beauties and excellent Scenes of Hamlet were separated from
> the Improbabilities, strange Circumstances, and violent Transitions which
> have been always objected to that Tragedy, an Alteration, intending to
> remove the Chief of these Objections, and effected merely by Omissions
> and Restorations in the 5th Act, with the Addition of a very few Lines, is
> now in the Hands of the Managers of this Theatre, and will be humbly
> submitted to the Public. Hamlet by Mr. Garrick ...

Garrick's correspondence spread reports of his adaptation's success: to
Pierre-Antoine de Laplace he wrote on 3 [January] 1773: "I have ventur'd

to alter Hamlet, & have greatly Succeeded; I have destroy'd ye Grave diggers, (those favourites of the people) & almost all of ye 5th Act–it was a bold Deed, but ye Event has answer'd my most sanguine expectation: if you correspond with any of the Journalists, this circumstance will be worth telling, as it is a great Anecdote in our theatrical history – ."[2] Laplace obligingly placed an article in *L'Oberservateur François à Londres* and replied that surely it would be reprinted elsewhere.[3] Though later critics shuddered at them, and Arthur Murphy parodied them, Garrick's alterations proved a commercial success.[4]

This chapter considers Garrick's media-conscious business practices, moving outward from a discussion of the division of managerial labour at Drury Lane Theatre to consider in-house communications, and Garrick's prompts to change, as discernable in the diaries kept by the theatre's prompters Richard Cross and William Hopkins. It considers the prompter's intelligence during the Battle of the Romeos, in a case study concerning the effects of dramatized competition on celebrity; and peers into one of Garrick's anonymous newspaper columns, in which he took up the persona of a prompter. Finally, it examines Garrick's use of the prompter's persona outside the theatre, in two court cases where he acted as a character witness.

The Patentees' Relationship

King Charles II established London's theatrical business model in 1660 by issuing two warrants, later reframed as letters-patent. The theatre patents were brief but powerful legal instruments, inheritable or transferable by purchase. Patent-holders were granted the sole legal right to present comedy, tragedy, opera and other stage entertainments in London. While the London theatre business itself is most accurately described as a commercial monopoly, the existence of two patents often created a duopoly, in which two theatrical houses competed for audiences. Patent-holders had the ability to set actors' salaries and admission prices, and they were charged with a moral duty to reform the stage by presenting improving entertainments and removing offensive passages from any extant plays they produced. All those who worked in the theatre industry, from hairdressers and milliners to actors and musicians, were subject to the financial and aesthetic choices made by the patent-holders. Possessing a patent was the surest route to financial gain and artistic control within the limited market of London theatre.

Garrick purchased half of one of these valuable patents on 9 April 1747 for £12,000. James Lacy was the less-famous owner of the other half-patent; indeed, Lacy owned his share first, and invited Garrick into the partnership, in which they received equal shares of the theatre's profit, exclusive of Garrick's earnings as an actor.[5] Thomas Davies writes of Garrick's acquisition of his share in the patent in terms that lay open Garrick's commodity value to Lacy, and show the strategic value of securing the popular actor:

> Mr. Lacy knew that the possession of a patent was of little avail without the power to make it advantageous to him. He saw that the great theatrical loadstone [sic] was Mr. Garrick, who could, without the assistance of any great actors, always draw after him the best company, and fill the boxes. Lacy having too, about this time, prevailed on the duke of Grafton to promise renewal of the Drury-lane patent, he wisely thought, the best way to secure so valuable an acquisition as Mr. Garrick, would be to offer him the moiety of it. This he well knew was a proposition worthy of acceptance; and, in case he closed with the offer, would render the other moiety of greater value to himself than the whole would be without such a partner.[6]

The Irish actor Thomas Sheridan also recognized Garrick's value, and made him a proposal around the same time that Lacy invited Garrick to purchase half the Drury Lane Theatre patent. Writing on 21 April 1747, Sheridan confides:

> I have a scheme to propose to you, which at first view may seem a little extraordinary to you, but if rightly considered, must turn to both our advantages: if you could be brought to divide your immortality with me, we might, like Castor and Pollux, appear always in different hemispheres ... in plain English, what think you of dividing the kingdoms between us; to play one winter in London, and another in Dublin? ... it will make us always new in both kingdoms, and consequently always more followed; and I am satisfied that Dublin is as well able to pay one actor for the winter as London.[7]

Sheridan's whimsical scheme of rotating theatrical monarchies limits each partner's potential gain to whatever the novelty factor might add to each's usual performance earnings. Sheridan's proposal, viewed in the hindsight of Garrick's established celebrity, now reads as laughable hubris. Its timing and terms indicate that both Sheridan and Lacy saw Garrick's reputation and future labour as an actor as the commodity they hoped to secure. Lacy's offer had the most potential for Garrick. In acquiring the "great theatrical loadstone," Lacy got more than he bargained for, however.

In 1747, Lacy had deeper experience in the theatre industry than did Garrick. Lacy had played minor and middling parts on several London stages beginning in the 1720s, written an afterpiece (*Fame; or Queen Elizabeth's Trumpets*, 1737), built a theatre at Ranelagh, and acted as manager over Garrick.[8] Perhaps because of his experience or his residual feelings of authority from their former relationship, Lacy was not always as silent a partner or as removed from the business of the stage as Garrick would have liked. In a document endorsed by Garrick, "Some Letters that pass'd between Mr. Lacy & Me, upon a Difference between Us,"[9] the division of labour, formerly a verbal agreement between Garrick and Lacy, is newly articled with cool precision. The first four of the seven articles appear below:

> 1:st That the settling or altering the business of the Stage to be left entirely to Mr Garrick who shall immediately communicate the same to the Prompter for the information of Mr Lacy with this promise that whensoever Mr Lacy shall apprehend that Mr Garrick is pursuing measures injurious to his, Mr Lacy's property he shall state his objection to John Paterson Esq (who undertakes to act as the common Friend of both), and to him only; and Mr Garrick shall submit to his determination.
>
> 2dly: That all Actors Actresses Singers Dancers & other Servants shall be hired or discharged and their salaries or allowances settled or encreased by joint consent and not otherwise.
>
> 3:dly That the Accounts and all other business of the Copartnership shall be jointly carried on at the Office, Mr Garrick by reason of his attendance upon the Business of the Stage being at liberty to employ his Brother George Garrick to attend & act for him in the said Office; But to give his personal Attendance whensoever any Matter of importance shall in the judgement of Mr Lacy appear to require it.
>
> 4:thly That in case of any future difference the Partner who shall think himself injured shall (without venting any speeches in publick to the disadvantage of the other) state his complaint to Mr Paterson who shall decide thereon & finally settle the dispute between them.

This agreement continued without substantial legal intervention from its negotiation in 1749 until Lacy's death in 1774. Notably, the fourth article insists upon public silence in case of dispute between the patentees. Disagreements between Garrick and Lacy are not to be "vented" in public, but kept within the organization, and if necessary, brought to private arbitration.

The document interposes between the patentees three intermediaries for the purposes of communication within the theatre: the lawyer John Paterson is to hold the agreement and to be arbiter of any difference between the partners; David's brother George Garrick is to look after business transactions with Lacy; and the theatre's prompter is to communicate to Lacy information pertaining to management of the stage, which is to be decided by Garrick. The agreement demonstrates both parties' interest in presenting a united front in the public imagination. Rumours of insecurity in an organization's management make hiring for that business and marketing its products much more challenging. Lacy's previous failed theatrical triumvirate with the bankers Richard Green and Norton Amber no doubt still resonated in the public memory, and news of further instability in management would not have been beneficial to the theatre's business. Both parties contracted that the public story of Drury Lane should not include disruptive news of quarrelling patentees.

Their vow of media silence may have been the only article of the patentees' agreement that functioned (almost) as it was supposed to do. Garrick's correspondence shows that he had to rely upon intermediaries to retrench his partner's repeated incursions into the "business of the Stage," and to keep the theatre's marketing message – that Drury Lane was the home of Shakespeare – consistent. Garrick writes to Somerset Draper on 17 August 175[1], thanking him for looking in at the playhouse, and asking,

> Have you seen the *Great Lacy* lately? I wish, when you have that pleasure, that you would hint your great surprise and dislike to *Maddox*'s rope-dancing upon our stage. I cannot possibly agree to such a prostitution upon any account; and nothing but downright starving would induce me to bring such defilement and abomination into the *house of William Shakespeare*. What a mean, mistaken creature is this Par[tn]er of mine![10]

Recourse was had to the lawyer Paterson as mediator on several occasions; on others, George Garrick ran between his brother and "Timbertop" (Garrick's dismissive nickname for Lacy).[11] Garrick's letters bemoan Lacy's disagreements with George, his attempts at hiring personnel without consultation, and his demanding the cast book just as Garrick was trying to fill up the company.[12] The Garrick–Lacy relationship reverberated with mutual disrespect and dislike. Garrick remarked to George Colman in a letter of 10 March 1765, "[Lacy] will never forgive my being the means of his making a figure in the world – but this between Ourselves."[13]

Yet Garrick and Lacy's business partnership was an immediate financial success. Kalman Burnim observes that in "the first year of their management Garrick and Lacy realized a net profit of £6334 for the season. By the end of their third season (1749–50), they had their investment back. At the same time, each manager drew an additional £500 per year as salary. Garrick received another £500 per season as the leading actor, plus the profit of a clear benefit."[14] Partnership was profitable, just not pleasant.

Garrick and Lacy generally succeeded in keeping their mutual dislike out of public view. They appeared together on stage – the *Public Advertiser* for 23 January 1754 announces that Garrick will play "The Bastard, Being the First Time of his appearing in that Character," with Lacy as the Dauphin in a revival of Shakespeare's *King John*. The *Town and Country Magazine*'s column "British Theatre, No. 3" (1769) remarks on their harmonious relationship, "both are equally satisfied with their authority and power, and are too sagatious [sic] to enter into any altercation by which their mutual interest would be greatly injured." More convincingly, media representations of differences between the two are scant. Rumours of disagreement in 1766 were tersely dismissed: "Mr. Garrick and Mr. Lacey have entirely accommodated their affairs, and Drury-Lane Theatre is still to continue under the direction of its old Managers," which article appeared in *Owen's Weekly Chronicle and Westminster Journal*, the *Gazetteer and New Daily Advertiser* and the *London Evening Post* for 13–15 March 1766. Even in trenchant satires such as William Shirley's pamphlet *A Bone for the Chroniclers to Pick* (1758), "Jemmy" and "David," however rascally themselves, still support one another's stratagems. In response to Garrick's expressed desire for "Immortality," Jemmy assures him:

> "If they scoff at your *Prologues* and hiss at your *Farces*,
> I'll order our Bruisers to kick all their A–es.
> Then think how the Chroniclers trumpet your Name!
> Come you shall be immortal, immortal in Fame."[15]

The two patentees' presentation of a united front and their decision to maintain media silence regarding any differences in their management relationship can be glimpsed in the suppression of a potential scandal involving the actor Thomas Weston. Weston, who had got his theatrical start as a spouter, then a stroller, was a low comedian who specialized in a particular character: the "*dry, vulgar simpleton.*"[16] Less amusingly, off stage, he had the character of a drunken debtor, perpetually pursued by creditors. The anonymous posthumous *Memoirs of that Celebrated Comedian, and very Singular Genius Thomas Weston* (1776) describes several of his shifts to evade bailiffs, including scrambling into the Haymarket Theatre via a tennis court near the theatre's upper dressing room windows.[17] During the 1772 spring benefit season, Weston was caught by bailiffs for a debt the theatre managers at Drury Lane had refused to clear; they had already withheld money from Weston's benefit on 21 April to go toward previous debts. Weston convinced the bailiffs to accompany him to the theatre, where he was supposed to be on stage, playing his signature role, Jerry Sneak in *The Mayor of Garratt*, in a benefit for the dancers M. Daigueville and Signora Vidini. When the excuse was made that Weston was not able to appear due to illness, he popped up from amongst the gallery's audience, contradicted this excuse, and blackmailed the managers into clearing his debt by nearly causing a riot. The *London Evening Post* for 25–28 April 1772 reported:

> On Friday night, between the play and farce at Drury-lane Theatre, a disturbance arose, which continued for a full hour. A Comedian, it appeared, was in debt to the managers a sum of money, on which account they had stopt the cash received on his benefit night; this the Comedian did not like, and therefore on Friday sent word that he could not play, as he was arrested, and detained in a Spunging-house, but desired that no apology should be made use of his being suddenly taken ill (the usual Stage plea) as it would be an egregious falshood. After the play, a person came forward, and informed the audience, that Mr. W. was suddenly taken ill, and could not perform. W. instantly started up in the front of the upper gallery, and informed the house that he was not ill, but in the custody of an officer, and if the audience would have patience he would inform them of the whole affair; a long altercation ensued, Mr. Vernon went on repeatedly, and after much *pro* and *con.* Mr. W. came down and played his part. A publication of the whole affair was promised.[18]

The Daily Advertiser for 27 April, and the *General Evening Post* and the *Middlesex Journal: or, Chronicle of Liberty* for 23–25 April all printed similar accounts, the last two adding: "The managers promised the town a publication of the whole affair; 'till it appears, it will be impossible to know whether they or W—— are to blame."

The night's beneficiaries were two foreign dancers who were dancing between the acts of the mainpiece, *Twelfth Night*. Weston's disruption, which goes unnoted in the Cross-Hopkins Theatre Diaries, probably interfered with the dancers' climactic presentation, the "Grand Historical Ballet" of *Psyche*, which followed Act V of the mainpiece before the farce. If so, it was a shrewdly positioned bit of interference for the low actor to rise from amongst the lower-class, pro-British gallery audience to demand his due, timed so as not to interfere with the benefits of fellow actors, on whom Weston might have to rely in future, and disrupting only the efforts of foreign dancers.

The managers may have promised the turbulent audience publication of the "whole affair," as the newspaper account proclaims, but Garrick was careful to assess the public mood first. To his brother George, Garrick wrote on 27 April, asking about public reaction to Weston's "Advertisement." The so-called "Advertisement" probably refers to an occasional apology written by Garrick for Weston to speak in the theatre on the Saturday immediately following the near-riot. This "Advertisement," written in Garrick's hand, is to be returned to Garrick from Ralph Griffiths of the *Monthly Review*, and a few copies may, Garrick's letter says, be printed by George for distribution, but it is to be kept out of the newspapers if possible:

> I shd be glad to know by a Note sent with my Newspapers today, what ye folks say of Weston's Advertisement–I think Griffith shd absolutely get me ye Copy of ye Advertisement written in my hand–Weston may take a Copy if he will–you must I think get a few printed of ye acct–had it been publish'd in ye Papers, it wd have look'd as if we got him to ask pardon, & then at ye same time set ye Publick against him–in my opinion, & Mr Lacy shd know that, all theatrical Squabbles wth Actors shd be compris'd as soon as possible with honour to ye managers, & no Accounts produc'd– however if you are call'd upon, & are oblig'd to publish–it will not be our fault–the head piece to it may run thus–
> "As Mr Weston of Drury Lane Theatre was pleas'd to make a Complaint to ye Publick last Fryday Night in an unprecedented manner, the Managers are, as it were, call'd upon to publish ye following short account, this can be ye only excuse for giving ye Publick ye least trouble upon so impertinent a Matter:["]
> ——Something like this will be right–if there is no noise–it will be better as it is–our unwillingness to trouble ye Publick will appear right in Us– Weston's letter to ye Managers shd be full of distress & repentance–let Lacy see it if proper. I fear that he gave ye fool hopes of letting him have *all* ye Money –[19]

Garrick's prepared introduction to a managerial explication of Weston's "unprecedented" cheek was not used in the newspapers. While some form of apology may have been exacted from Weston (perhaps two: one "Advertisement" delivered live in the theatre, and one letter of "distress & repentance" to the managers, in which it seems George is to coach Weston, and to convey to Lacy only if it is "proper"), Garrick's concern is to not create additional media "noise," and to bring the managers out of this situation without troubling the public. George Garrick – one of the patentees' designated mediators – is to remind Lacy to keep the dispute in-house and undocumented. Even though Lacy and Garrick have disagreed about the amount to pay Weston, Garrick appears willing to concede the point to avoid altercations. Indeed, Weston's *Memoirs* relate that not only did they clear the debt, but the managers imitated Weston's bailiff-avoidance tricks: "To prevent the like accident in future [... the managers] had apartments allotted him [Weston] in Vinegar-yard, which communicated with the theatre, and here he lived during the winter season."[20]

What was the public response to the Weston incident? In the *General Evening Post* for 28 April 1772, 'ANIMADVERTOR' (George Steevens)[21] called out Weston's "late misbehaviour," writing, "he has endeavoured to create a riot in the theatre, has given a personal disturbance to the town, and to the extent of his influence endangered (as the consequences of a playhouse riot may be very fatal to the performers) the bread of all his brethren under the direction of Mr. Garrick." It was "unpardonable," Steevens opined, for actors like Weston and Ned Shuter to allow their vices to keep them from their responsibility to appear on stage, and "To admit *any* palliation, is to open a door for *every* possible misconduct in our actors." Steevens's letter was the only media notice to name Weston; other references are coyly oblique, referring only to a "Comedian." The *London Chronicle* for 25–28 April reports: "The debts of a certain Comedian, at present in durance, are said to amount to near 12,000*l*."[22] The same paper for 28–30 April jests that a new theatre is forming up in King's Bench Prison: "Many celebrated Performers, we are assured, are engaged for the entertainment of the Inhabitants of that place, particularly some *low* Comedians, who have lived so *high*, that they have not been able to support themselves on *eight* or *nine hundred* pounds a year!" The *General Evening Post* for 23–25 April cites a "correspondent" who reveals that the comedian's debt is "only 700*l*.," and consoles its readers, "we hear, that as he does not owe 1000*l*. to any single creditor, the act of insolvency will speedily restore him to the service of the public." Nothing appears in the *Monthly Review* for April or May 1772 about the Weston incident, so if Griffiths had access to Garrick's hand-written "Advertisement" as the letter above suggests, that article seems to have been returned to Garrick as requested, and suppressed.

Media noise of the Weston incident was muted. This is the more impressive as Garrick's reputation for avarice, upon which Weston's accusations that the managers had stopped his benefit proceeds played, would have made of this event low-hanging fruit for Garrick's foes. The Weston incident was soon eclipsed in the news cycle by greater scandal: the accusations of sodomy levelled at Isaac Bickerstaff, which began to appear in the news on 30 April, and the publication of William Kenrick's

Love in the Suds. While animosity continued to bubble between Garrick and Weston,[23] the public remained unaware of the differences between the patentees in this and other disputes. If in no other sense, in their agreement to keep their disagreements in-house, rather than airing them in the media, Lacy and Garrick were united.

Garrick's Prompters, Cross and Hopkins

The prompter is named in the 1749 agreement as another intermediary who might interpose between the patentees to communicate business intelligence within the theatre. The prompter's task was larger than his title, and his duties included much more than feeding actors their forgotten lines. David Hunter observes, in relation to the Covent Garden prompter's diary of John Stede, that the prompter was responsible for a variety of tasks crucial to running the theatre:

> First, control of text: copying out parts for actors; procuring performance licenses; and maintaining the house's collection of texts. Second, production direction: directing rehearsals – both individual and group; maintaining the production copy, so that all the cues, property hand-offs, scene changes, curtain lifts, and so on were marked; stage managing each performance; and maintaining the cast book and advising on casting. Third, publicity and response: writing out the publicity bills; and advising the manager/owner on public reaction. In other words, he was the stage manager, personnel director, public relations manager, librarian, and secretary.[24]

The two men who served as prompters during Garrick's tenure as co-patentee with Lacy performed these multiple duties, and served as intermediaries who could communicate the business of the stage from one patentee to the other. Fortunately, some of these communications were recorded in a series of notebooks now known as the Cross-Hopkins Theatre Diaries, after those prompters, Richard Cross and William Hopkins.[25]

The first of the two prompters was Richard Cross (d. 20 February 1760), whose career at Drury Lane spanned the years 1741–60. Cross was an actor who played on every London stage, in summer theatre in Richmond and Twickenham, and in booths in Bartholomew and Southwark fairs, beginning circa 1729. Even for a period in which actors were expected to learn and retain a large number of roles, Cross's versatility and utility as an actor are astonishing. Cross acted (at a conservative estimate) over 130 minor roles, and frequently served as an extra.[26] He could step in

as Surly or Face in *The Alchemist*; as Archer or Aimwell in *The Beaux'
Stratagem*; or as Duncan in *Macbeth*. Cross was less successful as an author.
His one novel, *The Adventures of John Le-Brun* (1739), sank under the
weight of its labyrinthine plots; and his attempt at farce, *The Henpeck'd
Captain*, performed 1 May 1749, was, in his own words, "damn'd before
half over."[27]

As Judith Milhous and Robert D. Hume have remarked, Cross's diary is
useful for its financial estimates of the house take and its recording of the
repertoire.[28] Other entries interpolated amongst these records enhance
understanding of mid-eighteenth-century drama's reception, for Cross
attends to the audience's hisses, groans and laughter. Cross's diary entries
range from sensational and humorous to heart-wrenching. On a Friday the
thirteenth in 1758, during a performance of *Romeo and Juliet*, Cross
recorded a grim stage accident: "Mr. Fletewood in ye. fight with Paris in
ye last Act, having a Sword by his Side instead of a Foil, run Mr. Austin
[Paris] into the belly, he lay some time but at last call'd to be taken off – a
Surgeon was sent for – No harm, a Small wound, & he is recover'd." Cross
enjoyed, as did the audience, the joke of David Garrick playing Benedick
on 28 September 1749, in his first stage appearance after his marriage.

The prompter had a public identity, visible in newspaper advertisements
such as this for his benefit in 1753: *"Drury-Lane, Saturday, April 21. Mr.
Cross has been very indefatigable in his Business all this Season, as usual,
and though his constant Attendance in his Theatrical Employment,
renders it impossible for him to wait upon the Nobility, Gentry, and his
Friends, it is thought, as* EVERY MAN IN HIS HUMOUR *is to be
performed for the last Time this Winter, that the Town will* know their
Cue *to go there on his Night* without a Prompter.*"*[29] Cross figures as the
character Crouch in the satirical green-room drama *Hecate's Prophecy*
(1758), where he is shown in an active media-relations role, inserting
Fidget's (Garrick's) work anonymously into the print milieu:

FIDG: Has Type done that Pamphlet yet?
CRO: O, yes, Sir, and it'll be *publish'd* soon; on *Monday*, I believe.
FIDG: Hark you,–he don't know that -*I wrote* it, does he?
CRO: No, Sir, –not for the World, no, no, no.[30]

From his entries in the Theatre Diaries, Cross emerges as a loyal, valuable
servant of the theatre, vigilantly observing audience response to maintain
theatrical productions' quality, and advising the manager upon productions' financial viability. After recording the performances and incidents of
thirteen seasons, Cross's notation ends on 23 January 1760, with

Hopkins's hand resuming the journal the next day. Cross died less than a month later. The *Public Advertiser* for 21 February 1760 announced Cross's death, praising him as a man whose "Abilities in his Station were equal to any in the Theatre, and whose Integrity might have done Credit to any Profession."

William Hopkins (d. 1780), who succeeded Cross as prompter at Drury Lane in 1760, was "more remarkable for writing a neat expeditious hand, and being conversant in the regulation of the internal business of a Theatre, than for great abilities as an Actor," but was "perfectly qualified to superintend in getting up Plays."[31] Hopkins experimented with format: his diary entries are less orderly and uniform than those of Cross. Unlike Cross, Hopkins does not record estimates of the house take. Hopkins carefully observes the number of times each piece appeared in a season in his running notes, and his end-of-season notes add up the number of different plays, the number of different farces, and the total number of performing nights in a given season, indicating an interest in the repertoire's extent and variety.

Hopkins often includes insightful reception notes that show he paid at least as much attention to the audience as to the players. At an early-in-the-run command performance of George Colman's *The Deuce is in Him* he remarks: "The King & Queen Laugh'd much at the Farce" (6 November 1763). On 1 October 1772, Hopkins records a new actor's reception: "Mr. Dimond made his first appearance upon the Stage in the Part of Romeo, he is very young. a Smart Figure good Voice & made a very tolerable first appearance. he met with great Applause." The next day's *Morning Chronicle* puffed the actor in its "Theatrical Intelligence" column:

> Mr. Diamond [sic], the young gentleman who appeared for the first time in the character of *Romeo*, at Drury-lane theatre last night, was received with great applause. His figure is neat and smart, his features expressive, and his voice pleasing ... He trod the stage with a degree of ease, dignity, and firmness necessary for a Tragedian, but rarely seen on a first appearance. Mr. Garrick has evidently tutored him in his mode of delivery and actions ...

The puff so closely echoes the prompter's diary entry that it suggests that Hopkins's notes informed the newspaper's theatrical intelligence, and that like Cross before him, Hopkins assisted in creating and placing theatre news. Garrick apparently agreed with Hopkins's assessment of the young actor's potential, as William Wyatt Dimond was offered a contract for the next season.[32]

Hopkins's comments in the Theatre Diaries yield an impression of an acerbic, demanding person, fully committed to promoting and supporting the manager. He observes when actors are "imperfect" in their parts, as in a 4 November 1771 performance of *Tamerlane*: "Mr. Barry being Ill Mr. Reddish play'd Bajazet not the thing Miss Hayward Shamefully imperfect in Selima." When performers aim for roles above their usual ambit, he is apt to damn them with faint praise, as in this entry from 1 October 1771, when *As You Like It* and *The Padlock* were on the bill: "Mrs. Hunt Daughter of Mr. Dunstall her first appearance in Leonora a tolerable Voice figure & face so, so, pretty well receiv'd." When Mr. Cautherly chose to appear as Don John in *The Chances* for his benefit on 22 April 1772, Hopkins trolled out a deadpan "La, la!" Francis Gentleman neatly captures Hopkins's influence, calling him "the Lord Bute of Drury-Lane theatre."[33]

Only Garrick came up to Hopkins's exacting standards. Hopkins recorded that Garrick "play'd divinely" (on 18 December 1772, as Hamlet) and frequently enthused that "Mr. G" was "never better" (as on 19 February 1773, when he received "monstrous Applause" as Lear). This may have been politic praise, for Garrick checked the prompter's diary regularly: as James Winston recorded in "The Manager's Note-Book" (1838), Hopkins "took special care that [the diary] should always lie in his [Garrick's] way *accidentally*."[34] Figure 6 shows Hopkins's account of Garrick's intervention with the riotous audience at Henry Bate's comic opera, *The Blackamoor Wash'd White* (1776).

The prompter's role in observing a play's reception and financial viability, and in assisting the manager in media relations, is well illustrated by Cross's part in a theatrical competition known as "the battle of the Romeos."

"Pox on both your Houses": The Battle of the Romeos[35]

Early in the 1750 theatre season, *Romeo and Juliet* was the only show in London: Garrick's passionate yet cerebral Romeo, on stage at Drury Lane, was pitted against that of Covent Garden's handsome Spranger Barry for a tense twelve-night run.[36] Kalman Burnim summarizes critical commentary on the two performers as tending "to award Barry superiority in the first three acts, Garrick the final two. Some spectators . . . made a practice of leaving Covent Garden after Act III to catch the wind-up at Drury Lane."[37] The spectators' mobility facilitated comparative reviews that focused on the differentiation of the two male leads, such as this one, written by a female spectator: "Had I been Juliet to Garrick's Romeo,–so

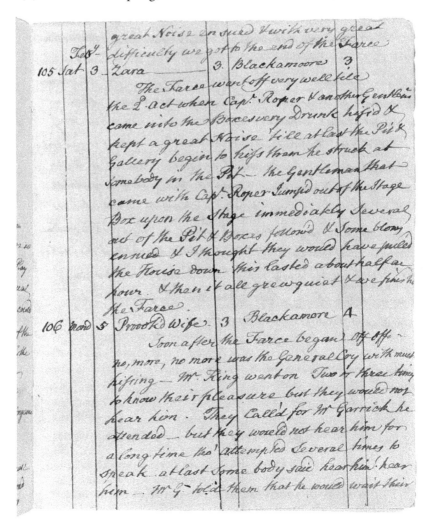

Figure 6   This page from the Cross-Hopkins Theatre Diaries (Folger Wa.104 (13)) shows prompter William Hopkins's account of audience unrest and Garrick's intercession at Henry Bate's *The Blackamoor Wash'd White*, 5 February 1776. After much hissing, Garrick told the audience "that he would wait their [sic] all Night with pleasure if they requir'd it–hear him! again was bellow'd out–he told them he waited to know their pleasure–whether they would have the Blackamoor go on or if they would have any other Farce then a great Noise ensued; assoon [sic] as they were quiet Mr. G. told them that his Theatrical Life would be very Short + he should be glad to end it in peace–A man in the Pit said if you have a mind to die in Peace don't let this Farce be play'd again." By permission of the Folger Shakespeare Library.

ardent and impassioned was he, I should have expected he would have come up to me in the balcony; but had I been Juliet to Barry's Romeo,–so tender, so eloquent, and so seductive was he, I should certainly have gone down to him!"[38] Francis Gentleman, who, with admirable even-handedness, saw the play three times at each house, perceived that "Mr. GARRICK commanded most applause – Mr. BARRY most tears."[39]And the *Gentleman's Magazine* that October wound up its theatrical review with an epigrammatic close: "At *Covent Garden* I saw JULIET *and* ROMEO; and at *Drury Lane*, ROMEO *and* JULIET."[40]

That spectators were at pains to oppose the two principals' performances, is not, however, to say that Garrick's and Barry's performances were so widely differential as to constitute opposites, as the balanced syntax of the spectators' accounts just referred to might at first suggest. Extant media coverage pertaining to the Battle of the Romeos suggests not just product differentiation and the production of celebrity by means of profitable competition, but an abiding public interest in mimicry and its place within theatrical representation.

While comparative, often lineage-like reviewing of actors' interpretations of the same role was common practice, Barry's and Garrick's Romeos prompted an unusually aggressive mode of comparative critical discourse, and it is worth considering why – aside from the simultaneity of the performances – the 1750 Battle was characterized as a battle. David Brewer locates the beginning of such theatrical contests in productions of *The Beggar's Opera* in 1728, and writes that competing productions imply a "challenge to interpretive monopolies."[41] This is true: however, I will suggest that a challenge to interpretive monopoly is carried out in this case, not only by differentiation in performance, but also by repetition and non-parodic performative imitation.

Spranger Barry and Susannah Maria Cibber had first acted *Romeo and Juliet* as Garrick's faithful servants at Drury Lane in 1748, when Garrick, then in his second season as manager, offered the public his new adaptation of the play. Garrick's adaptation appeared as a relative novelty; though Theophilus Cibber had produced his adaptation of the play at the Haymarket in 1744, it ran for only ten performances before the Licensing Act was invoked and further performances prevented.[42] An earlier treatment of the story in Thomas Otway's play *The History and Fall of Caius Marius* (1679) had last been performed in 1735.[43] In 1748, with Garrick's adaptation and Barry and Cibber in the leads at Drury Lane, the play enjoyed a successful run of almost identical length to that of the later 1750

Battle. The piquancy of the 1750 Battle of the Romeos derived in part from public knowledge that Barry had defected[44] from Garrick's self-proclaimed House of Shakespeare at Drury Lane to Rich's gaudy home of pantomime in Covent Garden, taking Garrick's Juliet (Mrs. Cibber), and Garrick's adaptation of the play with him, and thus, that their contest enacted the play's thematic obsession with filial disobedience meta-dramatically.

Alongside this grand gesture of defection, there was a series of smaller gestural thefts: to judge by descriptions of rehearsal technique at Drury Lane, Garrick was, in a very real sense, the parent of Barry's gestures and interpretation of the role. Thomas Davies recounts in *Dramatic Miscellanies* that it was Garrick's practice to instruct players in their roles by reading "a new or revived piece" to them and, as Garrick "took infinite pains to inform, he expected an implicit submission to his instructions."[45] Arthur Murphy is still more direct about the debt Barry's performance owed to Garrick. Of the 1748 production in which Barry and Cibber were the leads, Murphy writes:

> Having with great care prepared this play for the stage, he [Garrick] behaved to Barry in the most liberal manner. He knew, that in the lover's parts, he was a great favourite; and, to give him a fair opportunity, assigned to him the part of *Romeo*, with Mrs. Cibber to second him in the character of *Juliet*. Solicitous for the success of his alterations, he attended the rehearsals, and communicated all his ideas to the performers.[46]

What ideas did Garrick communicate to Barry in those rehearsals? Following Peter Holland's charge to be attentive to the aural dimension of theatre history,[47] we might speculate that Garrick's rehearsal practice of reading aloud influenced Barry's delivery. Garrick's characteristic rapidity of speech; his pauses; his sudden transitions in volume and mood; all of these would have been keenly observed by Barry. Both actors were praised for their vocal flexibility and quick transitions or breaks. The anonymous author of *The Theatrical Review for the Year 1757* termed Barry's voice "clear, and distinct" and declared "its greatest perfection is its prodigious flexibility, whereby it may be brought to bend at will, to the most sudden and most difficult transitions, from one passion to another; from despair, to a transport of joy; from the extreme of tender love, to the extreme of jealousy, etc." [48] Garrick, the writer suggests, has not one, but several "different voices, now tender and melting, now terrible and severe, then weak and broken, and sometimes whimpering, when the part requires it."[49]

Aside from their shared ability to project and break well, there are indications that Barry's and Garrick's Romeos shared certain gestural and vocal tricks. According to Luigi Riccoboni, each actor's response in the tomb scene of *Romeo and Juliet* was identical. In a plea for more variety across performances on the English stage, Riccoboni moans:

> With us the same Scene is always play'd in the same Manner, not only by the same Actor, but by every Actor who performs it: We know, therefore, before it comes, all that we are to admire ... that beautiful, though perhaps not proper, Attitude of *Romeo* at the Tomb, is always the same, not only in Mr. *Barry* and in Mr. *Garrick*, every Time each plays, but 'tis the same in both: On the contrary, let an *Italian* please ever so greatly once in his Scene, he never courts a second Applause by the same Attitude.[50]

Though Riccoboni does not specify what this wearyingly consistent "Attitude of Romeo at the Tomb" looked like, Theophilus Cibber does:

> the Actor, with folded Arms, advances about three or four Steps,—then jumps, and starts into an Attitude of Surprize:–At what?–Why, at the Sight of a Monument, he went to look for:—And there he stands, 'till a Clap from the Audience relieves him from his Post. Is this not forced? Is it not misplaced?[51]

Yet Romeo's reluctant, over-awed approach to the tomb was admired by some audience members, as an appreciative poem, "*On seeing Mr.* Barry *and Mrs.* Cibber *in* ROMEO *and* JULIET," attests:

> WHEN *Barry* fraught with all the rage of woe,
> His accents broken, and his paces slow,
> Tow'rds *Juliet's* tomb in desperation moves,
> Each look, each gesture shews how much he loves.[52]

Not only had Garrick instructed Barry in the role (as he later did again, with Dimond), but the public was predisposed to consider Barry Romeo's epitome, both because of his precedence, and because he was tall, handsome and well cast as the lover. William Kenrick observed, "the Impression the first Person in ev'ry Part gives us, is of such Force, that we think him an Original, and the very Person the Poet has describ'd ... no one that ever saw him [Barry], could form a Wish for a Person more suited to the Idea the Poet gives us of Romeo."[53] John Hill, who like Kenrick nourished a grudge against Garrick, rationalized his preference for Barry with convincing plot references: in Romeo, "It is the figure and the address that strike [Juliet]; for heaven's sake therefore let us have address and figure in the player. Here is no family, no past distress, nor any remembrance of past services: it is the love of a girl for a youth; founded only on his external accomplishments; for she has seen no other. The whole character therefore is out of nature, if we have not all that can charm a woman in the lover." Hill concludes: "Among the heroes of tragedy rage or grief are the two great passions . . . in parts where violence and fury are the great characteristics, Mr. Garrick succeeds best, and Mr. Barry in these distinguished by tenderness; and in the character of Romeo, where there is a great deal of both, they are both so amazingly eminent: if, upon the whole, we see Mr. Barry with the greatest pleasure, it is not because Mr. Garrick is the inferior actor, but because Romeo is more distinguished by love than rage."[54] Those persons who purchased Garrick's 1748 edition of the play saw Barry's name at the top of the Dramatis Personae, further reinforcing this identification in print. Garrick's name does not appear in this edition.[55]

In the public view, Barry owned the part. In 1750, Garrick was in effect waging an uncanny competition with his own textual and gestural interpretation of the play. One may read Gentleman's agonized division of the play into parts in which each actor excelled not as a testament to variety, but as evidence of similarity: if both Garrick and Barry played the tomb scene similarly, which actor did it best? Gentleman splits it between them: "Mr. BARRY first part of the tomb scene, and Mr. GARRICK from where the poison operates to the end."[56]

Given Barry's pre-eminence in the role, Garrick's motivation for taking it on in 1750 after Barry's defection to Covent Garden demands explication and for that, I turn to Garrick's correspondence, and to the financial side of the battle. Garrick's correspondence with his co-patentee Lacy in July of 1750 figures an early staging of *Romeo and Juliet* as the opening salvo in a season of revenge: "I have been informed that Barry and Cibber are certainly engaged with Rich, which neither amazes nor intimidates me:–Let them do their worst, we must have the best company, and by a well layed regular plan, we shall be able to make them as uneasy with Rich, as Rich will be with them."[57] However pleasant the prospect of revenge, the success of the company and the season is of primary importance to Garrick as manager. How much did *Romeo and Juliet* contribute to the success of both the 1748 and 1750 seasons, and how did such direct competition affect the estimated house take at Drury Lane in 1750? Was spending so much time "cut[ting] their combs" good business?

Here, I will show some of the effects that competition was perceived to have upon theatre income by the prompter, Cross. In the theatrical season of 1748, Barry and Cibber appeared in the title roles of Garrick's adaptation of *Romeo and Juliet* at Drury Lane on 29 November. The play reappeared two nights later on 1 December, and ran for thirteen consecutive performances, and then appeared at intervals throughout the remainder of the season. *Romeo and Juliet* was Drury Lane's most frequently performed mainpiece in 1748, and amongst 48 different mainpieces, *Romeo and Juliet* occupied a 12 per cent share of receipts when receipts are grouped by title. It was also the most profitable, drawing in £2,990; the second most profitable play, *Much Ado about Nothing*, made about £1,000 less. The profitability factor, or the quotient of a show's seasonal profits divided by its seasonal appearances, shows that the play is more profitable than average (~1.06); when we subtract benefit performances, the profitability factor goes up to 1.11. With Barry and Cibber as the leads, Garrick's adaptation was a hit. Losing this repertoire to Covent Garden in 1750 along with the players would have been a significant blow.

In the 1750 theatrical season, with Garrick and Bellamy in the leading roles, at no point in the Battle of the Romeos did the Drury Lane house take drop below £90, according to Cross's estimates, with the high points being the opening night at £180, and the closing night at £160. Excluding benefits, the profitability factor is even slightly higher than it was in 1748: 1.13. Once again, the play accounted for a significant 12 per cent of Drury Lane's receipts when receipts are grouped by repertoire in 1750.[58] Retaining the repertoire was the right choice, as it proved even more profitable with Garrick in the lead, in direct competition with his former protégé, than it had with Barry. Though audiences perceived similarities across Barry's and Garrick's performances (such as their hesitant approach to the tomb), their perception of imitation did not impede the profitability of the performance at Drury Lane.

In both 1748 and 1750, *Romeo and Juliet* was the most frequently performed play, brought in the most net income, and, correcting for benefit performances, was among Drury Lane's most profitable titles. Even if Garrick was unsuccessful in damaging Rich's take at Covent Garden, he kept his very profitable adaptation of *Romeo and Juliet* in Drury Lane's repertoire. Garrick also published a new print adaptation in 1750, making some textual changes: famously, he jettisoned mention of Rosaline, presenting Romeo as Juliet's faithful lover throughout the play, a move consonant with Garrick's own off-stage domestic fidelity, while the unfaithful, mutable Barry continued to portray a changeable Romeo. Of all the textual changes made to the 1750 edition of the play, however, perhaps none was so crucial as Garrick's replacement of Barry's name in the Dramatis Personae with his own – a shrewd and unusual move at a time when old cast lists frequently lingered in print editions long after the roles had been taken up by other actors.[59] Garrick's firm purchase on the play, exerted in print and performance, demonstrated that the loss of Barry and Cibber to the company was not so great or irreparable as those actors had perhaps imagined. Cross's notations concerning the house take, intended for the managers' information, challenge George Anne Bellamy's later contention that Garrick only won the contest by papering the house.[60]

Garrick's final vengeful pleasure was in turning his competitors into an unwilling audience. He wrote to the Countess of Burlington, "our Antagonists yielded last thursday Night & we play'd ye Same Play (Romeo & Juliet) on ye Fryday to a very full house to very great applause; Mr Barry & Mrs Cibber came incog to see Us, & I am very well-assur'd they receiv'd no little Mortification –."[61] Garrick's delight in the play's business success and at his competitors' chagrin in slinking in to watch his performance "incog" is palpable. Revenge is not always profitable, but it seems that this well-laid plan was. To complement these financial portraits, we also have the qualitative observations from Cross's Theatre Diary, which in reference to *Romeo and Juliet* is particularly attentive to the reception of performative paratexts.

The Battle of the Romeos occurred early in Garrick's managerial career, and was fought out over a more restricted mediascape than that of the 1760s and 1770s, when Garrick had remarkable media coverage, thanks to his relationships with the bookseller Thomas Becket and newspaper publishers Henry Bate and William and Henry Sampson Woodfall, amongst others; and in part to his proprietary interests in newspapers. Of the newspapers then publishing in London, the *London Gazette*, the *Penny Post or the Morning Advertiser* and *Read's Weekly Journal or British Gazetteer* have nothing to say of the Battle during its run.

Newspaper coverage of the Battle is largely limited to playbills, advertisements for related print publications, and reprintings of the two productions' occasional prologues and epilogues, with little overt commentary or reviewing. These items appear in four papers: the thrice-weekly *Whitehall Evening Post; Or, London Intelligencer*, the *London Evening Post*, the *General Evening Post* and the daily *General Advertiser*, which had the most extensive coverage, as it was the authorized publisher of the theatres' bills. Exemplary advertisements of publications related to the Battle include such things as notices for the *British Magazine*, which contained prologues delivered by Barry and Garrick,[62] and promotions of an occasional number of *The Kapélion, or Poetical Ordinary* which promised "A Parallel between Mr. Barry and Mr. Garrick in the Character of

Romeo."[63]Advertisements for print editions of *Romeo and Juliet*, including Theophilus Cibber's adaptation, also appear.[64] Spectators of the staged contest were encouraged to look for variety, not on stage, but in print, as the last stanza of a poetic Fable published in the *Westminster Journal* for 27 October 1750 suggests:

> At home, if on your books you feed,
> Variety, at least, you read:
> When Shakespear tires, if he can tire,
> Others, new pleasure may inspire.
> A sermon, or a pastoral letter,
> (The dullest of their kind) is better,
> Or law reports, or quack physicians,
> Than players mouthing repetitions.[65]

Notably, media representation of the Battle was a war of words: though Garrick was adept at commissioning and distributing images of himself *en rôle*, the best-known images of Barry and Garrick as Romeo post-date the contest.[66] The words with the widest media distribution were the competing productions' prologues and epilogues.

Novelties, including fresh prologues, epilogues, spectacles, music, personnel and scenes, snowballed as the contest wore on, and these have been documented by scholars including Kalman Burnim, Vanessa Cunningham[67] and Michael Burden.[68] These novelties were not just observable to spectators of the drama, but to readers of newspapers. Generally, advertisements for Drury Lane and Covent Garden appear together, like conjoined twins, in the *General Advertiser*, offering the reader a chance to compare the two houses' bills, and make a choice of entertainment based on repertoire, performers or divertissements. What is notable about the proliferation of novelties is the parity across the two productions. The advertisements in the *General Advertiser* for 28 September 1750, for instance, juxtapose Garrick's appearance in the role of Romeo as a novelty ("The Part of Romeo to be performed by Mr. GARRICK, *Being the First Time of his Appearing in that Character*") with the novelty of Barry's first appearance on a new stage.

While some novelties, such as the funeral dirges composed by Thomas Arne (for Covent Garden) and William Boyce (for Drury Lane) to accompany the new scene of Juliet's funeral procession,[69] undoubtedly affected each theatre's bottom line, the parity of the two spectacles on stage and as staged for the press in duelling advertisements ultimately threw attention back to the performers' interpretations and to the metatheatric pleasure inherent in comparing two performances. Oddly, the least costly of these novelties, the prologues and epilogues, seem to be most significant in shaping the play's reception.

From the perspective of Drury Lane's prompter, Cross, the performative paratexts – not the interpretations of the mainpiece by the lead actors – seem to be the crucial point of differentiation amongst performances at his house. Cross was attentive to the role of prologues and epilogues in fashioning public reception of the Battle. On the first night, 28 September, Cross writes: "The Audience excus'd Mr. Garrick speaking ye. prologue"; on the second, "They oblig'd him to speak it" (29 September); on the third night, 1 October, "Nothing said about ye. prolog:" In the margin, Cross notes: "Both ye. Houses play'd on ye. same day, Romeo & Juliet, Mr. Barry & Mrs. Cibber at Covent Garden against Mr. Garrick & Miss Bellamy at Drury Lane – Miss Bellamy never appear'd upon this Stage before, & was greatly receiv'd – both houses too added a Scene of Juliet's funeral." This paratextual differentiation, literally demanded by spectators during the Battle ("They oblig'd him to speak"), stretched not only from one playhouse to the next, but also longitudinally, widening the competition to include spectators' memories of past performances in the same house, to the point where Cross's entry on the second-last night of the run, 11 October, records "a new Epilogue upon the two Occasional prologues spoken by Mrs. Clive – Great App:" – an epilogue that referred to both Garrick's and Barry's earlier-delivered prologues.[70] Examination of a few of these performative paratexts demonstrates why Cross was so interested in noting their reception alongside his financial data. These not-so-ephemeral pieces show the circulation of critical opinion often begins with actors commenting on stage on their own performances.

Drury Lane's 1750 season opened on 8 September with a prologue in which Garrick set the conditions through which Barry's defection to Covent Garden could be seen as a movement from high to low. The Battle of the Romeos is presaged with a magazine of martial metaphors: Drury Lane's actors are prepared to best their foes "Arm'd cap-a-pie in self-sufficient merit" (line 16); they fight for the audience's presumed appetite for "the nobler scene" of Shakespearean entertainment: "To keep the field, all methods we'll pursue; / The conflict glorious! For we fight for you" (lines 37–38). Garrick acknowledges the "commotions in our mimick state" (line 4), and takes notice of the advance publicity surrounding Barry and Cibber's defection: "To shake our souls, the papers of the day / Drew forth the adverse power in dread array; / A power, might strike the boldest with dismay" (lines 12–14). The Battle of the Romeos was publicly perceived as a battle because Garrick's "New Occasional Prologue Spoken at the Opening of Drury-Lane Theatre" was widely reprinted – in at least six different venues in September alone. It was also frequently delivered: Garrick's prologue was repeated in Drury Lane on 8, 11, 13, 15 and 18 September; its publication announced on the 21st; delivered again on 27 and 29 September.[71] In this prologue, as we have seen, Garrick brands Drury Lane as the house of Shakespeare: "Sacred to Shakespeare, was this spot design'd, / To pierce the heart, and humanize the mind" (lines 25–26).

Yet Barry's responding prologue of 28 September 1750, also delivered frequently, announced 29 September, and "every day to 11 October, being omitted only on 9 October,"[72] lays claim to Shakespeare with equal determination, and emphasizes Covent Garden's reputation and market advantage in offering audiences variety:

> If Shakespear's passion, or if Johnson's art,
> Can fire the fancy, or can warm the heart,
> That task be ours:———But if you damn their scenes,
> And heroes must give way to Harlequins,
> We, too, can have recourse to mime and dance,
> Nay there, I think, we have the better chance.[73]

There is justice in Barry's claim to Shakespeare as a shared property of both theatric houses. Paul Sawyer observes that in production of works by Shakespeare, the competition was not far behind Drury Lane: "The frequency of productions is not significantly different, with Drury Lane staging a total of 1,759 Shakespearean plays to its rival's 1,627 from the 1715–16 season to the 1760–1 season, an average of about 38 to 35 per season ... Rich did not neglect Shakespeare."[74] Barry's prologue dramatizes the power imbalance between himself, a mere player, and managerial "Monarchs" like Garrick who have "out Heroded" Herod in the green room, by characterizing himself as an heroic figure of resistance (Bajazet) and Garrick, not as Tamerlane, but as the ridiculous, interfering playwright Bayes: "O! they can torture twenty-thousand ways: / Make bouncing Bajazet retreat from Bayes" (lines 13–14, 15–16). Barry cites lines from Garrick's occasional prologue with heavy irony, rejecting the self-positioning of those "Managers of Merit" who claim to "'take the Field with spirit'" (lines 11–12). However, against Garrick's frequent delivery of the original lines in print and performance, Barry's bitter citation may have begun to sound less ironic than derivative; his self-positioning less heroically rebellious than sulky and subordinate.

Garrick's twenty-day jump on Barry's prologue meant that his prologue was printed in September papers and journals; Barry's in October. This delay, along with Barry's citation of lines from Garrick's prologue, gives Barry's prologue the appearance of stale wit. While Covent Garden's market position and ability to cater to the public desire for novelty may have been stronger, Barry's prologue withered after a short outing in the contemporary press.[75] Garrick's "Occasional Prologue" outlived its occasion; it was reprinted and reproduced by the amateur actors known as spouters[76] even after Garrick's retirement, as it appears in spouting companions such as *The Theatrical Bouquet*, published in 1778, with the performative directive "Spoken by Mr. Garrick."[77] John Thieme correctly cites "hero-worship of Garrick" as an "important factor contributing to the rise of spouting-clubs."[78] More than 13 per cent of spouting companions' content acknowledges Garrick as speaker or author, and of course, much of Garrick's repertoire was so well known as to not need attributions, so this number would only rise if all the works identified with Garrick were included. The *Modern London Spy* (1781) mentions excerpts from *Romeo and Juliet* as favoured spouting pieces, so it is possible that the Battle of the Romeos continued, in smaller scale, in spouting clubs, with spouters imitating Garrick's Romeo and delivering his prologue as "Spoken by Mr. Garrick," long after his death.[79]

The third and last performative paratext I will discuss is the epilogue written by Garrick and delivered by Catherine Clive on 11 October 1750 at Drury Lane, and repeated on 13, 15, 16, 18 and 19 October, after different plays.[80] Garrick plotted the epilogue's content and tone carefully, as he wrote to the Countess of Burlington on 13 October: "I have written an Epilogue for Clive, which is an Answer to Barry's almost universally Exploded prologue – We have got ye Laugh on our Side, & by turning the whole to Joke, We are at present in ye highest Spirits."[81] Having "exploded" Barry's prologue through the printed and performed repetition of his own, Garrick exploited Clive's reputation as a feisty comedienne, which positioned her well to deliver the epilogue. Clive was not part of the cast of *Romeo and Juliet*. Her entrance is staged as an intervention on behalf of the house: Clive "*Enters hastily, as if speaking to one who would oppose her,*" demanding to be let in to the quarrel: "I *Catherine Clive* come here t'attack 'em all, / And aim alike at *little* and at *tall* " (lines 11–12). Of course, Clive does not aim quite alike at Garrick and Barry: while "little" Garrick has a "cholerick disposition" (line 26) and a love of gain (line 31), Garrick's shortness is cited to point up the ridiculousness of Barry's complaints:

> He [Barry] tells you tales how cruelly THIS [Garrick] treats us,
> To make you think the little monster beats us.
> Wou'd I have whin'd in melancholy phrase,
> *How bouncing* Bajazet *retreats from* Bays!
> I, who am woman! would have stood the fray;
> At least, not snivell'd thus, and run away! (lines 38–43)

Barry comes off as an emasculated crybaby in comparison to the Amazonian Clive, who spears him on a line from his own prologue. Garrick's exploitation of negative advertising appears again, as the epilogue introduces and dismisses his shortness and reputation for avarice. The repetition of Clive's epilogue, long past the conclusion of the Battle of the Romeos, reinforced Garrick's victory.

The battle's end seems to have been occasioned by exhaustion. Unlike Drury Lane's energetic teenage ingénue, George Anne Bellamy, Susannah Maria Cibber was a woman in her thirties who was frequently unwell, as Garrick knew, having often played opposite her. The Battle of the Romeos may have halted because Covent Garden's Juliet could not or would not continue such a gruelling performance schedule: James Winston's dramatic register records that the run concluded "because Mrs Cibber would act in Romeo no longer."[82] The town's patience with just one theatrical offering was exhausted, too, as this satiric verse from the 12 October *Daily Advertiser* hints:

> Well – what's tonight, says angry Ned,
> As up from bed he rouses,
> Romeo again! and shakes his head,
> Ah! Pox on both your houses.[83]

The Battle of the Romeos produced considerable media coverage for both Garrick and Barry. But as weary Ned, and Garrick, in his letters, saw it, this was also a contest between theatres for a place in public discourse. Garrick wrote to the Countess of Burlington on 18 October: "We go on vastly well at Drury Lane, Nothing is talk'd of now but ye Theatres, & I have ye Pleasure of assuring yr Ladp that we don't loose Ground in ye Contest."[84] In playing Romeo, Garrick not only expanded his list of roles and enhanced his growing reputation, he retained his adaptation of the play in Drury Lane's repertoire, sustained a profitable competition, and enjoyed personal revenge. The Battle of the Romeos revealed the value of the timely release and sustained reprinting of paratextual material in the media.

"*The* Prompter *Before the Curtain!*"

Prompters like Cross and Hopkins were known by the public to be attuned to theatrical productions' quality, observant of actors' interpretations of roles, and of plays' financial and popular success; understanding this perception, alongside the prompter's role in communications within the theatre and with the media, suggests why Garrick chose a prompter as his persona in a newspaper column. Garrick assumed the pseudonym, "*The* Prompter *before the Curtain!*" in an occasional column in the *Morning Post, and Daily Advertiser*, James Boaden confirms: "Mr. Garrick's retirement from the management did not estrange him from the interests of the stage, and he undertook to become 'the prompter *before* the curtain,' by a series of essays so signed, which his friend Bate published in the *Morning Post*, at the close of the year 1776. He insinuates his *complaints* in the course of an attack upon the late manager, Mr. Garrick."[85] Short synopses of these columns demonstrate that Garrick continued to reinforce aspects of his personal brand in the media even after retirement. Garrick's "Prompter" persona stresses his identifications with variety and British (especially Shakespearean) drama, and expresses concern with the state of the English stage.

The first "Prompter" column of 19 November 1776 shows Garrick relishing the dramatic irony pseudonymity offers: "The Criticks upon our theatres, are so apparently influenced, that I never knew a more fit time for a calm, impartial spectator to make his appearance; and when I assure you, that no privilege in the power of a MANAGER to give – can bribe me, nor that any art of any performer, or even part of his, or her salary shall guide my pen, my unbiased judgment will make no bad figure among the present writers upon the same subject." Referring to the "late *Manager* of old Drury," he smirks, "nobody can be more sensible of that Manager's merits than myself." Garrick was, the Prompter tells the public, too indulgent to his actors, which has led to many "pretended *indispositions*" amongst the present performers. Garrick accuses such malingerers of setting up "a mock-importance" for there is now "no actor or actress who can draw an audience, by his, or her own peculiar strength" – a statement sure to bring to mind one Mr. Garrick, who did have such strength, and who issued numerous health bulletins. Clearly, the "sport" of anonymity, which Garrick had enjoyed with the "Mouse in the Green Room" columns and his earlier pamphlets, had not lost its appeal.

Garrick continues the theme of actresses' "pretended *indispositions*" through several numbers. In the Prompter's second essay on 26 November he writes, "these mistaken Ladies injure their own consequence, by falsely imagining, that they support it, in appearing seldom." He cautions Mrs. Yates and Mrs. Barry that performance is their duty, and the road to fame: "Ladies, the more you are *seen*, the more you'll be admired." He promises to "account for the decline of the Stage, and offer some proposals for raising it" in future numbers. The Prompter's third column of 5 December hints that, because of actors' absenteeism and want of "*variety*" in the bills, the fashionable world will soon bring in foreign players and the theatres will suffer a "*French invasion.*" Garrick cannot resist puffing his own consequence as manager, actor, leader and stage icon, and remarking on the gap left by his retirement: "When the late Manager left the stage, his place as an actor made certainly a considerable chasm; which should have been supplied by the *joint merit* of the best performers. If this had been done, I will assert, what will be thought a paradox by some *idol worshippers*,—that an excellent play, perform'd in the strength of the company, without their old leader, would be preferable to the same play, only assisted by the performance of Mr. *Garrick*." The fourth column of 21 December 1776 reiterates that excuses of illness are hurtful to the company. Garrick insists that he is a "sincere friend" who "much esteems their profession, and only opposes himself to the ruinous endeavours of some, against *themselves*. Real talents stand not in want of daily, hurtful, nauseous panegyrics in prose and verse; which, not content with giving common praise, must even – to deserve their hire – change the *full of the leaf*, into the very *budding of the spring*!" Here, Garrick displays none of the sportive self-aware irony that characterizes his self-descriptions in the first column. His italics level unseemly animosity at aging actresses. The inference is that his talent was real and ageless, meriting panegyrics, while their self-promotion is delusional, even sickening.

There is no fifth number; number v of "*The* Prompter *before the Curtain!*" is advertised on 4 January to be printed on the next Monday, when it appears as No. VI, of 6 January 1777. This number sees Garrick aligning himself with Hopkins, a real prompter, in an extended parallel. On 31 January, Garrick introduces a new persona, the "Deputy Prompter," who commends the Prompter on his project of stage reform, but wishes to turn the conversation to consider authors, not actors. The Deputy Prompter fulminates against "the poison of *French* criticism" spread by Voltaire, and in the next day's paper, offers a sketch of Shakespeare, who is "excellent" "in the sock and the buskin," and whose tragedies are especially worthy of idolatry. No. IX on 3 and 6 March 1777 continues the biographical sketches of English dramatists, concluding that no worthwhile tragedies have been written in the last twenty years. The Prompter returns to claim the superiority of English over French drama, and to refute Voltaire and claim Shakespeare as the "*Magna Charta* of the English stage!" on 5 April 1777 in no. xi.[86] These remarks conclude Garrick's occasional column.

These anonymous media interventions by Garrick in the persona of a prompter demonstrate that he was still concerned, post-career, to manage his representation by prompting the public memory, supplying the right words to keep his celebrity ever bright. The columns' obsessive attentiveness to feigned illnesses also attempts to foreclose upon other actors and actresses imitating Garrick's strategic media representation of illness to establish public "consequence."

Prompting Public Opinion: Garrick as Witness in Two Courtroom Dramas

Prompters' role as communicators of theatrical intelligence within and without the theatre, preparing not only actors' lines, but audiences' expectations, is also a visible influence in some actions undertaken by the actor-manager outside the theatre. The last part of this chapter considers two legal cases in which Garrick served as a character witness: first, behind the scenes; and second, in open court. In both cases, there were positive consequences for the defendant and the actor. Garrick's acting ability and social influence made him a convincing and valuable witness in the King's Bench court and in the court of public opinion; his interventions were almost certainly the decisive factor in preventing the execution of two men. Garrick's reputation as a man of probity, charity and consequence profited from his media exposure in these cases. Garrick's ownership of newspaper shares and ties with the publishing trade aided circulation of reports of his extra-theatrical acts of charity. Recirculation of news of these cases in later biographies solidified Garrick's reputation for clemency and loyalty, and ameliorated charges of penurious self-interest.

The first of the two men for whom Garrick intervened as a witness to character was [Benjamin] Robert Turbot.[87] Turbot was accused of theft from a specified place on 18 September 1765. He had stolen a silver cup valued at £3 7s. from George White, publican of the Rising-Sun in Covent Garden on 20 August.[88] This act, as Blackstone's *Commentaries on the Laws of England* suggests, was an offence against private property known as "*mixt* or *compound* larceny, which also includes in it the aggravation of a taking [property] from one's house or person."[89] From statements of the crime's location and the value of the stolen cup it would have been possible for contemporaries to predict the case's outcome should the accused be judged guilty. Benefit of clergy, meaning the substitution of a lesser penalty for the death penalty, Blackstone writes, was not granted in "larcinies committed in an house in almost every instance"; nor in "all larcinies above the value of twelvepence, from ... a dwelling-house, or booth, any person being therein."[90] Death, with slim chance of reprieve, was the certain verdict should Turbot prove guilty.

Robert Turbot's trial at the Old Bailey was straightforward. The publican, George White, produced the stolen silver cup, which had been recovered from a pawnbroker. The cup was clearly marked with White's name. White and his servant testified that the cup was kept in a cupboard near the bar, and established that no one had opportunity to steal it but the accused. A pawnbroker next testified that Turbot had offered him the cup for sale, and as Turbot did not know its true value, he grew suspicious; his suspicions were confirmed the next morning when he read of a missing cup in the *Daily Advertiser*.[91] Turbot was taken up and committed by Sir John Fielding.

Turbot's brief defence was flimsy: he protested his innocence, pleaded his youth, and mentioned his wife and children. Three rather noncommittal character witnesses (all proprietors of coffee-houses or public houses themselves) appeared for Turbot. The first testified to his "sober and honest" character; the next said "his character is in general very good"; and the last said that "he bore the character of a diligent sober servant," but all of these character references, each increasing in wariness, were three years out of date, and did not exhibit knowledge of Turbot's current character or circumstances. The verdict: guilty. The punishment: death.

The *Gentleman's Magazine* for September 1765 records that the Old Bailey sessions ending 24 September included nine criminals receiving sentence of death, among them, "*Robert Turbut* for stealing a silver cup."[92] The three murderers in this lot were executed immediately; Turbot entered into Newgate Prison under sentence of death. Surprisingly, the next issue of the *Gentleman's Magazine* states that "report was made to his majesty of the prisoners under sentence of death in *Newgate* when *Benj. Robert Turbot*, a young man son to the Comedian of that name, for stealing a silver cup from a public house; *John M Kenzie*, for the like crime; and *James Haines*, for a highway-robbery, were ordered for execution. *Turbot* has since been respited."[93] Why was Turbot respited (his sentence postponed or never carried out), when another man convicted "for the like crime," was executed?

Turbot was saved by the combinatory force of obligation, interest and flattery. As the second *Gentleman's Magazine* account suggests, he was the son of an actor. The thief's father, also named Robert Turbot or Turbutt, "the Old Comedian," had worked on the London stage since 1733. Turbot generally played secondary comic parts, such as Lockit or Peachum in *The Beggar's Opera*, though he attempted more substantial roles (such as Falstaff) in summer theatre in the Haymarket.[94] Garrick and Turbutt were members of the Drury Lane company together for three seasons, and occasionally played together.[95] At the time of his death, Turbutt was said to be a member of the Drury Lane company, and master of the Swan Tavern in Smithfield.[96] One of Garrick's letters, dated 7 September 1772, mentions "Bob Turbot" as a legendary glutton – actors used to set him salivating in the green room by describing delicious imaginary dinners.[97] After the actor's death in 1746, there was supposed to be a benefit for his wife and children performed on 29 April 1746, but Philip Highfill *et al.* suggest this benefit was deferred and may never have taken place.[98] Why would Garrick, by the 1760s a theatre manager constantly besieged by requests from hopeful actors and writers, respond to an appeal from a young thief?

Garrick may have been motivated to help his former colleague's son out of a sense of fraternity amongst actors. Perhaps he was additionally motivated by a sense of obligation or guilt, considering the first deferral of charity towards the Turbot family, as poverty was a clear motive for Turbot's crime. Or perhaps he was moved by this soul-wrenching letter from young Robert Turbot, dated from Newgate Cells, 7 October 1765:

> Most ever good and gracious sir,
>   Since I find it is the will of Almighty God that I must die, I here take this last opportunity to return you, good Sir, my ever-sincere and last thanks for your kind endeavours and good intention. I own I flattered myself too much with hopes of my life being saved by the news my poor unhappy wife brought me last Tuesday; but when the dreadful summons came to me last night to prepare to die on Wednesday next, the shock at first overpowered me; but, thanks be to God! I am something easier in my mind, which as I fear there is no possibility now of saving my life, and no mercy to be found in this world, I hope God will have mercy upon my poor soul in the next. But then here comes another heavy blow, which is my poor wife, but God and all good friends I hope will be her comfort. Oh! I could say a great deal on this head, but that my heart is too full; and for fear I be too troublesome, I here return you my last thanks for all your goodness to me in this world,
>   And am, with due respect, your dying and ever obliged humble servant,
>   Robert Turbutt.

P.S. Pardon me, good Sir, but here I hope God in Heaven will bless you and all your good family.[99]

From the prisoner's letter, we can deduce that Garrick had made some "endeavours" on Turbot's behalf before "last Tuesday" (1 October 1765), when Turbot's wife brought him hopeful news of potential salvation. How had Garrick intervened? The actor-manager used a form of appeal with which he was familiar from the actors' revolt led by himself and Charles Macklin against Charles Fleetwood in the 1740s – group petition by an acting company. Turbot's wife must have brought him news of the actors' petition on 1 October; indeed, by 3 October, the petition had been touted in the papers and was public knowledge:

> A petition to his Majesty has been signed by all the principal actors of Drury-lane house, in favour of the unfortunate Turbutt, now under sentence of death in Newgate, for stealing a pint mug. This unhappy young man was son to the Comedian of that name; and was, it seems, at the time of committing this first fact, in the utmost distress, his wife being just brought to bed.

This notice in the *London Chronicle* for 1–3 October appeared above a note that Drury Lane was next playing *The Foundling*. The *Public Ledger* for 3 October printed a similar notice of the actors' petition, but expanded on the pathos of Turbot's domestic situation:

> A petition to his Majesty has been signed by Mr. Garrick, and all the principal actors of Drury-lane House, in favor of the unfortunate Turbot, now under sentence of death in Newgate for stealing a pint mug. This unhappy young man is son to the Comedian of that name, who formerly played at one of our theatres; and was, it seems, led into this, his first fact, by the pressing necessities of a most unutterable distress; his wife being just delivered of a child, and he not only out of all manner of business, but without a six-pence in the world to furnish either of the miserable wretches with the smallest sustenance in so affecting a situation.

Both accounts stress extenuating circumstances and aspects of Turbot's character (poverty, unemployment, first offence and childbirth expenses) not visible in the trial transcripts of Turbot's ineffectual character witnesses.

This petition, however industriously drawn up and circulated in the newspapers, was not successful. On the night of 7 October, along with Turbot's piteous letter of resignation to his fate, Garrick received news that more intervention was required, and quickly:

Sir,

   I beg pardon for troubling you with this, but is with concern that I acquaint you the Report was this day made by the Recorder[100] to his Majesty, in consequence of which the dead warrant was brought this afternoon to prepare (among the rest) the unhappy Robert Turbott for execution next Wednesday.

   I hope, if not too late, your goodness will interest itself in behalf of the life of that unfortunate youth, as a petition signed by a nobleman only can save him,

   From, Sir, your devoted and most obedient and humble servant,
   Robert Bristow, for W. Bristow, being absent[101]

News of the Recorder's report and the order for Turbot's execution were duly printed in the *St. James's Chronicle* for 3–5 October.

   Garrick went straight to the top for the requisite noble signature: sometime between 7 October, when he received news of the actors' petition failing, and publication of the 8 October *St. James's Chronicle*, which announced Turbot's respite, he intervened on Turbot's behalf with Charles Watson-Wentworth, second Marquis of Rockingham. At the time of Turbot's trial, Rockingham was leader of the Whigs and Britain's prime minister. As Mary E. Knapp observes, Garrick had many friends in the Rockingham ministry: "Edmund Burke was Rockingham's private secretary; Charles Townshend was paymaster of the forces; Charles Pratt was created Lord Camden; William Fitzherbert was appointed to the Commission for Trade and Commerce."[102] That Garrick made use of friends in high places is not surprising; what is intriguing is the way that he subsequently publicized his act of intercession.

   Garrick's verses, "Advice to the Marquis of Rockingham, Upon a late occasion. By an Old Courtier," allude to and enlarge upon this intervention. The poem's nine six-line stanzas praise Rockingham's clemency, and raise his and Garrick's social capital. Garrick's poem proposes that as Rockingham is young, he will not "Sink, in the Minister, the Man" as older statesmen do, but prove sympathetic and "to a wretch be kind" (lines 5, 3). Rockingham is, with Garrick's characteristic heavy irony, counselled against such kindness, which will only lead to the annoyance of further petitions. Neither Turbot's name nor the case is directly referred to in the poem. The third stanza instead highlights Garrick's dramatic skill in playing upon young Rockingham's feelings. It encourages the reader to imagine a pleasing meeting between the two men, in which a deferential Garrick, emboldened by Rockingham's smiles, makes a "strange appeal" to spare Turbot's life:

You should have sent, the other Day,
G———*k*, the Player, with frowns away;
Your Smiles but made him bolder;
Why would you hear his strange Appeal,
Which dar'd to make a Statesman feel?
I would that you were *older*!

(lines 13–18)

As Knapp's *Checklist* and article on these verses show, this poem received sustained media attention. It first appeared in the 24–26 October 1765 *St. James's Chronicle*; was reprinted in *Lloyd's Evening Post* for 1–4 November; and was later collected in the *Annual Register* (1765) and Moses Mendez's *Collection of the Most Esteemed Pieces of Poetry That Have Appeared for Several Years* (1767). The poem became part of Garrick's posthumous reputation as a humane man of influence by its inclusion in *The New Foundling Hospital for Wit* (1769, 1785) and Garrick's *Poetical Works* (1785).[103]

Knapp does not note the significance of the poem's first point of publication, however. The *St. James's Chronicle*, as we have seen, was a newspaper in which Garrick was a proprietor, and one which frequently printed his occasional verse and prose; thus, the poem's appearance in the *St. James's Chronicle* cannot be said to confer public recognition or approbation of either Garrick's or Rockingham's intervention in Turbot's case. Its appearance in print does reinforce Garrick's access to the media to shape public perception of his own reputation. In publishing this poem, Garrick demonstrated his influence with Rockingham, and at the same time furnished content for a paper in which he was invested, providing a satisfying ending to a story the public had followed through the media for several weeks – the arrest, imprisonment and improbable respite of Robert Turbot.

The date of the poem's first publication likewise deserves attention: as amazing as it would be to argue that occasional poetry saved a man's life, there is no evidence that Garrick solicited his favour of Rockingham in rhyme. The poem was certainly not printed in time to sway Rockingham. Its "occasion" is not the appeal itself, but Rockingham and Garrick's success. Turbot's respite had already been reported in the *St. James's Chronicle*'s 5–8 October issue: "Last Night a Respite was sent for Benjamin-Robert Turbot, convicted last sessions of stealing a Silver Cup from the Sun-Alehouse in Covent-Garden."[104] One might also consider that in the fall of 1765, Garrick had only recently returned from a long absence on the Continent, and was carefully negotiating his re-entry onto the Drury Lane stage so that it appeared to be the result of a public clamour for his appearance. He did not appear, in fact, until summoned by royal command, making a late entry into the theatrical season on 14 November, playing Benedick in *Much Ado About Nothing*.[105] The poem celebrating Garrick's agency in prompting Rockingham to effect Turbot's release forms part of Garrick's pre-appearance campaign for positive public opinion.

News of Garrick's success spread quickly amongst his friends. Dr. John Brown wrote to Garrick on 27 October, "I think you acted a truly humane and charitable part in getting the reprieve for poor Turbott; and I am glad to hear that Lord R.[ockingham] is so considerable a man: I am sure I shall not endeavor to make him appear less so."[106] Knapp, whose article on these verses stresses Garrick's humanitarianism, cuts off Brown's "I am sure I shall not endeavor to make him appear less so" in her account, thereby suppressing part of Garrick's motivation for publicizing his role in the event: strengthening his networks of influence. One effect of this appears to be tying up Brown, a trenchant political writer, from writing negatively about Rockingham in future, from a sense of friendly obligation.

Garrick's initial intervention on Turbot's behalf may have been prompted by benevolence and charity, but distribution of his poem on the subject was more likely to have been prompted by ambition and interest. Stone and Kahrl's assertion that Garrick's "humanitarianism alone prompted him to write to the Marquis of Rockingham to save Turbot's son from death for stealing a silver goblet"[107] must be taken with a grain of salt. Having committed himself publicly to the actors' petition supporting Turbot, Garrick could not be seen to fail. The manuscript copy of Garrick's verses in the Harvard Theatre Collection bears a tantalizing Latin tag from Virgil's *Aeneid*: "Solve metus; feret haec aliquam tibi fama salute[m]."[108] This tag, appended at the bottom of the poem, may not be attributable to Garrick, but its intimation of the lasting protective quality garnered by fame for worthy actions speaks to one possible motivation for the poem's wide distribution.

Another intriguing case involved Garrick appearing openly in the court of King's Bench as a character witness for Joseph Baretti, who had been charged with the wilful murder of Evan Morgan in the autumn of 1769. Baretti, a writer, had recently published an *Account of the Manners and Customs of Italy*, printed by Thomas Davies and advertised in the *St. James's Chronicle* for 3–6 June 1769. Baretti's trial, which ended happily for him in a verdict of not guilty by reason of self-defence, involved a defence as elaborately plotted as any Drury Lane comedy – perhaps not surprisingly, given Garrick's role in the trial, and the presence of playwright Arthur Murphy on Baretti's three-man legal team.[109] A dissertation by Matthew Rusnak focuses on the history of the provocation defence and the effects of Baretti's Italian identity on the case.[110] I therefore include only such details of the inquest and trial and their depiction in the media as are conducive to understanding Garrick's role in prompting public response.

From the plaintiffs' perspective, it was a simple story: Morgan and his companions saw Baretti abusing a woman in the street and intervened.[111] However, the corroborating witnesses were unconvincing. The woman whom Baretti allegedly struck was a prostitute who did not turn up for the trial; so was the first witness, Elizabeth Windsor or Ward. Ward testified that her companion that evening, a woman who wore a brown or a black dress, whom she alleged never to have seen before, asked Baretti for a glass of wine and put her hand towards him, "by way of inducing him to go with her," and then – probably – touched him. According to Ward, Baretti then turned and struck the woman with a "double fist." Three young men saw the blow, demanded how he could strike a woman, and shoved Baretti off the pavement. Ward testified that she saw Baretti take his knife out, and the men give chase. She first denied, then admitted that someone called Baretti "buggerer, or some such name," but could not say whether it was the woman or one of the men. Ward's equivocal answers and admission that she recognized one of the men because he "had kissed her the night before in the Haymarket" did not make credible testimony.

Morgan's companion, Patman, then described the evening of 6 October, when he, Morgan and a third man named Clark had drunk three pints of beer. They were walking along the Haymarket to another location where Morgan desired to sing them a song, when they saw a gentleman strike a woman. They pushed up against Baretti, and first Patman, then Morgan, was stabbed. Baretti then ran up Panton Street.

Constable John Lambert next testified that he saw Baretti run into a grocer's shop, and nine or ten persons gathering at the door; he secured Baretti and brought him to Sir John Fielding. Baretti did not resist detention, Lambert noted: "Mr. Barretti said he was very willing to go before him [Fielding]." Lambert's testimony also established that Baretti "appeared to be very near sighted," as he could not even see the constable's staff. These themes (Baretti's co-operation with the law, and his nearsightedness) were later elaborated upon by Baretti and his character witnesses. Lambert questioned several prostitutes in the Haymarket, but could not find the instigator of the incident.

The last witness was a surgeon at the Middlesex Hospital (a charity, incidentally, that often received a substantial sum from a Christmas season benefit performance at Drury Lane Theatre).[112] Surgeon John Wyatt testified that Morgan had been stabbed in the abdomen and lungs. Morgan's companion Clark suggested to Wyatt that Morgan knew the instigating prostitute's identity – an admission Clark denied moments later, though both remarks had been overheard by a third party, who called Clark a "rascal" for lying.

After the testimony of the prostitutes, liars and rascals, recoverable only from trial transcripts, as none of their testimony appeared in the newspapers, it was Baretti's turn. He read a prepared written statement. This was a superb choice. The Old Bailey transcripts reveal a convincing narrative, presented as a moving whole, not fractured and uncertain, as was the testimony of those who spoke on behalf of Morgan. The effect of Baretti's statement received intense media commentary. The *Independent Chronicle* for 18–20 October 1769 declared it "so pathetic in many parts, as to draw tears from several of the spectators, as well as himself"; while the *London Chronicle* for 19–21 October asserted it was "composed and pronounced with so much force, as to melt into tears the greatest part of his audience." This phrase was published widely, also appearing in the *Gazetteer and New Daily Advertiser* for 23 October, the *Dublin Mercury* for 26–28 October, and the *St. James's Chronicle* for 19–21 October, and the *Town and Country Magazine* for October 1769. The rationale for the media focusing on the dramatic effect, rather than on the content of Baretti's statement, becomes clear when one reads Baretti's allegation of an undignified attack upon his person.

Baretti's statement begins by establishing the defendant as a man of letters. He had spent 6 October at home revising his Italian-English Dictionary, "which is actually reprinting and working off, and upon another book in four volumes, which is to be published in February next, and has been advertised in the News-papers."[113] Baretti invokes the style of newspaper advertisements of his work as proof of his sober industry. He may even have been cool enough to use his testimony as advertisement, for along with the rest of his testimony, this announcement of forthcoming publications was reported in the *Independent Chronicle* for 18–20 October.[114] Robinson and Roberts, the printers of the *Independent Chronicle*, were amongst the conger of printers of Baretti's *Dictionary*.

Baretti then tells that on his way to the Royal Academicians' club, a destination that reminds all present of his status in literary society, a woman "clappe[d] her hands with such violence about [his] private parts, that it gave ... great pain." He returned a blow and angry words, and the woman, hearing his foreign accent, called him "French bugger, D—mned Frenchman, and a woman-hater." A group of men asked him how he dared strike a woman, and knocked him from the pavement. Baretti's misinterpreted foreign identity intensified the mob's violence: "I was a Frenchman in their opinion, which made me apprehensive I must expect no favour nor protection" from the "great number of people."

It is doubtful whether the mob's knowledge of his true nationality would have helped Baretti at the time; in the trial, however, Baretti gained credit from declining a legal measure that was due to him as a foreign national. He drew the jury's attention to this voluntary gesture in his closing:

> Equally confident of my own innocence, and English discernment to trace out truth, I did resolve to wave the privilege granted to foreigners by the laws of this kingdom: nor was my motive a compliment to this nation; my motive was my life and honour; that it should not be thought I received undeserved favour from a Jury part my own country. I chose to be tried by a Jury of this country; for if my honour is not saved, I cannot much wish for the preservation of my life.

Baretti's statement convincingly establishes his intelligence, social status and probity. The defendant's dress and demeanour were also approved by the 18–20 October *Independent Chronicle*: "Mr. Baretti was dressed in a Suit of Black, and behaved with great Propriety."

The fact that Baretti had stabbed Evan Morgan with a small knife was never disputed. The defence was that Baretti was extremely short-sighted, and alarmed at an attack from many persons, had been struck first, and struck back in self-defence. This defence was supported by references to Baretti's genteel academic character by some very credible witnesses. *The St. James's Chronicle*'s (19–21 October) list of these august persons reads like a roll call for Johnson's literary club or the Royal Academy: "The following Gentlemen spoke to his Character: Mr. Beauclerk, Sir Joshua Reynolds, Dr. Johnson, Mr. Fitzherbert, Mr. Burke, Mr. Garrick, Dr. Goldsmith, Mr. Stevens [sic], and Dr. Hallifax." Samuel Johnson reinforced Baretti's studiousness and near-sightedness during his testimony. When questioned, "How is he [Baretti] as to his eye-sight?" the equally near-sighted Johnson quipped, "He does not see me now, nor do

I see him. I do not believe he could be capable of assaulting any body in the street, without great provocation."[115]

Garrick's contributions to the proceedings appear in the trial transcripts. Garrick is first questioned about Baretti's character and reputation, and responds:

> I was not very intimate with Mr. Baretti till about the year 54, though I knew him before. I never knew a man of a more active benevolence. He did me all the civility he could do to a stranger, as indeed he did so to every Englishman that came in the course of my acquaintance with him. When I was at Paris, I was very inquisitive about men of literature. I asked who they thought was the best writer in their language; they told me Mr. Baretti. He is a man of great probity and morals. I have a very particular instance of his great friendship to me. Mrs. Garrick got a lameness, and we tried every method in order for a remedy to no purpose; and Mr. Baretti was the person that restored her.

Garrick first reinforces Baretti's social and literary value, then establishes his moral character by referring to a past act of kindness to a woman (Mrs. Garrick). Garrick next employed his comic powers to turn a repugnant object – the murder weapon – back into a diminutive dinner knife:

Q.   Look at this knife. (He takes it in his hand.)
MR. GARRICK   I cannot say I ever saw one with a silver sheaf before. I had one, but I have lost mine. Mrs. Garrick has one now, with a steel blade, and gold.
Q.   When you travel abroad, do you carry such knives as this?
MR. GARRICK   Yes, or we should have no victuals.

Assuming that Johnson's witty remark about near-sightedness raised a laugh from the courtroom audience, one might imagine that Garrick's statement built on that goodwill, and then neatly upstaged Johnson's performance, using the murder weapon almost as a prop. Just as he rendered Macbeth's imagined dagger larger than life on stage by recoiling from it as though it were already redolent of horror, Garrick's reaction to counsel's intimate handling of Baretti's knife, which he admires aesthetically ("I cannot say I ever saw one with a silver sheaf before"), combined with his domestic references to his wife, reinforce the small scale and unsuitability of such an undignified weapon as an instrument of intentional murder. Garrick's dry final line, "Yes, or we should have no victuals," reportedly brought down the house, even as it established the knife as a quotidian object one might reasonably expect a European to carry on his person.[116] The *Independent Chronicle's* account of 23–25 October implies that Garrick was playing to the crowd, and that his antics even raised a dangerously inappropriate smile from the accused: "Mr. G_____k ... did not seem to be sufficiently aware of the difference between a *Court of Justice* and the *Court of Drury*. It was cruel in him to make a man smile who was before a judge, in a matter that so nearly concerned his life and reputation."

After Garrick, Goldsmith and Hallifax each spoke briefly; the transcripts conclude: "There were divers other gentlemen in court to speak for his character, but the court thought it needless to call them." According to Thomas Davies, deliberation took all of six minutes before the jury "brought it in self-defense."[117]

Throughout the trial and after, periodicals were largely pro-Baretti. The *Town and Country Magazine*, which did reprint pro-Baretti summaries, desired "*to shew ... impartiality*," and reprinted a letter from the *Independent Chronicle* signed "*A Lover of Truth and Justice*," penned by someone in the Morgan camp, if not Morgan's brother. This shocking letter alleged that the victim's brother was excluded from Middlesex Hospital while his brother was dying, and shut out of the courtroom while his case was being heard, despite offering money for admittance. Most remarkable is this writer's insistence that the coroner's inquest that preceded Baretti's trial was rigged in a manner vividly reminiscent of a theatrical claque. On 10 October, Morgan's brother "attended the coroner's inquest, which sat in the afternoon. Before three the room was crowded with a great number of well dressed gentlemen (besides the jury) whose conversation proved them to be warm friends to Mr. Barretti. They took no small pains with the jury before they were sworn; they extolled the *meekness* and *peaceableness* of Mr. Barretti, and deprecated the character of the deceased."[118] Not only did these gentlemen tamper with the jury, the writer alleges, but the prosecutor's attempts to reply to the coroner's questions were disrupted "by a general laughter of the by-standers."[119] Garrick was one of these well-dressed gentlemen: "One of the gentlemen (Mr. G——) being asked if Mr. Barretti, was a *peaceable man*, upon his oath, replied, *he never knew an Italian who was otherwise*."[120]

Apart from the *Independent Chronicle* letter, the trial's press coverage generally reinforced Garrick's reputation as a humane man of social consequence. The *London Chronicle* for 12–14 October reported that Garrick, Reynolds, Burke and Fitzherbert "gave bail before Lord Mansfield for Mr. Joseph Barretti's appearance at the ensuing sessions." Garrick's charitable role as bail was also reported in *Lloyd's Evening Post* for 13–15 October, which gave the amount as a bond of £400 per each of the four gentlemen who stood bail; and the *Gazetteer and New Daily Advertiser* for 14 October gave the amount, but not the gentlemen's names. Besides his financial contribution, Garrick's presence as bail put Lord Mansfield in a good mood. In a strange reversal, Mansfield reportedly tried to impress Garrick with his interpretation of a line in *Othello*, according to Joshua Reynolds: "When Sir J. Reynolds, Mr. Garrick, Mr. Burke, and others went to Lord Mansfield's house to bail Baretti, his lordship, without paying much attention to the business, immediately and abruptly began with some very flimsy and boyish observations on the contested passage in *Othello*, 'Put out the light,' &c. This was by way of showing off to Garrick, whose opinion of him however was not much raised by this impotent and untimely endeavour to shine on a subject with which he was little acquainted."[121] The trial transcripts, the newspaper intelligence and Reynolds's report all show that Garrick's presence prompted a positive outcome for Baretti inside and outside the court.

After the results of Baretti's trial were announced, the *Independent Chronicle* for 23–25 October 1769 reported sourly that "the *little* manager has looked so very *little*, within these few days, that he has not been *visible* behind the scenes." This criticism was just: Garrick's stage pageant, *The Jubilee*, began its long run on 14 October, and as cast lists in the *London Stage* volumes show, from the date of Baretti's arrest to that of the criticisms in the *Independent Chronicle*, Drury Lane audiences would have only seen Garrick in his walk-on part in *The Jubilee*: once delivering the *Jubilee* ode upon royal command; and once as Sir John Brute. Garrick was performing more behind the scenes than in front of them.[122]

One final effort at discrediting Garrick's involvement in the case appeared in the *Middlesex Journal* for 8–10 November 1770 in a letter "To DAVID GARRICK, Esq." from "D.K." The writer accuses Garrick of bribing Constable Lambert (a Panton Street tallow-chandler) who was admitted prosecutor against Baretti with "a silver ticket, which will admit the bearer *gratis* at any time into the play-house; and that the constable has such a ticket at this time in his possession, and has had it ever since the trial." The writer argues that Garrick, as he has "acquired a Peer's fortune, and more than a Peer's reputation in your province, will not, I dare say, hesitate to follow the noble example of a Peer, and an Alderman, by making a public defence to a public charge, and clear yourself of the imputation of having used indirect means to prevent justice, and screen the *peaceable* Italian, who stabbed an innocent Englishman." Despite the writer's shrill threat, "Your silence will be deemed guilt"; Garrick wisely made no response. 'Silurist' prodded Garrick to defend himself in the newspapers one last time in the 22–24 January 1771 *Middlesex Journal*, but sceptically remarked, "I am persuaded he never will."

In the case of the foreign fruit knife, as in other news of charity circulated through Garrick's network of tributary newspapers and print trade friends, reports of Garrick's generosity won the day. Coverage from Garrick-owned and -influenced papers like the *St. James's Chronicle* and *Lloyd's Evening Post* outpaced, in number, length and reprinted articles, the limited cavilling in the *Middlesex Journal* and *Independent Chronicle*. When called to account for his mediation in the Baretti case, Garrick maintained a judicious silence and returned to the stage.

David Garrick moved nimbly from acting upon the daily business intelligence provided him by the prompter inside Drury Lane Theatre to a more metaphorical realization of the prompter's role as communicator in his anonymous newspaper column and in preparing audience reception in the theatre and courtroom. The prompter's persona is emblematic of Garrick's media-centred approach to the theatre business, in which the audience is not only watching, but watched; prepared and prompted by media interventions to respond to Garrick and his theatre.

Conclusion: Garrick, Re-Collected

> I am so plagu'd here for my Prints or rather Prints of Me – that I must desire You to send me by ye first opportunity six prints from Reynolds's picture, You may apply to ye Engraver he lives in Leicester fields, & his name is Fisher, he will give you good ones, if he knows they are for Me – You must likewise send me a *King Lear* by *Wilson*, *Hamlet* do *Jaffier* & Belv[idera] by *Zoffani*, speak to him for two or 3, & what Else he may have done of Me – There is likewise a print of Me, as I am, from Liotard's picture Scrap'd by MacArdel, . . . & any other prints of Me, if tolerable, that I can't remember.
>
> – David Garrick, letter to George Garrick, from Paris, 20 November 1764

David Garrick repeatedly described the pursuit of print and performance success as a quixotic quest. References to Quixotes occur in his prologue to *Pamela* and his epilogue to *Regulus*; there are references to Dulcinea in the epilogue spoken by Mrs. Woffington at the opening of Drury Lane Theatre in 1747; the spouters in Murphy's farce *The Apprentice* are identified in Garrick's prologue as "young Quixotes," and so forth.[1] In the "Prologue to *The Gamester*," Garrick identifies himself as a Quixote:

> LIKE fam'd La Mancha's knight, who, launce in hand,
> Mounted his steed to free th'enchanted land,
> Our Quixote bard sets forth a monster-taming,
> Arm'd at all points, to fight that hydra—*gaming*.

There is deliberate humour in the misfit metaphor: at this point, Garrick's shape more closely resembled that of Sancho Panza than that of the gaunt knight, and as the prologue's writer, Garrick is more analogous to Cervantes than to his character Don Quixote. The piece is suffused with an amused, if weary, sense that the whole project of making drama is a quixotic enterprise. Garrick's use of this trope positions him as a valiant, persistent idealist who attempts to make good plays and reform audience tastes, despite constant, comic failures.

However, considering the care with which he attended to his public image on stage and in print, Garrick's self-representation as Quixote should be viewed sceptically. Some of his contemporaries may have believed with quixotic fervour that publishing rewarded literary merit, or that thespian talent drew disinterested accolades, but Garrick knew, from his managerial position and his involvement in publishing, that celebrity was a highly mediated production. In his interlude *The Farmer's Return from London*, acted at Drury Lane in March 1762, the innocent farmer-come-to-town, played by Garrick, says of newsmen:

> I ask'd for the Maakers [sic] o' News, and such Things!
> Who know all the Secrets of Kingdoms, and Kings!
> So busy were they, and such Matters about,
> That six Days in the Seven they never stir out.[2]

Political and theatrical news alike are manufactured fictions, created by critics, or "Cratticks" as the farmer calls them, who are "Like Watchmen in Town, / Lame, feeble, half-blind, yet they knowck Poets down."[3] Garrick knew the romance of merit to be a quixotic delusion.

This book demonstrates that Garrick's celebrity as actor and manager was produced by broad-based, frequently iterated media exposures and consistent marketing, and that Garrick was deeply involved in that process. One is always cautious to infer intent, but from the persistent recurrence of certain images, verbal tropes and patterns of action, it seems clear that Garrick acted, wrote and influenced others to act and write in a fashion that would enhance a particular public understanding of himself. In so doing, he shifted both the means and the terms by which theatrical culture was judged. Archibald Campbell's pamphlet *Lexiphanes* (1767) protests linguistic inflation, of which Garrick, as represented in the news, is the signal instance: "Instead of saying, as people did formerly, such a one is a person of talents, parts, or abilities, the word now is, he has great *powers*, and those *powers* are, according to the wares he deals in, either *theatrical, comical, tragical, poetical*, or *paradoxical*. The modern Roscius cannot step upon the stage, but in the next news-paper, our ears are stunned with the *amazing theatrical powers* of our inimitable Garrick."[4]

Garrick's shrewd use of vertical integration had lasting effects on the media's portrayal of the theatre, just as his centrality to the stage affected perceptions of actors. William Winter's speech, *The Press and the Stage* (1889), suggests that Garrick's success did not just drive lesser actors out of major roles and out of the newspapers, but right off the Continent:

> The stage in America has existed about one hundred and fifty years. One of
> the causes which especially promoted its growth on this continent was the
> sudden and brilliant ascendancy obtained in London by David Garrick ...
> His success was so prodigious that it soon overwhelmed the fortunes of
> every other theatrical notability of the time; and this force it was that
> dispersed the more ambitious players during a considerable period, driving
> them into the north, to York and Edinburgh, into Ireland, and even across
> the Atlantic into America.[5]

Attributing the genesis of all Irish, regional British and North American
theatre to a Garrickian exodus is oratorical hyperbole, but there can be no
doubt that Garrick's adept management of the media in constructing his
public image resulted in a lasting celebrity. His endurance as one of the few
pre-film-era actors to retain public recognition is due largely to the trove of
verbal and pictorial images of the actor generated during his lifetime, and
to their recirculation after his death. As a parting gesture, and as a means of
assessing how modern scholars arrived at our present image of David
Garrick, it is worthwhile examining what happened to Garrick's media
archive at his retirement, and after his death in 1779.

Retirement?

Biographies that focus on Garrick as an actor tend to skip from his final
performance to his death and the ensuing spectacular public funeral.
Eclipsing the few years of retirement in which Garrick enjoyed a genteel
lifestyle, replete with visits to influential friends' country houses, is problematic, however, for while Garrick may have sold his share of the patent,
he was still concerned with the theatre, and actively maintained his
reputation by intervening in the media. During this period, Garrick
penned his anonymous column, *"The* Prompter *before the Curtain!"*
(November 1776 – April 1777) in the *Morning Post*. It was also during
this time that, under the auspices of his friend, the bookseller and publisher Thomas Becket, that Garrick began writing a still more ambitious
anonymous newspaper column.

Becket, who had once held newspaper shares in secret for the actor-
manager, had, as previously discussed, a long association with Garrick that
extended almost to the moment of his death. On 10 January 1779, Becket sent
Garrick some newspapers and theatre news, and a cryptic copy-editing note:

> I have this night received your letter dated *Friday night*, and have made the
> alterations as you desired: "it was after they had drew," & c. I have made it
> *drawn*. I have struck out *Sir H. P.* and put in Dr. H—t–y; *spiritual* instead of
> ecclesiastical, and added the two new ones. It is a good one, but how you could

write it in your state is astonishing: it will make a noise. Woodfall is in high spirits about it, but very low to hear you have been so ill. You will see by my note last night there are two answers in yesterday's paper, which is now sent you. I send you the magazine and review, and the St. James's of last night. I cannot find the others at the Adelphi, nor what they have done with them.[6]

Becket was editing a piece from a new series Garrick was secretly writing for Henry Sampson Woodfall's paper, the *Public Advertiser*: a column called "The Whisperer." The column, ostensibly written by one "Matthew Mum," took as its premise the idea that as in modern society everyone was overexposed, secrecy had become the most valuable commodity. As the first column, in the 26 December 1778 *Public Advertiser*, put it, the news industry depended as much upon mystery and the containment of information as it did upon revelation:

> one of the Curses of the present Times is, that there are no Secrets . . . universal Communication of all our Affairs, public and private . . . will most assuredly accomplish what hitherto the most daring Minister could never effect, viz. the Destruction of the Liberty of the Press. By destroying all Secrets, we destroy Curiosity, and when Curiosity is dead, or even lethargic, as it is at present you, Mr. *Sampson*, and your *Brother William*, and all your *Brother Editors* of News-papers, may go into deep mourning . . . You must, with your Brethren, bring back Secrets into Fashion again.

Becket was enlivened at the column's success and alarmed at his friend's ailing health when he updated Garrick with dashing secrecy later that December on the column's reception: "Do not think of the W——; we can do without til next Saturday. There are two good letters in to-day's paper addressed to the author; the printer has made an apology for not sending them to the author, who, he, hopes, will be satisfied. We carry on this affair charmingly together, and not a soul knows it."[7]

In "The Whisperer," Garrick was to take a sweeping satiric look at society's secrets. The *Public Advertiser* for 12 January 1779 listed a comprehensive range of topics:

1. Court Whispers
2. State Whispers
3. Spiritual (in which are included Right Reverend) Whispers
4. Law Whispers
5. Army and Navy Whispers
6. City Whispers
7. Intriguing Whispers
8. Rebel and Loyal Whispers
9. Stage Whispers, including the *Operatical* and *Theatrical*, which are now one and the same Thing.

"Stage Whispers" were the last-mentioned of Matthew Mum's intended subjects. Yet even in this initial categorization, Garrick cannot bite back criticism of what the stage had become without him: over-reliant upon music and spectacle.

Garrick's newfound leisure and impressive social circle, which included the fourth Earls of Sandwich and Rochford, Richard Rigby, the Countess Spencer and other nobles and persons of influence, would have afforded him access to some truly dazzling whispers of national import.[8] The column, as Becket's letter indicates, had already generated several responses when Garrick died on 20 January. "The Whisperer," a sensational idea scarcely begun, was swept away by waves of epitaphs. Becket and Woodfall kept the secret of Garrick's authorship, and neither his biographers nor the editors of his correspondence uncovered this, his final media manoeuvre.

It may be that Garrick, already superbly positioned for public office by virtue of his celebrity, was preparing for a second act in public life, and "The Whisperer" heralded his broadening interest in public affairs. As two of the former manager's tributary papers announced, Garrick was poised for appointment as a public magistrate just prior to his death. The *St. James's Chronicle* for 5–7 January and the *Public Advertiser* for 7 January 1779 reported: "On Tuesday the Quarter Sessions of the Peace for the City and Liberty of Westminster, was held at Guildhall in King-Street, when the new Commission for Magistrates for the above City and Liberty was read ... and 25 new Magistrates added to the Commission, among whom [was ...] David Garrick, Esq." A letter protesting this appointment, signed "HARDWICKE," appeared in the *Public Ledger*, on 17 January, asking if

> the comic or tragic powers of Garrick qualify him for a justice of peace? Is there any thing farcical or tragical in the administration of justice? What ideas must judicious foreigners have of our *police*, when they hear that the tragic powers of a theatrical genius are exerted *magisterially*? His worship will be stiled the theatrical, or, perhaps, the tragical justice of peace; a description so ludicrous as to excite the mirth of some men, and the indignation of the more serious part of the community, at so absurd, useless, and unnecessary a nomination.[9]

Death foreclosed upon the possibility of David Garrick becoming one of the first actors to employ his celebrity to slip from the stage into public office, and upon whatever debate might have ensued from his appointment. Epitaphs and notices of death, many of which reverently cited the

Figure 7   The *General Evening Post* for 28–30 January 1779. Newspaper columns funnel Garrick's funeral procession past the reader's eye in an uncanny match of form with content. This representation may be modelled on William Pitt's less impressive funeral procession, as mapped out in the 6–9 June 1778 *St. James's Chronicle*. Harry Ransom Center, The University of Texas at Austin.

verbal images of the actor Garrick promulgated as attributes of his personal brand, surged into the newspapers, where they buried the news of Garrick's last new role.

Occasional verse lamenting Garrick's death poured into all of the papers associated with the actor-manager. Indeed, Garrickian epitaphs were the *only* poetry published in the *St. James's Chronicle* until 9–11 February 1779, and this trend (barring verses on Keppel and one prologue) continued into March. Garrick's infinite variety, natural genius, brilliant eyes and association with Shakespeare are all reflected in this public mourning. Wrote one correspondent in the 21–23 January 1779 *St. James's Chronicle*:

> A Reflexion on the Death of Mr. GARRICK.
>
> WHAT different Signs express our Heart-felt Cares? –
> On Garrick's Death see Comedy all Tears! –
> While bursting Tragedy – so great her Grief –
> Can't call a single Tear to her Relief.

The *Morning Post* for 25 January carried verses uniting all aspects of Garrick's public image by one "W.," including these lines:

> Clos'd are those eyes, which shone with magic fire;
> Mute is that tongue which made the world admire!
> By Nature tutor'd, he, in every part,
> Express'd the passions, with a feeling heart.
>   . . .
> His country's boast, and Phoenix of the age,
> The great restorer of the drooping stage;
> Ten thousand suns may run, yet run in vain,
> Nor shall mankind *behold his like again.*
> SHAKESPEAR and GARRICK – an illustrious pair –
> Who Nature's powers so equally did share;
> Hail! happy Britain, thou canst call them thine,
> Who did thy morals, and your taste refine.

The *Public Advertiser* for 22 January carried an extempore epitaph which concluded with a reflection upon Garrick's physical and cultural stature: "God bless your Soul, my *great*, my *little* David." These epitaphs bear powerful testimony to the efficacy of Garrick's sustained, consistent media management, for their words echo back the associations he so assiduously cultivated in the newspapers in which he bore an interest.

Extra, Extra! Extra-Illustration

Shearer West's foundational book, *The Image of the Actor* (1991), attends to the theatrical portrait industry's development, and notes that Garrick's retirement in 1776 was one of the "most fecund periods of theatrical print production in the 18th century."[10] West's work highlights "the proliferation of public art exhibitions" during this period, and stresses that the importance of public art display "cannot be overestimated."[11] More recently, Heather McPherson's *Art and Celebrity in the Age of Reynolds and Siddons* (2017) beautifully illustrates the role of Royal Academy exhibitions and related prints in constructing theatrical celebrity.[12]

Garrickiana of all sorts enjoyed a considerable afterlife and vigorous recirculation following the actor's death. Many prints of the actor are now bound up in extra-illustrated books that are the unsung sources of much modern Garrick scholarship.[13] One must consult these volumes to access original letters, prints and other ephemera, yet material found within their marbleized covers is often treated without reference to the mediating effects of the book-sized archives that house it. It is a myth, Diana Taylor writes, that the archive "is unmediated . . . What makes an object archival is the process whereby it is selected, classified, and presented for analysis. Another myth is that the archive resists change, corruptibility, and political manipulation."[14] Extra-illustrated books present a potent challenge to the myth that archival materials are stable and unmediated, for they are consciously selected and designed pastiches. If, as Taylor has argued, we need to attend to "the process whereby" an archival object "is selected, classified, and presented for analysis,"[15] then it is time to look at the extra-illustrated book as archive, and to consider its illustrators' visceral interactions with the original text. By looking at selected extra-illustrated texts pertaining to David Garrick, we can consider what such archives reveal about received notions of Garrick's iconic status.

An extra-illustrated book is one into which has been drawn, bound or otherwise inserted pictorial or textual material not in the original volume. It is not a scrapbook. The difference between the two, as Erin Blake succinctly puts it, is that extra-illustration extends an extant printed book whereas "scrapbooks do not serve a pre-determined text."[16]

Extra-illustration's heyday extends from the 1770s into the early twentieth century,[17] beginning with the work of the Reverend James Granger. Indeed, the practice of extra-illustrating books was and sometimes still is called "grangerizing." The full title of Granger's book is *A Biographical History of England, from Egbert the Great to the Revolution: Consisting of*

Characters Disposed in Different Classes, and Adapted to a Methodical Catalogue of Engraved British Heads: Intended as an Essay Towards Reducing Our Biography to System, and a Help to the Knowledge of Portraits; Interspersed with Variety of Anecdotes, and Memoirs of a Great Number of Persons, Not to Be Found in Any Other Biographical Work: With a Preface, Shewing the Utility of a Collection of Engraved Portraits to Supply the Defect, and Answer the Various Purposes, of Medals. Granger argued for years with his publisher Thomas Davies about this title (Davies felt it could be shorter),[18] mainly because it is not just a title, but Granger's "agenda" for collectors, as Marcia Pointon notes.[19] Granger's system of biography illustrated by portraits promotes a scheme for "ordering society and making visible the body politic."[20]

Granger states his didactic aims in the preface:

> A methodical collection of engraved heads will serve as a visible representation of past events, become a kind of *speaking chronicle*, and carry that sort of intelligence into civil story, that in popish times was almost the sole support of religion: with this difference, that instead of those lying legends, and fabulous relations, which spread error and superstition through the minds of men; these, by short and accurate inscriptions, may happily convey, and that in a manner almost insensible, real and useful instruction. For such a collection will delight the eye, recreate the mind, impress the imagination, fix the memory, and thereby yield no small assistance to the judgment.[21]

His educational system of civil icons enforces periodicity, so that historical figures will be remembered "in the several periods in which they really flourished,"[22] and be inspirational, awakening "genius" in a pupil who "will presently perceive the true bent of his temper, by his being struck with a Blake or a Boyle, a Hyde or a Milton."[23] Granger divides English history by monarchical reigns up until James II; within each reign, he considers twelve categories of notable persons, and gives a brief, entertaining biography of each subject.[24] Each biography begins with a listing of extant prints of its subject, but no illustrations are included.

Some scholars assume that this is because collectors were meant to organize their prints separately, as Granger did with his own impressive collection.[25] However, it seems that from the first, either Granger or his publisher Thomas Davies imagined that collectors might want to juxtapose image and text, for, as their correspondence reveals, a small proportion of the quarto first edition of Granger's book was printed on "large paper" with "the paper on one side."[26] The second, octavo edition of the work continued the practice of a split run in which some volumes included blank paper, as Davies notes on 26 February 1774: "There are 20 setts with blank paper, as in the quarto, for the convenience of such gentlemen as may chuse to place the heads near to the lives in your work."[27] It is unclear whether Granger or Davies originated the idea of including blank paper in the copy. This decision represents a financial risk for the publisher, given the expense of paper, and Davies's caution is evident in the size of this run: he imagines a small demand, amongst "gentlemen."

Whether Davies or Granger was responsible, the idea of producing a volume of biography with blank pages for collectors to customize with their own prints dates to Granger's first edition (1769). Representation of historical persons, Granger opined, ought to include "variety of prints of the same person," "done at different periods of his life, or by different hands," for "by comparing the several portraits, the true likeness may with more certainty be determined." While his primary selection principle, as Pointon observes, seems to be "true likeness" (however illusory that goal), Granger is also concerned with variety and comprehensiveness.[28]

As Granger's *Biographical History* concludes with the reign of James II, one might imagine that David Garrick would not appear in it. However, at a passing mention of Shakespeare, Garrick rises up from the footnotes' trapdoor: "Mr. Garrick, who thoroughly understands Shakespeare, has exhibited a thousand of his beauties, which had before escaped the mob of actors and of readers; and has carried his fame much higher than it was ever raised in any former period. It is hard to say whether Shakespeare owes more to Garrick, or Garrick to Shakespeare."[29] Garrick's appearance momentarily ruptures Granger's careful chronology. This encomium aside, Granger pens no biography of Garrick with attendant list of prints. Even the Reverend Mark Noble, who in 1806 continued Granger's *Biographical History*, did not carry Granger's project forward far enough to include the actor. Noble expressed fears about recent history's ability to "excite uneasy apprehensions or sensations in the minds of those whose families and near connections might be affected by the relation"[30] and extends the *History* only to the end of George I's reign. Granger's publisher Davies apparently did not suffer from such anxieties about recent history – at least, they did not prevent him from writing and publishing Garrick's biography in 1780. But Davies evidently did not see enough market potential for grangerizing his biography of Garrick to print it with blank paper, as he had with Granger's book. While the practice of grangerizing can be dated to 1769, when Garrick still had seven seasons left to play and prints of the actor were abundant, the extra-illustration of David Garrick occurred posthumously.

Though, as Erin Blake notes, many illustrators used the terms inter-changeably,[31] 'extra-illustrated' is a more capacious term than 'granger-ized,' and more accurately describes Garrickian extra-illustrators' practices, which are not exclusively focused on portraiture or "heads." There are busts and half-length portraits of Garrick, true, but many images of Garrick *en rôle* were designed to show his acting's energy and plasticity through whole-body poses. These stand out particularly in extra-illustrated volumes where they are frequently juxtaposed with heads of other persons mentioned in the text. Garrick sometimes appears to be the only moving figure, granting him a kind of liveness within the extra-illustrated archive. These images of the actor's body include a variety of recognizable costumes tied to particular roles, such as the fur hat and frogged hussar's jacket associated with Garrick's turn as Tancred – another notable difference from Granger's text, which includes information on dress as an aid to historical periodization, a purpose confounded by eclectic eighteenth-century theatrical costuming practices (fourteenth-century Italian garb might have been more appropriate to Tancred, for example, as James Thomson adapted the story from Boccaccio's *Decameron*). A complete set of illustrations of Garrick would exceed the space Granger allots to even his comprehensive image descriptions. Whereas in Granger's scheme there might be one iconic portrait of a statesman, with representative back-ground and allegorically significant props, for Garrick, variability of dress, countenance, pose, and setting in his images were crucial components of his identity as the actor who embodied variety. In Garrick's theatrical portraits, likeness is not just resemblance in basic physiognomy, but something more elusive – likeness to the audience's memory of Garrick in a particular role. Likeness in theatrical portraiture comprehends the expression of a characteristic movement or pose, or a particular dramatic moment, associated with the actor's portrayal of that character. The 'Remarks on the Exhibition by the Society of Artists in Spring Gardens' in the *St. James's Chronicle* for 29 May – 1 June 1762 shown in Figure 8 suggest that such images could even call particular lines to mind.

Images of Garrick were produced during his lifetime for promotional purposes, creating a market rather different than the antiquarian market in which circulated prints of long-dead kings and bishops. While the anti-quarian market, to Horace Walpole's disgust, grew more competitive and certain portraits grew ever more rare and expensive after the publication of Granger's book, new prints of actors multiplied.[32] Not surprisingly, images of Garrick occupied a large portion of the theatrical portraiture market. In John Boydell's *Catalogue of Prints* (1773), Garrick rules the

Figure 8 *St. James's Chronicle*, 29 May – 1 June 1762. The benefits of media convergence: this review of an art exhibition, praising Johann Zoffany's image of Garrick in a dramatic role, appears in a newspaper in which Garrick was a proprietor. Permission British Library Board.

category of "Metzotintoes" of "Players, and Scenes in Plays": five of seven images are of Garrick, and Benjamin Wilson's "Mr. Garrick and Mrs. Bellamy in the Character of Romeo and Juliet" is cross-indexed in the history category. These prints are not priced like antique curiosities, but neither are they cheap. The least expensive, after the Wilson (5s.), is Zoffany's "Mr. Garrick in the Farmer's Return," at 7s. 6d.; and 10s. 6d. is the price for Dixon's print, "Mr. Garrick in Richard the Third, after Dance," "Mr. Garrick between Tragedy and Comedy, after Sir Joshua Reynolds" and "Mr. Garrick, with Shakespeare's Bust, after Gainsborough. By Valentine Green."[33] Though images of Garrick were numerous, it does not follow that they were inexpensive. In contemporary printsellers' catalogues such as Boydell's, Garrick is often represented by artists and engravers of the first rank, in mid-to-high-priced print offerings, though less expensive images are also available. By promoting his relationship with recognized artists of merit, Garrick ensured that his print image could become popular, yet never downmarket cheap. As part of the assessment of Garrick's place in the portraiture print market depends not only on pricing and the artists' reputations, but upon the media employed, I will outline the most frequently used techniques in print media: line engraving, etching and mezzotint.

Variety in Visual Representation

Garrick's expressive range as an actor is mirrored in the variety of his visual representations, beginning with various means of artistic production. As Timothy Clayton explains, line engraving was "the most prestigious, the most time-consuming, and therefore the most expensive printmaking process. Lines were incised on a copper plate 1 or 2 mm thick with a burin or graver. When the image had been engraved, the plate would be inked, wiped clean so that the ink remained only in the incisions, and printed under great pressure. The plate was re-inked and re-wiped for each impression, and printing was a skillful, time-consuming and expensive procedure."[34] If the initial process was expensive and time-consuming, still, "several thousand impressions could be printed from a plate that had been engraved and printed carefully."[35] A line engraving such as "David Garrick Esqr." (1776, engraved by J. Collyer based on the portrait by Thomas Gainsborough; Figure 3) exemplifies what Clayton terms engraving's visual "vocabulary" of "linear patterns appropriate to different textures,"[36] with its density of hatching to darken the drapery behind Garrick, and its subtle handling of highlights on Garrick's nose and forehead, and the lively glint in his eyes. The choice of a line engraving for this portrait suggests that its publisher anticipated a strong market for the work in the year of Garrick's retirement, and thus invested in a line-engraved plate that could withstand numerous impressions.

The printing process for etching is the same, but the design was first drawn with a needle on an acid-resistant (usually wax) surface. Clayton notes "it was possible to draw far more freely on the wax than an engraver could with a burin. Sudden changes of direction and little squiggles were difficult for the engraver but characteristic of etching. The plate was then immersed in acid which bit into the copper only where the lines had exposed it ... compared with the subtlety and variety of engraving, only crude tonal graduation could be achieved by the etcher."[37] "David Garrick in 'Richard III,'" with engraving and etching by William Hogarth and Charles Grignion, after Hogarth's painting of 1746 (Figure 9), takes

Figure 9   "David Garrick in 'Richard III,'" engraving and etching by William Hogarth and Charles Grignion, after Hogarth's painting of 1746. Garrick's friendship with numerous artists aided the growth of his impressive visual archive. By permission of the Folger Shakespeare Library.

advantage of the fluid lines made possible by etching for the draperies of the tent, and the tonal variation and textures of engraving for the pallid face and ermine trim of the cape.

The third choice in the print market, and an attractive one, was mezzotint. As Clayton explains, mezzotint is a

> tonal rather than a linear process, and was worked from black to white rather than from white to black, making it particularly appropriate for dark designs. It became popular as a medium for producing the appearance of oil paintings and, being relatively cheap, was favoured by painters who wished to give currency to their creations and for private commissions for portraits. The plate was first 'ground' all over with a spiked tool called a rocker, until thoroughly roughened. Graduated high-lights were then smoothed out with a 'scraper' or burnisher . . . printing of a mezzotint plate was a highly skilled operation. The burr thrown up by the rocker was fragile and would wear down quickly, however skillful the printer.[38]

Figure 10   "David Garrick with Mrs Cibber as Jaffier and Belvidera in Otway's 'Venice Preserv'd,'" engraving by James McArdell after painting by Johann Zoffany, 1764. Mezzotint's velvety depths emphasize the drama of this scene. © Victoria and Albert Museum, London.

Mezzotints were suitable for small runs, for though they could be re-engraved, the "yield was much smaller than that of a line engraving. On the other hand, a mezzotint could be engraved much more quickly and cheaply than an engraving … For economic reasons it was preferred for subjects for which a small sale was expected, and where relatively rapid publication was desirable."[39] Mezzotint's expressive, painterly quality, association with a small run and exclusivity, and timeliness made it ideal for promotional images of Garrick. James McArdell's "David Garrick with Mrs Cibber as Jaffier and Belvidera in Otway's 'Venice Preserv'd,'" 1764 (Figure 10), is a superb example. Johann Zoffany's dramatically lit night scene, in which Garrick's Jaffier draws back an arm to kill his wife Belvidera (Mrs Cibber), is perfectly suited to a mezzoint's velvety darkness. As Rosie Broadley observes, Garrick commissioned this painting, "and hung it in the dining room at his house in the Adelphi," though not before Zoffany exhibited it in his studio from January to February 1763 to collect subscriptions for prints to be made of it, as announced in the *Public Advertiser* that January.[40] The painting was also exhibited at the Society of Artists in 1763, where its fame presumably added to the subscriptions for the mezzotint made by McArdell, one of London's most skilled printmakers.[41]

Advertising, Exhibiting, Acquiring

While the original paintings on which prints were based sold to an upper echelon of collectors for large sums, collectors of more modest means were invited to subscribe to prints through the newspapers, or through public displays of art at which print subscription lists were promoted, as the Zoffany/McArdell example indicates. Newspapers make visible moments of multi-media convergence, and demonstrate the print market's tremendous potential to reinforce Garrick's celebrity.

One such moment occurred in 1746, when prints of Hogarth's "David Garrick in 'Richard III'" (Figure 9) became available to subscribers. The image's release converged with a command performance of the play, and a poem on the picture appearing in the September 1746 *British Magazine*. Hogarth advertises in the 22 July 1746 *London Evening-Post*: "Mr HOGARTH hereby gives Notice, that the Print of Mr. GARRICK, in the Character of Richard the Third, is now finish'd, and ready to be deliver'd to Subscribers. The said Print will continue to be sold at 7s. 6d. each, at the Golden Head in Leicester-Fields; where also may be had, all his other Works." The print was announced as published "this day" on

20 September 1746. The related poem in the *British Magazine* was advertised in the *General Advertiser* on 1 October as an inducement to buy the 3*s*. magazine, and the moment was crowned by a command performance on 31 October: "By Command of Their Royal Highnesses the DUKE, the Princesses Amelia, and the Princess of HESSE ... At the Theatre-Royal in Covent-Garden, this Day, will be presented the Tragical History of King RICHARD the Third ... The Part of King Richard to be perform'd by Mr. GARRICK." The poem, print, performance and publicity vigorously cross-promoted one another. That they did so was not coincidence: Garrick was interested in the progress of Hogarth's picture, and in the possibility of prints issuing from it. Garrick questioned his friend Somerset Draper repeatedly about Hogarth's painting, writing from Lichfield on 23 October 1745, "Mr. Wyndham sends me a great account of *Hogarth*'s Picture; have you seen it lately?" and from Dublin on 1 December 1745: "Pray, does *Hogarth* go on with my picture, and does he intend a print from it? Pray, when you see him, give him my services."[42] Garrick's interest in the production of prints hints at the actor's early recognition of the value of visual print media in establishing his reputation, particularly when allied with an already successful artist like Hogarth.

Hogarth's print, which, Kalman Burnim attests, was reproduced at least fourteen times,[43] shaped theatrical portraiture in unexpected ways: Ravenet's engraving of Garrick as Romeo was advertised as matching it in size, suggesting that the images were of comparable quality and might be displayed together, and promoting the idea of a collection centred on the actor. The advertisement in the 2 March 1753 *Public Advertiser* reads:

> at 5s. PRINT of Mr. GARRICK and Miss BELLAMY, in the Characters of Romeo and Juliet, in the Monument Scene, engraved from a Painting of Mr. B. WILSON, by Mr. RAVENET, will be ready to be delivered to Subscribers the beginning of next month. The Subscription will be closed the last Day of this Month; after that the Price will be 7*s*. 6*d*. The Size of the Print is the same with Mr. Hogarth's Garrick in Richard.

The paper advertised the print thrice more, and then Garrick appeared as Romeo in a benefit for Mr. Havard on 19 March 1753. Once again, visual image, newspaper advertising and theatrical appearances cross-promoted one another.

Besides booksellers' shops, public exhibitions provided another way for contemporaries to see and purchase images of Garrick. Catalogues of the Society of Artists of Great Britain reveal that images of Garrick featured in eleven of seventeen of the Society's annual exhibitions between its first exhibition in 1760 and 1776.[44] As McPherson and Clayton show, these exhibitions were unabashedly opportunistic in exploiting viewers' enthusiasm, with subscription lists for prints of the works on display at the ready. Clayton remarks: "It quickly became standard practice to launch a subscription for an engraving at the time that the picture was exhibited or, alternatively, to time publication to coincide with the public showing of the original painting or the print."[45] Garrick was a member of this society,[46] and actively promoted it and its members. His extensive coverage as a subject in works shown in the Society's exhibitions reciprocates that patronage; both the artists and their attractive sitter benefited from exposure at this prestigious venue with its unique cachet combining patriotism, commercial opportunity and high art.

The Extra-Illustrated David Garrick

Theatrical prints' timeliness, variety, emphasis on the body; their association with a range of roles (as opposed to a stable professional, historical or class-based identity); and their emphasis on commercial entertainment value rather than instruction, significantly diverge from Granger's ideas about the educative value of collecting heads. However, Granger's ideals and methodology left a legacy for later extra-illustrators, especially his love of comprehensiveness and variety. Having established the kinds of print available to extra-illustrators, and some ways in which this archive was shaped by Garrick's patronage, I will now look at examples of extra-illustrated works concerning Garrick, observing some illustrators' approaches to the challenges of illustrating his life.

The most frequently extra-illustrated books about Garrick are Percy Fitzgerald's gossipy biography (1868), and James Boaden's selected and regularized *Private Correspondence of David Garrick* (1831), which also includes a biography. Their publication dates place these books near the height of the nineteenth-century fashion for extra-illustration and probably made them less expensive host texts than earlier works, such as Davies's biography. Boaden's and Fitzgerald's works were printed on larger pages than was Davies's book, and could easily incorporate large eighteenth-century prints – though unfortunate Procrustean results sometimes still occur when illustrators trim images to fit. The degree to which illustrators extended their texts varies considerably, from small inclusions pasted into the original volumes, to a daunting expansion from an original two to seventeen folios.[47]

Typically, extra-illustrating does to books what strip-mining does to landscape. As Robert Shaddy explains, illustrations "were usually removed from other publications, ideally, owned by the collector, but ... [o]riginal bindings, signatures, and importantly, intentions of the authors and printers yielded to the personal preference of the collector/extra-illustrator."[48] The words "bibliomania" and "craze" haunt most academic articles concerning extra-illustration as brief apologetics for these rapacious practices. J.M. Bulloch sums it up best: "Little did Granger, as he led his blameless life in Oxfordshire, at war with no man, dream of the turmoil that he was to raise and the vista of annihilation that his admirable enthusiasm was indirectly to create, for by a curious irony his desire to record the existence of certain prints has led to the destruction of thousands of books."[49] Extra-illustrated books express competing nostalgias: that of the illustrator for the biographical subject, and that of the forlorn bibliophile for the mutilated books illustrators left behind. However, thanks to the plethora of prints of Garrick and other theatrical personnel that circulated outside the covers of contemporary books, extra-illustrated lives of Garrick are relatively benign projects, at least as regards their material construction: only a few frontispieces and magazines appear to have been harmed in their making – though indices of Fitzgerald's book are rare, suggesting their probable employment as collectors' shopping lists.[50] The illustrator's nostalgic access to Garrick is less burdened by guilt than other projects: less destructive, and more editorial or curatorial, gathering loose objects together and preserving them in a book-shaped archive. This plenitude and the idea of choice it implies provides extra-illustrators with the illusion of exercising taste and agency within what is an already well-managed visual archive mediated by Garrick.

With the huge selection of portraits of Garrick available, how many ought one to include, and where to position them? In some volumes, portraits of Garrick predominate: the Folger Shakespeare Library's copy 6 of the Fitzgerald biography contains 178 inserted plates, "many of which are very rare and all good impressions – Included in these are thirty-six Portraits of Garrick – Collected and inlaid by JW Poinier for Dec. 1872." In Harvard University Houghton Library: Hyde *2003J-SJ632, an extra-illustrated copy of Davies's biography, portraits of Garrick are inserted without reference to age – a 1776 portrait (Gainsborough) occurs early in volume 1, for instance. Extra-illustrators were working with a pictorial archive with a distinct chronological skew: there are simply more images of Garrick in late than in early career,[51] which works against the equitable illustration of all stages of biography's progressive narrative. To illustrate Garrick's first appearance on the London stage, prints of Hogarth's painting of Garrick as Richard III (his first London role) are used often, despite the image's later date and use of naturalistic, rather than stage scenic background. Images of Garrick as Richard III by Thomas Bardwell and Bartholomew Dandridge predate Hogarth, but these earlier prints (both c. 1741) are scarce. Images of a young, thin Garrick are rare, and usually occur in the extensively expanded volumes that betoken a collector or purchaser of means. In most copies, the insertion of images of a mature Garrick early in the biographies supports his origin story of instant stage success, suggesting pictorially an equally instant maturity and gentility. Hogarth's arresting, skillful depiction of the actor mirrors Garrick's skillful, arresting portrayal of Richard III, and the cultural and commercial value of a Hogarth print or other "very rare" items adds to the reader's "good impressions" of the subject's value.

Biography's focus on Garrick as actor tends to emphasize roles, and images of Garrick as actor do predominate in most extra-illustrated texts, though there are nearly as many images of Garrick in civilian garb as in costume. *The Catalogue of Engraved British Portraits Preserved in the Department of Prints and Drawings in the British Museum* divides portraits of Garrick into two categories: "In private dress," for which there are eighty entries, including copies, later states and reversals of originals; and "In character," for which there are ninety-five entries.[52] Within the "character" archive, some images of Garrick appear in extra-illustrated volumes in disproportionate relation to the performance record. Garrick played Tancred just twenty-three times between 1745 and 1762 (often in benefits to oblige Susannah Cibber)[53] in *Tancred and Sigismunda*, but pictures of Garrick in Tancred's furred hat were popular or readily obtainable, and appear in over half the volumes surveyed.[54] There are abundant representations of Sir John Brute from Vanbrugh's *The Provok'd Wife*, especially the scene in which Garrick appeared in women's clothes – yet hardly any of Garrick as Ranger, one of his most frequently performed roles. Abel Drugger in Jonson's *The Alchemist*, a part for which Garrick was famous thanks to his own early self-promotion, but a minor role, is another common illustration, and extra-illustrators had numerous prints of this role from which to choose.[55] In the Houghton Hyde *2003J-SJ632 extra-illustrated Davies, the illustrator inserts multiple Druggers opposite Davies's contention that "Garrick's Abel Drugger was of a different species from Cibber's."[56] Multiple states of the same print, or different artists' representations of Garrick in the same role, are not usually grouped together, except in particularly large expansions or in the works of illustrators whose collections bespeak certain thematic obsessions within the archive of personal references suggested in the original text.

The usual emphasis amongst extra-illustrators is upon exemplarity, or affixing one apt image per role.

A collection of exemplary images is adept at visually articulating range, but not depth or repetition. Such a collection might reflect its host text – having mentioned a role or a play once, biographers tend not to dwell on its recurrence in the repertoire – but is this an effective way of illustrating performance? Extra-illustrators who rejoice in multiples may be said to intervene in biography's tendency to think of a single example as truly representative of the ephemeral, yet repetitive, art of acting, in the sense that their inclusion of different states of a print, or different images of an actor in the same role, can stand in visually for the concept of performative repetition. The more common and economically feasible practice of illustrating with one exemplary print per role stresses Garrick's variety across numerous tragic and comic roles, not his longevity in or repetition of roles, which heightens the reader's sense of his virtuosity as an actor.

Throughout his career, Garrick enjoyed friendships with artists including William Hogarth, Benjamin Wilson, Johann Zoffany, Nathaniel Dance, Sir Joshua Reynolds, Thomas Gainsborough, Mary Darly, Francis Hayman, Robert Edge Pine and Angelica Kauffman, to name but a few friends and correspondents who were also his portraitists. Desmond Shawe-Taylor observes a pattern in these relationships: Garrick "finds established painters (or painters of obvious proficiency) and helps them to venture outside their normal patch. He gives Hogarth a 'leg up' into history painting, he tempts Reynolds into mock-heroic comedy, and he sets Zoffany up as a master of the glancing parody."[57] The artists gained a popular model whose familiar visage could advertise their aptitude for taking a likeness and make their prints saleable; and the actor could shape public perception of himself by commissioning paintings or distributing prints. Articulating the mutually beneficial socioeconomic relations underlying the trade in prints reveals the ways in which extra-illustration, while it may be said to offer a visual 'reading' of the host text, is distinct from reader response, because of the way in which the archive of extant textual and pictorial materials shapes that response.[58]

As many illustrations were first commissioned, created or influenced by Garrick, their new habitus in extra-illustrated books might best be described as re-mediated. Consider this chapter's epigraph: Garrick's 20 November 1764 letter from Paris to his brother George in London, asking George to send him particular prints for his French friends.[59] Garrick makes five requests: six copies of Reynolds's recent allegory "David Garrick between Tragedy and Comedy" (1761); then three tragedy roles, two from Shakespearean plays, as Lear (1761) and Hamlet (1754) in single copies, and two or three prints as Jaffier (1764); and "2 or 3" of himself "as I am" in private dress (1751). His diction reveals his expertise in prints: the word "Scrap'd" is not colloquialism or denigration, but a knowledgeable reference to the process of making mezzotints, which were scraped, rather than hatched with a graver, as in an engraving.[60] Garrick takes an obsessive level of care in ordering these prints, down to counselling George to consult with Dance in "chusing" good impressions.

Garrick recalls the images of himself then in print with impressive exactness. Garrick's association with Zoffany only went back two years at this point, and Garrick lists all the work by Zoffany available.[61] Likewise, Garrick has listed everything McArdell had "Scrap'd" of him to date: McArdell was the engraver and publisher of the Lear and Jaffier images as well as the Liotard portrait (Figure 11). George might have also plucked up copies of Hogarth's "David Garrick in 'Richard III'," not named here, but Garrick's requests cover the existing stock of images by the artists named in the letter comprehensively.[62] His general request for "any other prints of Me ... that I can't remember" may be a feint at modestly pretending not to know the full extent of his print presence, or perhaps expressive of a hope that more images have been generated in his absence. The letter orders six copies of the Reynolds print (Figure 4), but does not make clear whether its popularity was driven by Garrick's distribution of it abroad, or by the requests of persons whom Garrick supplied; in either case, Garrick is the agent of their distribution. The image of Garrick portrayed in the set of Paris requests is one of a serious tragic actor (see Figure 12) and a sophisticated man; the picture of Garrick that emerges from his letter to George is of a man who has a ready, comprehensive knowledge of his own print representations, and who is keen to employ them to enhance his reputation abroad. Extra-illustrators who pasted copies of the ubiquitous Reynolds print into biographies were following a path Garrick laid out for them years earlier.

Mention of Hogarth brings up a curious and notable point about Garrick's visual representation: the eighteenth century's most pictured man is scarcely ever caricatured. Such caricatures as do exist are remarkably positive. "The Theatrical Steel-Yards of 1750" (Patrick O'Brian, sculpt.; 1752) for example, shows Garrick's enormous popularity visually: his small figure astride one end of a scale is sufficient to outweigh all Covent Garden's best players (Mrs. Cibber, Barry, Quin Mrs. Woffington) dangling on the other side. Hogarth sketched Garrick's proportions, and did portray him as the rough-hewn Farmer in "The Farmer's Return,"

Figure 11   James McArdell, after Jean-Étienne Liotard, "David Garrick Esqr.
Done from the Original Picture Painted at Paris," 1751. Garrick wrote from Paris to his
brother George, to send "a print of Me, as I am, from Liotard's picture Scrap'd by
MacArdel, . . . & any other prints of Me, if tolerable" to distribute. Harry Ransom Center,
The University of Texas at Austin.

Figure 12   Benjamin Wilson and James McArdell, "Mr. Garrick in *Hamlet*, Act I, scene 4," 1754. Another of the "Paris requests" personally distributed abroad by Garrick. By permission of the Folger Shakespeare Library.

(engraved by J. Basire as a frontispiece to the published interlude; 1762) but he never skewered his friend with a caricature as he did with Charles Churchill. Renowned caricaturist Mary Darly's work, *Darly's Comic-Prints of Characters, Caricatures, and Macaronies* (1776), is dedicated to Garrick – a dedication engraved into a rondel on the title page, in the midst what may be two bust portraits of the actor, as Mary Dorothy George suggests (the bust on the right seems a likely candidate)[63] – but he is not ridiculed in its pages. Matthew Darly created the frontispiece "Behold the Muses Roscius sue in Vain, Taylors & Carpenters usurp their Reign" (1772),[64] but though the pamphlet it adorns, Gentleman's *The Theatres: A Poetical Dissection*, is satirical, Darly's Garrick is a graceful figure and a good likeness. Not even a handful of the hundreds of images of Garrick extant are caricatures. This is a truly strange gap in his representation: a proud, socially aspirational short man with a recognizable face and a rich supply of costumes and previous visual iconography must have tempted caricaturists greatly. Patronage of and friendship with the best artists of the day may have preserved Garrick from caricature. Extra-illustrated texts concerning Garrick are thus largely untroubled by caricature's deflating pricks, as is the visual archive of the eighteenth century more broadly considered. If we have always taken Garrick seriously, it is in part because he has always been depicted seriously.

While most extra-illustrating is pictorial, there are exceptions. Stuart Sillars writes that by the mid nineteenth century, collectors became more interested in "unique items – letters from leading actors, signed playbills ... which could define the uniqueness of their volumes in a way that collections of prints, now so easily available, could not."[65] One illustrator of Boaden's edition of Garrick's *Private Correspondence* (Harvard University Houghton Library, TS 937.3.3) who seems attuned to the possibilities of illustrating words with more words[66] begins with a bravura move: a 7 December 1830 letter from Boaden to his publishers, relative to seeking out a source for his nearly completed book. The illustrator thus draws attention to the making of the edited letters with another letter. This illustrator includes other letters and news clippings, and landscapes referring to the letters' origins or places mentioned therein, in an expansion so enthusiastic that it disrupts Boaden's two-volume division. The illustrator concludes the new volume 1 with a Cruikshank caricature showing prospective purchasers peering in the windows of F. Harvey, Book and Print Seller – a nineteenth-century print that is neither temporally appropriate, nor illustrative of any content in Boaden's text. Again, our attention is drawn to the extra-illustrating process, this time to the work of the illustrator, now off to the shops for prints to finish the next volume. Less fancifully, changing the volume division changes its dynamics, especially the time one spends reading and considering various correspondents. Boaden dumps Garrick's foreign correspondence into the back of his second volume, removing it from the chronology. This illustrator's division of Boaden's text into six parts gives new weight to the foreign correspondents, as does his or her careful attention to their illustration, not, as some others do, treating the foreign language letters as illegible and unimportant by leaving them pictorially unglossed.

This illustrator's intelligence and thoroughness, however, are not just evident in the clever placement of well-selected images and volume divisions. The sixth volume, which functions as an appendix to Boaden's collection, pushes extra-illustration closer to edition by including thirty-eight new letters, twenty newspaper clippings and several complete pamphlets. The collector offers a reading experience that focuses on theatrical criticism, and on letters perhaps too indelicate or unheroic for Boaden, such as Lady Bathurst's letter of 24 August [no year], returning a play to Garrick, wrapped in with a nice cut of meat: "I have taken a hint from my Sons Fable, and have had recourse to the Greasy Spit as the only probable way perhaps I can ever hope to entertain you ... [I] shall venture to put a Haunch of Venison in the Basket with Lethe, if it serves to convey any part of the gratitude I feel for the entertainment you have given me, it will make me very happy."[67] Inserting authentic material letters invests the correspondence with the 'private' titillation promised by Boaden's title, but lacking from his sanitized edition. This volume in particular exemplifies the Boswellian urgency underlying extra-illustrated biographies of Garrick, as if only by the illustrator's interventions can one "entirely preserve" the actor, and show him "completely."[68]

The images inside these curated micro-archives draw from a visual archive that was itself shaped by Garrick's patronage of and friendships with particular artists. The emphasis on Garrick as actor – not as manager, writer or media mogul – begins in the biographies that are the host texts, and is reinforced by extra-illustration practices that concentrate our gaze on the actor's body. Our understanding of Garrick as a serious actor of infinite variety is a construction driven in part by this nineteenth-century mode of collection and reading. Once extra-illustrators move mass-produced prints into the elite environment of historical biography, they create by the everyday alchemy of cut and paste a precious object, or in Granger's terms, a civil icon. When we in turn cut these images free, their curation needs to be acknowledged if we are to avoid recirculating the same assumptions that governed their inclusion in the extra-illustrated text. As Peter Thomson has remarked, Garrick "could never be entirely contained by the theatre whose artistic status he elevated. That is the whole point about him."[69] The voluminous circulation of print images of David Garrick, during his lifetime and posthumously, exemplifies Thomson's point about Garrick's extensive cultural reach, but also hints at a corollary: containment, or shaping, of the visual archive, had already taken place at the source, instigated by Garrick himself. There was no need to contain a visual archive that had already received impetus, patronage and aid in distribution from the archive's own subject.

Last Words

Of all of the glimpses of Garrick's media involvement afforded by extant letters, memoirs and other sources, none is quite so tantalizing as an undated sketch he recorded in a notebook for a new afterpiece about the newspaper trade. His notes for a five-scene farce appear below:

> The Newspaper – a Farce.
> Scene Ist-Between ye. Publisher <u>Sharp</u> & his <u>Wife</u>
> rejoicing over ye Success of ye Paper & ye Causes
> of it-but some bickerings to shew her Char
> acter of a jealous fretful woman-some
> Talk of their Neice-She wd. marry her
> but he declines it as ye fortune must be pd.
> directly-his Character any thing for Money.
>
> ――――――――
>
> 2d Scene-When <u>Neice</u> [sic] L complains of her uncle's
> Severity in not suffering Young <u>Spout</u> ye Silver
> Smith to keep her Company—Aunt goes out
> & Spout Enters from Concealmt. love. &c.
> distress—Sharp may surprise them—
> Scene 3d. the Chronicle Office—here various
> Characters may appear about ye News–
> Scene 4th- the meeting of Booksellers &
> authors Proprietors-a wrangle-go to fighting
> prevented. Sharp call'd away to ye widow
> Scene 5th. The widow's Scene & end –[70]

The unwritten farce seems to be completely realized in Garrick's mind. The widow, not mentioned in the notes until the fourth scene, is in the fifth accorded a sparse memo, "The widow's Scene," indicating that her character and action are already fully conceived. The third scene shows the interests of the "Booksellers & authors [&] Proprietors" to be at odds, causing a wrangle, set in the offices of "the Chronicle."

Did Garrick base this planned farce on his experiences with the *St. James's Chronicle* or another newspaper in which he was proprietor? What might have been the scenario causing this clash of interests? What events or scandals might have been the "Cause" of "ye Success of ye Paper" to make the money-hungry publisher Sharp and his shrewish wife rejoice in the opening scene? Was there a role for the author, and if so, was Garrick to play the avaricious Sharp, young Spout the silversmith or one of the Chronicle crowd? The splendid comic potential of the farce is easily grasped; what is less clear is why it was never realized. Perhaps Garrick felt that Murphy's farce, *The Upholsterer*, had already plumbed the news trade's comic potential. Or perhaps, given the inevitable presence of commentators like Murphy, Kenrick, Reed, Davies and others in the house, Garrick feared to introduce the subject of newspapers to critics who would surely feast upon the spectacle, reading his farce as allegory. Garrick's sketch of *The Newspaper – a Farce* is a poignant reminder of the ephemerality of the news, and of our limited capacity to reconstruct fully the intricate relationship between the news and the theatre that existed in Garrick's day.

The last words belong to Catherine Clive, so often called upon to close a performance at Drury Lane Theatre with a witty epilogue. Clive, or "the Pivy," as she calls herself in this friendly letter to Garrick upon his retirement, writes on 23 January 1776:

> In the height of the public admiration for you, when you were never mentioned with any other appellation but the Garrick, the charming man, the fine fellow, the delightful creature, both by men and ladies; when they were admiring everything you did, and every thing you scribbled,–at this very time, *I, the Pivy*, was a living witness that they did not know, nor could they be sensible, of half your perfections. I have seen you, with your magical hammer in your hand, *endeavouring* to beat your ideas into the heads of creatures who had none of their own–I have seen you, with lamb-like patience, endeavouring to make them comprehend you; and have seen you, when that could not be done–I have seen your lamb turned into a lion: by this your great labour and pains the public was entertained; *they* thought they all acted very fine, -they did not see you pull the wires.
>
> There are people *now* on the stage to whom you gave their consequence; they think themselves very great; now let them go on in their new parts without your leading-strings, and they will soon convince the world what their genius is ...[71]

Clive's words are often cited (appropriately so) in reference to Garrick's rehearsal techniques, but they might with equal justice be turned to show

Garrick's media influence in "pulling the wires" to establish his own and others' reputations. The gift of "consequence" Clive describes was not only a product of Garrick's stage management, but of his media management, which gave him the ability to nurture or destroy actors' and authors' reputations in print. "In some cases," Diana Taylor observes, "the emphasis on the constructedness of performance reveals an antitheatrical prejudice; in more complex readings, the constructed is recognized as coterminous with the real."[72] Garrick's self-fashioning as a celebrity does not detract from his stature as an innovator in acting technique, or his role in shaping Britain's dramatic canon: instead, I hope that by tracing some aspects of Garrick's close association with the media, this book enables us to appreciate his acumen and his work anew, by revealing him as the first actor to exploit the power of the press in the production and mediation of celebrity.

Notes

Introduction

1 For studies of Garrick's iconicity, see Shearer West, *The Image of the Actor: Verbal and Visual Representation in the Age of Garrick and Kemble* (New York: St. Martin's Press, 1991); and Michael S. Wilson, "Garrick, Iconic Acting, and the Ideologies of Theatrical Portraiture," *Word & Image: A Journal of Verbal/Visual Enquiry*, 6/4 (1990), 368–94.

2 Recent studies of Garrick's role in Shakespeare studies include Vanessa Cunningham's *Shakespeare and Garrick* (Cambridge University Press, 2008); Peter Sabor and Paul Yachnin's essay collection, *Shakespeare and the Eighteenth Century* (Aldershot: Ashgate, 2008); and Peter Holland's article on Garrick in Holland (ed.), *Great Shakespeareans*, vol. II: *Garrick, Kemble, Siddons, Kean* (London: Continuum, 2010).

3 Mary Luckhurst and Jane Moody, *Theatre and Celebrity in Britain, 1660–2000* (New York: Palgrave Macmillan, 2005), 1.

4 Joseph R. Roach, *It* (Ann Arbor: University of Michigan Press, 2007).

5 Joseph R. Roach, *The Player's Passion: Studies in the Science of Acting* (London: Associated University Presses, 1985).

6 Fred Inglis, *A Short History of Celebrity* (Princeton University Press, 2010), 42–46.

7 Leo Braudy, *The Frenzy of Renown: Fame and Its History* (Oxford University Press, 1986), 444.

8 Antoine Lilti, *The Invention of Celebrity*, trans. Lynn Jeffress (Cambridge: Polity Press, 2017; French edn 2015), 4, 29.

9 Cheryl Wanko, *Roles of Authority: Thespian Biography and Celebrity in Eighteenth-Century Britain* (Lubbock: Texas Tech University Press, 2003), 189.

10 Thomas Davies, *Memoirs of the Life of David Garrick, Esq., Interspersed with Characters and Anecdotes of His Theatrical Contemporaries*, new edn, 2 vols., vol. I (London: the author, 1780), vol. II, 380.

11 Ibid., vol. I, 16–17.

12 The *Quarterly Review*'s review of Percy Fitzgerald's biography, *The Life of David Garrick* (1868), expresses the detriments of Garrickian biography to date: "Garrick has not been fortunate in his biographers . . . Murphy's, besides

231

being venomous, is inaccurate, and, what is more surprising in a man whose dialogue in comedy was terse and sparkling, it is extremely prosy. That of Davies, while much less coloured by prejudice, and upon the whole sensibly and agreeably written, is often incorrect in its details, and far from complete in its treatment of the subject." James Boaden's work the reviewer dismisses as "colourless and jejune," and of Fitzgerald's biography, he complains that its Methuselah-like length is not its worst fault: "It wants accuracy, judgment in selection, and method in arrangement; and is, besides, at once tawdry and slovenly in style." Anon., "Review of *the Life of David Garrick; from Original Family Papers, and Numerous Published and Unpublished Sources*. By Percy Fitzgerald ... London, 1868," *Quarterly Review*, 125 (1868), 1–47 (at 1–3).

13 Wanko, *Roles of Authority*, 208.
14 George Winchester Stone, Jr. and George M. Kahrl, *David Garrick: A Critical Biography* (Carbondale: Southern Illinois University Press, 1979), 340, 343.
15 Ibid., 339.
16 Ibid., 340.
17 James Boaden (ed.), *The Private Correspondendence of David Garrick with the Most Celebrated Persons of His Time; Now First Published from the Originals, and Illustrated with Notes and a New Biographical Memoir of Garrick*, 2 vols. (London: Henry Colburn and Richard Bentley, 1831), vol. II, 136.
18 Ibid., vol. I, 585.
19 Hannah Barker, *Newspapers, Politics, and Public Opinion in Late Eighteenth-Century England* (Oxford: Clarendon Press, 1998), 65.
20 Woodfall is responding to Garrick's letter of 13 February 1776, which tellingly speaks of the "compensation" Woodfall owes Garrick: "I own that I may differ wth you in what is call'd ye impartial publication of letters which are brought to You – ... You will say yr Paper is open for vindication, indeed friend Woodfall, I cannot think that a sufficient answer from You, or fit compensation for Me" (*The Letters of David Garrick*, ed. David M. Little and George M. Kahrl, assoc. ed. Phoebe deK. Wilson, 3 vols. [Cambridge, MA: Harvard University Press, 1963], vol. I, xxiv, vol. III, 1071).
21 [David Williams], *A Letter to David Garrick, Esq. On His Conduct as Principal Manager and Actor at Drury-Lane* (London: S. Bladon, 1772), 3.
22 Ibid., 4.
23 Ibid., 4.
24 Robert R. Bataille, "The Kelly-Garrick Connection and the Politics of Theatre Journalism," *Restoration and Eighteenth-Century Theatre Research*, 4/1 (1989), 39–48 (at 45).
25 Ian McIntyre, *Garrick* (London: Penguin, 1999), 142.
26 [David Garrick], *An Essay on Acting: In which will be consider'd the Mimical Behaviour of a Certain fashionable faulty Actor, and the Laudableness of such unmannerly, as well as inhumane Proceedings. To which will be added, A short Criticism On His acting Macbeth* (London: W. Bickerton, 1744), 2, 12.
27 McIntyre, *Garrick*, 274.

28 Ibid., 303.

29 Ibid., 476–80.

30 John Pruitt, "David Garrick's Invisible Nemeses," *Restoration and Eighteenth-Century Theatre Research*, 23/1 (2008), 2–18 (at 6).

31 Stuart Sherman, "Garrick Among Media: The 'Now Performer' Navigates the News," *PMLA*, 126/4 (2011), 966–82 (at 967).

32 Ibid., 979.

33 Davies, *Memoirs*, vol. 1, 42.

34 Ibid., vol. 1, 43.

35 Robert D. Hume, "Garrick in Dublin in 1745–46," *Philological Quarterly*, 93/4 (2014), 507–40. See 513–14 for Hume's explanation of Garrick's time in Ireland as a strategic gambit to gain managerial control over Drury Lane Theatre.

36 Denis Diderot, *L'origine du Paradoxes sur le comédien: La partition intérieure*, 2nd edn (Paris: J. Vrin, 1980; 1st edn 1773), 32–33, quoted in Roach, *Player's Passion*, 152.

37 Roach, *Player's Passion*, 152.

38 Lucyle Werkmeister, *The London Daily Press 1772–1792* (Lincoln: University of Nebraska Press, 1963), 448.

39 Ibid., 447.

40 Richard Schoch, *Writing the History of the British Stage, 1660–1900* (Cambridge University Press, 2016), 16, 18. These references are drawn from Schoch's subheadings detailing certain "thematic recurrences" in theatre historiography.

41 *Letters of David Garrick*, vol. 1, xxiv.

42 Ibid.

43 Ibid., xxv.

44 For insight into the methodological rationale for assemblages, I am indebted to David Worrall, *Celebrity, Performance, Reception: British Georgian Theatre as Social Assemblage* (Cambridge University Press, 2013).

1 A View of London's Mediascape, circa 1741–1776

1 "1850 Biblical Repertory Jan. 131 Our periodicals are now the media of influence. They form and mould the community." See "medium, n. and adj.". *OED Online* (accessed 5 February 2015).

2 Harry William Pedicord, *The Theatrical Public in the Time of Garrick* (New York: King's Crown Press, 1954), 6.

3 Ibid., 14.

4 [Samuel Foote], *A Treatise on the Passions, So Far as They Regard the Stage; with a Critical Enquiry into the Theatrical Merit of Mr. G–K, Mr. Q–N, and Mr. B—Y. The First Considered in the Part of Lear, and the Two Last Opposed in Othello* (London: Corbet, [1747]), A2.

5 Allardyce Nicoll, *The Garrick Stage: Theatres and Audience in the Eighteenth Century* (Manchester University Press, 1980), 8.

6 Foote, *Treatise on the Passions*, A2.

7 Michael Harris, *London Newspapers in the Age of Walpole: A Study of the Origins of the Modern English Press* (London: Associated University Presses, 1987), 190.

8 Barker, *Newspapers*, 23.

9 As James Raven puts it, booksellers published "not just by themselves but also as part of syndicates holding shares in initial publication and in reprinting rights." James Raven, *The Business of Books: Booksellers and the English Book Trade 1450–1850* (New Haven, CT: Yale University Press, 2007), 125. Booksellers were divided "between those who invested and dealt in the ownership of the rights to publication, those who printed, sold, or distributed books for existing copyright-owners, and those who traded partly or fully outside the bounds of copyright materials. In addition to investment in publication by the individual or collaborative financing of a new copyrighted work, existing copyright shares became major tradable assets" (126).

10 John Feather, *A History of British Publishing*, 2nd edn (New York and London: Routledge, 1988, 2006), 52.

11 Ibid., 53.

12 Ibid., 53–54.

13 For more on the Stationers' Company, see Cyprian Blagden, *The Stationers' Company: A History, 1403–1959* (Cambridge, MA: Harvard University Press, 1960).

14 Harris, *London Newspapers*, 92–93.

15 Michael Harris, "The Structure, Ownership and Control of the Press, 1620–1780," in George Boyce, James Curran and Pauline Wingate (eds.), *Newspaper History from the Seventeenth Century to the Present Day* (London: Constable; Beverly Hills, CA: SAGE, 1978), 82–97 (at 93); see also J.A. Downie, "Periodicals, the Book Trade and the 'Bourgeois Public Sphere,'" *Media History*, 14/3 (2008), 261–74 (at 265), for the *Grub Street Journal's* earlier similar use of advertisements.

16 Jeremy Black, *The English Press in the Eighteenth Century* (London: Croom Helm, 1987). Black quotes Murphy's *Gray's-Inn Journal* of 4 May and 21 September 1754.

17 The documents to which Haig refers are British Museum (now British Library) Add. MS 38729, nos. 126 and 128.

18 Robert L. Haig, *The Gazetteer 1735–1791: A Study in the Eighteenth-Century English Newspaper* (Carbondale: Southern Illinois University Press, 1960), 22–23.

19 Robert Bataille similarly objects to Haig's conclusion, and Stone and Kahrl's generalization from it: "Stone and Kahrl (340), quoting Robert Haig's study of the *Gazetteer*, note that the *Gazetteer's* contracts prohibited shareholders from owning interests in other papers. But clearly that contractual situation was unusual … Kelly, while owning a share in the *Packet*, still edited the *Ledger*. Henry Baldwin and Henry Sampson Woodfall were also involved in other papers." Bataille, *The Writing Life of Hugh Kelly: Politics, Journalism, and*

Theatre in Late-Eigteenth-Century London (Carbondale: Southern Illinois University Press, 2000), 171–72). I agree with this assessment, and suggest multiple proprietary holdings were not perceived as conflicts of interest, provided that the periodicals appeared at different frequencies, or addressed different markets.

20 C.Y. Ferdinand, *Benjamin Collins and the Provincial Newspaper Trade in the Eighteenth Century* (Oxford: Clarendon Press, 1997), 52–53.

21 Ibid., 52–53.

22 Richmond P. Bond and Marjorie N. Bond, "The Minute Books of the *St. James's Chronicle*," *Studies in Bibliography: Papers of the Bibliographical Society of the University of Virginia*, 28 (1975), 17–40.

23 Harry M. Solomon, *The Rise of Robert Dodsley: Creating the New Age of Print* (Carbondale: Southern Illinois University Press, 1996), 107.

24 Ibid., 264.

25 Ferdinand, *Benjamin Collins*, 51.

26 Harris, *London Newspapers*, 162.

27 Black, *English Press*, 87.

28 Yale University Lewis Walpole Library: G286.1–2: "General Evening Post Minutes of Committee of Partners. May 31, 1754 – Aug. 9, 1786," 9.

29 See "costume, n." *OED Online* (accessed 17 January 2017). The earliest cited instance of "costume" in the *OED* is 1777.

30 William Zachs, *The First John Murray and the Late Eighteenth-Century London Book Trade* (Oxford University Press for the British Academy, 1998), 26.

31 Ibid., 46–47.

32 Ibid., 46.

33 Sherman, "Garrick Among Media," 966–67.

34 Ferdinand, *Benjamin Collins*, 43.

35 George Colman and David Garrick, *The Clandestine Marriage, a Comedy*, 2nd edn (London: T. Becket and P.A. De Hondt, R. Baldwin, R. Davis and T. Davies, 1766), 58.

36 University of North Carolina at Chapel Hill: 11004-z items 1–3: "Minute Books of St. James's Chronicle (London, England), 1761–1815."

37 Advertising space was sold to Cordial Cephalic Snuff in the *St. James's Chronicle* at least once (see 5–7 July 1764); this is not an instance of a total blockade of the product by its rivals.

38 Harris, *London Newspapers*, 7.

39 Arthur Murphy, *The Life of David Garrick, Esq.*, 2 vols. (London: J. Wright, J.F. Foot, 1801), vol. II, 197.

40 Ibid., vol. II, 201.

41 Performances of *The Drunken News-Writer* took place at the Haymarket on 1 October 1770 and 11 March 1771; see George Winchester Stone, Jr. (ed.), *The London Stage 1660–1800: A Calendar of Plays, Entertainments & Afterpieces Together with Casts, Box-Receipts and Contemporary Comment Compiled from the Playbills, Newspapers and Theatrical Diaries of the Period*, Part 4:

1747–1776, 3 vols. (Carbondale: Southern Illinois University Press, 1962), vol. III, 1501, 1531.

42 Anon., *The Drunken News-Writer: A Comic Interlude. As It Is Performed at the Theatre-Royal in the Haymarket* (London: G. Smith, 1771), 13.

43 Ibid., 8–9.

44 "An undated Secret Service account, evidently for the year 1784, suggests that during the first year of Pitt's ministry, he 'bought' the support of the press with subsidies paid via Thomas Harris, a printer and proprietor of the Covent Garden Theatre." Barker, *Newspapers*, 48; refers to *The Later Correspondence of George III*, ed. A. Aspinall, 5 vols. (Cambridge, 1962), vol. I, 116–18.

45 P.M. Handover, *A History of the London Gazette 1665–1965* (London: Her Majesty's Stationery Office, 1965), 53.

46 Ibid., 58.

47 See Harris, *London Newspapers*, 33.

48 Barker, *Newspapers*, 9.

49 Ibid., 9–10.

50 Andrew Pettegree, *The Invention of News: How the World Came to Know About Itself* (New Haven, CT: Yale University Press, 2014), 364, 366.

51 Robert D. Hume, "The Value of Money in Eighteenth-Century England: Incomes, Prices, Buying Power – and Some Problems in Cultural Economics," *Huntington Library Quarterly*, 77/4 (2015), 373–416 (at 385).

52 "The seventeenth-century coffee houses were sometimes referred to as the 'penny universities'; because they were great schools of conversation, and the entrance fee was only a penny. Two pence was the usual price of a dish of coffee or tea, this charge also covering newspapers and lights." William Ukers, *All About Coffee* (New York: Tea and Coffee Trade Journal Company, 1922), 73.

53 Judith Milhous, "Company Management," in Robert D. Hume (ed.), *London Theatre World, 1660–1800* (Carbondale and Edwardsville: Southern Illinois University Press, 1980), 1–34 (at 17–18).

54 Hume, "Value of Money," 380.

55 Markman Ellis, "Coffee-House Libraries in Mid-Eighteenth-Century London," *The Library: Transactions of the Bibliographical Society*, 10/1 (2009), 3–40 (at 13, 16).

56 Ibid., 19, 23.

57 Ibid., 37.

58 Ibid., 33.

59 Brian Cowan, *The Social Life of Coffee: The Emergence of the British Coffeehouse* (New Haven, CT: Yale University Press, 2005), 104–05. Though women were involved in the coffee trade, the coffee-house was predominantly a place for conversation amongst men.

60 Yale University Lewis Walpole Library: G286.1–2: "General Evening Post Minutes of Committee of Partners. May 31, 1754 – Aug. 9, 1786."

61 *Letters of David Garrick*, vol. I, 23.

62 Ibid., vol. I, 253.

63 Ellis, "Coffee-House Libraries," 16.
64 Anon., *"D-ry-L-ne P-yh-se Broke Open. In a Letter to Mr. G——"* (London: Cooper, 1758), 19–21.
65 Ibid., 2.
66 Ibid., 1–2.
67 [William Shirley], *Brief Remarks on the Original and Present State of the Drama: To Which Is Added Hecate's Prophecy, Being a Characteristic Dialogue Betwixt Future Managers, and Their Dependents* (London: S. Hooper, J. Morley, J. Scott, 1758), 30.
68 Ibid., 39–40.
69 Jürgen Habermas, *The Structural Transformation of the Public Sphere: An Inquiry into a Category of Bourgeois Society*, trans. Thomas Burger and Frederick Lawrence (Cambridge: Polity Press, 1989).
70 Davies, *Memoirs*, vol. II, 134.
71 Michael Harris, "Scratching the Surface: Engravers, Printsellers and the London Book Trade in the Mid-18th Century," in Arnold Hunt, Giles Mandelbrote and Alison Shell (eds.), *The Book Trade and Its Customers 1450–1900: Historical Essays for Robin Myers* (New Castle, DE: Oak Knoll Press; Winchester: St Paul's Bibliographies, 1997), 95–114.
72 See Boaden (ed.), *Private Correspondendence of David Garrick*, vol. I, 50.
73 Foote, *Treatise on the Passions*, 6.
74 Harris, *London Newspapers*, 92, fn. 66.
75 See the letter of 2 September [1754?], *Letters of David Garrick*, vol. I, 206–07.
76 Ibid., vol. III, 1154, 1205.
77 Ibid., vol. III, 1153–54.
78 Stephanie L. Barczewski, "Yorke, Philip, Second Earl of Hardwicke (1720–1790)," in H.C.G. Matthew and Brian Harrison (eds.), *Oxford Dictionary of National Biography* (Oxford University Press, 2004). The embedded reference is to HoP, Commons, 1715–54.
79 [Henry, Earl of Bathurst], *The Case of the Unfortunate Martha Sophia Swordfeager* (London: Anon., 1771), iv.
80 Barker, *Newspapers*, 23–24.
81 *Letters of David Garrick*, vol. I, 391, 403, 411.
82 Ibid., vol. I, 144.
83 Ibid., vol. II, 568–69.
84 This is a sampling, not an exhaustive index of references to periodicals in Garrick's correspondence. The periodicals listed in auction catalogues of the Garricks' library include many titles not mentioned in the correspondence. See Nicholas D. Smith, *An Actor's Library: David Garrick, Book Collecting and Literary Friendships* (New Castle, DE: Oak Knoll Press, 2017).
85 *Letters of David Garrick*, vol. III, 1205.
86 Ibid., vol. II, 432; the footnote mentions the August issue of the *London Magazine* as the locale for this letter.
87 Ibid., vol. I, 235.
88 Ibid., vol. II, 449–50.

89 Ibid., vol. i, 95.
90 Boaden (ed.), *Private Correspondence of David Garrick*, vol. i, i.
91 Ibid., vol. ii, 8.
92 References are to the Huntington 48879 copy of Robert Saunders, *A Catalogue of the Library, Splendid Books of Prints, Poetical and Historical Tracts, of David Garrick, Esq. Removed from His Villa at Hampton, and House on the Adelphi Terrace, with the Modern Works Added Thereto by Mrs. Garrick* (London: Robert Saunders, 1823).
93 For the sad story of how Garrick's uniformly bound collection of books was broken up, rebound and dispersed in accordance with library collection policies, see Dorothy Anderson, "Reflections on Librarianship: Observations Arising from Examination of the Garrick Collection of Old Plays in the British Library," *British Library Journal*, 6 (1980), 1–6.
94 Saunders, *Catalogue of the Library of David Garrick*, 61–63, 99.
95 Black, *English Press*, 27.

2 Proofs: Garrick's Involvement in the Mediascape

 1 British Library: Add. MSS 38728 and 38729: "Minutes of the London Packet."
 2 Ibid., Add. MS 38729.165.
 3 Ibid., Add. MS 38728.130.
 4 This column's title calls the article a continuation of one in "last Friday's *London Packet*," but that issue is not extant in the *17th–18th Century Burney Collection Newspapers*.
 5 *Letters of David Garrick*, vol. i, 248–49.
 6 Ibid., vol. ii, 861–62.
 7 Davies's previously unpublished letter is Item #1, in the Forster Collection, National Art Library, Victoria and Albert Museum, 48.F.20.
 8 Bond and Bond, "Minute Books," 18.
 9 Stone and Kahrl, *David Garrick*, 340.
10 Garrick Club: unaccessioned four-volume scrapbook titled "David Garrick: A Memorial. Memoir, Autograph Correspondence, Shakespere [sic] Plays, Illustrated": item 25, vol. i, receipt of Henry Baldwin. The receipt also shows Garrick's dividends from the newspaper, beginning with £7 in the first quarter of 1763, to £15 in the second quarter of 1765.
11 *Letters of David Garrick*, vol. iii, 1020.
12 Ibid., vol. ii, 583.
13 Elizabeth Griffith, *The School for Rakes: A Comedy*, 2nd edn (London: T. Becket and P. De Hondt, 1769).
14 Sir Nicholas Nipclose [Francis Gentleman], *The Theatres: A Poetical Dissection* (London: John Bell and C. Etherington, 1772), 33.
15 Ibid., 33, fn. 49.
16 George Saville Carey was accused of being the *Theatrical Monitor*'s author, and denied it in a letter to Garrick of 20 November 1767. Boaden, *Private*

Correspondence of David Garrick, vol. i, 276–77. Robert Bataille suggests that Mr. Monitor may have been William Kenrick, to judge by the 16 December 1767 issue, which focuses on reviews of Kenrick's play, *The Widow'd Wife*. I concur with this identification. See Bataille, *Writing Life of Hugh Kelly*, 40.

17 Lines 1–4, 13–16.

18 *Theatrical Monitor*, 19 December 1767, 3.

19 *Westminster Magazine*, March 1773, 177–78 (at 177).

20 *Letters of David Garrick*, vol. ii, 859.

21 [George Colman], *A Letter of Abuse, to D—d G———k, Esq.* (London: J. Scott, 1757), 15.

22 Boaden (ed.), *Private Correspondence of David Garrick*, vol. i, lxiii.

23 Quoted in Lance Bertelsen, *The Nonsense Club: Literature and Popular Culture, 1749–1764* (Oxford: Clarendon Press, 1986), 163.

24 John Hainsworth's volume of Garrick's *Selected Verse* (1981) was the first edition of Garrick's poetry since George Kearsley's publication of *The Poetical Works of David Garrick, Esq.* in 1785. Hainsworth is interested in the prologues and epilogues that offer evidence of actors' characters and those delivered by Garrick that demonstrate his ability to physically transform himself; in poems associated with important historical figures; and in Garrick's witty occasional verse. Published and manuscript poems are included. The fifty-nine selected poems are representative of Garrick's range, though edited with typography and spelling modernized and without full reference to all publication venues. David Garrick, *Selected Verse*, ed. John Hainsworth (Armidale, Aus.: University of New England, 1981).

25 Mary E. Knapp, *A Revision of a Checklist of Verse by David Garrick* (New Haven, CT, 1974).

26 *Letters of David Garrick*, vol. i, 268. Garrick's complimentary verses, "*To* Mr. GRAY, *upon his* ODES" ("Repine not, Gray"), appeared in the *London Chronicle* for 29 September – 1 October 1757, in the left-hand corner on the last page.

27 Richard Cumberland, *Memoirs of Richard Cumberland, Written by Himself* (Philadelphia, PA: Parry and McMillan, 1856), 153–54.

28 Boaden (ed.), *Private Correspondence of David Garrick*, vol. i, 437.

29 "Between Oct. 30, 1775, and April 26, 1776, eight contributions or letters addressed to Woodfall and signed 'the Mouse in the Green Room' were published in the *London Packet*. In the last, of April 26, the 'Mouse' gave his last will and testament and apparently terminated the series. However two additional contributions appeared signed 'The Mouse': one on Sept. 30, the second on October 30; both are almost certainly by Edward Thompson (see Letter 1078). That these two were not by Garrick is confirmed by the signature to the Dec. 11 letter as 'The Original Mouse in the Green Room,' and by the fact that in the letter itself the contributor asserts that he (the Mouse) had written nothing since the 'abdication of my royal master and manager, King David,' that is, since Garrick's retirement in June 1776." *Letters of David Garrick*, vol. iii, 1143–44 fn. Though unsuccessful in

locating the Mouse columns in the *Burney Collection*'s incomplete run of the *London Packet*, I have found many more Mouse columns in the *Morning Post* than the eight Little and Kahrl state were in the *Packet*. There are at least seventeen contributions that employ the Mouse's name; one of the last, printed 10 May 1777, is almost certainly by Garrick, coming as it does immediately after an "Ode" ostensibly written by Dragon, Garrick's dog.

30 See British Library: C.61.e.2: George Daniel, "The Jubilee Volume (a Scrapbook)," for a news clipping hand-dated 26 December 1857 that refers to a sale of autograph letters, including the letter from Clive (using the pet name "Pivy") to Garrick.

31 See the 1 November 1775 *Morning Chronicle, and London Advertiser*.

32 *Letters of David Garrick*, vol. III, 1143.

33 *Morning Chronicle, and London Advertiser*, 12 December 1775. Note William Woodfall's ironic use of the term "impartiality."

34 *Letters of David Garrick*, vol. II, 558–59.

35 Ibid., vol. I, 75; a note at 76 identifies this paper as George Faulkner's *Dublin Journal*; for Garrick's verses "To the Author of the Farmer's Letters" see Knapp, *Revision of a Checklist of Verse*, no. 151.

36 McIntyre, *Garrick*, 90.

37 *Letters of David Garrick*, vol. I, 188–89.

38 Ibid., vol. II, 441.

39 Ibid., vol. II, 463.

40 British Library: Add. MS 38169: "Accounts in Public Advertiser (1765–1771)."

41 Andrews represents this amount as "200l. a-year." Alexander Andrews, *The History of British Journalism, from the Foundation of the Newspaper Press in England to the Repeal of the Stamp Act in 1855, with Sketches of Press Celebrities*, 2 vols. (London: Richard Bentley, 1859), vol. I, 192. However, the accounts show the amount varied.

42 Harris, *London Newspapers*, 54.

43 F. Knight Hunt, *The Fourth Estate: Contributions towards a History of Newspapers, and of the Liberty of the Press*, 2 vols. (London: David Bogue, 1850), vol. II, 190.

44 Ibid., vol. II, 91.

45 Boaden (ed.), *Private Correspondendence of David Garrick*, vol. II, 173–74.

46 Wilfred Hindle, *The Morning Post 1772–1937: Portrait of a Newspaper* (London: George Routledge & Sons, 1937), 35.

47 John Genest, *Some Account of the English Stage from the Restoration in 1660 to 1830*, 10 vols. (New York: Burt Franklin, 1832; 1965), vol. V, 488–89.

48 Bataille, *Writing Life of Hugh Kelly*, 36.

49 For Kelly's letters, see Boaden (ed.), *Private Correspondence of David Garrick*, vol. II, 104–05.

50 Ibid., vol. II, 310.

51 Ian Hargreaves, *Journalism: A Very Short Introduction* (Oxford University Press, 2005), 17.

52 This incomplete clipping from an article in the Forster Collection (FL4–3321.488) suggests an origin in the *Morning Chronicle*; the source remains unknown.

53 Quoted in Charles Harold Gray, *Theatrical Criticism in London to 1795* (New York: Benjamin Blom, 1931), 236–37.

54 John Brewer, "'The Most Polite Age and the Most Vicious': Attitudes towards Culture as a Commodity, 1660–1800," in Ann Bermingham and John Brewer (eds.), *The Consumption of Culture 1600–1800: Image, Object, Text* (London and New York: Routledge, 1995), 341–61 (at 346).

3   Advertising and Brand Garrick: "Infinite Variety"

1 [Thomas Lowndes], *The Theatrical Manager: A Dramatic Satire* (London: T. Lowndes, 1751).

2 The poem appears in the *Ladies Magazine: or, The Universal Entertainer*, 3/28 (December 1752), 444; and in the *Gentleman's Magazine*, 22 (November 1752), 530.

3 Black, *English Press*, 60.

4 Ibid., 61.

5 James Raven, *Publishing Business in Eighteenth-Century England* (Woodbridge: Boydell Press, 2014), 264.

6 For a discussion of "moderate length," see ibid., 129–30.

7 Quoted in Roy M. Wiles, *Freshest Advices: Early Provincial Newspapers in England* (Columbus: Ohio State University Press, 1965), 160–61.

8 Boaden (ed.), *Private Correspondendence of David Garrick*, vol. 1, 497.

9 [Edward Purdon], *A Letter to David Garrick, Esq; on Opening the Theatre. In Which, with Great Freedom, He Is Told How He Ought to Behave* (London: I. Pottinger, 1769), 22.

10 "Mr Neither-Side," *An Impartial Examen of the Present Contests between the Town and the Manager of the Theatre. With Some Proposals for Accommodating the Present Misunderstandings between the Town and the Manager, Offer'd to the Consideration of Both Parties* (London: M. Cooper, 1744), 7.

11 "A Dramatic Author" [Arthur Murphy], *A Defence of Mr. Garrick, in Answer to the Letter-Writer. With Remarks Upon Plays and Players, and the Present State of the Stage* (London: R. Stevens, [1759?]), 22.

12 A. Aspinall, "Statistical Accounts of the London Newspapers in the Eighteenth Century," *English Historical Review*, 63/247 (1948), 201–32 (at 205).

13 Ibid., 201.

14 Ibid. See Table I, 208.

15 "Puff" in *OED Online* (accessed 10 March 2017).

16 Ibid.

17 "[S]ums received by the paper for the sale of newspapers and advertising are unlikely to have been exaggerated, since tax was payable on both, and any illegitimate income from the selling of puffs and paragraphs and from political

subsidy would only have increased the paper's income (if such sums did not go straight into the editor's pocket)." Barker, *Newspapers*, 50.

18 *Morning Chronicle*, "The Scenic Spectator," by "Lemuel Launce," no. 2 in occasional series. See the 5 October 1776 issue.

19 Foote, *Treatise on the Passions*, 4.

20 Ibid., 4.

21 Ibid., 5.

22 Shirley, *Brief Remarks*, 12–13, 18.

23 Ibid., 18.

24 Prologue to Samuel Foote's play *Taste* (1752), line 12, "Written by Mr. Garrick, and spoken by him in the Character of an *Auctioneer*." The prologue's first quatrain is visible in Hogarth's 1757 double portrait, "David and Eva Maria Garrick." Hogarth's image of the prologue-smith at work did not circulate in print during Garrick's life. Garrick holds out two fingers, as if in the midst of composing the prologue's next couplet, while Eva Maria tries to steal his quill. A volume of Shakespeare is visible behind the pen.

25 Charles Fleetwood is accused of a premeditated, violent claque during Garrick's pre-managerial period by the pamphlet author "B.Y.," who describes the technique of placing, "dispers'd in the Pit, several Men of doughty Valour, and undoubted Fame; and, that they might appear thoroughly disguised, procured them the Habits of Gentlemen, to sit by the Parties whom he was fearful would give these Sons of Thunder an Opportunity of exerting those excellent and useful Talents, their noble rough-hewn Natures had endowed them with." "B.Y.," *The Disputes between the Director of D—Y, and the Pit Potentates: Being a Letter to a Friend, Concerning the Behaviour of the Melancholly Manager of the Suff'ring Theatre; and Some Considerations on the Late Disturbances and the Causes Thereof: With a Few Hints on the Heroes and Heroines, G-RR–K, C-BB–R, Etc. The Whole Relating to Some Remarkable Occurrences in the Year 1744* (London: M. Cooper, 1744), 6. Fleetwood denied that these boxers were employed to bruise, silence and throw out dissenters, insisting that they were only carpenters and scene men.

26 James Boswell, *Boswell's London Journal 1762–1763* (New York: McGraw-Hill, 1950), 154–55.

27 Edward Gibbon, *Gibbon's Journal to January 28th, 1763*, ed. D.M. Low (London: Chatto & Windus, 1929), 203.

28 Boswell, *London Journal*, 162.

29 Ibid., 161.

30 Ibid., 225–26.

31 James Boswell, *Critical Strictures on the New Tragedy of Elvira, Written by Mr. David Malloch* (London: W. Flexney, [1763]), 16.

32 Ibid., 22. Boswell was not wrong to hear a delicately turned insult: his epilogue to *Elvira*, Garrick writes, is a "sugar-plum" (line 35) to please the audience, in case they "should not cry and should be dull" (line 6) at Mallet's tragedy.

33 Boaden (ed.), *Private Correspondence of David Garrick*, vol. 1, xxxiii.

34 Ibid., vol. i, 436.
35 Arthur Murphy published essays under the pseudonym 'Charles Ranger' in the *Gray's-Inn Journal* in the *Craftsman* from 21 October 1752 for 49 weeks; and from 29 September 1753 – 21 September 1754, in the now separately published *Gray's-Inn Journal*. In 1754, the 52 new numbers of the *Gray's-Inn Journal* were reprinted as a single folio volume, and in 1756, they were published in a two-volume edition of 104 numbers, "which probably included those he had written for the *Craftsman.*" Philip H. Highfill, "Arthur Murphy," in Highfill, Kalman A. Burnim and Edward A. Langhans (eds.), *A Biographical Dictionary of Actors, Actresses, Musicians, Dancers, Managers & Other Stage Personnel in London, 1660–1800*, 16 vols. (Carbondale: Southern Illinois University Press, 1973–93), vol. x, 392.
36 Boaden (ed.), *Private Correspondence of David Garrick*, vol. i, 66.
37 Ibid. See also *Letters of David Garrick*, vol. i, 203.
38 *Letters of David Garrick*, vol. i, 204 fn.
39 Stone (ed.), *London Stage*, Part 4, vol. ii, 597–600, 604; 496–98 and *passim.*
40 For details of the dispute over *Cleone*, see James E. Tierney (ed.), *The Correspondence of Robert Dodsley 1733–1764* (Cambridge University Press, 1988), 12. See also Solomon, *Rise of Dodsley*, 178–201.
41 *Letters of David Garrick*, vol. i, 318–19.
42 Dodsley published Garrick's poem "Death and the Doctor" in Robert Dodsley, *A Collection of Poems by Several Hands*, 3 vols., 2nd edn (London: printed for R. Dodsley, 1748), vol. iii, 239–40; his "Inscriptions on a Monument to the Memory of a Lady's Bullfinch" was published in both Dodsley's *Collection* (vol. iii, 240–41) and the *London Magazine* (February 1747, 95); Garrick's verses "To Mr. Gray, on the Publication of his Odes in 1757" appeared in the *London Chronicle*, in which Dodsley was proprietor, and so on. For further instances of Garrick's publications in Dodsley's print holdings, see Mary E. Knapp, *A Checklist of Verse by David Garrick* (Charlottesville: University of Virginia Press for the Bibliographical Society of the University of Virginia, 1955).
43 Tierney (ed.), *Correspondence of Robert Dodsley*, 382–83.
44 George Anne Bellamy, *An Apology for the Life of George Anne Bellamy, Late of Covent-Garden Theatre*, 3rd edn, 5 vols. (London: John Bell, for the Author, 1785), vol. iii, 109.
45 Tierney (ed.), *Correspondence of Robert Dodsley*, 392.
46 [John Hill], *An Account of the Tragedy of Cleone* (London: M. Cooper, 1758), 4.
47 Ibid., 11, 16, 18.
48 Tierney (ed.), *Correspondence of Robert Dodsley*, 386.
49 "An Impartial Hand" [Charles Macklin?], *Stage Policy Detected; or Some Select Pieces of Theatrical Secret History Laid Open: In a Letter to a Certain Manager on His Imaginary Justification of His Late Conduct* (London: J. Robinson, 1744), 41.

50 George Belch and Michael Belch, *Advertising and Promotion: An Integrated Marketing Communications Perspective*, 9th edn (New York: McGraw-Hill, 2012), 59.

51 Fitzgerald remarks perceptively that Garrick's broken conversational speech, often parodied by critics, may have been strategic: "'Hey, now! now-what-all,' went on Mr. Garrick. 'How-really this-this-is—why, well, well, well, do call on me on Monday, and you may depend on my doing all I can for you.' This broken style of speech was Mr. Garrick's characteristic when addressing his inferiors, and was, in fact, his *managerial* manner, and may have been found very useful in helping him to a sort of vague generality, without committing him to any positive declaration. It was not a bad auxiliary for one who was asked for so much, and had to refuse so much." Percy Hetherington Fitzgerald, *The Life of David Garrick; from Original Family Papers, and Numerous Published and Unpublished Sources*, 2 vols. (London: Tinsley Brothers), 331–32.

52 Williams, *Letter to David Garrick*, 7, 22.

53 Anon., "A Collection of Original Letters from a Young American Gentleman in London, to His Friend, &c. Letter II," *Town and Country Magazine*, 6 (1774), 130–32 (at 131).

54 Ibid., 131.

55 Raven, *Publishing Business*, 123.

56 Purdon, *Letter to David Garrick*, 19.

57 Ibid., 21.

58 Genest, *Some Account of the English Stage*, vol. V, 498.

59 *The Early Journals and Letters of Fanny Burney*, ed. Lars Troide, 3 vols. (Oxford: Clarendon Press, 1988), vol. I, 151.

60 Murphy, *Life of David Garrick*, vol. I, 248–49.

61 Tobias Smollett, "The Character of Mr. Garrick," *Gentleman's Magazine*, 12 (October 1742), 527.

62 Garrick, *Essay on Acting*, 5.

63 Ibid., 9, 17.

64 Anon. [David Garrick], *Reasons why David Garrick, Esq; Should Not appear on the Stage, in a Letter to John Rich, Esq;* (London: J. Cooke, 1759), 11, 33–34. The British Library copy bears the words, "I believe by Garrick" on the page before the frontispiece; later observations on the French actress Mlle Clairon and other internal evidence substantiate the claim.

65 Ibid., 29–30.

66 Shirley, *Brief Remarks*, 39.

67 Williams, *Letter to David Garrick*, 33.

68 Harvard University Houghton Library: Theatre Collection f TS 1116.256.3: "David Garrick; Original Manuscripts, Etc. [of and Relating to David Garrick]," item 19, lines 18–27.

69 Fixity is a distressing element of all death masks, but it is especially disturbing on the face of a man legendary for the prodigious mobility of his features. The medium of print alone cannot be held responsible: it is the observable drape

and pull of gravity on a recumbent face, rather than the downward pull of gravity on a vertically disposed face that drains the features of even the potential of mobility visible in prints of Garrick as a living actor. For more on death masks, see Marcia Pointon, "Casts, Imprints, and the Deathliness of Things: Artifacts at the Edge," *Art Bulletin*, 96/2 (2014), 170–95.

70 Cunningham, *Shakespeare and Garrick*.

71 See, for example, Holland (ed.), *Great Shakespeareans*; Peter Holland, "David Garrick: '3dly, as an Author,'" *Studies in Eighteenth-Century Culture*, 25 (1996), 39–62; Jean I. Marsden, "Improving Shakespeare: From the Restoration to Garrick," in Stanley Wells and Sarah Stanton (eds.), *The Cambridge Companion to Shakespeare on Stage* (Cambridge University Press, 2002), 21–36; Michael Dobson, *The Making of the National Poet: Shakespeare, Adaptation and Authorship, 1660–1769* (Oxford: Clarendon Press, 1995).

72 Richard Rolt, *A Poetical Epistle from Shakespear in Elysium, to Mr. Garrick, at Drury-Lane Theatre* (London: J. Newbery and W. Owen, 1752), lines 50–53.

73 Murphy may have stolen this phrase from MacNamara Morgan, who wrote, "I look upon a good Player, as the best Commentator; he calls forth latent Beauties from the Poet's Works, that a common Reader, tho' deeply learned, cou'd never have imagined." See MacNamara Morgan, "A Letter to Miss Nossiter. Occasioned by Her First Appearance on the Stage: In Which Is Contained Remarks Upon Her Manner of Playing the Character of Juliet; Interspersed with Some Other Theatrical Observations" (London: W. Owen, G. Woodfall, 1753), 13. Morgan's use of the phrase stresses the importance of a new, skilled young actress like Miss Nossiter in interpreting roles afresh; Murphy (if he was aware of Morgan's phrase) turned it to Garrick's account.

74 Arthur Murphy, "Letter of 20 April 1754 to Charles Ranger"; No. 79 of the *Gray's-Inn Journal*, in *The Works of Arthur Murphy, Esq*, 7 vols. (London: T. Cadell, 1786), vol. VI, 255.

75 Murphy, *Defence of Mr. Garrick*, 28–29. Other internal evidence of Murphy's authorship includes a spirited defence of *The Orphan of China*: "Mr. *Murphy* must at least be allowed to have some Merit as an Improver of the *Frenchman's* Plan, by lopping off all the Love-Parts, (which must have proved disgustful to an *English* Audience)"; and an allusion to the *Gray's-Inn Journals*, which "the Author only play'd with, and never intended them to be as exact, and finished as their Cotemporaries, the *World* or the *Connoisseur*" (14, 16).

76 *Works of Arthur Murphy*, vol. IV, 402–03.

77 *The Works of Ben. Jonson*, ed. Peter Whalley (London: D. Midwinter, W. Innys and J. Richardson *et. al.*, 1756), vol I, xxiv.

78 Elizabeth Robinson Montagu, *An Essay on the Writings and Genius of Shakespear, Compared with the Greek and French Dramatic Poets. With Some Remarks Upon the Mistrepresentations of Mons. De Voltaire* (London: J. Dodsley, Mess. Baker and Leigh, J. Walter, T. Cadell, J. Wilkie, 1769), 15–16.

79 John Monck Mason (ed.), *The Dramatick Works of Philip Massinger Complete*, 4 vols. (London: T. Davies, T. Payne, L. Davis, J. Nichols, T. Evans, W. Davis, H. Payne, 1779). vol. I, xvi.

80 Ibid., xviii.
81 David Erskine Baker, *The Companion to the Play-House: Or, an Historical Account of All the Dramatic Writers (and Their Works) That Have Appeared in Great Britain and Ireland, from the Commencement of Our Theatrical Exhibitions, Down to the Present Year 1764. Composed in the Form of a Dictionary, for the More Readily Turning to Any Particular Author, or Performance*, 2 vols. (London: T. Becket and P.A. Dehondt, C. Henderson, T. Davies, 1764), vol. 1, xxviii.
82 [Francis Gentleman], *The Dramatic Censor; or, Critical Companion*, 2 vols. (London J. Bell, C. Etherington, 1770), vol. 1, 107.
83 Garrick's role as Shakespeare's best commentator appears in Jane Gomeldon's series of humorous essays *The Medley* (Newcastle: J. White and T. Saint, 1766), in the surest sign of widespread cultural understanding of a trope: a joke. In "All the World Acts the Player" the narrator explains that to see Garrick play Shakespeare's characters eliminates the need for costly higher education or arduous study: "All People are not made to read, or to understand what they read, without something more than a Book to give them a Hint," the narrator begins; fortunately, "*Garrick* 's Action makes all sure: None can mistake, when *Garrick* acts what *Shakespeare* means," and "taken as a Study, with *Garrick* for his Expositor, he might save a Student his Course of Ethics, at College, or a pretty Genius his Study of an Encyclopedia." (136, 7, 138).
84 Murphy, *Life of David Garrick*, vol. ii, 181–82.
85 Ibid., 183.
86 Ibid., 183.
87 For reprintings of this poem, see *European Magazine, and London Review*, May 1784, 37; *Edinburgh Magazine, or Literary Miscellany*, 17 n.s. (1801), 204; *Gentleman's Magazine*, 77 (January 1807), 38. It appeared in London newspapers, and in provincial papers such as *Adams's Weekly Courant* of Chester for 29 February 1780. Throughout the nineteenth century, it appears in publications pertaining to the educability of deaf persons, as a testament to their capacity. Murphy's claim that Whiteford wrote the verses seems to have been overlooked, beginning with the poem's second appearance in the *Public Advertiser* for 2 August 1783, where it is touted as a "SPECIMEN *of the* Degree *of* PERFECTION *in* written Language *to which* THE NATURALLY DEAF *are capable of arriving. Written by a* DEAF *Pupil of* Mr. Braidwood's, *without Assistance or Amendment.*"
88 See, for example, the *Monthly Epitome* for January 1802, 96.
89 *Letters of David Garrick*, vol. 1, 242 fn.; citing Joseph Warton, *Essay upon the Genius and Writings of Pope*, 2 vols. (London: M. Cooper, 1756), vol. 1, 123.
90 See William Shakespeare, *Antony and Cleopatra; an Historical Play, Written by William Shakespeare: Fitted for the Stage by Abridging Only; and Now Acted, at the Theatre-Royal in Drury-Lane, by His Majesty's Servants* (London: J. and R. Tonson, [1758]), 7.
91 Oliver Goldsmith, *Retaliation: A Poem. Including Epitaphs on the Most Distinguished Wits of This Metropolis* (London: G. Kearsly, 1774), 6.

92 *Letters of David Garrick*, vol. I, 34.

93 Robert D. Hume, "John Rich as Manager and Entrepreneur," in Jeremy Barlow and Berta Joncus (eds.), *The Stage's Glory: John Rich (1692–1761)* (Newark: University of Delaware Press, 2011), 29–60 (at 46–48).

94 Ibid., 55.

95 Pierre Danchin (ed.), *The Prologues and Epilogues of the Eighteenth Century: The Third Part: 1737–1760*, vol. v (Nancy: Éditions Messene, 1990), 268. See also Dodsley, *Collection of Poems By Several Hands*, vol. III, 150–52; and Samuel [Johnson *et al.*], *Miscellaneous and Fugitive Pieces*, 3 vols., vol. II (London: T. Davies, 1773).

96 Danchin (ed.), *Prologues and Epilogues*, 336–37.

97 *Letters of David Garrick*, vol. I, 35n.

98 *The Journal of David Garrick, Describing His Visit to France and Italy in 1763*, ed. George Winchester Stone (New York: Modern Language Association of America, 1939), 8.

99 David Erskine Baker and Isaac Reed, *Biographia Dramatica: Or, a Companion to the Playhouse*, 3 vols. (London, 1812), vol. I, 264–65.

100 [William Cooke], *Memoirs of Charles Macklin, Comedian, with the Dramatic Characters, Manners, Anecdotes, &c. of the Age in Which He Lived: Forming an History of the Stage During Almost the Whole of the Last Century*, 2 vols. (London: James Asperne, 1804), vol. I, 247–48.

101 *Letters of David Garrick*, vol. I, 172.

102 Garrick, *Essay on Acting*, 7–8.

103 Anon., *A Letter to Mr. Garrick on the Opening of the Theatre, with Observations on the Conduct of Managers, to Actors, Authors, and Audiences: And Particularly to New-Performers* (London: J. Coote, 1758), 5–6.

104 Purdon, *Letter to David Garrick*, 18–19.

105 Desmond Shawe-Taylor *et al.*, *Every Look Speaks: Portraits of David Garrick* (Bath: Moore Stephens, 2003), 57–58.

106 David Mannings, "Reynolds, Garrick, and the Choice of Hercules," *Eighteenth-Century Studies*, 17/3 (1984), 259–83.

107 Ibid., 261, 262.

108 *Letters of David Garrick*, vol. II, 433.

109 "An original Critique on the Merits of Mr. Garrick as an Actor," *London Museum*, January 1770), 48.

110 Murphy, *Life of David Garrick*, vol. I, 296–97.

111 Ibid., vol. I, 261–62.

112 "Old Comedian," *The Life and Death of David Garrick, Esq. The Celebrated English Roscius*, 2nd edn (London: J. Pridden, S. Bladon, J. Mathews, 1779), 2–3.

113 Lewis [Luigi] Riccoboni, *A General History of the Stage, from Its Origin*, 2nd edn (London: W. Owen and Lockyer Davis, 1754), iii.

114 Ibid., ii. For mention of Garrick's managerial and writing skills, see vi, x.

115 Robert Sayer and John Smith, *Dramatic Characters, or Different Portraits of the English Stage*, (London: Robert Sayer and Jo[h]n Smith, 1770).

116 *Epigrams of Martial, &c. With Mottos from Horace, &c. Translated, Imitated, Adapted, and Addrest to the Nobility, Clergy, and Gentry*, trans. Rev. Mr. Scott (London: J. Wilkie, J. Walter and H. Parker, 1773). Scott promises that if readers find a riddle too hard, they may write the *Public Advertiser*, "which he sees every day," for a solution, and he "will not fail telling them what it is, the very next day, or the day after at farthest" (30). He thus attempts to engage newspaper readers in promoting his work without incurring advertising costs.

117 Rev. Mr. William Scott, *A Sermon Preached at the Court End of the Town and in the City, on Sunday October 25, 1772. On the King's Accession to the Throne of These Realms. Dedicated to Mr. Garrick* (London: J. Wilkie, J. Walter and H. Parker, 1773), vii–viii.

118 William Shakespeare, *Bell's Edition of Shakespeare's Plays, as They Are Now Performed at the Theatres Royal in London; Regulated from the Prompt Books of Each House*, 5 vols. (London: John Bell and C. Etherington, 1774), vol. 1.

119 *[Illustrated Plates for] Bell's Edition of Shakespeare's Works Compleat, Including His Poems ... To Complete the First Five Volumes* (London: John Bell, [1773–76?]).

120 H.R. Plomer, E.R. McC. Dix, G.J. Gray and G.H. Bushnell, *A Dictionary of the Printers and Booksellers Who Were at Work in England, Scotland and Ireland, from 1726 to 1775* (Oxford University Press for the Bibliographical Society, 1968), 111.

121 Isaac Bickerstaff, *The Padlock: A Comic Opera. As It Is Perform'd by His Majesty's Servants, at the Theatre-Royal in Drury-Lane* (London: W. Griff[i]n, at Garrick's Head, [1768?]).

122 No numbers of this short-lived journal appear to survive. See "Gentleman's Journal, or Weekly Register," in George Watson (ed.), *The New Cambridge Bibliography of English Literature*, vol. II (Cambridge University Press, 1971).

123 *Letters of David Garrick*, vol. 1, 124. Griffin may have raised this sign over his earlier shop in Fetter Lane, or Garrick may refer to another bookseller's sign; the letter predates title-page references to Garrick's Head functioning as Griffin's sign.

124 Garrick did send the poem to the Countess of Burlington, as noted in his letter of 19 September 1749, but it has not been found, as the *Letters'* editors note. Ibid., vol. 1, 128–29.

125 Heather McPherson, "Theatrical Celebrity and the Commodification of the Actor," in Julia Swindells and David Francis Taylor (eds.), *The Oxford Handbook of the Georgian Theatre 1737–1832* (Oxford University Press, 2014), 192–212 (at 193).

126 Ibid., 196.

127 Ibid., 201–02. As McPherson notes, Garrick's image was also available on tin-glazed earthenware tiles, manufactured by Liverpool printer John Sadler and his partner Guy Green in the 1770s, based on the engravings in Bell's *British Shakespeare*. Of the set of twenty tiles featuring actors and actresses, three represent Garrick: as Abel Drugger, Sir John Brute and Don John. These tiles may be viewed at the Victoria and Albert Museum.

4 A Short History of Negative Publicity

1 *Letters of David Garrick*, vol. ii, 905.
2 McIntyre, *Garrick*, 127, fn. McIntyre estimates Garrick's height at "not much more than 5' 3"."
3 Garrick, *Essay on Acting*, 2, title page.
4 In *The Thespian Dictionary; or, Dramatic Biography of the present Age; Containing Sketches of the Lives, Lists of the Productions, Various Merits, etc., etc. of All the Principal Dramatists, Composers, Commentators, Managers, Actors, and Actresses of the United Kingdom: Interspersed with Numerous Original Anecdotes, Forming a Complete Modern History of the English Stage* (London: James Cundee, 1805; 1st edn 1802). Quin's remark appears in the "Garrick" entry, which notes that when Quin similarly disparaged Garrick's shortness in the character of "Jacky Brute," Garrick persisted with the character.
5 Foote, *Treatise on the Passions*, 14.
6 Smollett, "Character of Mr. Garrick," 527.
7 Jonah Berger, Alan T. Sorensen and Scott J. Rasmussen, "Positive Effects of Negative Publicity: When Negative Reviews Increase Sales," *Marketing Science*, 29/5 (2010), 815–27 (at 816).
8 Ibid., 819–20.
9 Ibid., 820.
10 Janine Barchas, *Graphic Design, Print Culture, and the Eighteenth-Century Novel* (Cambridge University Press, 2003), 158.
11 Charles R. Duke and Les Carlson, "Applying Implicit Memory Measures: Word Fragment Completion in Advertising Tests," *Journal of Current Issues and Research in Advertising*, 16/2 (1994), 29–39 (at 29).
12 Garrick, *Essay on Acting*, 2, 6, 3.
13 Ibid., B.
14 Ibid., A2.
15 Ibid., 14–15.
16 Ibid., 16.
17 Rohini Ahluwalia, Robert E. Burnkrant and H. Rao Unnava, "Consumer Response to Negative Publicity: The Moderating Role of Commitment," *Journal of Marketing Research*, 37/2 (2000), 203–14 (at 204).
18 Ibid., 204.
19 Garrick, *Essay on Acting*, 6.
20 Davies, *Memoirs*, vol. ii, 80.
21 Ibid., vol. i, 55.
22 Fred K. Beard, *Humor in the Advertising Business: Theory, Practice, and Wit* (Lanham, MD: Rowman & Littlefield, 2008), 91.
23 Davies, *Memoirs*, vol. i, 163. Stone and Kahrl, *David Garrick*, 551, argue that the *Essay* is "Garrick's manifesto of a different concept of performing from that spelled out by the rhetoricians," written "to forestall criticism of the novelty and to advertise the new departure in Shakespearean productions." McIntyre, *Garrick*, 85, likewise considers the *Essay* as "intended to blunt any

possible criticism by anticipating it, and to signal some of the ways in which his interpretation and performance would be distinctive."

24 Garrick, *Essay on Acting*, 18.

25 Ibid., 2.

26 Lisa Freeman, *Character's Theatre: Genre and Identity on the Eighteenth-Century English Stage* (Philadelphia: University of Pennsylvania Press, 2002), 27.

27 Garrick, *Essay on Acting*, 13–14.

28 This pamphlet prints Macklin's and Garrick's responses: [Charles Macklin], *Mr. Macklin's Reply to Mr. Garrick's Answer. To Which Are Prefix'd, All the Papers Which Have Publickly Appeared, in Regard to This Important Dispute* (London: J. Roberts and A. Dodd, 1743).

29 Macklin's portrayal of Shylock is praised: "Another Comedian *now living*, tho' not upon the Stage (it being so replete with greater Geniuses) has been observ'd constantly to attend the *'Change* for *Weeks together*, before he exhibited one of *Shakespear's* most inimitable and *difficult* Characters, and so far succeeded by his *great Attention* and *Observation* of the *Manners, Dress*, and *Behaviour* of a *particular Tribe of People*, that the *Judgment, Application*, and *extraordinary Pains* he took to divert the Publick *rationally*, was amply return'd with crowded Theatres, and *unequall'd Applauses*; nay, to so *great a Degree* did they shew their Approbation to this *Pains-taking Genius*, that he is at present more known by the Name of the *Character he perform'd*, than by *his own*." Garrick, *Essay on Acting*, 10–11.

30 Foote, *Treatise on the Passions*, 15.

31 "Old Comedian," *Life and Death of David Garrick*, 9–10.

32 Murphy, *Life of David Garrick*, vol. II, 177–78.

33 *Letters of David Garrick*, vol. II, 557.

34 His attention to the costs of Garrick's advertising himself through news of illness suggests Burney was attuned to the import of this aspect of Garrick's self-fashioning. British Library: 939.d, 939.e, 937.g.95–96: "Burney Collection. A collection of notebooks … dealing with the life and work of David Garrick," cited clippings on microfilm 939.d.35.

35 Fanny Burney, *Early Journals and Letters*, vol. I, 172.

36 References in this paragraph are to "Burney Collection" clippings found on microfilm 939.d.25.

37 Ibid., microfilm 939.d.7.

38 Forster Collection, FL4–3321.

39 "Burney Collection," microfilm 939.d.21.

40 E.F. [Samuel Foote?], *Mr. Garrick's Conduct, as Manager of the Theatre-Royal in Drury-Lane, Considered. In a Letter Addressed to Him* (London: C. Corbett, [1747]), 12.

41 Ibid., 18.

42 Garrick Club: unaccessioned three-volume scrapbook by John Nixon titled "Dramatic Annals: Critiques on Plays and Performers. Vol. I. (–III). 1741 to 1845": clipping hand-dated 1773 from vol. I, 1741–1785.

43 [J.T.], *A Letter of Compliment to the Ingenious Author of a Treatise on the Passions, So Far as They Regard the Stage; with a Critical Enquiry into the Theatrical Merit of Mr. G—K, Mr. Q—N, and Mr. B—Y, &c. With Some Further Remarks on Mr. M–N. And a Few Hints on Our Modern Actresses, Particularly Mrs. C—R and Mrs. P——D* (London: C. Corbett, 1747), 38.

44 [William Combe], *Sanitas, Daughter of Aesculapius. To David Garrick, Esq. A Poem* (London: G. Kearsly, 1772), 16–17.

45 Ibid., 17, 22–24.

46 Anon., *A Letter to Mr. Garrick, on His Having Purchased a Patent for Drury-Lane Play-House* (London: J. Freeman, [1747]), 7.

47 Ibid., 8.

48 Sir William Ashburnham, *A Sermon Preached before His Grace William Duke of Devonshire, President, and the Governors of the London-Hospital, at Mile-End, for the Relief of All Sick and Diseased Persons, Especially Manufacturers, and Seamen in Merchant-Service, &c. At St. Lawrence Jewry, on Monday, April 11, 1763* (London: H. Woodfall, [1764]), 14.

49 See *Old England*, 9 April 1748, for articles on these developments.

50 Davis-Kendall TA ms, Harry Ransom Center, University of Texas at Austin.

51 Anon., *An Account of the British Lying-in Hospital, for Married Women, in Brownlow-Street, Long-Acre, from Its Institution in November 1749, to December the 31st, 1770* (London: C. Say, [1771]).

52 Thomas Francklin, *A Sermon Preached at the Parish-Church of St. Anne, Westminster, on Thursday, May the 10th, 1758. Before the Governors of the Middlesex-Hospital, for Sick and Lame; and for Lying-in Married Women* (London: Published at the Request of the Society, 1758). 19. A benefit offered by John Rich in 1755, listed in the charity's table of Benefactions, made more – over £215.

53 Garrick appears as a "Perpetual Governor," for example, in John Nicols, *A Sermon Preached at the Parish Church of St. Andrew, Holborn, on Thursday, March 26, 1767, before the President, Vice-Presidents, Treasurer, and Governors, of the City of London Lying-in Hospital for Married Women, at Shaftesbury-House in Aldersgate-Street* (London: Published at the Request of the Society by C. Say, for the charity, [1767]).

54 Anon., Folger Shakespeare Library, Scrapbook B.26.2.

55 *Letters of David Garrick*, vol. III, 1054.

56 Thomas Morell, *A Sermon Preached at the Anniversary Meeting of the Sons of the Clergy, in the Cathedral Church of St. Paul, on Thursday, May 14, 1772 … Published at the Request of the Stewards. To Which Is Added, a List of the Several Amounts Arising from the Collections Made at the Anniversary Meeting of the Sons of the Clergy, since the Year 1721* (London: John and Francis Rivington, [1772]).

57 Linda E. Merians, "The London Lock Hospital and the Lock Asylum for Women," in Linda E. Merians (ed.), *The Secret Malady: Venereal Disease in Eighteenth-Century Britain and France* (Lexington: University Press of Kentucky, 1996), 128–46 (at 129).

58 Brian Vickers identifies Steevens as the author of the 'Animadvertor' theatrical criticisms. Brian Vickers (ed.), *William Shakespeare: The Critical Heritage*, vol. v: *1765–1774* (London: Routledge, 1979), 487.

59 Pedicord, *Theatrical Public*, 137, estimates that 23 authors had a single play only accepted by Garrick, writing, "of the 84 tragedies and histories brought forward by Garrick, 60 could be termed successful and had a better than average chance of gaining a place in her repertoire. Of the 60, we see that 32 were stock plays, revivals, alterations or adaptations, while 28 plays written and produced within the limits of his management were also successful. Thirty-three authors are represented in the successful dramas, but 23 of them are limited to a single winning entry."

60 Davies, *Memoirs*, vol. I, 211.

61 Ibid., 208–09.

62 *Letters of David Garrick*, vol. II, 471.

63 One of Kenrick's most popular works was the uncharacteristically pious *Whole Duty of Woman* (1753) which according to the *DNB* went into "at least five editions in his lifetime and remained popular well into the next century." C.S. Rogers and Betty Rizzo, "Kenrick, William (1729/30–1779)," in Matthew and Harrison (eds.), *Oxford Dictionary of National Biography*.

64 See Michal Kobialka, "Words and Bodies: A Discourse on Male Sexuality in Late Eighteenth-Century English Representational Practices," *Theatre Research International*, 28/1 (2003), 1–19; Robert Fahrner, "A Reassessment of Garrick's *The Male Coquette: Or, Seventeen-Hundred Fifty Seven* as Veiled Discourse," *Eighteenth-Century Life*, 17/3 (1993), 1–13; Charles Conaway, "'Thou'rt the Man': David Garrick, William Shakespeare, and the Masculinization of the Eighteenth-Century Stage," *Restoration and Eighteenth-Century Theatre Research*, 19/1 (2004), 22–42.

65 For Kenrick's representations of these quarrels, see William Kenrick, *A Letter to David Garrick, Esq., Occasioned by His Having Moved the Court of King's Bench against the Publisher of Love in the Suds, or the Lamentations of Roscius for His Nyky* (London: J. Wheble, 1772), 13, 28 (for references to *Falstaff's Wedding*), 20–22 (regarding *The Widow'd Wife*).

66 Alan Kendall identifies a Puttick and Simpson catalogue (1862) as the source of the letter from Garrick to Thompson in which Garrick promises to beat Kenrick for his infamy. Alan Kendall, *David Garrick: A Biography*, 1st US edn (New York: St. Martin's Press, 1985), 156. Garrick's proposed seconds in this meeting were the printer William Griffin, who published Isaac Bickerstaff's work, and the printer Thomas Becket. "Your Suggestion about Griffin Becket & Yr Publisher is a poor tale from ye beginning to ye End," Garrick scoffs at Kenrick. In the same unsent letter, he denies instigating Goldsmith and others to publish against Kenrick in the *Morning Chronicle* [post 15 June 1772]. *Letters of David Garrick*, vol. II, 806–07.

67 Boaden (ed.), *Private Correspondence of David Garrick*, vol. I, 473.

68 The poem refers to Sodom (9); to "Platonic love" (8); to Catamites (24), etc.

69 William Kenrick, *A Letter to David Garrick, Esq. From William Kenrick, LL.D.* [Containing *Love in the Suds: A Town Eclogue. Being the Lamentation of Roscius for the Loss of His Nyky*] (London: J. Wheble, 1772), 15 (hereafter *Love in the Suds*).

70 Kenrick is almost certainly the author of the anonymous epigrammatic response to the poem, published in the *General Evening Post*, 23 May 1771, later a footnote in *Love in the Suds:*

> When mincing masters, met with misses,
> Pay mutual compliments for kisses,
> Miss Polly sings, no doubt, divinely!
> And Master Jacky spouts as finely!
> But odious such a fulsome greeting,
> When two old stagers have a meeting:
> Foh! how I hate the filthy pother!
> What! Men beslobber one another!

71 Kenrick, *Love in the Suds*, 18.

72 A letter [19 October 1778] from Garrick to Ralph Griffiths refers to a review of Henry Brooke's *A Collection of Pieces* (1778) which Garrick wrote for the *Monthly Review*, vol. LIX, October 1778, 241f., November 1778, 357f. He tells Griffiths, "if you think any Note necessary pray insert it, & I beg that You will never give YrSelf ye trouble to send proofs of my stuff to me, unless you may have some doubts – I shall Endeavor to do something better for yr next –" *Letters of David Garrick*, vol. III, 1248.

73 See Boaden (ed.), *Private Correspondence of David Garrick*, vol. I, 256: Garrick asks his brother George to send him the *Monthly Review*, and mentions Becket is already sending a *Gentleman's Magazine*.

74 "In his old age Joseph Cradock said that 'Garrick rendered his life miserable by believing & encour[ag]ing tale-bearers & feeling hurt in the extreme at every little squib that appeared in the daily prints & novels of the day. Tom King, the actor, & Becket the bookseller, were the persons who brought Garrick every disagreeable paragraph & tittle-tattle of the day. Becket was a sort of runner for Garrick. I have called on Garrick in the morning & no person could be in higher spirits & when I have repeated my visit about an hour or two after I have found him quite the reverse; depressed by the daily tales &c of the above gentlemen.'" Alan S. Downer, "The Diary of Benjamin Webster," *Theatre Annual* (1945), 47–64 (at 64).

75 One such endorsement to the Baron von Diede, 22 [September 1768], read: "Mr Garrick takes the liberty of recommending the Bearer of this, Mr Becket the Bookseller, as a most Worthy, honest Man in his profession, & who is very desirous to be honour'd with the King of Denmark's commands, if his Majesty Should have any Occasion for English or Other books–Mr Garrick begs pardon for this impertinence, & should not have taken the Liberty he has but for One, (Mr Becket), for whom he has the greatest regard." *Letters of David Garrick*, vol. II, 630.

76 Ibid., 447–48.

77 "I call him the *Worm*, from an agreeable vermicular Motion he has with his arms & Legs," Garrick writes of Becket. Ibid., 684.

78 Kenrick, *Love in the Suds*, 16–18.

79 Ibid., 16.

80 Harris traces the development of this relationship: the *London Daily Post*'s "first issue in 1734 announced that the managers of the five principal houses had, for convenience, decided to advertise in one publication, and a notice in each advertisement showed that the paper was to be used exclusively for performances at Drury Lane, Covent Garden, and Goodman's Fields, and regularly for those at the Haymarket. During the 1760s the ledger of the *Public Advertiser*, the amended title of the same paper, showed payments to the London theatres of up to £200 per annum." The ledger is December 1766, British Library Add. MSS 38, 169; see *also London Daily Post*, 1 and 4 November 1734, *passim*. Harris, *London Newspapers*, 54.

81 Kenrick, *Love in the Suds*, 18.

82 Ibid.

83 Ibid.

84 Ibid.

85 Barker, *Newspapers*, 57, mentions one such case, in which Henry Bate of the *Morning Herald* received government money despite his paper's bias against Pitt.

86 Kenrick, *Love in the Suds*, 19.

87 "*This Day is published*, LOVE in the SUDS for John Wheble, 24 Paternoster Row," reads the advertisement in the *Morning Chronicle* of 1 July 1772.

88 "The King's Bench was the highest court of common law in England and Wales, with jurisdiction over both civil and criminal actions. Civil business was conducted on the 'Plea Side' and criminal business on the 'Crown Side' . . . Crown Side had three separate jurisdictions:

 • Original jurisdiction over all matters of a criminal and public nature as the *custos morum* of all the subjects of the realm;
 • Supervisory powers over inferior courts;
 • A local jurisdiction, in that its presence within any county extinguished the rights of all other courts to hear and try criminal cases. In practice, since the court had become fixed at Westminster by the fifteenth century, its local jurisdiction was over Middlesex and its subordinate jurisdictions (principally Westminster and the Tower Hamlets)."

National Archives, "Court of King's Bench," www.nationalarchives.gov.uk/records/research-guides/kings-bench.htm.

89 Barker, *Newspapers*, 65, characterizes William Woodfall's *Morning Chronicle* as "a self-consciously uncommitted paper," and his brother Henry Woodfall's *Public Advertiser* as not as "neutral as that of his brother [. . . but] not nearly as partisan as other newspapers." She observes, "impartiality did not mean a lack of bias in all coverage, but a willingness to publish letters and paragraphs partisan to both sides of the political debate."

90 Haig, *Gazetteer*, 137.
91 Black, *English Press*, 35–36.
92 George Crabbe, *The News-Paper: A Poem* (London: J. Dodsley, 1785), 16.
93 Barker, *Newspapers*, 59; Werkmeister, *London Daily Press*, 5.
94 This appears to be reprinted from the 8 July 1772 *Daily Advertiser*.
95 Kenrick, *Love in the Suds*, A2.
96 Ibid., A2.
97 *Letters of David Garrick*, vol. ii, 810. The Latin translates as: 'and served not without renown' (Horace, *Odes*, iii.xxvi.2).
98 Reed writes: "Our reconciliation continued about two Years in which interval under the signature of Benedick I attack'd Dr. Kenrick on account of an infernal insinuation laid to Mr Garricks charge. My Letters with the Doctors answers first appear'd in the Morning Chronicle and were afterwards published by him by way of Appendix to his scandalous Town Eclogue call'd Love in the Suds." Folger Shakespeare Library: T.a.112: Joseph Reed, "Theatrical Duplicity, or a Genuine Narrative of the Conduct of *David Garrick* Esqr. To *Joseph Reed* on His Tragedy of *Dido* Containing All the Letters and Several Conversations Which Passed between the Manager, Author, and Others on That Subject. By the Author of the Register Office," 95.
99 The *Morning Chronicle* for 7 October 1772 prints a Kenrickian account of the withdrawal of motion.
100 There are insufficient numbers extant to determine if the apology might also have been printed in the *London Packet*; Say does not appear to have repeated the apology in his *Craftsman or Say's Weekly Journal* issues that November.
101 Goldsmith, *Retaliation*, 13–14.
102 Thomas Whincop lists Joseph Reed as "a Tradesman at *Stockton* in the Bishoprick of *Durham*, and, having some Genius for Poetry, has printed one Dramatic Piece, called, *The Superannuated Gallant;* a Farce." Thomas Whincop, *Scanderbeg: Or, Love and Liberty. A Tragedy. To Which Are Added a List of All the Dramatic Authors, with Some Account of Their Lives, and of All the Dramatic Pieces Ever Published in the English Language, to the Year 1747* (London: W. Reeve, 1747), 274.
103 Much of what is known of Reed is drawn from a ninety-nine-page-long unpublished manuscript called "Theatrical Duplicity." There are two copies. Folger Shakespeare Library: T.a.112, is an undated fair copy written on paper watermarked 1832 and 1833 (Reed died in 1787). The other copy, Harvard University Houghton Library: Theatre Collection GEN TS 1253.8, has an inscription on its flyleaf: "The Author's Original Copy Given to me by his Son John Watson Reed Isaac Reed" and is in a different hand than the Folger copy. It seems that Isaac Reed, the Shakespeare scholar, owned Joseph Reed's mss at one point. The Houghton manuscript's emphatic underscores are more copious, eg.: "The Great reputation which Mr. Garrick hath deservedly acquir'd as an Actor, his Success as an Author, & his Abilities as a Manager have plac'd him in so high a degree of estimation, that it is a

kind of <u>critical</u> heresy to call in question his <u>Infallibility</u> in dramatic affairs. But notwithstanding the partiality of the Public in his favor, I shall endeavor to prove, that the supposed <u>Infallibility</u> of the theatrical <u>Pontiff</u> of Drury Lane is not always to be depended upon" (1). The manuscript quotes several external documents, including newspaper articles. The Houghton copy was accepted as genuine by the editors of Garrick's letters: letter 454 in *Letters of David Garrick*, vol. II, 567–68, uses this document as its copy-text, for example. Quotations of the work refer to the Folger manuscript's pagination.

104 Writes Reed (as "Dramatis Persona"): "I hired, at the important sum of two-pence a week, a queer, obsolete author, that you may perhaps have heard of, one William Shakespear, a great play-wright; but unluckily while I was perusing the first volume, I was detected by a dissenting clergyman, who ... was of opinion, that the knowledge of Shakespear was altogether unnecessary to a halter-maker. Well, what was to be done? I was so charmed with my cousin Shakespear, that I could not forget him; and to read him openly was downright defiance to my mother and her ministry. In this exigence I had recourse to a variety of wiles, by which I secured to myself the pleasure of perusing my favourite author without discovery" (582).

105 The opera *Tom Jones* ran for fourteen performances, and "Fielding encouraged Reed to construct the adaptation and was quite vocal in praising Reed's work and celebrating the achievements of the piece." L. Lynette Eckersley, "Joseph Reed," in Matthew and Harrison (eds.), *Oxford Dictionary of National Biography*.

106 Murphy, *Life of David Garrick*, vol. II, 47.

107 Eckersley, "Joseph Reed."

108 Reed, "Theatrical Duplicity," 17.

109 The first refusal Reed resolved by writing a mad scene for Dido, as Garrick requested. It is worth citing Reed's compositional method, as it shows how much of a presence (and a nuisance) Reed was in the theatre. To write the mad scene, Reed informs Mrs. Cibber that he must "first take <u>measure</u> of her" (15). He says, "'Madam I must see you in the Character Alicia: your various attitudes & revolutions of countenance will greatly assist me.' When therefore Jane Shore was next play'd I went to the House, & saw Mrs Cibber as she came off the stage in the 4th act. She desired me to go into the front, as I should there have a better view of her, I told her I should be more private behind the prompter* & desired her to turn herself as much as she could to the prompt-side–She went on for the mad scene ... When she had finished her part, She ask'd 'Have You had a good view?' 'Madam' says I, clapping my right hand on my forehead 'I have you here: I will write the mad scene before I breakfast to morrow.'" Reed, "Theatrical Duplicity," 15, 16.

110 Ibid., 24. Johnson apparently agreed with Garrick about the dubiousness of the quasi-Shakespearean language; Reed hints that Churchill was threatened by Evan Lloyd with publication of his opinion if it was positive and backed down, for "this great Satirist was even afraid of giving offence to Garrick" (18, 20). Reed wrote to "King David's Fort," 12 August 1761: "Will Mr.

Garrick so far give up his judgment and his power, as to refer the merits of "Dido" to the decision of Mr. Capel, Mr. Mason, and Mr. Paul Whitehead? or to Mr. Whitehead only? They are gentlemen with whom I have not a twentieth part of your intimacy ... You may prudently reply, that, as a manager, you may run a risk which you ought not to hazard on other people's judgment ... produce the receipts of the managers' six nights for any new tragedy you have played these seven years, and I shall give you sufficient security to make up the sum. If the play should be damned on the first night, I will engage to pay half the expense of dressing it." Boaden (ed.), *Private Correspondendence of David Garrick*, vol. I, 127.

111 John Nichols (ed.), *Illustrations of the Literary History of the Eighteenth Century. Consisting of Authentic Memoirs and Original Letters of Eminent Persons; and Intended as a Sequel to the Literary Anecdotes*, 8 vols. (London: J.B. Nichols and Son, 1828), vol. v, 116.

112 Reed, "Theatrical Duplicity," 25–26. For the complete, dismal saga of the play's rejections, see 23–27.

113 [Joseph Reed], "To the Printer," *Universal Museum, Or Gentleman's and Ladies Polite Magazine of History, Politicks, and Literature for 1764*, 581–83.

114 Reed, "Theatrical Duplicity," 23–24.

115 Samuel Johnson, *A Dictionary of the English Language: in which The Words are deduced from their Originals, and Illustrated in their Different Significations by Examples from the best Writers*, 2nd edn, 2 vols. (London: W. Strahan, for J. Knapton; C. Hitch and L. Hawes; A. Millar; R. and J. Dodsley; and M. and T. Longman, 1756).

116 Reed, "Theatrical Duplicity." See the letters of 2 November 1765 (30) and 29 September 1766 (44).

117 Garrick tells Reed that he should bring *Dido* out as a benefit, for "'In giving it to Holland or Powell you will add the Interest of the Actor to that of the Author & thereby in all likelyhood secure its success'" (ibid., 45). But Garrick told Reed his author's night would be the fourth, not the third night (50). Reed surmised that this was intended to draw an argument, so that Garrick would have an excuse to cancel the play (51), but it seems to reassert the customary author–house balance: usually the house gets two nights, then the author, one. By giving the first night's proceeds to Holland for his benefit, the house is down one, and needs to recoup.

118 Ibid., 33.

119 Ibid., 42. Davies, sympathetic to the ropemaker, later wrote that this arrangement was extraordinary: "It was thought an unusual favour to give the first night of a play to an actor; nor does the public know why Dido was not played more than three nights. If the managers pleaded that the season was too far advanced to act it successively, as was usual in other new pieces, it might have been resumed the next winter; and that it merited such favour, if it really was a favour, may be presumed for the applause bestowed upon it. The author is certainly a man of genius; his farce of the Register Office

contains a variety of characters aptly drawn and it has accordingly met with great and deserved approbation." Davies, *Memoirs*, vol. II, 127–28.

120 Sylas Neville's diary establishes that Garrick's refusal of Reed's play was widely known. Neville writes: "To see *Dido*, a Tragedy in Shakespere's style, performed for the first time . . . This piece is the production of a Ropemaker of Chadwick, and being refused by the managers, was given to Holland to be played for his benefit. It went off with considerable applause and is by desire to be performed again. Powel and Yates were good in Aeneas and Dido. Holland played Narbel, Havard Bilias, and Bensley Anchises. We had a *prologue* spoken by King and an *Epilogue* spoken by Mrs Abington. Before the play began, by the light of my wax taper read No. 1564 of the *London Chronicle*, in which was "Night" a pretty good ode." Quoted in Stone (ed.), *London Stage*, Part 4, vol. II, 1231.

121 Folger Shakespeare Library: W.b.467: "Collection of prologues and epilogues and other miscellaneous verses by David Garrick." The name "Reed" is written in the margin opposite the name "Crab."

122 Reed, "Theatrical Duplicity," 46, 48. Reed's revisions may have included new speeches vindicating his honesty; in the play's 1808 edition, Achates is interpretable as a Reed figure, refusing to bow to Drury Lane's monarch: "I cannot mould / My rugged looks into a simpering leer, / Nor, with lip-adoration, deify / A mere, mere mortal, swell'd into a monarch." *Dido; a Tragedy. As It Was Performed at the Theatre Royal in Drury Lane, with Universal Applause* (London: Nichols and Son, 1808), 10.

123 Reed may have tried this tactic again, in a different newspaper: "Mr. Joseph Reed, the author of those celebrated pieces the tragedy of Dido and the farce of the Register Office, has finished an English Opera called Tom Jones; and we hear it is to be brought out next season at Drury-lane Theatre" (*Gazetteer and New Daily Advertiser*, 29 August 1767). This anticipatory puff failed: *Tom Jones* was brought out at Covent Garden.

124 Mary Ann Yates played Medea for her benefit on 24 March; the prologue to *Medea* appeared in the *Public Advertiser* on 25 March 1767. Her benefit was not particularly rich: £54 10*s.* 6*d.* in profit, after a deduction of £64 17*s.* house charges. Stone (ed.), *London Stage*, Part 4, vol. II, 1230.

125 Reed, "Theatrical Duplicity," 49.

126 Ibid., 50.

127 Shakespeare, *Bell's Edition of Shakespeare's Plays*, vol. III, 189 (*Hamlet*, 3.3). Garrick changes the King's words "our faults" to "his faults," sharpening the gibe at Reed.

128 Reed, "Theatrical Duplicity," 54.

129 A Halter-Maker [Joseph Reed], *A Sop in the Pan for a Physical Critick: In a Letter to Dr. Sm*ll*t, Occasion'd by a Criticism on a Late Mock-Tragedy, Call'd Madrigal and Trulletta* (London: W. Reeve, 1759), 9.

130 J.[oseph] Reed, *Madrigal and Trulletta. A Mock-Tragedy. Acted (under the Direction of Mr. Cibber) at the Theatre-Royal in Covent-Garden. With Notes*

by the Author, and Dr. Humbug, Critick and Censor-General (London: W. Reeve, 1758), 6.

131 Knapp, *Checklist of Verse by David Garrick*, 62, notes the prologue to Joseph Reed's *Dido* exists in a transcript at the Folger Shakespeare Library, and in *The Poetical Works of David Garrick, Esq. Now First Collected into Two Volumes. With Explanatory Notes*, ed. George Kearsley (London: George Kearsley, 1785), vol. II, 225–26, but she did not locate it in published form. For a review which pans the play but puffs the prologue, see *Lloyd's Evening Post* for 30 March – 1 April 1767: "the Author seems to have followed (rather too closely) the Dido of Metastasio in the conduct of his piece. In point of language, I cannot say any thing particularly struck me ... The Prologue spoken by Mr. King, and the Epilogue by Mrs. Abington, were well delivered, and afforded entertainment."

132 *Poetical Works of David Garrick.*

133 "Garrick's "Prologue to [Reed's] *Dido.** Spoken by Mr. King," 22–27, 36–37. The footnote reads: "A Tragedy, by Mr. Reed, acted at Drury-lane, March 28, 1967, for Mr. Holland's Benefit." *Poetical Works of David Garrick*, vol. II, 225–26.

134 "What is to become of *Dido*? now I talk of Dido, I have heard a Bird sing, that there were some scoundrel suspicions that I wrote a long copy of verses against *Dido* in ye St James's Chrone I shall be very angry, if I hear ye least hint of it from my Partner–it is well known that they are *Kenrick's*, & I shall speak to Reid about 'Em as soon as I see him–do You know any thing about this? don't mention *Kenrick's* name, for *Becket* told me in Secresy ..." *Letters of David Garrick*, vol. II, 564–65.

135 Lacy calls the verse-writer "a villainous bush fighting scoundrel" and promises to "reprimand Woodfall and hear who is the Author" (Reed, "Theatrical Duplicity," 54). Then Mrs Yates fell ill, and Dido was not played again for four weeks (ibid., 57). Meanwhile, Reed wrote to Garrick, saying he would like to publish the play, but wants to hear Garrick's thoughts first. Garrick responds, "the longer you defer publication you will strengthen the representation of your play–my reasons are these–The price of the Copy will be the same this season or the next; and if it is not printed; the curiosity of the Public will be greater when it is brought out again, than if they were well acquainted with it by publishing it now. Besides by deferring publication you escape all criticism till you have reaped the benefits of representation ... I desire you to have no more regard of my opinion than will be agreeable to your own and consistent with your interest." Garrick adds a postscript, "If you don't print immediately you will have an opportunity, when Mr Barry is in England to make some profitable Bargain with him for his Theatre and with some Irish Bookseller at the same time" (ibid., 59–60).

136 Reed's response to the occasional poem by "J.K." in the *St. James's Chronicle* for 16–19 May 1767 appeared in the same paper, 21–23 May:

> As my poor *Tyrian* Princess hath been most outrageously *belaboured* with Billins-gate [sic] and Brutality, by that *Scalper*, J.K. your Correspondent, I am advised to

stop his Mouth; I have therefore sent him a Present, the Application of which *to his own Use* will undoubtedly *silence* him.
I am, Sir, your humble Servant,
The Author of DIDO.
N.B. *This short Letter was accompanied with* a Halter, *which, according to the Maker's Desire, who is likewise the Author of Dido, is ready to be delivered to* J.K. *whenever he shall please to call for it.*

"J.K." thanks Reed for the noose in the 16–18 June issue, noting that he will defer using it until he too has written a tragedy in imitation of Shakespeare's style.

137 As shown in *London Stage*, the Treasurer's Book notes that £2 2*s.* was paid for licensing *Dido*; *Dido* played again 1 April 1767 (second time); *Dido* was deferred on account of the indisposition of Mrs Yates on 9 April 1767; *Dido* featured in a double bill with *The Register Office* on 14 May 1767, which was announced as a benefit for the author of the mainpiece, and had house charges of £76 19*s.* 6*d.* See Stone (ed.), *London Stage*, Part 4, vol. II, 1232, 1233, 1235, 1246.

138 Boaden (ed.), *Private Correspondendence of David Garrick*, vol. I, 252.

139 Accordingly, on 12 February 1768, *The Register Office* played as the farce to Garrick and Colman's *Clandestine Marriage*. Stone (ed.), *London Stage*, Part 4, vol. III, 1311.

140 George Colman [Jr.], *Posthumous Letters, from Various Celebrated Men: Addressed to Francis Colman, and George Colman, the Elder: With Annotations and Occasional Remarks, by George Colman, the Younger* (London: T. Cadell and W. Davies; W. Blackwood, 1820), 144–45, 145fn.

5 Prompting, Inside and Outside the Theatre

1 *Works of Arthur Murphy*, vol. II, 35.
2 *Letters of David Garrick*, vol. II, 840.
3 Boaden (ed.), *Private Correspondendence of David Garrick*, vol. II, 601.
4 For evidence of commercial success, see George Winchester Stone, Jr., "Garrick's Long Lost Alteration of *Hamlet*," *PMLA*, 49/3 (1934), 890–921. For Murphy's parody of the alterations, see Dobson, *Making of the National Poet*, 172–76. For detailed analysis of Murphy's parody, see Richard Schoch, "'A Supplement to Public Laws': Arthur Murphy, David Garrick, and 'Hamlet with Alterations,'" *Theatre Journal*, 57/1 (2005), 21–32.
5 For an impressionistic memoir of Lacy: Anon., "James Lacy, Esq. Late Patentee of the Theatre Royal, Drury Lane [with a Portrait]," *European Magazine, and London Review*, 1809, 274–78 (at 277).
6 Davies, *Memoirs*, vol. I, 103.
7 Boaden (ed.), *Private Correspondence of David Garrick*, vol. I, 15–16.
8 Charles Brayne, "Lacy, James (1696–1774)," in Matthew and Harrison (eds.), *Oxford Dictionary of National Biography*.

9 Victoria and Albert Museum National Art Library: Forster Collection 48. F.30: David Garrick and James Lacy, "Some Letters that pass'd between Mr. Lacy & Me, upon a Difference between Us," 3.

10 *Letters of David Garrick*, vol. I, 172.

11 Ibid., vol. I, 185. For instances of John Paterson's interventions, see vol. I, 495, and vol. II, 622–23.

12 Garrick complains to his brother George on 25 August [1752], "our Company is over loaded already, thanks to my Partner *Timbertop*." Ibid., vol. I, 185.

13 Ibid., vol. II, 449.

14 Kalman A. Burnim, *David Garrick, Director* (University of Pittsburgh Press, 1961), 4.

15 [William Shirley], *A Bone for the Chroniclers to Pick; or a Take-Off Scene from Behind the Curtain. A Poem* (London: J. Coote, J. Scott, 1758), 9.

16 Anon., *Memoirs of that Celebrated Comedian, and Very Singular Genius Thomas Weston* (London: S. Bladon, 1776), 51.

17 Ibid., 30.

18 The editors of Garrick's letters also suggest that this account appeared in the *London Chronicle* for 25 April 1772. *Letters of David Garrick*, vol. II, 798.

19 Ibid., vol. II, 797–98, fn.: "Evidently the managers found it unnecessary to publish an account."

20 Anon., *Memoirs of Thomas Weston*, 38.

21 Vickers (ed.), *William Shakespeare*, 487, identifies Steevens as the author of the 'Animadvertor' theatrical criticisms.

22 This Comedian is identified as Weston by the editors of Garrick's *Letters*. However, Ned Shuter was in debt at the same time, and it is not clear to which "Comedian" this debt belongs. See *Letters of David Garrick*, vol. II, 798 fn. 2. Weston continued unrepentant in his course of debt and drinking, as the *London Chronicle* for 30 April – 2 May 1772 indicates: "A few days ago a celebrated Comedian in the King's Bench was indulged with the rules, and now receives company at the Dog and Duck."

23 Weston was still impecunious months later, when Samuel Foote accorded him a benefit in the summer season at Theatre Royal in the Haymarket, with Foote playing Bayes. However, Garrickians disrupted Weston's benefit. "CAESAR" in the *London Evening Post* for 22–25 August 1772 reports that "this condescension from the *summer favourite* [Foote], was surely sufficient to fill poor *Weston*'s house, without any other exertion. But for some theatrical reasons of state, the confidential bookseller, that parasite of the manager, was ordered to proclaim (though with the appearance of profound secrecy) that Mr. *Garrick* was to come under the lash of *Bayes* that night, for some little meannesses that he had been guilty of. The report flew through the town like wild-fire. The political intent of these stage secrets, is always fully answered by the public curiosity being doubly excited. The friends of Mr. *Foote*, and the enemies of Mr. *Garrick*, in course, attend to idolize the one, and sacrifice the other."

A footnote to the affair appeared after Weston's death in 1776, when a joke will, published in the *Memoirs*, was reprinted in several papers. In it, Weston leaves his money (non-existent) to Garrick: "I owe some obligations to Mr. Garrick, I therefore bequeath him all the money I die possessed of, as there is nothing on earth he is so very fond of." Weston's common-law wife, Martha, refuted this in *Lloyd's Evening Post* and the *General Evening Post* for 14 February 1776, and the *Morning Post* for 12 February, stating that she, not Garrick, had received Weston's "ALL." One Richard Hughes added a postscript to Martha Weston's newspaper article stating that Weston "died in peace with all mankind, frequently acknowledging the obligations he was under to a few friends, Mr Garrick in particular." Garrick, who may have kindly sent the dying Weston a doctor (see *Letters of David Garrick.*, vol. III, 1276), got the last word.

24 David Hunter, "The Diary of John Stede, London Theatre Prompter from about 1710 to the 1760s," *Theatre Notebook: A Journal of the History and Technique of the British Theatre*, 62/3 (2008), 163–66 (at 163).

25 Folger Shakespeare Library: W.a.104 (1–13): Richard Cross and William Hopkins, "Cross-Hopkins Theatre Diaries, Drury Lane," 1747–60, 1762–64, 1768–76.

26 "Richard Cross," in Highfill, Burnim and Langhans (eds.), *Biographical Dictionary of Actors*, vol. IV, 66–70.

27 Richard Cross, *The Adventures of John Le-Brun*, 2 vols. (London: G. Hawkins, 1739).

28 Regarding Cross's notations, see Judith Milhous, and Robert D. Hume, "David Garrick and Box-Office Receipts at Drury Lane in 1742–43," *Philological Quarterly*, 67/3 (1988), 323–44; Robert D. Hume and Judith Milhous, "Receipts at Drury Lane: Richard Cross's Diary for 1746–47," *Theatre Notebook*, 49 (1995), 12–26, 69–90; and Judith Milhous, "Reading Theatre History from Account Books," in Michael Cordner and Peter Holland (eds.), *Players, Playwrights, Playhouses: Investigating Performance, 1660–1800* (Basingstoke: Palgrave Macmillan, 2007), 101–34.

29 Victoria and Albert Museum National Art Library: Forster Collection L4 to 3321: "Printed and ms. extracts from newspapers, magazines, &c. relating to Garrick," 3.C.11.

30 Shirley, *Brief Remarks*, 32.

31 James Winston, "The Manager's Note-Book. – No. V," *New Monthly Magazine and Humorist*, 52/207 (1838), 379–87.

32 Stone (ed.), *London Stage*, Part 4, vol. III, 1742.

33 Nipclose, *The Theatres*, 58, fn. 74.

34 Winston, "Manager's Note-Book," 380.

35 Previously published as: Leslie Ritchie, "Pox on Both Your Houses: The Battle of the Romeos," *Eighteenth-Century Fiction*, 27/3–4 (2015), 373–94.

36 Eva Maria Garrick evidently felt that Barry lacked the mental maturity and complexity requisite to portray Romeo: "I was at the Play Last Saturday at Coven-garden, all what I can Say of it is, that Mr Barry is to jung (in his ha'd)

for Romeo, & Mrs Cibber to old for a girl of 18 . . . I wish thie woold finish both, for it is to much for My Little Dear Spouse to Play Every Day." Burnim, *David Garrick, Director*, 132, quoting a letter dated from London, 6 October 1750, Folger Shakespeare Library.

37 Ibid., 131.
38 "Spranger Barry," in Highfill, Burnim and Langhans (eds.), *Biographical Dictionary of Actors*, vol. I, 330.
39 Gentleman, *Dramatic Censor*, vol. I, 190.
40 Anon., "Rev. of Romeo and Juliet, by William Shakespeare," *Gentleman's Magazine*, 20 (October 1750), 438.
41 David Brewer, *The Afterlife of Character, 1726–1825* (Philadelphia: University of Pennsylvania Press, 2005), 69.
42 Theophilus Cibber's adaptation was staged at the Little Haymarket "until the patent theatres required Sir Thomas de Veil to enforce the Licensing Act and interdict the performances." Arthur Hawley Scouten (ed.), *The London Stage, 1660–1800: A Calendar of Plays, Entertainments & Afterpieces Together with Casts, Box-Receipts and Contemporary Comment Compiled from the Playbills, Newspapers and Theatrical Diaries of the Period*, Part 3: *1729–1747*, 2 vols. (Carbondale: Southern Illinois University Press, 1961), vol. II, 1115. It was performed 11, 12, 14, 17, 19 and 29 September; 2 and 13 October; 1 November (with a reversion to 'concert' form advertising); and a final benefit for fifteen-year-old Jenny Cibber, who played Juliet to her father's Romeo, was acted 17 December 1744. Cibber emphasized the novelty of his revival in the media, as in this advertisement from the 12 September 1744 *Daily Advertiser:* "Will be reviv'd a Play Not acted these 100 Years."
43 Otway's play *Caius Marius* (1679) has a pair of lovers (Lavinia and Marius) who awake in the tomb before Marius expires – "a revision which both Theophilus Cibber and Garrick later adopted in their respective versions, and which was until well into the nineteenth century preferred by most audiences as an ending superior to Shakespeare's original," notes Burnim, *David Garrick, Director*, 127–28. At the time of Garrick's 1748 adaptation, *Caius Marius* had last been performed at Lincoln's-Inn-Fields in 1735. Scouten (ed.), *London Stage*, Part 3, vol. I, 504.
44 Barry's move to Covent Garden was experienced as a defection, to judge by the tone of Richard Cross's diary entry for 8 September 1750: "Mr. Barry flew from his Articles & engag'd with Mr. Rich; Mrs. Cibber (who did not play last Season) is also engag'd there—."
45 Thomas Davies, *Dramatic Miscellanies: Consisting of Critical Observations on Several Plays of Shakspeare: With a Review of His Principal Characters, and Those of Various Eminent Writers, as Represented by Mr. Garrick, and Other Celebrated Comedians*, 3 vols. (London: Printed for the Author, 1783–84), vol. II, 68.
46 Murphy, *Life of David Garrick*, vol. I, 95.
47 Peter Holland, "Hearing the Dead: The Sound of David Garrick," in Cordner and Holland (eds.), *Players, Playwrights, Playhouses*, 248–70 (at 248).

48 Anon., *The Theatrical Review: For the Year 1757, and Beginning of 1758. Containing Critical Remarks on the Principal Performers of Both the Theatres. Together with Observations on the Dramatic Pieces, New, or Revived; That Have Been Performed at Either House within That Period. To Which Is Added, a Scale of the Comparative Merit of the above Performers* (London: J. Coote, 1758), 23. Retrospectively, Arthur Murphy described the contest: "He had lectured Barry and Mrs. Cibber in that play, and now expected that they would employ his own weapons against himself. Accordingly he was determined to contend with them for victory. Though he had imparted his ideas to his antagonists, yet such a genius was not exhausted. To strike out new beauties in passages, where the most penetrating critic could not expect them, was his peculiar talent." Murphy, *Life of David Garrick*, vol. 1, 102.

49 Anon., *Theatrical Review*, 4.

50 Riccoboni, *General History of the Stage*, xiv–xv.

51 Theophilus Cibber, *Cibber's Two Dissertations on the Theatres* (London: Printed for the Author, [1757]). Cibber objects, with equal wit, to Romeo's managing to "shift his Cloaths" between his visit to the apothecary and the tomb, "that he may die, with the Decency of a Malefactor, in a Suit of Black" (68), and to a piece of stage business in which Romeo threatens Paris with the iron crow rather than with a sword, as a gentleman ought to do (70).

52 Anon., *Original Prologues, Epilogues, and Other Pieces Never before Printed* (London: Printed for and sold by the Booksellers in Pater-Noster-Row, 1756), 12, lines 1–4.

53 Archimagírus Metaphoricus [William Kenrick], *The Kapélion, or Poetical Ordinary; Consisting of Great Variety of Dishes in Prose and Verse; Recommended to All Who Have a Good Taste or Keen Appetite* (London, [1750–51]), 130.

54 John Hill, *The Actor: Or, a Treatise on the Art of Playing* (London: R. Griffiths, 1755), 212. For a detailed account of Hill's earlier altercations with Garrick, see Leslie Ritchie, "Garrick's *Male-Coquette* and Theatrical Masculinities," in Shelley King and Yaël Schlick (eds.), *Refiguring the Coquette* (Lewisburg, PA: Bucknell University Press, 2008), 164–98.

55 William Shakespeare, adapted by David Garrick, *Romeo and Juliet. By Shakespear. With Some Alterations, and an Additional Scene: As It Is Performed at the Theatre-Royal in Drury-Lane* (London: J. and R. Tonson, and S. Draper, 1748).

56 Gentleman's division of the beauties of Garrick's and Barry's Romeos rivals a sportscast for competitive immediacy: "those scenes in which they most evidently rose above each other are as follow—Mr. BARRY in the Garden scene of the second act—Mr. GARRICK the friar scene in the third – Mr. BARRY the Garden scene in the fourth – Mr. GARRICK in the first scene, description of the Apothecary, &c. fifth act – Mr. BARRY first part of the tomb scene, and Mr. GARRICK from where the poison operates to the end." Gentleman, *Dramatic Censor*, vol. 1, 189.

57 *Letters of David Garrick*, vol. 1, 152–53.

58 Thanks to Maya Bielinski for her work in calculating these statistics.

59 Differences between Garrick's 1748 and 1750 editions have been detailed by
    Cunningham, *Shakespeare and Garrick*, 63–75. Garrick's "Advertisement" to
    the 1750 edition appears below, with changes from the 1748 edition noted, to
    demonstrate his repositioning of Romeo as a faithful lover.

> "September 29, 1750. Advertisement. [1748: To the Reader.]
>   *The Alterations in the following Play are few* [1748: few and trifling], *except in the
> last act; the Design was to clear the Original as much as possible, from the Jingle and
> Quibble which were always thought a great Objection to performing it* [1748: the great
> Objections to reviving it].
>   *When this Play was reviv'd two Winters ago, it was generally thought, that the sudden
> Change of* Romeo's *Love from* Rosaline *to* Juliet *was a Blemish in his Character,
> and therefore it is to be hop'd that an Alteration in that Particular will be excus'd; the only
> Merit that is claim'd from it is, that it is done with as little Injury to the Original as
> possible"* (A3).
>   [The 1748 edition, in place of the second paragraph, has the following: "*Many
> People have imagin'd that the sudden Change of* Romeo's *Love from* Rosaline *to* Juliet
> *was a Blemish in his Character, but an Alteration of that kind was thought too bold to be
> attempted;* Shakespear *has dwelt particularly upon it, and so great a Judge of Human
> Nature, knew that to be young and inconstant was extremely natural:* Romeo *in the
> Third Scene of the Second Act makes a very good Excuse to the* Friar *for the quick
> Transition of his Affections:*
>
>   '————————She whom now I love,
>   Doth give me grace for grace, and love for Love.
>   The other did not so—'
>
> *However we shall leave this to the Decision of abler Criticks; those, I am sure, who see the
> Play will very readily excuse his leaving twenty* Rosalines *for a* Juliet.
>   *The favourable Reception the new Scene in the fifth Act has met with, induc'd the
> Writer to print it, and if he may be excus'd for daring to add to* Shakespear, *he shall think
> himself well rewarded in having given* Romeo *and* Juliet *an opportunity of shewing their
> great Merit"* (v–vii).]

60 Bellamy, *Apology for the Life of George Anne Bellamy*, vol. II, 114. Bellamy
    wrote, "The piece was performed so many nights, that the public as well as the
    performers were tired and disgusted with it. We, however, got the advantage
    of some nights. But this was not done without a great deal of paper, which was
    bestowed upon the occasion."

61 *Letters of David Garrick*, vol. I, 156–57.

62 One such advertisement appears in the 29 September – 2 October *Whitehall
    Evening Post; Or, London Intelligencer*, which is not surprising, as the *British
    Magazine* was printed by C. Corbett, who also printed the *Whitehall Evening
    Post*. Corbett is cross-promoting, using the time-sensitive newspaper to adver-
    tise his magazine, and capitalizing on the Battle to promote both.

63 Advertisements for no. 3 of the *Kapélion*, containing the comparison of
    Garrick's and Barry's depiction of Romeo, written anonymously by William
    Kenrick, appear in the *General Advertiser* for 10 and 11 October; the 9–11
    October *Whitehall Evening Post*; the *General Evening Post* for 6–9 October;
    and the *London Evening Post* for 9–11 and 11–13 October 1750.

64 William Shakespeare, adapted by Theophilus Cibber, *Romeo and Juliet,
    a Tragedy, Revis'd, and Alter'd from Shakespear ... To Which Is Added, a*

Serio-Comic Apology, for Part of the Life of Mr. Theophilus Cibber, Comedian. Written by Himself (London: C. Corbett, 1748). Cibber, whose *Romeo and Juliet* had disappeared from the stage thanks to the Licensing Act intervention described above, gamely advertised his print edition of the play in the 1 October 1750 *General Advertiser*, as "now acted at the Theatre-Royal in Drury Lane."

65 The verses were reprinted in the *Gentleman's Magazine*, 20 (October 1750): Anon., "Rev. of Romeo and Juliet, by William Shakespeare," 438.

66 These images are "Mr. Garrick and Miss Bellamy in the Characters of Romeo and Juliet," showing Act v, sc. iii, from a painting by Benjamin Wilson, engraved by Ravenet (1753); and "Mr. Barry and Miss Nossiter, in the Characters of Romeo and Juliet," showing Act ii, sc. ii, by R. Pyle; Wm. Elliott, Sculp. (1759). They were not released concurrently with the Battle. Wilson returned to England from Ireland in 1750, and wrote hazily in his memoirs: "About this time I painted Mr. Garrick in the character of Romeo, along with Miss Bellamy in the Tomb scene this was at the time, when the two Theatres were contending who played it best. Mrs. Cibber, had by far, the advantage over Miss Bellamy, and I think, upon the whole, that Mr. Barry excelled Mr. Garrick in Romeo: the latter having not that plaintive softness in his voice, which the character of Romeo seems to require. I had an engraving made of that picture which sold very well; and brought me in some money." Andrew Graciano, "The Memoir of Benjamin Wilson, F.R.S. (1721–88): Painter and Electrical Scientist," *Walpole Society*, 74 (2012), 165–244 (at 191). Wilson's painting is dated 1753 by the Victoria and Albert Museum. It is unlikely, even had it been started in 1750, that the painting could have been completed and prints made of it and distributed during the play's twelve-night run in 1750.

67 Cunningham, *Shakespeare and Garrick*, 63–75.

68 Michael Burden, "Shakespeare and Opera," in Peter Sabor and Fiona Ritchie (eds.), *Shakespeare in the Eighteenth Century* (Cambridge University Press, 2012), 204–26.

69 Ibid.

70 "Cross-Hopkins Theatre Diaries."

71 Danchin (ed.), *Prologues and Epilogues*, 336.

72 Ibid., 338.

73 Spranger Barry, "The Occasional Prologue Spoken at Covent-Garden Theatre, by Mr. Barry [to *Romeo and Juliet*]," *London Magazine*, October 1750, 473.

74 Paul Sawyer, "John Rich's Contribution to the Eighteenth-Century London Stage," in Kenneth Richards and Peter Thomson (eds.), *The Eighteenth-Century English Stage: The Proceedings of a Symposium Sponsored by the Manchester University Department of Drama* (London: Methuen, 1972), 85–104 (at 98).

75 For the prologue's distribution, see Danchin (ed.), *Prologues and Epilogues*, 338.

76 "For the information of our country Readers we must observe, that the spouters are in general the journeymen and apprentices of barbers, taylors, and other crafts, who, to the grief of their masters and parents, meet once a week to guzzle porter and imitate the speeches and attitudes of that wicked wight, Garrick, who has done more mischief than the king of Prussia." Anon., "Rev. of *the Sentimental Spouter*," *Monthly Review; or Literary Journal*, 51 (July–December 1774), 486. For more about spouters, see Leslie Ritchie, "The Spouters' Revenge: Apprentice Actors and the Imitation of London's Theatrical Celebrities," *Eighteenth Century: Theory and Interpretation*, 53/1 (2012), 41–71.

77 Anon., *The Theatrical Bouquet: Containing an Alphabetical Arrangement of the Prologues and Epilogues, Which Have Been Published by Distinguished Wits, from the Time That Colley Cibber First Came on the Stage, to the Present Year* (London: T. Lowndes, 1778), 27.

78 John Thieme, "Spouting, Spouting-Clubs and Spouting Companions," *Theatre Notebook*, 29/1 (1975), 9–16 (at 11). See also Dane Farnsworth Smith and M.L. Lawhon, *Plays About the Theatre in England, 1737–1800, or, the Self-Conscious Stage from Foote to Sheridan* (Lewisburg, PA: Bucknell University Press, 1979), 149.

79 One example of spouters enjoying this play: "Romeo and Juliet next made their appearance, but such a matchless pair I never saw. Romeo was frequently asleep, till Juliet awaked him by the affected violence of her love, when he threw himself into some very unnatural attitudes, and ranted away, in order to make amends for his former apathy." Richard King, reviser, *The Complete Modern London Spy, for the Present Year, 1781; or, a Real New, and Universal Disclosure, of the Secret, Nocturnal, and Diurnal Transactions, in and About the Cities of London and Westminster, and the Borough of Southwark* (London: Alex. Hogg, T. Lewis, 1781), 114.

80 Stone (ed.), *London Stage*, Part 4, vol. I, 212–13. See also Danchin (ed.), *Prologues and Epilogues*, 342.

81 *Letters of David Garrick*, vol. I, 156–57.

82 Folger Shakespeare Library: T.a.49–64: James Winston, "A dramatic register of theatres and dramatic performances from the beginning to the present," 16 vols., vol. VII (1744–52).

83 The verses were attributed to "I. H——tt" in the *Daily Advertiser* for 12 October 1750, but least one person felt that "Garrick wrote [it] himself, in order to get rid of a contest, in which he was sensible he had the worst of, both in fame and profit." See Cooke, *Memoirs of Charles Macklin*, vol. I, 159–60.

84 *Letters of David Garrick*, vol. I, 158.

85 Boaden (ed.), *Private Correspondence of David Garrick*, vol. I, lix.

86 This date range expands the number of "Prompter" articles noted by Charles Gray, who suggests that the column began 18 November 1776, continuing irregularly until 6 March 1777. Gray also speculates that Garrick may have written two letters signed "The Ghost of Gay," published in the *Morning Post*

on 24 and 28 December 1776, and a series of letters 14–21 December 1776, entitled "Theatres du Paris." Gray, *Theatrical Criticism*, 228.

87 For a transcript of the trial, see *Old Bailey Online*, "Benjamin Robert Turbot, Theft," 18 September 1765 (t17650918–24), www.oldbaileyonline.org. I use the trial transcripts' spelling; in other sources, Turbot's name is spelled variously Turbot, Turbut, Turbutt, etc., and he used his middle name, Robert, rather than his first name, in correspondence with Garrick.

88 The address appears in the *Old Bailey Online* as Vine Street; the Covent Garden location and other sources suggest Vere Street.

89 William Blackstone, Esq., *Commentaries on the Laws of England*, 4th edn, 4 vols. (Dublin: John Exshaw, Henry Saunders *et al.*, 1770), vol. IV, 229.

90 Ibid., vol. IV, 240.

91 The *17th–18th Century Burney Collection Newspapers* database unfortunately does not have any issues of the 1765 *Daily Advertiser*.

92 Sylvanus Urban, "Historical Chronicle," *Gentleman's Magazine*, 35 (1765), 442 (September) and 489 (October). See also the *Public Advertiser* for Friday 20 September 1765, which reports Benjamin-Robert Turbot's capital conviction for "stealing a Silver Cup, Value 3*l.* and 7*s.* in Money, the Property of George White, in his Dwelling-house, the Rising Sun in Vere-street, Covent-garden."

93 Boaden (ed.), *Private Correspondence of David Garrick*, vol. I, 202n., repeats this account: "Robert Turbott, a young man, son of the Comedian, was tried at the Old Bailey for stealing a silver cup from a public-house, and found guilty. He received sentence of death, Sept 24, 1765, and from the Report made to the King, Oct. 5, he was ordered for execution, but, owing to the intercession of powerful friends, he was afterwards respited. –*Gentleman's Magazine*, 1765."

94 "Robert Turbutt," in Highfill, Burnim and Langhans (eds.), *Biographical Dictionary of Actors*, vol. XV, 54.

95 For instance, on 17 February 1743, when Garrick played the lead Millamour and Turbutt played the minor character Dr Crisis in Henry Fielding's comedy, *The Wedding Day*; see Scouten (ed.), *London Stage*, Part 3, vol. III, 1035.

96 "Robert Turbutt," in Highfill, Burnim and Langhans (eds.), *Biographical Dictionary of Actors*, vol. XV, 55.

97 *Letters of David Garrick*, vol. II, 814–15.

98 "Robert Turbutt," in Highfill, Burnim and Langhans (eds.), *Biographical Dictionary of Actors*, vol. XV, 55.

99 Boaden (ed.), *Private Correspondence of David Garrick*, vol. I, 202–03.

100 The Recorder of London was the "chief legal officer of the City of London. He was one of the judges who heard cases at the Old Bailey. He sent reports to the King (later the Home Office) about all the cases in which convicts were sentenced to death, so that the King or his ministers could decide whether or not to pardon them." Clive Emsley, Tim Hitchcock and Robert

Shoemaker, "Historical Background – Glossary", *Old Bailey Proceedings Online*, www.oldbaileyonline.org (accessed 6 April 2016).

101 Boaden (ed.), *Private Correspondence of David Garrick*, vol. I, 202.

102 Mary E. Knapp, "Garrick's Verses to the Marquis of Rockingham," *Philological Quarterly*, 29/1 (1950), 78–81 (at 79).

103 Ibid.

104 News of Turbot's respite also appears in the *Public Advertiser* and the *Public Ledger* on 9 October.

105 Stone (ed.), *London Stage*, Part 4, vol. II, 1137.

106 Boaden (ed.), *Private Correspondence of David Garrick*, vol. I, 205.

107 Winchester and Stone, *David Garrick*, 346.

108 "David Garrick; Original Manuscripts, Etc."

109 *Lloyd's Evening Post* for 11–13 October names Baretti's legal team as Mr. Cox, Mr. Murphy and Mr. Lucas.

110 Matthew Rusnak, "The Trial of Giuseppe Baretti, October 20th 1769: A Literary and Cultural History of the Baretti Case," PhD thesis, Rutgers University (2008).

111 For a transcript of this trial, see *Old Bailey Online*, "Joseph Baretti, Killing," 18 October 1769 (T17691018-9), www.oldbaileyonline.org.

112 The Cross-Hopkins Theatre Diaries indicate that the Middlesex Hospital received benefit takings from Drury Lane Theatre on 21 December 1757 (£280); on 17 December 1759 (£160); on 20 December 1763 (no amount given); and on 18 December 1770 (no amount given).

113 References are to the trial transcript noted above.

114 In 1771, when Baretti's revised *Dictionary* was printed, Garrick's frequent collaborators Davies and Becket were amongst its printers; the book in four volumes, *A Journey from London to Genoa, through England, Portugal, Spain, and France*, published in 1770, was printed for T. Davies and L. Davis.

115 Sir Joshua Reynolds's portrait, c. 1773, presents Baretti, as the Tate Gallery's notes put it, "as a myopic scholar, in an attempt to counteract his public image which was still coloured by his trial for murder in 1769. Baretti narrowly escaped hanging after stabbing a pimp to death in a violent street brawl." www.tate.org.uk/whats-on/tate-britain/exhibition/joshua-reynolds/joshua-reynolds-creation-celebrity-room-guide-3 (accessed 12 April 2016). The victim, Evan Morgan, judging by accounts in the 23–25 October 1769 *Independent Chronicle*, was a singer at the Grotto Gardens.

116 The *Independent Chronicle* for 20–23 October 1769 gives a sense of Garrick's delivery of these lines: "at the trial of Mr. Baretti last Friday, the modern Roscius was so great an *actor* that he *over-topt* his part; for being called to the character of the prisoner, he enlarged much on his tenderness and humanity, saying, that Mrs. G—— having some uncommon disorder (while they were on their tour in Italy) which baffled the skill of the most eminent physicians, Mr. B. had cured her without the least expectation of reward; and, that as he acknowledged himself under the greatest obligations to Mr. B—, the court could not but consider him as an impartial evidence. Mr. Murphy (who was

council for the prisoner) then desired that as Mr. G – was a *travelled* gentleman, to look at the knife, and tell the court whether it was like those usually worn in Italy, and whether he made use of such a one when abroad? To which he replied, O yes, Sir, or else we could not have eat; that his indeed had not a silver case, but simpering said that Mrs. G–'s had a gold one, and that she still carefully preserved it; upon which it was observed, by a person in court, that there was no doubt of that, as it was composed of a *metal* they both had a particular affection for."

117 Davies, letter to Granger, *Letters* ... (1805), 28.

118 "A Lover of Truth and Justice," "Particular Relation of a Late Remarkable Affair and Particulars of Mr. Barretti's Trial," *Town and Country Magazine* (1769), 510.

119 Ibid., 511.

120 Ibid., 511.

121 Sir James Prior, *Life of Edmund Malone, Editor of Shakespeare* (London: Smith, Elder, 1860).

122 Stone (ed.), *London Stage*, Part 4, vol. III, 1429 and *passim*.

Conclusion: Garrick, Re-Collected

1 See lines 80–81, 85, 97, 22 of these works respectively for references to Quixotes.

2 [David Garrick], *The Farmer's Return from London. An Interlude* (London: Dryden Leach, for J. and R. Tonson, 1762), 9–10.

3 Ibid., 12.

4 Archibald Campbell, *Lexiphanes, a Dialogue. Imitated from Lucian, and Suited to the Present Times* (London: J. Knox, 1767), 124–25.

5 William Winter, *The Press and the Stage: An Oration* (New York: Lockwood & Coombes, 1889), 21.

6 Boaden (ed.), *Private Correspondendence of David Garrick*, vol. II, 329–30.

7 Ibid., vol. II, 323.

8 *Letters of David Garrick.* Relaxed, though still courteous, letters to the fourth Earl of Sandwich (vol. III, 1247) and the fourth Earl of Rochford (vol. III, 1222) demonstrate Garrick's growing ease with his genteel social status in retirement.

9 This newspaper clipping from the *Public Ledger*, manuscript-dated 17 January 1779, appears in Forster, "Scrapbook."

10 Shearer West, *The Image of the Actor: Verbal and Visual Representation in the Age of Garrick and Kemble* (New York: St. Martin's Press, 1991), 48.

11 Ibid., 28.

12 See especially the first two chapters of Heather McPherson, *Art and Celebrity in the Age of Reynolds and Siddons* (University Park: Pennsylvania State University Press, 2017).

13 For a recent study that attends to extra-illustration's relation to theatrical celebrity, see Amanda Weldy Boyd, *Staging Memory and Materiality in Eighteenth-Century Theatrical Biography* (London: Anthem Press, 2018).

14 Diana Taylor, *The Archive and the Repertoire* (Durham, NC: Duke University Press, 2003), 19.

15 Ibid., 19.

16 Erin C. Blake and Stuart Sillars, *Extending the Book: The Art of Extra-Illustration* (Washington: Folger Shakespeare Library, 2010), 6.

17 Robert Shaddy dates the end of the extra-illustrating craze to 1930, when collectors began to prefer "to collect works in original condition, first editions, association copies, rather than create the multi-volume sets that were in vogue during an earlier period." Robert A. Shaddy, "Grangerizing: 'One of the Unfortunate Stages of Bibliomania,'" *Book Collector*, 49/4 (2000), 535–46 (at 546).

18 On 26 December 1767, Granger conveys Horace Walpole's suggestions about the title to his publisher, Thomas Davies. Davies and Granger are still arguing politely over the title in a letter of January 1769. The first edition was published 16 May 1769. See James Granger, *Letters between the Rev. James Granger, M.A. Rector of Shiplake, and Many of the Most Eminent Literary Men of His Time: Composing a Copious History and Illustration of His Biographical History of England with Miscellanies, and Notes of Tours in France, Holland, and Spain, by the Same Gentleman* (London: Nicols and Son, for Longman, Hurst, Rees, and Orme, 1805).

19 Marcia Pointon, *Hanging the Head: Portraiture and Social Formation in Eighteenth-Century England* (New Haven, CT: Yale University Press, 1993), 54.

20 Ibid., 58.

21 Rev. James Granger, *A Biographical History of England, from Egbert the Great to the Revolution: Consisting of Characters Disposed in Different Classes, and Adapted to a Methodical Catalogue of Engraved British Heads: Intended as an Essay Towards Reducing Our Biography to System, and a Help to the Knowledge of Portraits; Interspersed with Variety of Anecdotes, and Memoirs of a Great Number of Persons, Not to Be Found in Any Other Biographical Work: With a Preface, Shewing the Utility of a Collection of Engraved Portraits to Supply the Defect, and Answer the Various Purposes, of Medals*, 2nd edn, 4 vols. (London: T. Davies, J. Robson, G. Robinson, T. Becket, T. Cadell, and T. Evans, 1775; 1st edn 1769), vol. I, vi–vii.

22 Ibid., vii.

23 Ibid., viii.

24 Had Granger's biography appeared in his own volume, he might have been classified under category four, "inferior Clergymen," or nine, "ingenious Persons, who have distinguished themselves by their Writings."

25 "When one compares the physical dimensions of Granger's book to those of most of the prints he includes in his lists, it is clear he never thought of the actual incorporation of those prints in a copy of his book. He was providing a guide for the acquisition and ordering of a collection of portrait prints that would be physically independent of the book." Granger had over 14,000 prints, but these were kept as separate sheets, not in books, Wark writes. See Robert R. Wark, "The Gentle Pastime of Extra-Illustrating Books," *Huntington Library Quarterly*, 56/2 (1993), 151–62 (at 154).

26 Granger, *Letters*. See Thomas Davies's letter to Granger of 21 October 1769 (28).

27 Ibid., 58.

28 Granger, *Biographical History*, Preface, [ix]. Shaddy, "Grangerizing," 537, perceptively hypothesizes that the availability of images drove Granger's selection of individuals: "One of the crucial criteria for selecting persons for inclusion in this biographical history was the availability of engraved portraits." In other words: no icon, no saint.

29 Granger, *Biographical History*, vol. II, 9–10.

30 Rev. Mark Noble (ed.), *A Biographical History of England, from the Revolution to the End of George I's Reign; Being a Continuation of the Rev. J. Granger's Work: Consisting of Characters Disposed in Different Classes, and Adapted to a Methodical Catalogue of Engraved British Heads; Interspersed with a Variety of Anecdotes, and Memoirs of a Great Number of Persons, Not to Be Found in Any Other Biographical Work*, 3 vols. (London: W. Richardson, Darton and Harvey, W. Baynes, 1806), vol. I, iv.

31 Blake and Sillars, *Extending the Book*, 4.

32 See Horace Walpole's letter to T. Mann, 6 May 1770, *The Yale Edition of Horace Walpole's Correspondence*, ed. W.S. Lewis, 48 vols. (New Haven, CT: Yale University Press, 1937–83), vol. XXIII, 465. Both Pointon, *Hanging the Head*, 70, and Wark, "Gentle Pastime," 158, cite this letter.

33 John Boydell, *A Catalogue of Prints Published by J. Boydell, Engraver in Cheapside, London* (London: J. Boydell, 1773), 16, 24–25.

34 Timothy Clayton, *The English Print 1688–1802* (New Haven, CT and London: Yale University Press for the Paul Mellon Centre for Studies in British Art, 1997), 13–14.

35 Ibid., 14.

36 Ibid., 14.

37 Ibid., 14.

38 Ibid., 16.

39 Ibid., 16.

40 Shawe-Taylor *et al.*, *Every Look Speaks*, 52. Broadley's catalogue notes identify this as one of the prints Garrick requested while in Paris (53).

41 A further print technique, 'dotted' or 'chalk manner' stippling, sometimes printed in colour, came to dominate English output in the late 1770s, writes Clayton, *English Print*, 218. A point is used upon wax, and the design is then bitten in with aqua fortis, with or without the use of a graver, punches or roulettes. Stipples have a finely grained, pointillist appearance. Few images of Garrick use this format.

42 *Letters of David Garrick*, vol. I, 65, 70.

43 Kalman A. Burnim, "Looking Upon His Like Again: Garrick and the Artist," in Shirley Strum Kenny (ed.), *British Theatre and Other Arts, 1660–1800* (Washington, DC: Folger Shakespeare Library; London: Associated University Presses, 1983), 182–218 (at 187).

44 The 1769 Society exhibition catalogue features Mr. Finlayson's "Mr. Garrick in the character of Sir John Brute, a mezzotinto." Royal Society of Artists of Great-Britain, *A Catalogue of the Pictures, Sculptures, Designs in Architecture, Models, Drawings, Prints, &c. Exhibited at the Great Room in Spring-Garden, Charing-Cross, May the First, 1769* (London: William Bunce, 1769), 18.

45 Clayton, *English Print*, 198.

46 See Burnim, "Looking Upon His Like Again," 189. For the Society's history, see Matthew Hargraves's book, *Candidates for Fame: The Society of Artists of Great Britain 1760–1791* (New Haven, CT: Yale University Press, 2006).

47 Fitzgerald, *Life of David Garrick*. The seventeen-volume expansion is Folger Shakespeare Library, PN2598G3F5 (copy 4).

48 Shaddy, "Grangerizing," 539.

49 J.M. Bulloch, *The Art of Extra-Illustration*, ed. T.W.H. Crossland (London: Anthony Treherne, 1903), 14.

50 Ironically, given that his biography of Garrick is the most frequently extra-illustrated of any, Fitzgerald "viewed the Grangerite as one who slaughtered books [for their pictures], 'just as an epicure has had a sheep killed for the sweetbread'" (quoted in Shaddy, "Grangerizing," 168, 174). Folger Shakespeare Library, PH2598G3F3 (copy 5) retains an index; in other copies it is conspicuously absent.

51 In the catalogue by Shawe-Taylor *et al.*, *Every Look Speaks: Portraits of David Garrick* (2003), for instance, only thirteen of the sixty-six portraits listed predate 1762, slightly after the half-way point of Garrick's thirty-five year career.

52 Freeman O'Donoghue, *Catalogue of Engraved British Portraits Preserved in the Department of Prints and Drawings in the British Museum*, 6 vols. (London: By order of the Trustees, 1908).

53 The role of Tancred, during the regular season, passed to Charles Holland, 19 April 1759. See Stone (ed.), *London Stage*, Part 4, vol. II, 721.

54 Price may be one reason for its ubiquity: John Simco's catalogue for 1792 lists for sale at 2s, "Mr. Garrick, in the Character of Tancred" [no indication of artist or engraver], which makes it one of the least expensive prints of Garrick on the resale market. John Simco, "A Catalogue of Books, Prints, and Books of Prints, for 1792" (London: John Simco, [1792]), 4.

55 John Thane's 1773 catalogue lists a print of Garrick as Abel Drugger (no artist attribution) at 1s. (75); also for sale, Garrick's image on one of his "English Medals in Copper," where Garrick rubs shoulders with Oliver Cromwell, George II, Mary II and the Duke of Cumberland (92). John Thane, *Thane's Catalogue for 1773, of a Curious and Valuable Collection of Prints, Drawings, and Books of Prints, Both Ancient and Modern* ([London], 1773).

56 Harvard University Houghton Library: Hyde *2003j-Sj632 Extra-Ill.: Thomas Davies, *Memoirs of the Life of David Garrick*, 2 vols., 3rd edn (London: The author, 1781), vol. I, 61.

57 Shawe-Taylor *et al. Every Look Speaks*, 27.

58 Blake and Sillars, *Extending the Book*, 4, suggest, "Readers' interactions with texts are rarely as physically evident as they are in extra-illustrated books. The concept is simple: identify significant people, places, and things in a printed text, collect pictures of them, then insert the pictures as visual annotations to the text." I agree that readers' interactions are made visible, but extra-illustration's acts of interpretation often exceed simple identification.

59 *Letters of David Garrick*, vol. ii, 433–34.

60 Carington Bowles recommends mezzotint for its "amazing Ease" to those familiar with drawing, and makes clear the distinction between engraving and mezzotint: "Mezzotinto Prints are those which have no Hatching or Strokes of the Graver, but whose Lights and Shades are blended together, and appear like a Drawing of *Indian* ink." Carington Bowles, *The Artist's Assistant in Drawing, Perspective, Etching, Engraving, Mezzotinto Scraping, Painting on Glass, in Crayons, in Water-Colours, and on Silks and Sattins*, 5th edn (London: T. Kitchin, 1775), 37.

61 The print of Zoffany's "The Farmer's Return" (1762, 1766) is by J.G. Haid; see O'Donoghue, *Catalogue of Engraved British Portraits*, 284.

62 Garrick kept copies of many of these prints, as shown by *A Catalogue of a Valuable and Highly Interesting Collection of Engravings, Consisting chiefly of English and Foreign Portraits, Including the Scarce Portrait of Sir T. Chaloner, By Hollar, and Others ... The Property of the Late David Garrick, Esq which Will be Sold by Auction, By Mr. Christie ...* on 5 May 1825. Page 8 lists "item 104. Fourteen. Garrick in Richard III. Garrick, after Pine, &c. Mezz 105. Eight. After Zoffany, by Dixon, &c ditto." Similarly, under Drawings, page 9 lists "Item 132 Garrick in the character of Ranger, ditto in Abel Drugger, on vellum," and item 133, "Liotard. An original Partrait [sic] of Garrick, in black-lead, highly finished." One copy of this catalogue is pasted into an extra-illustrated Davies, *Memoirs*, Folger Shakespeare Library, W.b. 473, vol. iv, 486.

63 See Mary Dorothy George, *Catalogue of Political and Personal Satires Preserved in the Department of Prints and Drawings in the British Museum*, vol. v: *1771–1783* (London: By Order of the Trustees, 1935), item 5369: "two profiles of Garrick are given in medallion bust portraits on the engraved title page of 'DARLY's Comi-Prints of Characters. Caricature, Macaronies &c.' Price £4 4s.0 Dedicated to D. Garrick Esq."

64 Ibid., item 5063: "Behold the Muses Roscius sue in Vain, Taylors & Carpenters usurp their Reign [MD[arly] [1772]."

65 See Sillars's essay in Blake and Sillars, *Extending the Book*, 17.

66 Bulloch, *Art of Extra-Illustration*, is one of the first writers to advocate the use of newspapers in extra-illustration: "the newspaper ... cries loudly for disintegration at the hands of every particular reader so far as future use is concerned; and it is there that the grangerite comes in and serves a most useful purpose" (23). Newspapers, lower in cost than prints, will not exclude persons of limited means (37) who might receive pleasure and instruction from extra-illustration. Bulloch identifies the newspaper, "co-extensive with every

possible aspect of human activity" (24–25), as a plentiful, guilt-free source of illustrations, and suggests that while "No one pretends that the newspaper is authentic or final … the very diversity of its views contains the ultimate germ of truth" (31).

67 See item 36 in Boaden (ed.), *Private Correspondence of David Garrick*, Harvard University Houghton Library, TS 937.3.3 937.3.3, vol. VI.

68 Boswell famously argues for the inclusion of telling details in biography: "Had his [Samuel Johnson's] other friends been as diligent and ardent as I was, he might have been almost entirely preserved … he will be seen in this work more completely than any man who has ever yet lived." James Boswell, *The Life of Samuel Johnson, L.L.D.*, 2 vols. (London: Henry Baldwin, for Charles Dilly, 1791), vol. I, 4.

69 Peter Thomson, *On Actors and Acting* (University of Exeter Press, 2000), 96.

70 Folger Shakespeare Library: W.b.492 (30): David Garrick, "The Newspaper – a Farce."

71 Boaden (ed.), *Private Correspondendence of David Garrick*, vol. II, 128.

72 Taylor, *The Archive and the Repertoire*, 4.

References

Manuscript Works and Extra-Illustrated Books

British Library: 939.d, 939.e, 937.g.95–96: "Burney Collection. A collection of notebooks … dealing with the life and work of David Garrick."

British Library: Add. MS 38169: "Accounts in Public Advertiser (1765–1771)."

British Library: Add. MSS 38728 and 38729: "Minutes of the London Packet."

British Library: C.61.e.2: George Daniel, "The Jubilee Volume (a Scrapbook)."

Folger Shakespeare Library: B.26.2: Anon., Scrapbook.

Folger Shakespeare Library: T.a.49–64: James Winston, "A dramatic register of theatres and dramatic performances from the beginning to the present."

Folger Shakespeare Library: T.a.112: Joseph Reed, "Theatrical Duplicity, or a Genuine Narrative of the Conduct of David Garrick Esqr. To Joseph Reed on His Tragedy of Dido Containing All the Letters and Several Conversations Which Passed between the Manager, Author, and Others on That Subject. By the Author of the Register Office."

Folger Shakespeare Library: W.a.104 (1–13): Richard Cross and William Hopkins, "Cross-Hopkins Theatre Diaries, Drury Lane," 1747–60, 1762–64, 1768–76.

Folger Shakespeare Library: W.b.467: "Collection of prologues and epilogues and other miscellaneous verses by David Garrick."

Folger Shakespeare Library: W.b.492 (30): David Garrick, "The Newspaper – a Farce."

Garrick Club: unaccessioned four-volume scrapbook titled "David Garrick: A Memorial. Memoir, Autograph Correspondence, Shakespere [sic] Plays, Illustrated": item 25, vol. 1, receipt of Henry Baldwin.

Garrick Club: unaccessioned three-volume scrapbook by John Nixon titled "Dramatic Annals: Critiques on Plays and Performers. Vol. 1. (–III). 1741 to 1845": clipping hand-dated 1773 from vol. 1, 1741–1785.

Harvard University Houghton Library: Hyde *2003j-Sj632 Extra-Ill.: Thomas Davies, *Memoirs of the Life of David Garrick*. 2 vols. 3rd edn. London: The author, 1781.

Harvard University Houghton Library: Theatre Collection f TS 1116.256.3: "David Garrick; Original Manuscripts, Etc. [of and Relating to David Garrick]."

Harvard University Houghton Library: Theatre Collection GEN TS 1253.84: Joseph Reed, "Theatrical Duplicity: Or a Genuine Narrative of the Conduct of <u>David Garrick</u> Esq: To <u>Joseph Reed</u> on His Tragedy of <u>Dido</u>. Containing All the Letters, & Several Conversations, Which Pass'd between the Manager, Author, & Others on That Subject. By the Author of the Register-Office."

University of North Carolina at Chapel Hill: 11004-z items 1–3: "Minute Books of *St. James's Chronicle* (London, England), 1761–1815."

Victoria and Albert Museum National Art Library: Forster Collection 48.F.30: David Garrick and James Lacy, "Some Letters that pass'd between Mr. Lacy & Me, upon a Difference between Us."

Victoria and Albert Museum National Art Library: Forster Collection L4 to 3321: "Printed and ms. extracts from newspapers, magazines, &c. relating to Garrick."

Yale University Lewis Walpole Library: G286.1–2: "General Evening Post Minutes of Committee of Partners. May 31, 1754 – Aug. 9, 1786."

Published Works

Anonymously published works attributed in this volume to an author are listed alphabetically under the attributed author's name in square brackets. Works published under a pseudonym but attributed in this volume to an author are listed twice, both under the pseudonym and under the author's real name.

Ahluwalia, Rohini, Robert E. Burnkrant and H. Rao Unnava. "Consumer Response to Negative Publicity: The Moderating Role of Commitment." *Journal of Marketing Research*, 37/2 (2000), 203–14.

Anderson, Dorothy. "Reflections on Librarianship: Observations Arising from Examination of the Garrick Collection of Old Plays in the British Library." *British Library Journal*, 6 (1980), 1–6.

Andrews, Alexander. *The History of British Journalism, from the Foundation of the Newspaper Press in England to the Repeal of the Stamp Act in 1855, with Sketches of Press Celebrities*. 2 vols. London: Richard Bentley, 1859.

Anon. *An Account of the British Lying-in Hospital, for Married Women, in Brownlow-Street, Long-Acre, from Its Institution in November 1749, to December the 31st, 1770*. London: C. Say, [1771].

"A Collection of Original Letters from a Young American Gentleman in London, to His Friend, &c. Letter II." *Town and Country Magazine*, 6 (1774), 130–32.

The Drunken News-Writer: A Comic Interlude. As It Is Performed at the Theatre-Royal in the Haymarket. London: G. Smith, 1771.

D-ry-L-ne P-yh-se Broke Open. In a Letter to Mr. G———. London: Cooper, 1758.

"James Lacy, Esq. Late Patentee of the Theatre Royal, Drury Lane [with a Portrait]." *European Magazine, and London Review*, 1809, 274–78.

A Letter to Mr. Garrick, on His Having Purchased a Patent for Drury-Lane Play-House. London: J. Freeman, [1747].

A Letter to Mr. Garrick on the Opening of the Theatre, with Observations on the Conduct of Managers, to Actors, Authors, and Audiences: And Particularly to New-Performers. London: J. Coote, 1758.

Memoirs of that Celebrated Comedian, and Very Singular Genius Thomas Weston. London: S. Bladon, 1776.

Original Prologues, Epilogues, and Other Pieces Never before Printed. London: Printed for and sold by the Booksellers in Pater-Noster-Row, 1756.

"Review of *The Life of David Garrick; from Original Family Papers, and Numerous Published and Unpublished Sources*. By Percy Fitzgerald ... London, 1868." *Quarterly Review*, 125 (1868), 1–47.

"Rev. of Romeo and Juliet, by William Shakespeare." *Gentleman's Magazine*, 1750, 437–38.

"Rev. of *The Sentimental Spouter*." *Monthly Review; or Literary Journal*, 51 (July–December 1774), 486.

The Theatrical Bouquet: Containing an Alphabetical Arrangement of the Prologues and Epilogues, Which Have Been Published by Distinguished Wits, from the Time That Colley Cibber First Came on the Stage, to the Present Year. London: T. Lowndes, 1778.

The Theatrical Review: For the Year 1757, and Beginning of 1758. Containing Critical Remarks on the Principal Performers of Both the Theatres. Together with Observations on the Dramatic Pieces, New, or Revived; That Have Been Performed at Either House within That Period. To Which Is Added, a Scale of the Comparative Merit of the above Performers. London: J. Coote, 1758.

The Thespian Dictionary; or, Dramatic Biography of the present Age; Containing Sketches of the Lives, Lists of the Productions, Various Merits, etc., etc. of All the Principal Dramatists, Composers, Commentators, Managers, Actors, and Actresses of the United Kingdom: Interspersed with Numerous Original Anec-dotes, Forming a Complete Modern History of the English Stage. 2nd edn. London: James Cundee, 1805 (1st edn 1802).

Archimagírus Metaphoricus [William Kenrick]. *The Kapélion, or Poetical Ordin-ary; Consisting of Great Variety of Dishes in Prose and Verse; Recommended to All Who Have a Good Taste or Keen Appetite*. London, [1750–51].

Ashburnham, Sir William. *A Sermon Preached before His Grace William Duke of Devonshire, President, and the Governors of the London-Hospital, at Mile-End, for the Relief of All Sick and Diseased Persons, Especially Manufacturers, and Seamen in Merchant-Service, &c. At St. Lawrence Jewry, on Monday, April 11, 1763*. London: H. Woodfall, [1764].

Aspinall, A. "Statistical Accounts of the London Newspapers in the Eighteenth Century." *English Historical Review*, 63/247 (1948), 201–32.

Baker, David Erskine. *The Companion to the Play-House: Or, an Historical Account of All the Dramatic Writers (and Their Works) That Have Appeared in Great Britain and Ireland, from the Commencement of Our Theatrical Exhibitions, Down to the Present Year 1764. Composed in the Form of a Dictionary, for the*

More Readily Turning to Any Particular Author, or Performance. 2 vols. London: T. Becket and P.A. Dehondt, C. Henderson, T. Davies, 1764.

Baker, David Erskine and Isaac Reed. *Biographia Dramatica: Or, a Companion to the Playhouse.* 3 vols. London, 1812.

Barchas, Janine. *Graphic Design, Print Culture, and the Eighteenth-Century Novel.* Cambridge University Press, 2003.

Barczewski, Stephanie L. "Yorke, Philip, Second Earl of Hardwicke (1720–1790)." In Matthew and Harrison (eds.), *Oxford Dictionary of National Biography.*

Barker, Hannah. *Newspapers, Politics, and Public Opinion in Late Eighteenth-Century England.* Oxford: Clarendon Press, 1998.

Barry, Spranger. "The Occasional Prologue Spoken at Covent-Garden Theatre, by Mr. Barry [to Romeo and Juliet]." *London Magazine*, 1750, 473.

Bataille, Robert R. "The Kelly-Garrick Connection and the Politics of Theatre Journalism." *Restoration and Eighteenth-Century Theatre Research*, 4/1 (1989), 39–48.

  The Writing Life of Hugh Kelly: Politics, Journalism, and Theatre in Late-Eigteenth-Century London. Carbondale: Southern Illinois University Press, 2000.

Beard, Fred K. *Humor in the Advertising Business: Theory, Practice, and Wit.* Lanham, MD: Rowman & Littlefield, 2008.

Belch, George and Michael Belch. *Advertising and Promotion: An Integrated Marketing Communications Perspective.* 9th edn. New York: McGraw-Hill, 2012.

Bellamy, George Anne. *An Apology for the Life of George Anne Bellamy, Late of Covent-Garden Theatre.* 3rd edn. 5 vols. London: John Bell, for the Author, 1785.

Berger, Jonah, Alan T. Sorensen and Scott J. Rasmussen. "Positive Effects of Negative Publicity: When Negative Reviews Increase Sales." *Marketing Science*, 29/5 (2010), 815–27.

Bertelsen, Lance. *The Nonsense Club: Literature and Popular Culture, 1749–1764.* Oxford: Clarendon Press, 1986.

Bickerstaff, Isaac. *The Padlock: A Comic Opera. As It Is Perform'd by His Majesty's Servants, at the Theatre-Royal in Drury-Lane.* London: W. Griff[i]n, at Garrick's Head, [1768?].

Black, Jeremy. *The English Press in the Eighteenth Century.* London: Croom Helm, 1987.

Blackstone, William, Esq. *Commentaries on the Laws of England.* 4th edn. 4 vols. Vol. IV. Dublin: John Exshaw, Henry Saunders *et al.*, 1770.

Blagden, Cyprian. *The Stationers' Company: A History, 1403–1959.* Cambridge, MA: Harvard University Press, 1960.

Blake, Erin C. and Stuart Sillars. *Extending the Book: The Art of Extra-Illustration.* Washington, DC: Folger Shakespeare Library, 2010.

Boaden, James (ed.). *The Private Correspondence of David Garrick with the Most Celebrated Persons of His Time; Now First Published from the Originals, and*

Illustrated with Notes and a New Biographical Memoir of Garrick. 2 vols. London: Henry Colburn and Richard Bentley, 1831.

Bond, Richmond P. and Marjorie N. Bond. "The Minute Books of the *St. James's Chronicle.*" *Studies in Bibliography: Papers of the Bibliographical Society of the University of Virginia,* 28 (1975), 17–40.

Boswell, James. *Boswell's London Journal 1762–1763.* New York: McGraw-Hill, 1950.

Critical Strictures on the New Tragedy of Elvira, Written by Mr. David Malloch. London: W. Flexney, [1763].

The Life of Samuel Johnson, L.L.D. 2 vols. vol. 1. London: Henry Baldwin, for Charles Dilly, 1791.

Bourne, H.R. Fox. *English Newspapers: Chapters in the History of Journalism.* 2 vols. London: Chatto & Windus, 1887.

Bowles, Carington. *The Artist's Assistant in Drawing, Perspective, Etching, Engraving, Mezzotinto Scraping, Painting on Glass, in Crayons, in Water-Colours, and on Silks and Sattins.* 5th edn. London: T. Kitchin, 1775.

Boyd, Amanda Weldy. *Staging Memory and Materiality in Eighteenth-Century Theatrical Biography.* London: Anthem Press, 2018.

Boydell, John. *A Catalogue of Prints Published by J. Boydell, Engraver in Cheapside, London.* London: J. Boydell, 1773.

Braudy, Leo. *The Frenzy of Renown: Fame and Its History.* Oxford University Press, 1986.

Brayne, Charles. "Lacy, James (1696–1774)." In Matthew and Harrison (eds.), *Oxford Dictionary of National Biography.*

Brewer, David. *The Afterlife of Character, 1726–1825.* Philadelphia: University of Pennsylvania Press, 2005.

Brewer, John. "'The Most Polite Age and the Most Vicious': Attitudes towards Culture as a Commodity, 1660–1800." In Ann Bermingham and John Brewer (eds.), *The Consumption of Culture 1600–1800: Image, Object, Text,* 341–61. London and New York: Routledge, 1995.

Bulloch, J.M. *The Art of Extra-Illustration,* ed. T.W.H. Crossland. London: Anthony Treherne, 1903.

Burden, Michael. "Shakespeare and Opera." In Peter Sabor and Fiona Ritchie (eds.), *Shakespeare in the Eighteenth Century,* 204–26. Cambridge University Press, 2012.

Burney, Fanny. *The Early Journals and Letters of Fanny Burney,* ed. Lars Troide. 3 vols. Oxford: Clarendon Press, 1988.

Burnim, Kalman A. *David Garrick, Director.* University of Pittsburgh Press, 1961.

"Looking Upon His Like Again: Garrick and the Artist." In Shirley Strum Kenny (ed.), *British Theatre and Other Arts, 1660–1800,* 182–218. Washington, DC: Folger Shakespeare Library; London: Associated University Presses, 1983.

"B.Y." *The Disputes between the Director of D—Y, and the Pit Potentates: Being a Letter to a Friend, Concerning the Behaviour of the Melancholly Manager of the Suffring Theatre; and Some Considerations on the Late Disturbances and the*

Causes Thereof: With a Few Hints on the Heroes and Heroines, G-RR–K, C-BB-R, Etc. The Whole Relating to Some Remarkable Occurrences in the Year 1744. London: M. Cooper, 1744.

Campbell, Archibald. *Lexiphanes, a Dialogue. Imitated from Lucian, and Suited to the Present Times*. London: J. Knox, 1767.

Cibber, Theophilus. *Cibber's Two Dissertations on the Theatres*. London: Printed for the Author, [1757].

Clayton, Timothy. *The English Print 1688–1802*. New Haven, CT and London: Yale University Press for the Paul Mellon Centre for Studies in British Art, 1997.

[Colman, George, the elder]. *A Letter of Abuse, to D—D G———K, Esq.* London: J. Scott, 1757.

Colman, George [the elder] and David Garrick,. *The Clandestine Marriage, a Comedy.* 2nd edn. London: T. Becket and P.A. De Hondt, R. Baldwin, R. Davis, and T. Davies, 1766.

Colman, George [the younger] (ed.). *Posthumous Letters, from Various Celebrated Men: Addressed to Francis Colman, and George Colman, the Elder: With Annotations and Occasional Remarks, by George Colman, the Younger.* London: T. Cadell and W. Davies; W. Blackwood, 1820.

[Combe, William]. *Sanitas, Daughter of Aesculapius. To David Garrick, Esq. A Poem.* London: G. Kearsly, 1772.

Conaway, Charles. "'Thou'rt the Man': David Garrick, William Shakespeare, and the Masculinization of the Eighteenth-Century Stage." *Restoration and Eighteenth-Century Theatre Research*, 19/1 (2004), 22–42.

[Cooke, William]. *Memoirs of Charles Macklin, Comedian, with the Dramatic Characters, Manners, Anecdotes, &c. Of the Age in Which He Lived: Forming an History of the Stage During Almost the Whole of the Last Century.* 2 vols. Vol. 1, London: James Asperne, 1804.

Cowan, Brian. *The Social Life of Coffee: The Emergence of the British Coffeehouse.* New Haven, CT: Yale University Press, 2005.

Crabbe, George. *The News-Paper: A Poem.* London: J. Dodsley, 1785.

Cross, Richard. *The Adventures of John Le-Brun.* 2 vols. London: G. Hawkins, 1739.

Cumberland, Richard. *Memoirs of Richard Cumberland, Written by Himself.* Philadelphia, PA: Parry and McMillan, 1856; first published 1806.

Cunningham, Vanessa. *Shakespeare and Garrick.* Cambridge University Press, 2008.

Danchin, Pierre (ed.). *The Prologues and Epilogues of the Eighteenth Century: The Third Part: 1737–1760.* Vol. 5. Nancy: Éditions Messene, 1990.

Davies, Thomas. *Dramatic Miscellanies: Consisting of Critical Observations on Several Plays of Shakspeare: With a Review of His Principal Characters, and Those of Various Eminent Writers, as Represented by Mr. Garrick, and Other Celebrated Comedians.* 3 vols. London: Printed for the Author, 1783–84.

Memoirs of the Life of David Garrick, Esq., Interspersed with Characters and Anecdotes of His Theatrical Contemporaries. New edn. 2 vols. London: The author, 1780.

[Davies, Thomas and Samuel Johnson]. *Miscellaneous and Fugitive Pieces.* 3 vols. Vol. II. London: T. Davies, 1773.

Diderot, Denis. *L'origine du Paradoxes sur le comédien: La partition intérieure.* 2nd edn. Paris: J. Vrin, 1980; 1st edn 1773.

Dobson, Michael. *The Making of the National Poet: Shakespeare, Adaptation and Authorship, 1660–1769.* Oxford: Clarendon Press, 1995.

Dodsley, Robert. *A Collection of Poems by Several Hands.* 3 vols. 2nd edn. London: Printed for R. Dodsley, 1748.

Downer, Alan S. "The Diary of Benjamin Webster." *Theatre Annual,* 1945, 47–64.

Downie, J.A. "Periodicals, the Book Trade and the 'Bourgeois Public Sphere.'" *Media History,* 14/3 (2008), 261–74.

"A Dramatic Author" [Arthur Murphy]. *A Defence of Mr. Garrick, in Answer to the Letter-Writer. With Remarks Upon Plays and Players, and the Present State of the Stage.* London: R. Stevens, [1759?].

Duke, Charles R. and Les Carlson. "Applying Implicit Memory Measures: Word Fragment Completion in Advertising Tests." *Journal of Current Issues and Research in Advertising,* 16/2 (1994), 29–39.

Eckersley, L. Lynette. "Joseph Reed." In Matthew and Harrison (eds.), *Oxford Dictionary of National Biography.*

"E.F." [Samuel Foote?]. *Mr. Garrick's Conduct, as Manager of the Theatre-Royal in Drury-Lane, Considered. In a Letter Addressed to Him.* London: C. Corbett, [1747].

Ellis, Markman. "Coffee-House Libraries in Mid-Eighteenth-Century London." *The Library: Transactions of the Bibliographical Society,* 10/1 (March 2009), 3–40.

England, Martha Winburn. "Garrick and Stratford." *Bulletin of the New York Public Library,* 66 (1962), 73–92, 178–204, 61–72.

Fahrner, Robert. "A Reassessment of Garrick's *The Male Coquette: Or, Seventeen-Hundred Fifty Seven* as Veiled Discourse." *Eighteenth-Century Life,* 17/3 (1993), 1–13.

Feather, John. *A History of British Publishing.* 2nd edn. New York and London: Routledge, 2006; 1st edn 1988.

Ferdinand, C.Y. *Benjamin Collins and the Provincial Newspaper Trade in the Eighteenth Century.* Oxford: Clarendon Press, 1997.

Fitzgerald, Percy Hetherington. *The Life of David Garrick; from Original Family Papers, and Numerous Published and Unpublished Sources.* 2 vols. London: Tinsley Brothers, 1868.

[Foote, Samuel?]. Under pseud. "E.F." *Mr. Garrick's Conduct, as Manager of the Theatre-Royal in Drury-Lane, Considered. In a Letter Addressed to Him.* London: C. Corbett, [1747].

[Foote, Samuel]. *A Treatise on the Passions, So Far as They Regard the Stage; with a Critical Enquiry into the Theatrical Merit of Mr. G–K, Mr. Q–N, and Mr. B—Y. The First Considered in the Part of Lear, and the Two Last Opposed in Othello*. London: Corbet, [1747]

Francklin, Thomas. *A Sermon Preached at the Parish-Church of St. Anne, Westminster, on Thursday, May the 10th, 1758. Before the Governors of the Middlesex-Hospital, for Sick and Lame; and for Lying-in Married Women*. London: Published at the Request of the Society, 1758.

Freeman, Lisa. *Character's Theatre: Genre and Identity on the Eighteenth-Century English Stage*. Philadelphia: University of Pennsylvania Press, 2002.

Garrick, David. *The Journal of David Garrick, Describing His Visit to France and Italy in 1763*, ed. George Winchester Stone. New York: Modern Language Association of America, 1939.

The Letters of David Garrick, ed. David M. Little and George M. Kahrl, assoc. ed. Phoebe deK. Wilson. 3 vols. Cambridge, MA: Harvard University Press, 1963.

The Poetical Works of David Garrick, Esq. Now First Collected into Two Volumes. With Explanatory Notes, ed. George Kearsley. 2 vols. London: George Kearsley, 1785.

Selected Verse, ed. John Hainsworth. Armidale, Aus.: University of New England, 1981.

An Essay on Acting: In which will be consider'd the Mimical Behaviour of a Certain fashionable faulty Actor, and the Laudableness of such unmannerly, as well as inhumane Proceedings. To which will be added, A short Criticism On His acting Macbeth. London: W. Bickerton, 1744.

The Farmer's Return from London. An Interlude. London: Dryden Leach, for J. and R. Tonson, 1762.

Reasons why David Garrick, Esq; Should Not appear on the Stage, in a Letter to John Rich, Esq; London: J. Cooke, 1759.

The Sick Monkey, A Fable. London: J. Fletcher, 1765.

Genest, John. *Some Account of the English Stage from the Restoration in 1660 to 1830*. 10 vols. New York: Burt Franklin, 1965; 1st edn 1832.

[Gentleman, Francis]. *The Dramatic Censor; or, Critical Companion*. 2 vols. London: J. Bell, C. Etherington, 1770.

George, Mary Dorothy. *Catalogue of Political and Personal Satires Preserved in the Department of Prints and Drawings in the British Museum*, vol. v: *1771–1783* (London: By order of the Trustees, 1935).

Gibbon, Edward. *Gibbon's Journal to January 28th, 1763*, ed. D.M. Low. London: Chatto & Windus, 1929.

Goldsmith, Oliver. *Retaliation: A Poem. Including Epitaphs on the Most Distinguished Wits of This Metropolis*. London: G. Kearsly, 1774.

Gomeldon, Jane. *The Medley*. Newcastle: J. White and T. Saint, 1766.

Graciano, Andrew. "The Memoir of Benjamin Wilson, F.R.S. (1721–88): Painter and Electrical Scientist." *Walpole Society*, 74 (2012), 165–244.

Granger, Rev. James. *A Biographical History of England, from Egbert the Great to the Revolution: Consisting of Characters Disposed in Different Classes, and*

Adapted to a Methodical Catalogue of Engraved British Heads: Intended as an Essay Towards Reducing Our Biography to System, and a Help to the Knowledge of Portraits; Interspersed with Variety of Anecdotes, and Memoirs of a Great Number of Persons, Not to Be Found in Any Other Biographical Work: With a Preface, Shewing the Utility of a Collection of Engraved Portraits to Supply the Defect, and Answer the Various Purposes, of Medals. 2nd edn. 4 vols. London: T. Davies, J. Robson, G. Robinson, T. Becket, T. Cadell, and T. Evans, 1775; 1st edn 1769.

Letters between the Rev. James Granger, M.A. Rector of Shiplake, and Many of the Most Eminent Literary Men of His Time: Composing a Copious History and Illustration of His Biographical History of England with Miscellanies, and Notes of Tours in France, Holland, and Spain, by the Same Gentleman. London: Nicols and Son, for Longman, Hurst, Rees, and Orme, 1805.

Gray, Charles Harold. *Theatrical Criticism in London to 1795.* New York: Benjamin Blom, 1931.

Griffith, Elizabeth. *The School for Rakes: A Comedy.* 2nd edn. London: T. Becket and P. De Hondt, 1769.

Habermas, Jürgen. *The Structural Transformation of the Public Sphere: An Inquiry into a Category of Bourgeois Society*, trans. Thomas Burger and Frederick Lawrence. Cambridge: Polity Press, 1989.

Haig, Robert L. *The Gazetteer 1735–1791: A Study in the Eighteenth-Century English Newspaper.* Carbondale: Southern Illinois University Press, 1960.

"A Halter-Maker" [Joseph Reed]. *A Sop in the Pan for a Physical Critick: In a Letter to Dr. Sm*ll*t, Occasion'd by a Criticism on a Late Mock-Tragedy, Call'd Madrigal and Trulletta.* London: W. Reeve, 1759.

Handover, P.M. *A History of the London Gazette 1665–1965.* London: Her Majesty's Stationery Office, 1965.

Hargraves, Matthew. *Candidates for Fame: The Society of Artists of Great Britain 1760–1791.* New Haven, CT: Yale University Press, 2006.

Hargreaves, Ian. *Journalism: A Very Short Introduction.* Oxford University Press, 2005.

Harris, Michael. *London Newspapers in the Age of Walpole: A Study of the Origins of the Modern English Press.* London: Associated University Presses, 1987.

"The Management of the London Newspaper Press During the Eighteenth Century." *Publishing History*, 4 (1978), 95–112.

"Scratching the Surface: Engravers, Printsellers and the London Book Trade in the Mid-18th Century." In Arnold Hunt, Giles Mandelbrote and Alison Shell (eds.), *The Book Trade & Its Customers 1450–1900: Historical Essays for Robin Myers*, 95–114. New Castle, DE: Oak Knoll Press; Winchester: St Paul's Bibliographies, 1997.

"The Structure, Ownership and Control of the Press, 1620–1780." In George Boyce, James Curran and Pauline Wingate (eds.), *Newspaper History from the Seventeenth Century to the Present Day*, 82–97. London: Constable; Beverly Hills, CA: SAGE, 1978.

[Henry, Earl of Bathurst]. *The Case of the Unfortunate Martha Sophia Swordfeager.* London, 1771.

Highfill, Philip H., Kalman A. Burnim and Edward A. Langhans (eds.). *A Biographical Dictionary of Actors, Actresses, Musicians, Dancers, Managers & Other Stage Personnel in London, 1660–1800.* 16 vols. Carbondale: Southern Illinois University Press, 1973–93.

Hill, John. *The Actor: Or, a Treatise on the Art of Playing.* London: R. Griffiths, 1755.

[Hill, John]. *An Account of the Tragedy of Cleone.* London: M. Cooper, 1758.

Hindle, Wilfred. *The Morning Post 1772–1937: Portrait of a Newspaper.* London: George Routledge & Sons, 1937.

Holland, Peter. "David Garrick: '3dly, as an Author.'" *Studies in Eighteenth-Century Culture*, 25 (1996), 39–62.

"Hearing the Dead: The Sound of David Garrick." In Peter Holland and Michael Cordner (eds.), *Players, Playwrights, Playhouses: Investigating Performance, 1660–1800*, 248–70. Basingstoke: Palgrave Macmillan, 2007.

(ed.). *Great Shakespeareans*, vol. II: *Garrick, Kemble, Siddons, Kean.* London: Continuum, 2010.

Hume, Robert D. "Garrick in Dublin in 1745–46." *Philological Quarterly*, 93/4 (2014), 507–40.

"John Rich as Manager and Entrepreneur." In Jeremy Barlow and Berta Joncus (eds.), *The Stage's Glory: John Rich (1692–1761)*, 29–60. Newark: University of Delaware Press, 2011.

"The Value of Money in Eighteenth-Century England: Incomes, Prices, Buying Power – and Some Problems in Cultural Economics." *Huntington Library Quarterly*, 77/4 (2015), 373–416.

Hume, Robert D. and Judith Milhous. "Receipts at Drury Lane: Richard Cross's Diary for 1746–47." *Theatre Notebook*, 49 (1995), 12–26, 69–90.

Hunter, David. "The Diary of John Stede, London Theatre Prompter from about 1710 to the 1760s." *Theatre Notebook: A Journal of the History and Technique of the British Theatre*, 62/3 (2008), 163–66.

"An Impartial Hand" [Charles Macklin?]. *Stage Policy Detected; or Some Select Pieces of Theatrical Secret History Laid Open: In a Letter to a Certain Manager on His Imaginary Justification of His Late Conduct.* London: J. Robinson, 1744.

Inglis, Fred. *A Short History of Celebrity.* Princeton University Press, 2010.

Johnson, Samuel. *A Dictionary of the English Language: in which The Words are deduced from their Originals, and Illustrated in their Different Significations by Examples from the best Writers.* 2nd edn. 2 vols. London: W. Strahan, for J. Knapton; C. Hitch and L. Hawes; A. Millar; R. and J. Dodsley; and M. and T. Longman, 1756.

Jonson, Ben. *The Works of Ben. Jonson.* 7 vols. Vol. I. London: D. Midwinter, W. Innys and J. Richardson *et al.*, 1756.

[J.T.]. *A Letter of Compliment to the Ingenious Author of a Treatise on the Passions, So Far as They Regard the Stage; with a Critical Enquiry into the Theatrical*

Merit of Mr. G—K, Mr. Q—N, and Mr. B—Y, &c. With Some Further Remarks on Mr. M–N. And a Few Hints on Our Modern Actresses, Particularly Mrs. C—R and Mrs. P——D. London: C. Corbett, 1747.

Kendall, Alan. *David Garrick: A Biography*. New York: St. Martin's Press, 1985.

Kenrick, William. *A Letter to David Garrick, Esq. From William Kenrick, LL.D.* [Containing *Love in the Suds: A Town Eclogue. Being the Lamentation of Roscius for the Loss of His Nyky*]. London: J. Wheble, 1772.

Kenrick, William. *A Letter to David Garrick, Esq., Occasioned by His Having Moved the Court of King's Bench against the Publisher of Love in the Suds, or the Lamentations of Roscius for His Nyky*. London: J. Wheble, 1772.

[Kenrick, William]. Under pseud. Archimagírus Metaphoricus. *The Kapélion, or Poetical Ordinary; Consisting of Great Variety of Dishes in Prose and Verse; Recommended to All Who Have a Good Taste or Keen Appetite*. London, [1750–51].

King, Richard (reviser). *The Complete Modern London Spy, for the Present Year, 1781; or, a Real New, and Universal Disclosure, of the Secret, Nocturnal, and Diurnal Transactions, in and About the Cities of London and Westminster, and the Borough of Southwark*. London: Alex. Hogg, T. Lewis, 1781.

Knapp, Mary E. *A Checklist of Verse by David Garrick*. Charlottesville: University of Virginia Press for the Bibliographical Society of the University of Virginia, 1955.

"Garrick's Verses to the Marquis of Rockingham." *Philological Quarterly*, 29/1 (1950), 78–81.

A Revision of a Checklist of Verse by David Garrick. New Haven, CT, 1974.

Knight Hunt, F. *The Fourth Estate: Contributions towards a History of Newspapers, and of the Liberty of the Press*. 2 vols. London: David Bogue, 1850.

Kobialka, Michal. "Words and Bodies: A Discourse on Male Sexuality in Late Eighteenth-Century English Representational Practices." *Theatre Research International*, 28/1 (2003), 1–19.

Lilti, Antoine. *The Invention of Celebrity*, trans. Lynn Jeffress. Cambridge: Polity Press, 2017 (French edn 2015).

"A Lover of Truth and Justice." "Particular Relation of a Late Remarkable Affair and Particulars of Mr. Barretti's Trial." *Town and Country Magazine*, 1769, 509–12.

[Lowndes, Thomas]. *The Theatrical Manager: A Dramatic Satire*. London: T. Lowndes, 1751.

Luckhurst, Mary and Jane Moody. *Theatre and Celebrity in Britain, 1660–2000*. New York: Palgrave Macmillan, 2005.

[Macklin, Charles]. *Mr. Macklin's Reply to Mr. Garrick's Answer. To Which Are Prefix'd, All the Papers Which Have Publickly Appeared, in Regard to This Important Dispute*. London: J. Roberts and A. Dodd, 1743.

[Macklin, Charles?]. Under pseud. "An Impartial Hand." *Stage Policy Detected; or Some Select Pieces of Theatrical Secret History Laid Open: In a Letter to a Certain Manager on His Imaginary Justification of His Late Conduct*. London: J. Robinson, 1744.

Mannings, David. "Reynolds, Garrick, and the Choice of Hercules." *Eighteenth-Century Studies*, 17/3 (1984), 259–83.

Marsden, Jean I. "Improving Shakespeare: From the Restoration to Garrick." In Stanley Wells and Sarah Stanton (eds.), *The Cambridge Companion to Shakespeare on Stage*, 21–36: Cambridge University Press, 2002.

Martial. *Epigrams of Martial, &c. With Mottos from Horace, &c. Translated, Imitated, Adapted, and Addrest to the Nobility, Clergy, and Gentry*, trans. Rev. Mr. Scott. London: J. Wilkie, J. Walter and H. Parker, 1773.

Massinger, Philip. *The Dramatick Works of Philip Massinger*, ed. John Monck Mason. 4 vols. London: T. Davies, T. Payne, L. Davis, J. Nichols, T. Evans, W. Davis, H. Payne, 1779.

Matthew, H.C.G. and Brian Harrison (eds.). *Oxford Dictionary of National Biography*. Oxford University Press, 2004.

McIntyre, Ian. *Garrick*. London: Penguin, 1999.

McPherson, Heather. *Art and Celebrity in the Age of Reynolds and Siddons*. University Park: Pennsylvania State University Press, 2017.

"Theatrical Celebrity and the Commodification of the Actor." In Julia Swindells and David Francis Taylor (eds.), *The Oxford Handbook of the Georgian Theatre 1737–1832*, 192–212. Oxford University Press, 2014.

Merians, Linda E. "The London Lock Hospital and the Lock Asylum for Women." In Linda E. Merians (ed.), *The Secret Malady: Venereal Disease in Eighteenth-Century Britain and France*, 128–46. Lexington: University Press of Kentucky, 1996.

Milhous, Judith. "Company Management." In Robert D. Hume (ed.), *London Theatre World, 1660–1800*, 1–34. Carbondale and Edwardsville: Southern Illinois University Press, 1980.

"Reading Theatre History from Account Books." In Michael Cordner and Peter Holland (eds.), *Players, Playwrights, Playhouses: Investigating Performance, 1660–1800*, 101–34. Basingstoke: Palgrave Macmillan, 2007.

Milhous, Judith and Robert D. Hume. "David Garrick and Box-Office Receipts at Drury Lane in 1742–43." *Philological Quarterly*, 67/3 (1988), 323–44.

Montagu, Elizabeth Robinson. *An Essay on the Writings and Genius of Shakespear, Compared with the Greek and French Dramatic Poets. With Some Remarks Upon the Misrepresentations of Mons. De Voltaire*. London: J. Dodsley, Mess. Baker and Leigh, J. Walter, T. Cadell, J. Wilkie, 1769.

Morell, Thomas. *A Sermon Preached at the Anniversary Meeting of the Sons of the Clergy, in the Cathedral Church of St. Paul, on Thursday, May 14, 1772 … Published at the Request of the Stewards. To Which Is Added, a List of the Several Amounts Arising from the Collections Made at the Anniversary Meeting of the Sons of the Clergy, since the Year 1721*. London: John and Francis Rivington, [1772].

[Morgan, MacNamara]. *A Letter to Miss Nossiter. Occasioned by Her First Appearance on the Stage: In Which Is Contained Remarks Upon Her Manner of Playing the Character of Juliet; Interspersed with Some Other Theatrical Observations*. London: W. Owen, G. Woodfall, 1753.

Murphy, Arthur. *The Life of David Garrick, Esq.* 2 vols. London: J. Wright, J.F. Foot, 1801.

The Works of Arthur Murphy, Esq. 7 vols. London: T. Cadell, 1786.

[Murphy, Arthur]. Under pseud. "A Dramatic Author." *A Defence of Mr. Garrick, in Answer to the Letter-Writer. With Remarks Upon Plays and Players, and the Present State of the Stage.* London: R. Stevens, [1759?].

National Archives of Great Britain. "Court of King's Bench." National Archives, www.nationalarchives.gov.uk/records/research-guides/kings-bench.htm.

"Neither-Side, Mr." *An Impartial Examen of the Present Contests between the Town and the Manager of the Theatre. With Some Proposals for Accommodating the Present Misunderstandings between the Town and the Manager, Offer'd to the Consideration of Both Parties.* London: M. Cooper, 1744.

Nichols, John (ed.). *Illustrations of the Literary History of the Eighteenth Century: Consisting of Authentic Memoirs and Original Letters of Eminent Persons; and Intended as a Sequel to the Literary Anecdotes.* 8 vols. London: J.B. Nichols and Son, 1828.

Nicoll, Allardyce. *The Garrick Stage: Theatres and Audience in the Eighteenth Century.* Manchester University Press, 1980.

Nicols, John. *A Sermon Preached at the Parish Church of St. Andrew, Holborn, on Thursday, March 26, 1767, before the President, Vice-Presidents, Treasurer, and Governors, of the City of London Lying-in Hospital for Married Women, at Shaftesbury-House in Aldersgate-Street.* London: Published at the Request of the Society by C. Say, for the charity, [1767].

Nipclose, Sir Nicholas [Francis Gentleman]. *The Theatres: A Poetical Dissection.* London: John Bell and C. Etherington, 1772.

Noble, Rev. Mark (ed.). *A Biographical History of England, from the Revolution to the End of George I's Reign; Being a Continuation of the Rev. J. Granger's Work: Consisting of Characters Disposed in Different Classes, and Adapted to a Methodical Catalogue of Engraved British Heads; Interspersed with a Variety of Anecdotes, and Memoirs of a Great Number of Persons, Not to Be Found in Any Other Biographical Work.* 3 vols. London: W. Richardson, Darton and Harvey, W. Baynes, 1806.

O'Donoghue, Freeman. *Catalogue of Engraved British Portraits Preserved in the Department of Prints and Drawings in the British Museum.* 6 vols. London: By order of the Trustees, 1908.

Old Bailey Proceedings Online, www.oldbaileyonline.org. October 1769, Trial of Joseph Baretti (T17691018–9).

Old Bailey Proceedings Online, www.oldbaileyonline.org. September 1765, Trial of Benjamin Robert Turbot (T17650918–24).

"Old Comedian." *The Life and Death of David Garrick, Esq. The Celebrated English Roscius.* 2nd edn. London: J. Pridden, S. Bladon, J. Mathews, 1779.

Pedicord, Harry William. *The Theatrical Public in the Time of Garrick.* New York: King's Crown Press, 1954.

Pettegree, Andrew. *The Invention of News: How the World Came to Know About Itself.* New Haven, CT: Yale University Press, 2014.

Plomer, H.R., E.R. McC. Dix, G.J. Gray and G.H. Bushnell. *A Dictionary of the Printers and Booksellers Who Were at Work in England, Scotland and Ireland, from 1726 to 1775*. Oxford University Press for the Bibliographical Society, 1968.

Pointon, Marcia. "Casts, Imprints, and the Deathliness of Things: Artifacts at the Edge." *Art Bulletin*, 96/2 (2014), 170–95.

Hanging the Head: Portraiture and Social Formation in Eighteenth-Century England. New Haven, CT: Yale University Press, 1993.

Prior, Sir James. *Life of Edmund Malone, Editor of Shakespeare*. London: Smith, Elder, 1860.

Pruitt, John. "David Garrick's Invisible Nemeses." *Restoration and Eighteenth-Century Theatre Research* 23/1 (2008), 2–18.

[Purdon, Edward]. *A Letter to David Garrick, Esq; on Opening the Theatre. In Which, with Great Freedom, He Is Told How He Ought to Behave*. London: I. Pottinger, 1769.

Raven, James. *The Business of Books: Booksellers and the English Book Trade 1450–1850*. New Haven, CT: Yale University Press, 2007.

Publishing Business in Eighteenth-Century England. Woodbridge: Boydell Press, 2014.

Reed, Joseph. *Dido; a Tragedy. As It Was Performed at the Theatre Royal in Drury Lane, with Universal Applause*. London: Nichols and Son, 1808.

Madrigal and Trulletta. A Mock-Tragedy. Acted (under the Direction of Mr. Cibber) at the Theatre-Royal in Covent-Garden. With Notes by the Author, and Dr. Humbug, Critick and Censor-General. London: W. Reeve, 1758.

[Reed, Joseph]. Under pseud. A Halter-Maker. *A Sop in the Pan for a Physical Critic: In a Letter to Dr. Sm*ll*t, Occasion'd by a Criticism on a Late Mock-Tragedy, Call'd Madrigal and Trulletta*. London: W. Reeve, 1759.

[Reed, Joseph]. "To the Printer." *The Universal Museum, Or Gentleman's and Ladies Polite Magazine of History, Politicks, and Literature for 1764*, 581–83.

Riccoboni, Lewis [Luigi]. *A General History of the Stage, from Its Origin*. 2nd edn. London: W. Owen and Lockyer Davis, 1754.

Ritchie, Leslie. "Garrick's *Male-Coquette* and Theatrical Masculinities." In Shelley King and Yaël Schlick (eds.), *Refiguring the Coquette*, 164–98. Lewisburg, PA: Bucknell University Press, 2008.

"Pox on Both Your Houses: The Battle of the Romeos." *Eighteenth-Century Fiction*, 27/3–4 (2015), 373–94.

"The Spouters' Revenge: Apprentice Actors and the Imitation of London's Theatrical Celebrities." *The Eighteenth Century: Theory and Interpretation*, 53/1 (2012), 41–71.

Roach, Joseph R. *It*. Ann Arbor: University of Michigan Press, 2007.

The Player's Passion: Studies in the Science of Acting. London: Associated University Presses, 1985.

Rogers, C. S. and Betty Rizzo. "Kenrick, William (1729/30–1779)." In Matthew and Harrison (eds.), *Oxford Dictionary of National Biography*.

Rolt, Richard. *A Poetical Epistle from Shakespear in Elysium, to Mr. Garrick, at Drury-Lane Theatre*. London: J. Newbery and W. Owen, 1752.

Royal Society of Artists of Great-Britain. *A Catalogue of the Pictures, Sculptures, Designs in Architecture, Models, Drawings, Prints, &c. Exhibited at the Great Room in Spring-Garden, Charing-Cross, May the First, 1769*. London: William Bunce, 1769.

Rusnak, Matthew. "The Trial of Giuseppe Baretti, October 20th 1769: A Literary and Cultural History of the Baretti Case." PhD thesis. Rutgers University (2008).

Sabor, Peter and Paul Yachnin (eds.). *Shakespeare and the Eighteenth Century*. Aldershot: Ashgate, 2008.

Saunders, Robert. *A Catalogue of the Library, Splendid Books of Prints, Poetical and Historical Tracts, of David Garrick, Esq. Removed from His Villa at Hampton, and House on the Adelphi Terrace, with the Modern Works Added Thereto by Mrs. Garrick*. London: Robert Saunders, 1823.

Sawyer, Paul. "John Rich's Contribution to the Eighteenth-Century London Stage." In Kenneth Richards and Peter Thomson (eds.), *The Eighteenth-Century English Stage: The Proceedings of a Symposium Sponsored by the Manchester University Department of Drama*, 85–104. London: Methuen, 1972.

Sayer, Robert and John Smith. *Dramatic Characters, or Different Portraits of the English Stage*. London: Robert Sayer and Jo[h]n Smith, 1770.

Schoch, Richard. "'A Supplement to Public Laws': Arthur Murphy, David Garrick, and 'Hamlet with Alterations.'" *Theatre Journal*, 57/1 (2005), 21–32.

Writing the History of the British Stage, 1660–1900. Cambridge University Press, 2016.

Scott, Rev. Mr. William. *A Sermon Preached at the Court End of the Town and in the City, on Sunday October 25, 1772. On the King's Accession to the Throne of These Realms. Dedicated to Mr. Garrick*. London: J. Wilkie, J. Walter and H. Parker, 1773.

Scouten, Arthur Hawley (ed.). *The London Stage, 1660–1800: A Calendar of Plays, Entertainments & Afterpieces Together with Casts, Box-Receipts and Contemporary Comment Compiled from the Playbills, Newspapers and Theatrical Diaries of the Period*, Part 3: *1729–1747*. 2 vols. Carbondale: Southern Illinois University Press, 1961.

Shaddy, Robert A. "Grangerizing: 'One of the Unfortunate Stages of Bibliomania.'" *Book Collector*, 49/4 (2000), 535–46.

Shakespeare, William. *Antony and Cleopatra; an Historical Play, Written by William Shakespeare: Fitted for the Stage by Abridging Only; and Now Acted, at the Theatre-Royal in Drury-Lane, by His Majesty's Servants*. London: J. and R. Tonson, [1758].

Bell's Edition of Shakespeare's Plays, as They Are Now Performed at the Theatres Royal in London; Regulated from the Prompt Books of Each House. 5 vols. London: John Bell and C. Etherington, 1774.

[Illustrated Plates for] Bell's Edition of Shakespeare's Works Compleat, Including His Poems ... To Complete the First Five Volumes. London: John Bell, [1773–76?].

Shakespeare, William, adapted by David Garrick. *Romeo and Juliet. By Shakespear. With Some Alterations, and an Additional Scene: As It Is Performed at the Theatre-Royal in Drury-Lane.* London: J. and R. Tonson, and S. Draper, 1748.

Shakespeare, William, adapted by Theophilus Cibber. *Romeo and Juliet, a Tragedy, Revis'd, and Alter'd from Shakespear ... To Which Is Added, a Serio-Comic Apology, for Part of the Life of Mr. Theophilus Cibber, Comedian. Written by Himself.* London: C. Corbett, 1748.

Shawe-Taylor, Desmond *et al. Every Look Speaks: Portraits of David Garrick.* Bath: Moore Stephens, 2003.

Sherman, Stuart. "Garrick Among Media: The 'Now Performer' Navigates the News." *PMLA*, 126/4 (2011), 966–82.

[Shirley, William.] *A Bone for the Chroniclers to Pick; or a Take-Off Scene from Behind the Curtain. A Poem.* London: J. Coote, J. Scott, 1758.

Brief Remarks on the Original and Present State of the Drama: To Which Is Added Hecate's Prophecy, Being a Characteristic Dialogue Betwixt Future Managers, and Their Dependents. London: S. Hooper, J. Morley, J. Scott, 1758.

Simco, John. *A Catalogue of Books, Prints, and Books of Prints, for 1792.* London: John Simco, [1792].

Smith, Dane Farnsworth and M.L. Lawhon. *Plays About the Theatre in England, 1737–1800, or, the Self-Conscious Stage from Foote to Sheridan.* Lewisburg, PA: Bucknell University Press, 1979.

Smith, Nicholas D. *An Actor's Library: David Garrick, Book Collecting and Literary Friendships.* New Castle, DE: Oak Knoll Press, 2017.

Smollett, Tobias. "The Character of Mr. Garrick." *Gentleman's Magazine*, 12, October (1742), 527.

Solomon, Harry M. *The Rise of Robert Dodsley: Creating the New Age of Print.* Carbondale: Southern Illinois University Press, 1996.

Stone, George Winchester, Jr. "Garrick's Long Lost Alteration of *Hamlet*." *PMLA*, 49/3 (1934), 890–921.

(ed.). *The London Stage 1660–1800: A Calendar of Plays, Entertainments & Afterpieces Together with Casts, Box-Receipts and Contemporary Comment Compiled from the Playbills, Newspapers and Theatrical Diaries of the Period*, Part 4: *1747–1776*, 3 vols. Carbondale: Southern Illinois University Press, 1962.

Stone, George Winchester, Jr. and George M. Kahrl, *David Garrick: A Critical Biography.* Carbondale: Southern Illinois University Press, 1979.

Taylor, Diana. *The Archive and the Repertoire*. Durham, NC: Duke University Press, 2003.

Thane, John. *Thane's Catalogue for 1773, of a Curious and Valuable Collection of Prints, Drawings, and Books of Prints, Both Ancient and Modern*. [London], 1773.

Thieme, John. "Spouting, Spouting-Clubs and Spouting Companions." *Theatre Notebook*, 29/1 (1975), 9–16.

Thomson, Peter. *On Actors and Acting*. University of Exeter Press, 2000.

Tierney, James E. (ed.). *The Correspondence of Robert Dodsley 1733–1764*. Cambridge University Press, 1988.

Ukers, William. *All About Coffee*. New York: Tea and Coffee Trade Journal Company, 1922.

"Urban, Sylvanus." "Historical Chronicle." *Gentleman's Magazine*, 1765, 442 and 489.

Vickers, Brian (ed.). *William Shakespeare: The Critical Heritage*, vol. v: *1765–1774*. London: Routledge, 1979.

Walpole, Horace. *The Yale Edition of Horace Walpole's Correspondence*, ed. W.S. Lewis, 48 vols. New Haven, CT: Yale University Press, 1937–83.

Wanko, Cheryl. *Roles of Authority: Thespian Biography and Celebrity in Eighteenth-Century Britain*. Lubbock: Texas Tech University Press, 2003.

Wark, Robert R. "The Gentle Pastime of Extra-Illustrating Books." *Huntington Library Quarterly*, 56/2 (1993), 151–62.

Warton, Joseph. *Essay upon the Genius and Writings of Pope*. 2 vols. London: M. Cooper, 1756.

Watson, George (ed.). *The New Cambridge Bibliography of English Literature*. vol. II. Cambridge University Press, 1971.

Werkmeister, Lucyle. *The London Daily Press 1772–1792*. Lincoln: University of Nebraska Press, 1963.

West, Shearer. *The Image of the Actor: Verbal and Visual Representation in the Age of Garrick and Kemble*. New York: St. Martin's Press, 1991.

Whincop, Thomas. *Scanderbeg: Or, Love and Liberty. A Tragedy. To Which Are Added a List of All the Dramatic Authors, with Some Account of Their Lives, and of All the Dramatic Pieces Ever Published in the English Language, to the Year 1747*. London: W. Reeve, 1747.

Wiles, Roy M. *Freshest Advices: Early Provincial Newspapers in England*. Columbus: Ohio State University Press, 1965.

[Williams, David]. *A Letter to David Garrick, Esq. On His Conduct as Principal Manager and Actor at Drury-Lane*. London: S. Bladon, 1772.

   A Letter to David Garrick, Esq. On His Conduct as Principal Manager and Actor at Drury-Lane. With a Preface and Notes, by the Editor. London: J. Williams and G. Corrall, [1778].

Wilson, Michael S. "Garrick, Iconic Acting, and the Ideologies of Theatrical Portraiture." *Word & Image: A Journal of Verbal/Visual Enquiry*, 6/4 (1990), 368–94.

Winston, James. "The Manager's Note-Book. – No. V." *New Monthly Magazine and Humorist*, 52/207 (1838), 379–87.

Winter, William. *The Press and the Stage: An Oration*. New York: Lockwood & Coombes, 1889.

Worrall, David. *Celebrity, Performance, Reception: British Georgian Theatre as Social Assemblage*. Cambridge University Press, 2013.

Zachs, William. *The First John Murray and the Late Eighteenth-Century London Book Trade*. Oxford University Press for the British Academy, 1998.

Index